The Organization of

Pupil Personnel Programs—

Issues and Practices

RAYMOND N. HATCH, EDITOR

MICHIGAN STATE UNIVERSITY PRESS

1974

★
　　★
★
　★
　★

Contents

Authors

Chapter 1   Raymond N. Hatch
             Professor, Michigan State University
             Ed.D., Oregon State University

Chapter 2   Donald G. Hays
             Administrator, Research and Pupil Services
             Fullerton Public Schools, Fullerton, California
             Ph.D., University of Wisconsin

Chapter 3   John F. Bancroft
             Director of Counseling, San Bernardino Valley College, San Bernardino, California
             Ph.D., University of Iowa

Chapter 4   Robert W. O'Hare
             Associate Director, Southwest Regional Laboratory for Research and Development, Los Alamitos, California
             Ed.D., University of South Dakota

Chapter 5   Kenneth W. Rollins
             Supervisor of Guidance, Montgomery County Public Schools, Maryland
             Ed.D., Harvard University

Chapter 6   Jane A. Bonnell
             Director of Research, Grand Rapids Public Schools
             Grand Rapids, Michigan
             Ph.D., Michigan State University

Preface

This book is designed as a textbook for college courses on the principles of administration as they apply to pupil personnel or guidance services. In addition, it has been prepared for the educational administrator of pupil personnel programs. It provides a thorough analysis of the major professional issues faced by administrators of pupil personnel services from kindergarten through the secondary school. The book also presents a complete description of the pupil personnel programs of five distinctly different school districts from varying areas of the United States.

The topics were chosen after a careful analysis of the content of contemporary professional periodicals and convention programs. The selections were made from those topics which appeared with greatest frequency during the past twelve months. The authors and the school districts, included in the book, were chosen, in part, by the method noted above plus a general survey of leaders in the field to obtain nominations and suggestions. The school districts were not selected because there was proof that they had the best programs but because they were considered to be both adequate and representative of typical programs in a given setting. Another factor having a bearing on the selection was that the school staff had a proven writer who was willing to describe the program.

A major assumption in support of the content of the book is that the current college instructor and program administrator seem to be more responsive to issue analysis in depth and to the organization and administrative approaches in other districts than to the detailed suggestions of one or two *authorities*. This book, therefore, attempts to meet that demand by using the writing of eleven different individuals, employed in seven different states, and trained in eleven different preparation programs to provide insight into current issues and practices.

The editor expresses his genuine thanks to the contributing authors for their excellent cooperation in developing a writing format and in meeting deadlines. In addition, he is grateful to all those professional colleagues who assisted in the selection of topics, programs, and authors. Finally, sincere appreciation is extended to those individuals and publishers who so generously consented to have their material reproduced in this book.

RAYMOND N. HATCH

PERSONNEL WORKER IDENTITY

Morris LeMay
ASSOCIATE DEAN OF STUDENTS
OREGON STATE UNIVERSITY

#1
wonder the students,
who are you?
faculty?
administration?
which?
you are,
yet,
you are not.
you must be
both,
   and even more.

#2
wonder the faculty,
what do you do?
queries the student,
what do you do?
asks even my son,
what do you do?
do you teach?
you work at a school,
why don't you teach?
I don't have time
   to teach,
   to prepare,
   to counsel,
   to advise,
   to research.

> must go to another meeting,
> write a report, answer the phone.
> no time
>   to do anything well.
> why? answered my son.
> you should, say the faculty
> you must, say the student
> I will.

The poem noted above illustrates the confusion that exists in our society as to the appropriate role of the personnel worker. The poem appeared in the *Personnel and Guidance Journal*, June 1970 (vol. 48, no. 10).

Permission to reproduce the poem has been given by the author and the American Personnel and Guidance Association.

*The Organization of Pupil Personnel
Programs—Issues and Practices*

CHAPTER 1

Introduction and Review

RAYMOND N. HATCH

THE concept of *Pupil Personnel Services* is a relatively new idea in the professional literature even though most of the elements that make up the services have been evident for over fifty years. It was not until after World War II that the term began to appear in journals and textbooks and was heard from the speaker's platform. The initial reaction was one of concern that the term was another "handle" for a program already operating under an older title. This was soon dispelled, however, as the professional fields of the "helping services" began to develop a conceptual model of what was needed to provide proper identity for a growing professional area in education.

CONTRIBUTIONS TO THE CONCEPT

A brief review of some of the contributing causes for the development of the concept may be in order. Each writer would probably select different factors or place the reasons in a different priority sequence, but the following related elements played a major role in the justification for the idea. The primary support for the term probably grew from the growing demand to have a semantic umbrella for a number of highly related services being offered to children with quite diverse identity in the school family. In the same vein, there needed to be not only an understanding of the term but an administrative framework which would result in the maximum effort of personnel serving in one or more of the pupil service areas. The principle of teamwork was presented on many fronts and accepted as a rationale approach to administrative organization. The need for

3

cooperation was presented succinctly by Mahoney[1] in the early 1960s at the Washington Interprofessional Conference on Pupil Personnel Services in Public Schools. His comments set the stage for the recognition of the uniqueness of the various services yet suggested the values inherent in cooperative effort through a common administrative channel. Others have addressed themselves to the same position in subsequent writing to the point that the arguments in favor of administrative cooperation in pupil personnel work often appear trite and unnecessary to the practitioner at this point in time. Although the value of cooperative effort is seldom challenged, there remain many unresolved issues as to the precise organizational patterns and related matters.

Another influence, frequently overlooked, upon the development of the pupil personnel concept in the schools is that of the personnel notion in business and industry. The importance of a personnel function in industry to improve production or marketing of merchandise has long been accepted in the business world. The value of knowing the employee, proper placement of the employee, plus the value of facilitating health and related services designed to improve both production and sales, is seldom questioned in the business world. The role of personnel services in business is similar to the role of personnel services in schools. If the parent, teacher, and administrator view the pupil personnel program as a means of improving the opportunity of each youngster to gain the most from his school experiences; the primary goal of education is achieved. All too frequently the incorrect perception of the proper role of the personnel worker on the part of the administrator, teacher, or even the specialist himself has inhibited the proper use of the services to help the school provide a maximum instructional effort. If the pupil services function within the framework noted above, it will be better understood and used by all concerned.

Other influences upon the growth of the *Pupil Personnel Services* concept are usually attempts at the refinement of roles and successful techniques which add support to the program. Suggestions of this kind are to be found in the subsequent chapters as the major issues facing the pupil personnel worker are reviewed.

A FRAME OF REFERENCE

The many-faceted educational enterprise that has emerged to provide for the education of the millions of children in the United States is usually referred to as the American Educational System. While such a broad title is accepted by the citizen of a foreign country as he views our educational activities from afar, it is surprising to learn that this title is also an expression commonly used by a vast majority of the lay public in our own country. The popular use of the title indicates that the educational program has preciseness that connotes an exact pattern of activity in every state, county, city, or hamlet throughout the nation. Such an interpretation appears to be contrary to the basic tenets upon which our educational programs have developed. It may also explain some of the confusion that prevails when educational inputs vary but common educational outcomes are expected.

Education in America seems to have prospered in the general permissive atmosphere of local control, influenced by community objectives and geared to adapt to the needs of the smallest group. In such a setting, staffing patterns, job descriptions, organizational models, and similar conditions of uniformity would be encouraged to vary in nature. This would be consistent with the pervading influence of local autonomy. It is at this point that the paradox becomes quite evident, since major elements of uniformity characterize the educational program. Instead of judging whether these developments have been desirable or not, it is important to analyze the conditions which gave rise to their acceptance. Should the conditions prove feasible, factors of educational conformity would then be justified in spite of the philosophical umbrella under which our program has developed.

In all probability the most significant factor influencing common patterns of educational practice was the acceptance of a common group of objectives. Most writers identify the *Cardinal Principles of Secondary Education,*[2] prepared by the Commission on Reorganization of Secondary Education in 1918, as the point of departure for a series of similar guidelines for our educational efforts. These objectives have been reordered and restated in subsequent studies by lay groups and professional educators; yet the primary gist of the original objectives remain intact. In all of these can be found the following broad objectives, projected in 1938 by the Educational Policies Commission that had been appointed by the National Education Association and the American Association of School Administrators to draft an up-to-date statement of the purposes of education: (1) self-realization, (2) human relationships, (3) economic efficiency, (4) civic responsibility.[3] The reiteration of this common set of objectives in all

5

the subsequent reviews and reports offers ample proof that the citizens of this nation are in general agreement on objectives even though they may question the route used to reach those objectives. It also suggests that many of the elements of the educational program are acceptable, with variations in patterns, to provide a more effective program.

The general endorsement of common educational objectives has resulted in the development of curricula, the institution of specific educational activities, the construction of facilities, the identification of organizational patterns, and the derivation of evaluative criteria common in all schools. One sometimes wonders, therefore, why there is so much criticism of education from time to time by both lay and professional leaders when there appears to be so much agreement with the goals of the enterprise. On closer observation we discover that the conflict probably develops from the relative significance given to one or more of the objectives and not from the objectives themselves. For example, the educational programs of the early 1970s have been condemned for not meeting the general objective of training young people to be economically efficient. This criticism has resulted in schools moving to a more viable career-oriented curriculum to expedite the attainment of skills and understandings so that the students enter the world of work in an efficient manner.

The implementation of such change has not been easy or without conflict, for there are many individuals both in the schools and out who have felt that the schools have been preparing young people to be economically efficient. It is interesting to note, however, that proponents for this change, as well as opponents to it, accepted the objective for education, but the matter became an issue when the relative emphasis was discussed and implemented. Nevertheless, the basic school pattern tends to remain intact as such adjustments are made in the programs being offered at a given time.

In addition to the importance of a common set of objectives in the shaping of educational patterns, has been the vast growth in urban population and the adoption of school consolidation programs, resulting in the housing of large numbers of students in one or several closely related school facilities. A situation of this nature gives rise to the need for specialists in certain unique educational areas and the identification of organizational patterns to provide leadership for the various educational functions. One may argue for or against school size. However, the fact remains that an educational program for a large school district requires definition of roles and delegation of specific responsibility, or chaos will prevail. This factor has, therefore, been a major determinant in the stabilization of organizational patterns along functional lines.

Other factors have contributed to a degree of conformity in the educational programs of our schools and will undoubtedly continue to exercise a similar influence in future years. Not the least of these factors is the natural tendency to perpetuate a satisfactory experience in an individual's personal life. Teachers are prone to teach as they have been taught, administrators tend to administer in a way that reflects their appreciation of a program they have experienced, and a majority of the lay public evaluates the current school program in terms of their own school life.

Here again one may debate the value or limitations of the influences, but these are facts of life in our culture with which the educator must contend. The number, kind, or value of such influences, however, may not be as important as the recognition of such conditions and the acceptance of those patterns which seem to hold the most promise for an effective school program. Fortunately, there still remains a degree of latitude in adjusting to accepted patterns and activities which is the great promise for the schools of tomorrow. The adoption of programs, organizational patterns, and similar educational elements that have a satisfactory rationale and result in a maximum school product then become the real challenge of educational leadership.

COMPONENTS OF THE EDUCATIONAL ENTERPRISE

The brief review of the evolving educational system, noted above, suggests that major components are to be found in the nation's schools. Such elements would inevitably be highly related yet have unique characteristics to insure the maximum effort in each area for the total school program. Many variations in the ingredients have been suggested, but there now seems to be general acceptance of three: instruction, management, and personnel.

The Instructional Component. This is the primary element of the educational enterprise. It is that part of the educational complex designed primarily to assist students to gain a mastery of subject matter and skills.

The Management, or Administrative, Component. This is a facilitating factor to insure that the primary component functions at maximum efficiency. The scope of this group includes a responsibility for planning, executing, staffing, and appraising the entire enterprise.

The Personnel Component. This includes all educational services designed primarily to insure that each student has an opportunity to gain the maximum from his instructional experience. It is within this ingredient that the "helping services" find a functional home.

Many values are to be found in a division of component responsibility as outlined above. First, such a division places the three major staff groups into proper focus in terms of major responsibility. A second value rests in the ease with which it lends itself to staffing; for example, the instructional staff function under the general supervision of a curriculum coordinator and the helping service personnel functions under the general supervision of a personnel coordinator. A third value rests in the fact that, by the delegation of responsibility in this manner, all three components have staffs committed to the completion of the scope of the components as a primary obligation. This discourages the slighting of one aspect due to the immediate demands of another. For example, if the administrative and personnel functions are vested in one individual or office, the pressure of management usually receives top priority in accordance with its overall responsibility.

Even though there is significant value in having three distinct elements for the provision of the school's educational program, there is also significant value in recognizing their interrelationships. The purpose of the three areas is to achieve a maximum educational experience for each child, and and the administrative and personnel components facilitate the primary element, the instructional component. A second conditioning factor is that staff members are assigned to one element as their primary responsibility, although there will be times when certain aspects of the other components may become their logical responsibility. The exact time and role will vary with the situation, but the acceptance of a secondary responsibility as part of each staff member's obligation removes many obstacles to educational programming. Implicit in the success of a scheme of this kind is the high premium placed on the value of compatibility among the three elements. Staff members who operate in an atmosphere of "self-containment" will contribute little to the total program or the educational well-being of the child. Delegation of responsibility to components suggests greater emphasis on given elements, but this will only happen if all three components function as a total program.

PROBLEMS OF IMPLEMENTATION

The introduction of the helping services into the public schools has not been without problems. For example, the impact of the traditional view that schools should demand academic excellence without regard for individual differences has discouraged help for individuals. This view has changed markedly in the past twenty-five years, consequently opening the door to help for the individual. Another block to growth in the services came from the professionals themselves. Many had been trained in clinical settings on a remedial one-to-one relationship and found it difficult to adjust to the broader demands of the total school environment. The type of training given to the various professionals in the several services proved to be an inhibitor to the rapid expansion of the pupil personnel programs. Liddle and Reighard[4] stated this problem very well, "Also, a number of the pupil personnel workers, particularly the psychologists, social workers and counselors, had overlapping skills and responsibilities which often led to jurisdictional disputes and a duplication of effort." The last named problem gave rise to a concerted effort on the part of schools and training institutions to define the proper scope of the services, and this will be discussed later in this chapter.

The three problems noted above have impeded the rapid development of programs of special help for students with the ever-present problem of a lack of adequate financial support. In addition, the inclination of the teacher to think of those youngsters in her room as "my pupils" slowed down the acceptance of another staff member who might bring a special element of expertise into the resolution of a unique learning problem. All these factors have been problems in the past and exist, to some degree, in the present. However, the degree of their influence has declined sharply in recent years. Professionals now have a better perception of their proper role, the current teaching staff has a far more sophisticated outlook in regard to individual differences, and even the lay public can usually be relied on to support tax issues for special services. Thus, the setting for continued growth is receptive and awaits leadership for improvement in the services offered.

THE PUPIL PERSONNEL PROGRAM

The various areas of the pupil personnel program have been active contributors to educational programs for many years. It has only been within the last two decades, however, that a review of their roles and relationships has resulted in some redefinition and reassignment. The process of redefining the scope of the services was touched off in a highly organized manner by the establishment of a commission to study the problem under the general auspices of the U.S. Office of Education in 1962. The unit was called the Interprofessional Research Commission on Pupil Personnel Services (IRCOPPS), and included representatives from eighteen professional associations. The Commission secured a grant from the National Institute of Mental Health in 1963 to carry out a five-year program of research and demonstrations. The goal of this project was an attempt to investigate and suggest ways by which the schools could make more effective use of the personnel services.

The research and reports of IRCOPPS made a significant impact on educational programs even though it was unable to obtain funding beyond the five-year period. Its publications, distributed throughout the country, served as a basis for reorganization and stablization of pupil personnel programs. Most of these publications were in mimeographed form and have become difficult to procure, since the Commission is now inactive. One publication, based in part on the findings of the Commission, has been written by Liddle and Ferguson[5], director and associate director respectively of the project, and it provides guidelines for programs in accordance with the findings of the project.

Definition

In most instances in this chapter, *Pupil Personnel Services* has been referred to as a group of services commonly alluded to as the "helping services." This may be too trite for current use, but for many decades it has conveyed a broad meaning to educators. For purposes of this presentation, however, a more precise definition is needed before the scope of the services can be identified.

Several excellent definitions have been proposed. One of the first and still very usable definitions has been offered by Liddle and Ferguson[6]—"a program of pupil services is comprised of a group or series of activities, functions, and services designed to help each pupil get the most out of his school program." This description at first appears to be a very adequate definition; however, there are limitations to such a definition. One could claim that the description could apply to all components of the educational emterprise, thereby not delineating the specific role of the personnel services. It may be helpful, therefore, to add appropriate terminology to insure greater uniqueness to the definition.

The personnel element was earlier defined as including all activities that are focused on the individual to insure that he gain the most from his school experience. If the pupil personnel program is to fulfill the demand of this factor, the definition should incorporate the thrust of individualization as the major obligation of the services. With this in mind, therefore, the following definition is submitted: *A program of pupil personnel services consists of those organized activities in education which have as their primary purpose the removal of any current or possible inhibitor to the educational progress of each individual student.*

A definition such as this sets the personnel services apart from those activities which are the primary obligation of either instruction or management. However, it must be borne in mind that, like the relationships among the three educational components, these services result in a multitude of activities complementary to the instructional and administrative services. The primary value in adopting this description lies in pinpointing those educational activities which gain their justification by assuring that every student has a major educational resource focused on him as an individual.

Typical Services

Given a definition for the services to be provided, an analysis of those educational activities may then be identified. Most writers tend to include about the same ones, with minor alterations in each case. Although there were a scattered number of writings related to the exact elements of the personnel services prior to 1960, the true scope of the program has taken shape since that time. The work of IRCOPPS offered the first generally accepted set of services for the program. One other publication also made a major impact on the precise areas to be included in such a group of services. This was prepared and distributed by the United States Office of Education under the title, *The Scope of Pupil Personnel Services.*[7] The following areas were noted in that publication as comprising the pupil personnel program:

Attendance	Psychiatric
Guidance	Psychological
Medical	Speech and Hearing
Nursing	Social Work

11

Later some alteration has been suggested in the make-up of the program. The National Association of Pupil Personnel Administrators lists the following services in its constitution and by-laws.[8]

Attendance	Social Work
Counseling and Guidance	Speech and Hearing
Health	Special Education
Psychological	Programs

One of the early enumerations of the personnel services was proposed by Hatch and Stefflre.[9] They proposed six services: attendance, guidance, health, psychological counseling, research, and social work. These authors did not include some of the special education areas, such as remedial programs of speech and hearing. Another significant difference in their suggestions is the inclusion of educational research in the pupil personnel area.

Some of the more recent writings include the areas noted in all other lists, with slight modifications and with varying degrees of emphasis and relationships. For example, Perrone and others.[10] note areas of psychological, social work, health, and guidance but expand the guidance services area in considerable detail. This same pattern of presenting the personnel programs tends to be common in many of the writings of the past five years and is probably due to the fact that the guidance function is so pervasive throughout the school staff that it requires greater attention than the other personnel services.

Hummel and Bonham[11] in 1968 developed a discussion of the pupil personnel services around eight general areas: (1) counseling and guidance, (2) school psychological services, (3) attendance and child accounting services, (4) school social work and visiting teacher services, (5) school health services, (6) speech and hearing therapy services, (7) pupil appraisal services, (8) remedial and special education services. The authors present a well-defined role for each service as a unique but highly related aspect to the other services of the program.

Another contemporary contribution to the analysis of the scope of the pupil personnel program has been presented by Mitchell and Saum.[12] The editors emphasize the concept of differentiated staffing, commonly called *The Youth Guidance System* (YGS). Here again recognition is given to various aspects of the personnel services, but the primary focus is on the services to be rendered, with limited delineation of the specific role of a given personnel area. One possible exception to this format is that of the role of the school counselor in the provision of guidance service.

A review of the various lists of services considered to be pupil personnel services reveals considerable agreement in most categories. There seems to be a general acceptance of the services of attendance, guidance, health, psychological and social work in a total program. Noted less often but yet receiving considerable prominence are areas usually identified as special education, such as remedial speech and hearing activities. Practice and precedent may have resulted in a combination of services with little thought given to a philosophical framework to justify the broader group. The larger number of services may also result from administrative convenience. In any event, the special education programs are frequently found in pupil personnel organization, which may suggest that a rationale for their inclusion should be assured.

The Inclusion of Special Education

The broad program of education usually identified as the special education services of the school may be divided into two major parts. One part is devoted to the instruction of pupils with special handicaps, such as blindness, deafness, or mental retardation. The second part is directed at the removal of special handicaps of pupils so that they can make better use of the regular instructional program of the school. Such areas as remedial speech, reading, or physical disabilities could be catalogued in this part of the program. The reader will see the potential conflict when these activities are grouped together for administrative purposes, since the first aspect is instruction and falls logically into the instructional component, while the second part is devoted to the removal of educational inhibitors and is thus completely compatible with the scope of the personnel component.

This conflict has created many difficulties for school administrators. They usually try to resolve the problem by keeping the special education staff in one administrative channel and by assigning individuals to either the personnel or the instructional component as a group. This may suggest that it is important to keep the entire special education staff together, regardless of their primary focus, and hope that their maximum contribution will not be hampered by local administrative organization. In all probability, however, the arguments will continue for years to come as each administrator attempts to resolve the obvious differences between the two primary thrusts of special education by proper assignment in the school program. Each school will have a slightly different alignment and in most cases will proclaim satisfaction with its plan. This might be best, since it is the

13

product of the service that is important, not the organizational plan or method by which the services are administered. A review of the five school districts presented in subsequent chapters should prove helpful in determining the true credence of a statement of this nature.

THE ORGANIZATIONAL FRAMEWORK

The primary purpose of an organizational framework is to provide the means by which the members of the organization may cooperate in the most effective manner. There is always need for structure when any group has a common task, since an unorganized and undirected group results in utter confusion. Such a group can neither determine its true purpose nor accomplish its ultimate objectives in spite of the fact that the common task is apparent. This need has given rise to various organizational frameworks designed to provide the most effective programs of pupil personnel services.

The organization selected by a school district, no matter how simple, must provide a means by which the staff can make decisions and take appropriate action. In the process of doing this, it must: (1) select its leadership, (2) determine the roles to be played, (3) determine the goals, (4) determine the methods to be utilized, (5) achieve the stated goals.

The precise pattern a given school may develop to accomplish these ends may vary greatly from that found in another district, but the need for a well-defined organization is accepted with little question.

Some Concepts of Organization

For many years authorities in the field of school administration have been guided by a general set of principles in the development of a workable organizational model. The relative value of the principles and methods by which they are implemented may differ from one writer to another, but the basic group of considerations are usually found in all their writing.

The interpretation that is sometimes given to the administrative emphasis in a school setting is the result of the improper application of the concepts. For example, there are administrators who seem to pride themselves in the efficiency of the organization as an end in itself. This would seem to justify criticism, since it is not the efficiency that is important but the effectiveness of the organization in the

14

attainment of its objectives. Efficiency plays an important role in the accomplishment of the latter, but it must not be the criteria by which the organization is judged.

Another problem that frequently hinders the success of effective educational services is staff ignorance of the proper role of the school administrator. This is to be expected, since few individuals preparing for a career in instruction or pupil personnel have had sufficient training in this area or any educational exposure of this kind. This lack of understanding prevents them from contributing to the administrative function in a meaningful way and may be the cause of hostility that reduces the impact of the total educational enterprise. Obviously, the members of the pupil personnel staff must become aware of some of the major ideas that undergird the organizational framework in education.

UNITY OF PURPOSE

The effectiveness of part of the school's activities is in direct proportion to the identification of goals and purposes. This is a shared responsibility of the administrator, staff, and other interested individuals, but it will not occur unless the administrator serves as the catalytic agent to the process.

SINGLE EXECUTIVE LEADERSHIP

The effectiveness of the organization is strengthened by a single executive leader. This concept has developed in the past fifty years as schools moved from the organizational pattern of an educational executive and a business executive in each district who reported independently to the board of education. This results in constant conflict and reduces the chances of the school system agreeing on common goals or the methods to be used in attaining those goals, since the business element of administration is inextricably related to the instructional elements and these cannot have separate leadership.

This idea sometimes results in the pupil personnel worker reneging on his proper role as a technical leader. If all members of the school staff could see themselves as competent technical leaders in their own areas and recognize the school administrator as the executive leader of the school, a more effective program would result. In this framework, the technical leader plays a vital role of developing goals, determining needs, implementing programs, and evaluating

15

results; but he does it in conjunction with the executive leadership. This would be consistent with the concept yet fulfill the requirements of an effective program in which the technical leader has a vested interest. Failure to follow this plan usually assures either conflict between technical and executive leadership or a school program that is ineffective. No dedicated pupil personnel worker dares to permit conditions of this kind to exist.

DELEGATION OF AUTHORITY AND RESPONSIBILITY

The effectiveness of an organization is enhanced when the superior officer delegates authority to the next in command. This concept has been one which has caused considerable confusion and concern among educational administrators. The exact cause for the confusion seems difficult to define, but is probably due to two different factors. First, the delegation to act may encourage the subordinate to become overly enthusiastic and make decisions that are contrary to the broad goals of the total enterprise. Such action usually results in conflict with the individual who delegated the authority and makes him apprehensive when similar action in the future is contemplated on educational matters. This may serve as a deterrent to total educational productivity and result in open conflict in the organization. Miller has developed an excellent discussion of this problem and hypothesizes that this concept increases conflict among subsystems of the organization.[13]

The second factor which may create confusion stems from misunderstanding relative to responsibility. In this case, the individual who has delegated the authority to act may feel completely removed from the responsibility for the actions of the individual to whom the authority has been delegated. This, of course, should not be the case, since the responsibility is very definitely shared by both parties. Nevertheless, some administrators fail to assume joint responsibility for staff action. The organization that prospers will not permit this type of interpretation to persist.

DIVISION OF LABOR

The effectiveness of an organization is increased by the designation of specific duties and by the identification of specific tasks. This factor is consistent with the discussion of the educational components and with the identification of the pupil personnel services noted earlier. It is an idea that suggests a maximum product can be obtained if specialization of tasks can be made and assignment of staff to those tasks is considered in the organization.

SPAN OF CONTROL

Greater effectiveness of the organization is achieved by assigning only the number of persons that an administrator can adequately supervise. This principle has been one of the more controversial of all organizational ideas. It is debatable since there is great differences in individuals and situations. In spite of these variables, there should be concern for the organization where progress is inhibited because too many must wait, to clear the matter with a busy supervisor before taking action. It is probably dangerous to suggest a desirable number of persons reporting to one supervisor, but the top executive must be alert to the possibility of administrative blockage due to too broad a span of control.

Elements that deal with providing stability as well as flexibility in the organization are usually noted in writing on the subject of administration. In addition, various personnel policies and evaluative ideas are likewise considered as basic ingredients of organization. All these factors are important, but it seems that the five reviewed here are the ones which should, if they are understood and accepted, enhance the development of the pupil personnel program.

Patterns of Organization

The early organizational plans for the administration of the personnel services tended to evolve in accordance with local needs, personnel, and similar factors, which indicated more of a response to administrative convenience than to a rational set of principles. It may also have been due to the rather recent acceptance of the pupil personnel idea as a major element of the educational enterprise. In any event, there now appears to be a rather firm set of principles emerging which seem to be acceptable in most school districts. The first of these is the acceptance of the three major educational components and the delegation of supervision in such a way as to insure system-wide leadership for all three components. The conceptualization of this principle is illustrated in Figure 1.1.

The designation of the number and title of individuals in the implementation of this principle is not so important as the separation of the components for leadership responsibility. In a plan of this kind each element is recognized and an individual is held responsible for

17

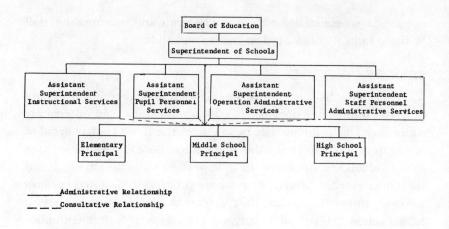

Fig. 1.1. Typical organization by components.

his part of the educational program. If this is followed, the number of individuals may be reduced in the smaller school district, provided each component is given a leader who has an equal amount of time to conduct the business of his assigned area.

Another organizational principle is that of bringing all the pupil personnel services into one administrative unit. This is shown in Figure 1.2 for six typical pupil personnel areas. It should be recalled, however, that not all school districts accept the same areas in this manner. Some, for example, will not include the guidance and counseling services in such a plan, since guidance work is done primarily by the staff assigned to a given building. This should not change the significance of the principle, however, since the point of the principle is to provide an administrative home for a group of related services, which should result in better services with a minimum of overlap and omission. The question that is sometimes raised about the role of counselors in relationship to the administration is another matter and is included in the next paragraph.

Another, less well-defined, principle has emerged to guide school

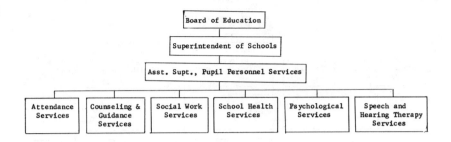

Fig. 1.2. Typical organization of related services.

districts in their organizational pattern for pupil personnel services. It includes both of those presented thus far but provides for the coordination of all of the pupil personnel services, with line relationships and advisory committees identified. This idea is illustrated in Figure 1.3, a plan which places the counselor in the building under the direct supervision of an assistant principal while allowing for building and district-wide coordination to develop through building committees and district-wide councils.

The three organizational designs reviewed here are illustrative of models that have been generally accepted for the management of pupil personnel services. The effectiveness of the models must be judged by the district attempting to provide an effective program. The demands of the local situation always dictate variations, and these will be noted in the five district models described later in this book. Arguments can be presented for almost any model, and counterproposals may sound equally valid. In most cases the proof of the value of one over another will never be revealed, since matters of this kind defy controlled and experimental study. Those responsible for the organizational model must make a decision and alter the plan when the effectiveness of the program appears to be in jeopardy due to the organizational structure.

19

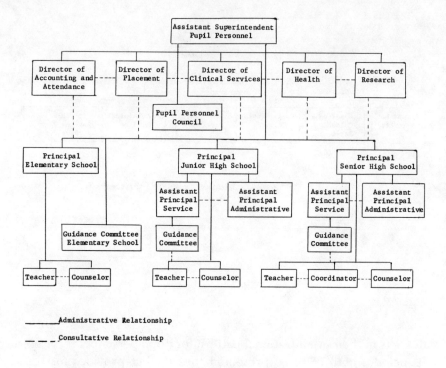

```
                          ┌──────────────────────┐
                          │Assistant Superintendent│
                          │   Pupil Personnel     │
                          └──────────────────────┘
```

Fig. 1.3. Typical organization by consultation and committee.

ROLE PERCEPTIONS

The growth of the pupil personnel services from a group of autonomous yet professionally related segments into an administrative unit with a common purpose has been surprisingly rapid but not without growing pains. The chief problem has been that of the wide range of role perceptions held by members of the various personnel areas. Not only have there been differences among the various groups but

20

significantly different interpretations of roles within the group itself. These differences are gradually being reduced and more generally accepted roles are being ascertained, but much is to be done before the administrator of the total program can make an assignment with the assurance that all parties involved have a common understanding of the role to be played.

The continuing attempts to find acceptable role definitions for service areas and individuals within a service area pales into almost insignificance when one compares it with the problem faced by the administrator of the entire program to define his role. The problem he faces is one that can be multiplied by the number of services involved, the individuals within each service, and the demands of an administrative superior who has his perception of the role of pupil personnel services. If the administrator of the pupil personnel area hopes to achieve any degree of success with the program under his jurisdiction, he must somehow bring all these facets into a compatible relationship. This represents a very unenviable task for the most enterprising administrator. Contemporary leaders of pupil personnel programs seem to be trained educators, and their efforts have been reviewed and reported in recent literature on the subject. Some of these reports are noted here to present more information about the work of many to determine an appropriate role for the program administrator, as well as for each of the major service areas.

Role of the Pupil Personnel Administrator

The role of the administrator of the pupil personnel program has, of neccessity, been defined as it has emerged. A development of this nature is an evolutionary process, which is characterized by changes in direction, definition, and scope. Frequently, the apparent vacillation has led the observor to criticize the program because there has been a lack of precise title, plan, or role specification. On second thought, however, the fair-minded critic has realized that it is only natural that the supervisor of a group of hitherto autonomous units would need to spell out his role as the shape of the emerging unit dictates a proper role. This explains much of the irresolution that has persisted during the past decade relative to the role of the administrator of the pupil personnel program. This situation will probably continue until a fairly precise program of services has general acceptance in most school districts. In the meantime, a role definition is needed which permits flexibility, yet allows for proper leadership.

Numerous studies have been conducted during recent years to

ascertain the title, duties, and role expectations of the individual responsible for the coordination of the pupil personnel program. Reports of the studies vary considerably, with a few trends to be noted in most cases. One of the early reports was prepared by Liddle and Reighard.[14] This study was designed, among other things, to determine who the coordinators were and what were their qualifications and duties. This study was conducted in the early 1960s and revealed several interesting factors relating to role and title. First, it seems significant to note that most of the coordinators surveyed were new in their job, with about one-third holding their positions for two years or less. Another important factor in the report suggests that a little over one-half of those reporting were responsible for the coordination of all services as usually defined in a pupil personnel program. About one-third of the over four hundred individuals surveyed, on the other hand, indicated they did not have system-wide responsibility for coordination.

This same study sought to pin down the most typical title for the coordinator of the program. About three-fifths were called directors or coordinators of pupil personnel services. The remaining titles were scattered widely, with the term pupil personnel usually in the title. This bench-mark study offered the professional field a frame of reference from which most duties and titles for the coordinator have emerged.

Subsequent studies have been conducted along the lines noted above. One of the most comprehensive reports of such studies has been reported by Hays,[15] who not only reviewed the reports of studies but projected a six-step approach to an improved definition of title as well as role.

Another study which has contributed much to the definition of role and title of the coordinator of the pupil personnel program has been reported by Warner.[16] This is a doctoral dissertation which provides a descriptive report of the supervisory and administrative programs in the area of guidance/pupil personnel services in each of the fifty state departments of education and of the agencies under their jurisdiction. This study, although directed at the state-wide level, provides some insight into the problem of defining the coordinator's role at the local level, since there were wide variations among the states as to title and the services to be coordinated into the pupil personnel unit. However, there appeared to be fairly general agreement among the states that whatever is coordinated should span the elementary and secondary school levels.

Various authorities have devoted considerable attention to the definition of role and title for the administrator of the pupil personnel program. One of the most comprehensive lists of duties has been suggested by Hummel and Bonham.[17] The list may include facets of responsibility that are shared by other educational leaders, but the administrator of the pupil personnel program must assume a primary role for those activities suggested by these authors. Hill[18] has also projected the role of the administrator in a similar manner and has suggested a role definition that appears to be consistent with a growing trend throughout the nation. The dilemma the reviewer of the reports faces is that of trying to ascertain the precise limit of those trends. It may be more meaningful to the reader to draw a rather general conclusion from current data and trust that future reviews will reveal more concise limits.

Title

Several conclusions can be drawn from the material currently available in which the title of the coordinator of the pupil personnel program is discussed. The following seem to be the most prominent:

1. The individual who has an administrative responsibility for two or more of the personnel services has the term pupil personnel in his title.
2. The descriptive term that is used in conjunction with the pupil personnel term depends on the status given to the personnel component in the school district. If it has equal status with instruction, it is given a comparable title. For example, if the coordinator of instruction is an assistant superintendent for instruction, the coordinator of pupil personnel services is an assistant superintendent for pupil personnel. Likewise, if the coordinator of instruction is the director of instruction, the coordinator of pupil personnel is the director of pupil personnel.
3. In school districts where size precludes the identification of anyone with the rank of an assistant superintendent, the individual responsible for leadership of the pupil personnel program is usually identified as a director or coordinator of the program.

Role

The definition of the role of the administrator, like his title, seems to have reached a point where several conclusions may be drawn. A brief list of these are reviewed here.

1. An individual who is given the coordination responsibility of two or more of the pupil personnel services has a vertical administrative duty that extends from kindergarten through the secondary school. This is consistent with accepted practice in the coordination of instruction.

2. The long debate in regard to the role of the coordinator as an administrative or professional leader seems to be academic at this point in time. Most authorities and administrators perceive such a person as being both an administrator and a competent leader of pupil personnel services. This suggests that the administrator be qualified as an executive leader and as a technical leader in one or more of the pupil personnel services. To be less than this may insure a block between the top administrator of the district and the professionals delegated the service responsibilities. Lacking executive competence, he is unable to relate to the administrative staff; and lacking professional qualifications in personnel, he finds it impossible to understand or determine the needs of an effective program.

3. The role of the coordinator in the smaller school district is not so clear-cut. There seems to be a tendency, however, to place the responsibility for coordination of the pupil personnel program in the same supervisory pattern as the instructional element. There may be merit in this type of arrangement provided there is a designation of supervisory responsibility to an individual who is competent to offer leadership in pupil personnel. The mere assignment of the pupil personnel component to the instructional component without the delegation of coordination of personnel services will probably assure little or no coordination, leadership, or a program of pupil personnel services.

4. The coordinator of the pupil personnel services should possess a number of personal characteristics which will enhance his role as a leader. The following are illustrative:
   a. responsive to staff suggestions,
   b. innovative in program development,
   c. solicitous of program support,
   d. aware of staff competency,
   e. cognizant of staff roles to insure an effective program,
   f. cooperative as a member of an educational administrative unit,
   g. understanding of the value of delegation, while at the same time accepting a mutual responsibility for the action taken.

Additional guides could be enumerated for the role of the administrator, but these may be of little value when a given school district appoints an individual to assume the leadership for the pupil personnel services. An awareness of the broad guidelines noted here and in light of the demands of a given situation, the role will take on the character needed to fulfill the job requirements of a specific position.

Failure to consider the guidelines or assess the situation will surely result in an ineffective program. The alert school superintendent interested in the best educational program his community can afford should find the guidelines adequate and will probably adapt them to his district.

Role of the Specific Services

The precise role of the various services has been projected by many writers, by the professional organizations representing the services, and by administrators of actual programs in operation. If there is a conclusion one can draw from all of these sources, it is that there appears to be general agreement on one or two unique functions for each service, but their duties seem to be so similar that the school administrator may find it most difficult to delegate responsibilities in such a way as to avoid duplication and major service omissions. The reason for this confusion was discussed earlier in the chapter, but the problem of proper delegation still remains unsolved.

Several authors have devoted major sections of their presentations to lists of duties for each of the major pupil personnel service areas. Hatch and Stefflre,[19] for example, devote considerable space to a discussion concerning the role of the school psychologist, school social worker, school nurse, and attendance coordinator. Many suggestions for the role of the individual services are to be found in a book of readings edited by Saltzman and Peters.[20] A comprehensive listing of duties assigned to the various services has been prepared by Hummel and Bonham.[21] All of these present a position for each member of the pupil personnel team and at the same time point out the need for defining precise roles where the same services may be rendered by two or more of the various service areas. This may be as far as a specific definition of roles can be made, but the reader is often left with a feeling of uncertainty when several professional areas profess competence and participation in the same service area. This presentation may not alleviate reactions of this kind, but an effort will be made to do so by stating a few specific duties for each area, discussing the roles and relationships in later chapters and reviews of the delegation of responsibility in five school districts. It is hoped that the professional field of pupil personnel services will find added direction in the proper delegation of responsibilities as the result of the material presented herein.

Two of the most common elements suggested for the roles of all pupil personnel staff members relate to consultation. In one form or another, it is usually suggested that the staff member should be a consultant to other school staff and serve as a consultant to parents in the school district. The exact conditions vary with the particular service, but this appears to be a logical role for such professionals to play in all situations. It may be assumed, therefore, that this should be a part of the primary activities of all staff members mentioned in the following brief review.

The School Psychologist

All the pupil personnel service areas find, in varying degrees, significant differences between role descriptions proposed by their professional groups and that set forth by state law or local job description. This may be expected since it is the obligation of the professional group to project an ideal setting, while state law or local assignment are conditioned by a number of factors calling for a type of concilatory action. All personnel services face this same problem, but in all probability the differences in the role of the school psychologist has been the most pronounced. This situation may be the result of many factors, and it may be the result of a general understanding in the professional field to maintain flexibility in role definition. The latter position would seem to gain support if the description of the school psychologist, described in a mimeographed paper distributed by the School Psychology Division (16) of the American Psychological Association, is typical of the role definition available to the pupil personnel administrator. The school psychologist is defined as follows:

A. A psychologist, a substantial proportion of whose professional knowledge, competencies, and time are spent:
(1) in collaboration, consultation, or conference with school personnel on enhancing the learning potential of school-age pupils or advancing their socio-emotional development; or
(2) in clinical work; or
(3) training and instruction of school psychologists as defined in (1) and (2) above; and/or
B. A psychologist, who through teaching, professional, or research activity, has made significant contributions to the training of school psychologists or the field of school psychology.

It would be very difficult to quarrel with such a description, but the latitude provided for local and individual interpretation of a precise role is very broad and could lead to considerable misunderstanding

26

and confusion. The potential disparity between acceptable role definition and training competence could easily lead to administrative misconception which could prove harmful to the service. It seems desirable, therefore, to enumerate the more significant elements of the role of a school psychologist which will utilize his competency to the maximum and reduce duplication of service that should be provided by other staff members.

Many attempts have been made to define a precise role for the school psychologist. One of the most thoughtful and comprehensive reviews has been presented by Magary.[22] Another publication which has proven helpful in role definition has been written by Attwell.[23] Both of these publications are extremely helpful in analyzing the proper role into which the school psychologist should be cast.

In the development of any role for a member of the pupil personnel team, it is imperative to analyze the unique elements of training usually provided the individual in a given service. This may sound trite, but all too often this is ignored and is one of the primary reasons for confusion in role designation. In the case of the school psychologist, for example, his training sequence includes major exposure to behavioral characteristics of children and techniques to bring about modification of behavior. Frequently, the ability is overlooked, and he may be delegated duties which can be done as well by another staff member, and his true value to the total program is diminished or lost. The specific roles noted below, therefore, give major weight to the kind of training provided the typical school psychologist.

As a Consultant
1. Assists teachers and administrators in understanding the behavioral characteristics of pupils with learning problems.
2. Aids the teacher, parent, and administrator in understanding certain antisocial behavior and how it may be modified.
3. Provides training for other staff members in the use of diagnostic tools and the proper placement and referrals for maximum pupil benefit.
4. Participates in case studies which have the dual purpose of aiding the student and providing added training for the other staff members actively involved in the study.
5. Assists group counseling leaders in process analysis and evaluation.

As a Coordinator and Participant
1. Serves as the chief coordinator of the staff assigned to the psychological services area. (The staff usually includes diagnosticians or similar personnel.)

2. Conducts applied research in all areas of school problems.
3. Participates in the work of the advisory council to the administrator of the pupil personnel services.

The School Social Worker

The movement that led to the rather common use of the social worker in the schools started in the major eastern cities and spread rapidly to the West. During the early 1900s communities recognized the value of assigning social workers from certain settlements to the schools in order to maintain a closer relationship between the settlement families and the schools. The early title for such workers was visiting teacher; but, with the rapid growth of the service, the positions have been fully incorporated into the regular school staff, and the title of school social worker is now the one most commonly used.

The school social worker is faced with a role designation problem much like that of the school psychologist. The primary difference is that many states reimburse the local school district for a part of the social worker's salary, which permits greater standardization of roles than in the case of the psychologist. This, however, may not in itself be a significant factor in controlling the school social worker's professional activity if the state leadership is weak or if the state level perception of a proper role is inconsistent with professional opinion. A factor that may have had a detrimental impact on a clear-cut role definition for the school social worker is that he is usually trained in a social work setting, with little or no contact with the school setting until he reports for his first assignment. This may or may not be a significant factor, but it does mean that, when first assigned, the social worker faces an adjustment period, which is usually characterized by some conflict and misunderstanding. The school administrator has his perception of the proper role, which usually differs from that of the social worker. It requires a period of working together before a mutual understanding is attained. This tends to create confusion and reduces the effectiveness of the pupil personnel worker during this adjustment period.

Authorities and national professional associations have attempted to define the role of the school social worker. The National Association of Social Workers, through its School Social Workers' Section, has been in the forefront in defining training programs and codes of ethical conduct for the social worker in the schools. These definitions have emerged in the last decade and have proven helpful to both the administrator and social worker in the determination of a proper role

28

for the professional in a school setting. Two recent articles by Williams[24] are especially helpful in ascertaining a proper role for the school social worker. The second article, in particular, contains a report of eighty-three items used by the author in interviews, which provide an excellent listing of activities that a social worker may perform. The study was conducted in one eastern city, and the population would, therefore, be a small sampling of current practice; but it is interesting to note that the author reported that administrators and professionals both reported greater role agreement than that which might be called areas of conflict as to proper role.

One of the more comprehensive discussions of the role of the school social worker is to be found in the material prepared by Hummel and Bonham.[25] Other writers have also devoted considerable attention to the same topic, so that it now seems that a rather specific role can be outlined for the school social worker in terms of the primary tasks this person should perform which are unique in the pupil personnel program.

As a Consultant
1. Assists in the organization and conduct of case studies.
2. Relates pertinent data to attendance officials regarding individuals included in personal case load.
3. Advises community agencies relative to school relationship.
4. Aids parents of students in personal case load in understanding particular problems faced by the student.

As a Coordinator and Participant
1. Provides special casework services for those students and families in need of such service.
2. Maintains an active relationship with community service agencies as the primary representative of the school district.
3. Serves as the major consultant to the staff in the development of case study technique.

The School Nurse
The health services vary considerably from one school district to another. The reason for the wide range of activities results from a number of factors. For example, legal or health policies set forth by agencies in the community or state may dictate the extent of the health program. In addition, the ever-present problem of budget priority may be a major determinant in the assignment of personnel to provide health services. In spite of such factors, however, there appears to be a developing health service program in the schools, and

the role of the school nurse is becoming better defined in the process.

Most authorities mentioned as resource information for the roles of school psychologist and social worker have also devoted considerable space to the role of the school nurse. Such discussions are helpful to the administrator of the pupil personnel program as a starting point in the delegation of duties in the school health program. Such reviews, however, may have less value in the health area than in most of the other pupil personnel services. The reason is that local conditions vary so much that the school administrator is required to tailor-make the role of the school nurse to fit the unique demands of his particular setting. An excellent example of this approach has been conducted in the Omaha Public Schools and published under the editorship of Lindsay.[26] This publication contains the role description for the nurse working in one school system and illustrates how a staff can adapt to the local conditions.

A school staff must, if it is to define a precise role for the school nurse, decide on the broad responsibilities of a person serving in this role as a frame of reference within which the role is specified. The Omaha school staff did this in the introduction of their publication, and it is reproduced here as a guide to those interested in developing a similar role definition.

> The role of the Omaha Public School Nurse is complex, demanding and rewarding.
>
> The object of her profession is the health of children. The health of a student is essential to her, for then she can utilize to the maximum all educational opportunities. The nurse's achievements in improving the health of the student are reflected in the increased effectiveness of the total school program.
>
> It is the nurse's responsibility to promote and exemplify healthful living in the school, home, and community for students, parents, and school personnel. Each contact with a student is used to further the student's health education.
>
> Her leadership in health activities is restricted to the limitations of the sphere of the school's responsibility. Always she aims for the ideal of mutual cooperation of home, school, and community for the maximum benefit of the child.
>
> As the school nurse works well with children and earns their confidence, she acquires a sympathetic understanding of their physical, intellectual, and emotional needs and problems.
>
> She is skilled in interpreting data from all related health appraisals and uses judgment and discretion to relate the significance of the findings for the individual student. She is available for guidance and counseling of students, teachers, and parents.

Broad definitions, such as the example noted here, may be as much as a given school district needs to obtain before defining the role of the school nurse in that district. There does appear to be merit, however, in looking at the rather unique contributions of the school nurse which will probably be common to all programs regardless of the local situation. A few of these are enumerated here.

As a Consultant

1. Assists the school staff in the identification and remediation of potential health problems in the district.
2. Provides referral advice to parents and teachers in regard to health problems of pupils.
3. Relates school health problems to local health authorities.

As a Coordinator and Participant

1. Coordinates the school health program.
2. Provides leadership in the promotion of good health practices.
3. Maintains an effective relationship with local health agencies and medical services.
4. Assists in emergency first-aid practices consistent with acceptable medical practice.

The School Attendance Coordinator

Historically, the school attendance services have been a viable part of the administrative component of education. In many school districts this condition still exists, but with the gradual shift from the philosophy of school attendance by compulsion to one of school attendance as a privilege the responsibility of coordinating the school attendance function has become more consistent with the role of the pupil personnel component. Many of the former elements of responsibility, however, still remain as a necessary part of the work of the attendance coordinator, since state attendance laws and accounting procedures are restrictions placed upon the school district by state statute. This sometimes results in some conflict and confusion, as the attendance official finds that the role he would like to play as a pupil personnel staff member is restricted by a law or regulation that he must enforce. It is not likely that this problem will change in the foreseeable future unless drastic changes are made in laws dealing with compulsory school attendance, child labor laws, and similar regulatory demands by the state.

Faced with the conditions noted above, the role of the school attendance worker becomes one of adjustment to the legal demands

31

while serving in the best interests of the pupil and the school program. To some this may appear to require a split personality, but this need not be the situation. The attendance coordinator can make a significant input into the pupil personnel program, which should result in improved assistance for pupils because he is a contributing member to the helping services in spite of the limits within which he must function.

Much like the role of the school nurse, the school attendance coordinator fits into a given school district in a manner unique to that district. Various writers have prepared rather lengthy lists of duties for such a role and various state organizations and authorities have specified very precise roles for the individual serving in such a capacity. There seems to be little value in reviewing the lists but rather to identify those responsibilities which the coordinator will probably be delegated in most school districts as a member of the pupil personnel staff.

As a Consultant

1. Provides the school staff with information obtained from parents and pupils as to causes for poor school attendance which may be correctable within the limits of good educational practice.
2. Relates to local youth and law enforcement agencies in such a way as to provide maximum understanding of the problems faced by pupils and how those problems can be handled in the most productive manner.
3. Assists other members of the pupil personnel staff in obtaining meaningful pupil information that his office can provide as a unique contribution.

As a Coordinator and Participant

1. Coordinates the total school accounting procedures and assists in making these compatible with pupil personnel records.
2. Provides a centralized service for the preparation of work permits and an information service to pupils and their parents relative to new regulations and interpretations in child labor laws.
3. Maintains student records as the registrar of the school district.

The School Counselor

In the past few years the role of the school counselor has been subjected to more attention than the roles of all other pupil personnel workers combined. The expressed concern of the lay public, the school administrators, and the counselors has resulted in some confusion as to the delegation of duties, the assessment of counselor productivity, and role expectations. Sharp criticism has been leveled at the counselor for, among other things, failing to provide relevancy in the guidance program, for failing to reduce social conflict, and for failing to prepare young people for productive careers upon graduation from high school. For many counselors, the criticism has been unjustified and far too harsh, for it appears that the critics have been trying to find a scapegoat for all the deficiencies of education, and possibly of society as well. The criticism has done little to reduce the confusion that pervades the profession as to the proper role of the school counselor.

Within the counselor training fraternity, some of the debates regarding the proper role for a school counselor have probably contributed much to the criticism. Most authorities seem to pledge their professional allegiance to the generally accepted role of a counselor as being a counselor, consultant, and coordinator. The questions of how much, of what, to whom, and when have left wide areas of difference in training and in the professional literature. Faced with this apparent lack of agreement among the authorities, counselors and administrators fell easy prey to the practice of shifting the role of the counselor to meet a new crisis or to provide a service which would result in a simple definition of activities much easier to explain to a questioning public.

A majority of school counselors themselves may be guilty of adding to the dilemma in which they find themselves today. Few counselors have assumed an aggressive role in helping the administrator define an appropriate role, report it to the individual to be served, or evaluate their service in accordance with that definition. Positions have been accepted on the fallacious assumption that the role as perceived by the counselor is viewed in the same manner by all individuals with whom he comes in contact. It is little wonder then that the administrator, teacher, pupil, and parent find it easy to be critical of the role of the school counselor when no agreed-upon role has been identified or explained.

Considerable space in the recent professional literature has been devoted to the proper role for a school counselor. For example, one of the most provocative articles has been written by Eckerson[27] as an outgrowth of the 1970 White House Conference on Children. One entire issue of *The Personnel and Guidance Journal*[28] was devoted to the role of counseling in a social revolution. A follow-up article to that presentation by Baker and Cramer[29] tended to sharpen the counselor's role in his current setting. Another significant concern affecting counselor role, that of sexism in the profession, has been reviewed in another complete issue of *The Personnel and Guidance Journal.*[30] These excellent presentations are but a handful of those available to the reader. Many will be noted later and should dramatize the current confusion relative to the proper role of the school counselor. It seems likely that it will be several years before agreement can be reached in the profession so that rather specific roles will be common in all settings. In the meantime, some generally accepted duties may be noted, and the exchange of experiences in other school districts may bring about a degree of acceptable uniformity.

As a Consultant

1. Shares with the classroom teacher, observations and suggestions designed to assist the pupil to gain the maximum from his school experience.
2. Devotes considerable time in helping the instructional staff with responsibilities for which the counselor may be uniquely prepared. Such activities as the conduct of the parent-teacher conference and the interpretation of the test profile are illustrative of this role.
3. Collects, distributes, and interprets materials of a guidance nature which may best be utilized in the regular curriculum sequence. Information about careers, social relationships, and training opportunities represent the type of information that the consultant can provide.

As a Coordinator and Participant

1. Assists the pupil assigned to him to understand and accept himself as an individual, thereby making it possible for the pupil to express and develop an awareness of his own ideas, feelings, values, and needs.
2. Provides leadership in the coordination of both pupil and environmental information so that the pupil data are cumulative and the information is comprehensive, with a minimum of significant omissions.
3. Evaluates and reports the status and needs of the guidance program to the proper school administrator in an attempt to insure a program of maximum effectiveness.

The Remedial Worker

Earlier in the chapter it was pointed out the members of the remedial or special education staff are frequently administered through the personnel group. It was also noted that the special services offered by such individuals may be more appropriately identified in the instructional group. This apparent conflict of service, however, appears to be of less concern when role definition is discussed, since the special contribution is so obvious that it requires little or no explanation. The role of the speech therapist, for example, would appear to be understood and accepted by all concerned. Likewise, the role of the reading specialist or of the teacher of the mentally retarded do not require role definitions but may demand some study of their proper relationships to the other pupil personnel workers. The latter will be noted in subsequent chapters and especially in the school district descriptions where actual practices are described.

MAJOR ELEMENTS OF THE GUIDANCE PROGRAM

The Guidance Program

Reference has been made in the preceding pages to the guidance program. Considerable space will be devoted to this topic in later material, particularly in Chapters 5 and 6, as well as in the school district descriptions. However, there does seem to be some value in identifying the broad limits of what constitutes a guidance program at this point.

Authorities tend to agree on the major elements of the guidance program of the school. Some of these use an approach they call developmental guidance, while others refer to guidance as a program of identifiable services. Sometimes the significant differences between the two approaches becomes academic if one views the elements to be found in both points of view. The following facets are the ones usually stipulated as making up the guidance program. All are vertical elements extending through all grade levels, with some being more pertinent at some levels than at others.

Student Appraisal

The various techniques used to gain a better understanding of the student and the methods used to record and report his unique characteristics constitute one of the major elements of the guidance program. Techniques of observation, anecdotal reporting, rating scales, and standardized testing represent techniques by which the individual data are collected, while the cumulative record or data processing printouts represent ways of reporting the data.

Career Planning Information

The collection, presentation, and analysis of information about social relationships, educational opportunities, and occupational outlets make up the second major element of the guidance program. The emphasis here is on the three areas of information as found in the pupil's current, as well as in his future, environment.

Counseling (Individual and Group)

Counseling consists of helping the individual, in both individual and group settings, to explore and understand himself so that he becomes a more self-directing individual.

Placement and Follow-up

Placement activities are related to assisting the student in obtaining a desirable job or in acquiring additional training in keeping with his interests and capabilities, as well as to the techniques used to give his evaluation of his educational experience in terms of his past school exposure.

Consultation to Staff

This area consists of various activities provided by the counseling staff to members of the administrative and instructional staff which improve the educational opportunities for all students.

EMERGING TRENDS AND ISSUES

This chapter has reviewed the status of pupil personnel services and defined the frame of reference within which the services will probably function in the foreseeable future. It has dealt very briefly with some of the more significant issues facing the administrator of a current and future program of pupil personnel services. These are reviewed in detail in the subsequent chapters but should be noted here in recognition of their importance in the organization of a personnel staff.

Accountability

The impact of the accountability concept on all facets of education has been both profound and demanding. There remains little doubt in the minds of school administrators and members of the governing boards as to the need for the educational enterprise to reassess its goals and to plan activities that evaluate progress toward those goals. This issue is reviewed in the next chapter.

Ethical and Legal Constraints

The present temper of the society which the educational system serves is one of great concern for the rights of the individual. Now, as never before in the history of the personnel movement, the helping services are faced with challenges which test their ethical or legal right to pursue a given course of action. This may eventually result in a far more healthy personnel program, but for the present it dictates the need for greater awareness of the limits within which the personnel worker performs. Such limits are to be noted in Chapter 3, "Ethical and Legal Aspects of Personnel Work."

The Impact of Technology

The past decade has been a period in which our society has accepted technology as a new and changing way of life. The personnel worker has seen great changes in the way his services are performed and he still faces unforeseen changes as the promise of technology is achieved. The significance of current and possible changes by the use of technology are covered in Chapter 4.

Developmental Programs

One of the most subtle, yet one of the most significant, issues facing pupil personnel workers is that of changing the relative role of the personnel worker from one of therapeutic action to one of problem prevention. This change has been described by many as a change from the corrective to the preventive. Others have suggested that the emphasis should be on the development aspects in contrast with the remedial components of a personnel program. The precise differences become most difficult to determine; yet there appears to be a recognized responsibility to develop a professional position that projects an image of individual development rather than one of therapy that has characterized the various personnel services of the past.

Projections and plans which present a development position in personnel work are most intriguing and have received general support throughout the profession. Such a shift has been, and will probably continue to be, plagued by crisis situations which cannot be anticipated in advance but which require action of a remedial nature. This should not, however, discourage the personnel worker from seeking ways and means of prevention and development as a desirable goal. Attempts at developmental activities are to be found in the chapters dealing with current programs.

The Team Approach

Another obvious trend in the professional writing of the past few years is that of giving added emphasis to the team concept. There appears to be little doubt that the personnel program of the future will be judged by the degree to which it can bring the various services into a cohesive functioning component of the total educational program. This suggests better definition of roles, better delegation of responsibility, and more functional relationships with administrators and teachers. Patterns of actual practices of this kind are reviewed in the school district descriptions, and guidelines are provided in the two chapters dealing with staff relationships.

Other trends and issues could probably be noted, but the several reviewed here appear to be the ones with the greatest potential for continued concern and direction in pupil personnel work. Crisis issues and educational fads have a way of making a dramatic impact on the educational scene and then fade into oblivion with little or no evidence of continuing concern or significant change of educational practice. The administrator, faced with such concerns, is sometimes hard pressed to evaluate the true depth of an issue or fad. He must address a new concern with the staff at his disposal and adjust to the immediate needs as the problem seeks a satisfactory resolution. This is not a very comforting solution, but it is probably the only feasible approach by which the administrator and his staff can cope with situations of this nature.

1. Harold J. Mahoney, "The Team Approach to Pupil Personnel Services," paper presented at the Interprofessional Conference on Pupil Personnel Services in Public Schools, Washington, D.C., 1961.
2. National Educational Association, *Cardinal Principles of Secondary Education* (Washington, D.C.: United States Department of the Interior, Bureau of Education, Bulletin No. 35, 1918).
3. Educational Policies Commission of the National Education Association, *The Purpose of Education in American Democracy* (Washington, D.C., 1938), p. 47.
4. Gordon P. Liddle and Gary W. Reighard, "Directors of Pupil Personnel Services, Who Are They? Where Are They Going?" *Psychology in the Schools* (Oct. 1956), 3(4): 342–48.
5. Gordon P. Liddle and Donald G. Ferguson, *Pupil Services Department, Functions Organization Staffing* (Washington, D.C.: Administrative Leadership Service, 1968).
6. Ibid., p. 3
7. Office of Education, Department of Health, Education, and Welfare, *The Scope of Pupil Personnel Services* (Washington, D.C.: Government Printing Office, 1966).
8. The National Association of Pupil Personnel Administrators.
9. Raymond N. Hatch and Buford Stefflre, *Administration of Guidance Services* (Englewood Cliffs, N. J.: Prentice-Hall, Inc., 1965).
10. Philip A. Peronne, Antoinette T. Ryan, and Franklin R. Zerau, *Guidance and the Emerging Adolescent* (Scranton, Pa.: International Book Co., 1970).
11. Dean L. Hummel and S. J. Bonham, Jr., *Pupil Personnel Services in Schools* (Chicago: Rand-McNally & Co., 1968), 331 pp.
12. Anita M. Mitchell and James A. Saum, eds., *A Master Plan for Pupil Services* (Fullerton, Calif.: California Personnel and Guidance Association, 1972).
13. James G. Miller, "Living Systems: Cross-Level Hypotheses," *Behavioral Science* (Oct. 1965), 10(4): 403
14. G. P. Liddle and G. W. Reighard, op. cit.
15. Donald G. Hays, "Administrator, Director, Supervisor—Would You Accept Chief?" *Counselor Education and Supervision* (Dec. 1971), 11(2):119–28.
16. Ray O. Warner, *Pupil Personnel Services in the 50 States* (Moravia, N.Y.: Chronicle Guidance Publications, Inc., 1969), 114 pp.
17. Hummel and Bonham, op. cit.
18. George E. Hill, *Management and Improvement of Guidance* (New York: Appleton-Century-Crofts, 1965), pp. 143–67.
19. Hatch and Stefflre, op. cit, pp. 116–47.
20. Glenn A. Saltzman and Herman J. Peters, *Pupil Personnel Services—Selected Readings* (Itasca, Ill.: F. E. Peacock Publishers, Inc., 1967..
21. Hummel and Bonham, op. cit., pp. 89–248.
22. James F. Magary, ed., *School Psychological Services*, (Englewood Cliffs, N.J.: Prentice-Hall, Inc., 1967).
23. Arthur A. Attwell, *A Handbook for School Psychologists* (Burbank, Calif.: The Eire Press, 1970).
24. Robert Bruce Williams, "The Helping Professions: Problems Only?", *The Journal of School Health* (Jan. 1970), 40(1):24–27; "The Role of the School Social

Worker," *The Journal of the International Association of Pupil Personnel Workers* (Sept. 1969), 13(4):171–77.

25. Hummel and Bonham, op. cit., pp. 179–97.
26. Vivian Lindsay, "Guidance for the School Nurse," publication of the Omaha, Neb., Public Schools, 1969, p. 2.
27. Louise O. Eckerson, "The White House Conference: Tips or Taps for Counselors," *The Personnel and Guidance Journal* (Nov. 1971), 50(3):161–74.
28. *The Personnel and Guidance Journal* (May 1971), 49(9):661–66.
29. Stanley B. Baker and Stanley H. Cramer, "Counselor or Change Agent: Support from the Profession," *The Personnel and Guidance Journal* (April 1972), vol. 50, no. 8.
30. *The Personnel and Guidance Journal* (Oct. 1972), vol. 51, no. 2.

SELECTED REFERENCES

Attwell, Arthur A. *A Handbook for School Psychologists*, chap. 1. Burbank, Calif.: The Eire Press, 1970.

Hummel, Dean L., and Bonham, S. J., Jr. *Pupil Personnel Services in Schools*, parts 3 and 4. Chicago: Rand McNally & Co., 1968.

Meisgeier, Charles H., and King, John D. *The Process of Special Education Administration*, Part 2. Scranton, Pa.: International Textbook Co., 1970.

Mitchell, Anita M., and Saum, James A., eds. *A Master Plan for Pupil Services*, chaps. 4 and 10. Fullerton, Calif.: California Personnel and Guidance Association, 1972.

Morphet, Edgar L., Johns, Roe L., and Reller, Theodore L. *Educational Organization and Administration*, 2nd ed., chap. 5. Englewood Cliffs, N.J.: Prentice-Hall, Inc., 1967.

Walz, Garry R., and Lee, James L. *Caps Current Resources Series Pupil Personnel Services*, pp. 1–43. Ann Arbor: ERIC Counseling and Personnel Services Information Center, 1968.

Warner, C. Ray. *Pupil Personnel Services in the 50 States*, part 5. Moravia, N.Y.: Chronicle Guidance Publications, Inc., 1969.

CHAPTER 2

Program Objectives and Assessment

DONALD G. HAYS

ALICE: Will you tell me, please, which way I ought to go from here?
CAT: That depends a good deal on where you want to get to.
ALICE: I don't much care where. . . .
CAT: Then it doesn't matter which way you go.
ALICE: . . . . so long as I get somewhere.
CAT: Oh, you're sure to do that if you only walk long enough.
Lewis Carroll, Alice in Wonderland

IT is not enough to get somewhere "if you only walk long enough."
Managers of pupil services do not have much time and they have
definite commitments to keep. They face new challenges daily. They
can continue to douse fires or they can begin to plan ways to prevent
those fires from starting. Any person who is responsible for the administration of a program of pupil services is a manager. This chapter
is written for new managers and for those experienced managers
who are seeking new ways to solve old, continuing problems. Pupil
personnel specialists may wish to consider the model of managing
offered here as a means of becoming more accountable.

RATIONALE

Man, in order to insure his survival and continuation, is concerned
with providing appropriate knowledge to his progeny—knowledge
that he has learned, modified by that which he is experiencing. The
knowledge, and its appropriateness, differs from one society to another and from one generation to another. Early man taught his son
skills in using primitive tools. How well the son learned those survival

skills was measured by his ability to find food, to make clothes, and to provide shelter for the family. In another time, the wealthy New England father employed a schoolmaster to teach his son that which the Puritan society valued. How well the son learned his lessons was measured by his ability to recite classical literature in Greek and Latin and to read and to interpret the Bible as expected by that society.

Traditionally, it has been the father's role to pass on to his son valued concepts and experiences. In some societies, the family, or tribe, assumed a major portion of the responsibility of raising young children to take their place in the society. The age of specialization saw the transfer of teaching go from the father to the tribe; from the tribe to the specialist. Accountability was known and practiced in the United States long before its current vogue. The educated man was held in high esteem by the society, and the schoolmaster had to produce results or he was "let go." The American dream, shared by the significant influx of emigrants, took for granted that formal education, taught by the specialist, would produce desired results about universally accepted subject matter thought needed for a democratic nation. Wise decisions and the democratic process were dependent upon a person's ability to read, write, and do calculations.

For the past decade the concept of accountability has been re-examined. As the typical American has become more consumer-conscious, as the cost of education has become increasingly more evident, as the willingness of Americans to pay additional taxes to support society's governments, at all levels, has dwindled, educators are being challenged to show evidence that what they produce is worth the cost involved. The halo of faith in American education has become tilted and tarnished. Too many of the young do not read, write, compute, nor value that which the older generation expects them to know and value. The rapid transition from an agrarian society through an age of industrialization into a nuclear era has reached a critical stage. Education is expected to project the young into an increasingly less-defined future, while keeping them firmly grounded in their heritage. The age of anxiety lingers, while an age of paradox grows. How is it possible for educators to be held accountable when society is not sure what it values or where it wants to go? There is evidence that some states are attempting to find the answers.[1]

Two concepts have been identified: society's expectations in educating its young and accountability. How the manager and his staff

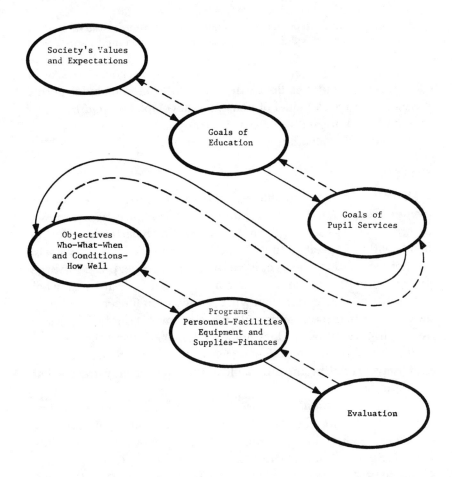

Fig. 2.1 Achieving greater accountability.

can become more accountable, and for what, can best be portrayed
by the diagram in Figure 2.1 and stated as follows:

Society's values and expectations become the goals of education. The
goals of pupil services must be compatible with, and serve as an extension of, the goals of education. Goals must be delineated and expanded
into specific objectives. Programs must be designed around the objectives. Finally, evaluation of the programs must take place to determine

43

if the objectives have been met which in turn determine if the desired goals which society values and expects are being accomplished.

It means the manager states what he wants and is going to do, does it, and then provides evidence that he did it. The remainder of this chapter describes a model of managing developed around this concept and is comprised of four major components: goals, objectives, programs, and evaluation.

GOALS

Man's expectations for himself and for his progeny are usually identified as *goals*. "A goal is a statement of broad direction, purpose, or intent that is general and is not concerned with particular achievements within a specified time frame."[2] Americans have many goals. As there are national goals of equality, justice, peace, prosperity, the pursuit of happiness, and other concepts that indicate that what should be must be better than what is now. Pronouncement of such goals means that the country values these concepts and will work to accomplish them, but it does not state how and when they will be attained. Individuals, also, have goals that they try to reach. These goals may be realistic and attainable or they may be only dreams that are desirable.

Goals of Education. Goals can be categorized, i.e., political, economic, social, and educational goals. Goals of education may vary from one person to another, from one group to another, and certainly from one generation, or period of time, to another. The importance of this diversity is recognized when one becomes aware that the goals of education have been discussed for centuries by some of the best minds of all time. The purposes of education reflect man's concern that he be able to perpetuate his species and, while so doing, seek the good life. As society changes, as the beliefs and values of people change, it seems reasonable that the future direction of the society and of its people would also change. Thus, educational goals change periodically. Yet, some ideas tend to remain constant.

A subcommittee of the Governor's Committee on Public School Education for the State of Texas reported that "the universal and continuing goals for public education may be grouped under six broad headings."[3] The subcommittee listed the six goals and traced each through more than three hundred years of historical landmarks for public education. Even though society's beliefs and values may change, it is conceivable that any future goals of education could be grouped under one of these six headings: (1) the ideal of intellectual discipline, (2) economic independence and vocational opportunity, (3) citizenship and civic responsibility, (4) social development and human relationships, (5) morals and ethical character, (6) self-realization, including health and psychological needs. Consider the pronounced statements that follow and see how they fit one or more of the categories above.

Participants of the National Conference of Pupil Personnel Services believed that the following were "the usual major needs of learners and that the satisfaction of those needs at a high level comprises the major goals of the new model":

1. A sense of one's self as a worthwhile person who is capable of making one's own life decisions.
2. Opportunities to participate in the process of identification of one's own needs, and the planning and evaluation of one's learning experiences.
3. Skills to survive in an oppressive environment and to bring about productive change.
4. Full opportunity to retain one's ethnic and cultural identity and to develop one's potentialities in harmony with the goals and values of one's family and community.
5. Skills in understanding, relating to, and communicating with others, irrespective of race, cultural and economic background, sex, and age.
6. Skills needed to learn and an attitude that learning is a life-long process.
7. Sound physical well-being.[4]

Another group of educational leaders devised a list of imperatives in education. They were not intended to be educational goals, but were "points at which the educational program must be revised and reshaped to meet the needs of the times."[5] However, on examining these imperatives, they could well be cast as goals.

1. To make urban life rewarding and satisfying.
2. To prepare people for the world of work.
3. To discover and nurture creative talent.
4. To strengthen the moral fabric of society.
5. To deal constructively with psychological tensions.
6. To keep democracy working.
7. To make intelligent use of natural resources.
8. To make the best use of leisure time.
9. To work with other peoples of the world for human betterment.[6]

Individuals, too, have spoken out about the purposes of education. It might be well to present the purposes of education from two contrasting points of view. While one approach looks specifically to the purposes, the other is stated in terms of tasks that confront the nation following the cessation of hositilities in Vietnam. Max Rafferty and John W. Gardner appear to be standing back-to-back at a given point in time, looking at their environment. One looks to the past and makes comments about the kind of education needed today, while the other is looking to the future and comments on the problems society must face and solve. In an editorial, Rafferty was asked, "What is the purpose of education?" he replied, "It doesn't have one, sir, it has five, and here they are (1) to pursue the truth . . ., (2) to hand down the cultural heritage of the race . . ., (3) to teach organized, disciplined, systematic subject matter . . ., (4) to help the individual realize his own potential . . ., (5) to ensure the survival of our country . . ."[7]

While not directly stating the purpose, or purposes, of education, Gardner wrote of the commitments society must make regarding ten problems. He portrayed a world society as it prepares to be projected into the twenty-first century. Although he stated a series of problems, they could be considered as goals for a nation if reworded.

1. The problem of building an enduring peace.
2. The problem of the developing nations.
3. The problem of population control.
4. The problem of equal opportunity.
5. The problem of creating an educational system that will provide the maximum individual fulfillment for each American.
6. The problem of bringing new life to our cities.
7. The problem of our natural environment.
8. The problem of reshaping of government.
9. The problem of economic growth.
10. The problem of the relationship of the individual to society.[8]

Kaufman, Corrigan, and Johnson state "that by far the most important goal of public education is to give citizens the requisite skills and knowledges to survive and contribute in the operational or real world."[9] Earlier, Gardner addressed himself to the ever-renewing society and identified three characteristics of the self-renewing man:

1. The self-renewing man is versatile and adaptive.
2. The self-renewing man is highly motivated and respects his own energy and motivation.

46

3. For the self-renewing man, the development of his own potentialities and the process of self-discovery never end.[10]

He continued by saying:

The ever-renewing society will be a free society. It will understand that the only stability possible today is stability in motion. It will foster a climate in which the seedlings of new ideas can survive and the deadwood of obsolete ideas be hacked out. Above all, it will recognize that its capacity for renewal depends on individuals who make it up. It will foster innovative, versatile and self-renewing men and women, and give them room to breathe.[11]

From these excerpts and quotations, it can be seen that goals of education vary, and yet there is a common thread running through each fabric. Words differ but the concepts tend to be universal.

Most school districts have a statement of goals or a philosophy of education. Some or all ideas presented here will be found in these statements. Pupil services personnel must examine these statements to know the direction their institution, community, and society wishes to go and to know the rationale behind each. Knowledge of the intent of the goals represents the first step in developing and managing an effective pupil services program.

Goals of Pupil Services. Pupil services are an integral part of the educational enterprise. Thus, the goals of pupil services emanate from the goals of education. They may be an extension or elaboration of the educational goals, but they are *not* different. It is essential that managers of pupil services programs consider the goals of their institution and identify those statements of goals for which they, and the services they manage, have a primary responsibility in accomplishing. An example of one district's efforts can be seen in Table 1.1. Personnel of the Fullerton, California, Union High School District examined recently adopted district goals of education and extracted six statements in which they felt they could make a positive contribution.[12] They recognized that the district's goals implied, but did not state specifically, goals in three strategic areas of concern to counselors. Thus, they added to their goal's statement and then reorganized the items in priority order.

Not all districts have a written statement of goals or if there is one, it may not be readily available. How does one begin to develop goals if a district does not have a statement? There appear to be at least

47

TABLE 1
Fullerton, California, Union High School District

GOALS OF EDUCATION

1. To improve in the individual the intellectual process of thinking accurately, critically, and clearly on the basis of all evidence available and arriving at logical conclusions.
2. To improve in the individual the basic skills: reading, writing, listening, computing, spelling, and speaking.
3. To assist each student in the acquisition of knowledge.
4. To develop, maintain, and improve the mental and physical health of the individual.
5. To assist each individual in preparing for a choice of a satisfying and useful vocation, and in many instances develop marketable skills in the individual.
6. To assist each individual in developing an acceptance and understanding of himself within his physical and mental potentials.
7. To instill within each individual an appreciation for the American heritage and a willingness to assume active responsibility for citizenship in a free democratic society.
8. To provide opportunities for each individual to develop special and creative talents.
9. To develop in each individual an appreciation for the beauty in nature and the creations of man.
10. To encourage each student toward enjoyment of leisure time.
11. To encourage each student to be a contributing member of society.
12. To assist each student to build a constructive, consistent, and compelling system of values and accompanying attitudes.

GOALS OF GUIDANCE AND COUNSELING

1. To help students become increasingly self-directed and self-disciplined.
2. To assist individuals in developing an acceptance and understanding of themselves within their physical and mental potentials.
3. To help students become more understanding of their aptitudes, abilities, interests, attitudes, and limitations.
4. To assist students to build constructive, consistent, and compelling system of values and accompanying attitudes.
5. To assist individuals in preparing for a choice of a satisfying and useful vocation, and in many instances, develop marketable skills in the individuals.
6. To encourage students to be contributing members of society.
7. To develop, maintain, and improve the mental and physical health of individuals.
8. To help students by interpreting students to their many environments.
9. To provide opportunities for individuals to develop special and creative talents.

two alternatives. Other organizations or groups have developed goal statements. The National Association of Pupil Personnel Administrators suggests that "the pupil personnel staff has a deep concern with the school's efforts to"

1. create an effective climate for learning;
2. integrate and utilize all available information on each child pertinent to the educational process;
3. provide educational experiences appropriate to the unique characteristics of the individual pupil;
4. help children develop appropriate aspirations and a positive self-concept;
5. protect each child's individuality, his right to self-determination and his right to be respected;
6. help each child achieve and to facilitate his optimal development.[13]

Wellman, in a study for the United States Office of Education, developed a taxonomy of guidance objectives.[14] While he used the term "objective," these statements are goals in the context of the definitions used in this chapter. He recognized the problem that universally applicable guidance (goals) had to be identified to the exclusion of other organized or incidental agents of behavior change. His taxonomy of guidance (goals) "are the *primary purpose* of *guidance* while they are only secondary or incidental purposes of other groups."[15] Wellman categorized his (goals) for research and program purposes to provide a structure which would define the scope, content, and, where appropriate, the sequence of expected outcomes. "The major areas of (goals) are referred to as the educational domain, the vocational domain, and the social domain."[16] Within each domain (goals) were classified in a hierarchy from perceptualization, through conceptualization, to generalizations. "This sequential classification may permit the specification of immediate, intermediate, and long-range (goals) of the guidance process, thus providing a basis for a longitudinal study of behavior change from the point of initial awareness to the point of behavior integration."[17]

The California State Department of Education developed a set of Objectives of Pupil Personnel Services.[18] Once again, the word "objective" is used when it should read "goal." The ten objectives were divided into two major sections.

A. *The Optimization of Learning*
   1. To assist each pupil to achieve at a level commensurate with his ability.
   2. To assist each pupil, his teacher, and his parents to agree generally on the achievements and behavior to be expected of him.

49

3. To promote effective interpersonal behavior.
4. To minimize learning problems.
B. *The Utilization of Learning*
5. To achieve an optimum level of education.
6. To effect a smooth transition from one educational level to another.
7. To create positive attitudes toward school.
8. To assist pupils in the development of positive but realistic self-perceptions.
9. To assist pupils in the development of appropriate levels of aspirations.
10. To promote the effective use of learning in problem-solving.

A second alternative is for the manager to develop his own unique goals for a particular program—but always within the context of the values and beliefs of the community to be served. A rather simple process to accomplish this activity is to consider what should be that is not now. What specific direction of change does the manager expect to see in pupil behavior? How should pupils be different at the end of an educational activity than at the beginning? Goal development tends to dwell in the realm of philosophy. A sound philosophic foundation is crucial to the development of a strong and positive pupil services program.

Goals of Individual Pupil Services. The goals of the attendance, guidance, health, psychological or social work services do not differ from the overall goals of pupil services. The goals of the total program should encompass all five services. Should subgoals be desired (this would depend on the size of the district, its organizational structure, and the personnel involved), each of the major goals can be extended and limited to the unique contributions of each service. These extended goals become the primary mission of that service. They provide the means to establish priorities and help to eliminate the possible overlapping of responsibilities of each service.

At the risk of oversimplification, consider how one goal listed above might be extended for each of the five services:

Pupil Services Goal: TO ASSIST EACH PUPIL, HIS TEACHER, AND HIS PARENTS TO AGREE GENERALLY ON THE ACHIEVEMENTS AND BEHAVIOR TO BE EXPECTED OF HIM.
Attendance service subgoal: To resolve problems that interfere with a pupil's school progress resulting from nonattending behavior.
Guidance service subgoal: To help each pupil understand himself in relation to the social and psychological world in which he lives.
Health services subgoal: To provide health counseling to each pupil,

50

his parents, and teachers that will help them plan corrective action for health problems which interfere with the pupil's effectiveness in learning.

Psychological services subgoal: To help parents and school personnel understand the causes underlying a pupil's behavior and to suggest methods of helping the pupil develop desirable behavioral patterns.

Social work services subgoal: To serve as liaison between a pupil's home, the school, and other community helping agencies in an effort to resolve family problems affecting a pupil's ability to learn or to function socially.

These are examples only. Each pupil services team must design goals that mesh with the goals of the district and the expectations of the community.

Summary. Goals provide a target. They help school people to determine what is important to the specific community they serve and to society in general. They establish a rationale for our activities and maintain relevancy. There are universally accepted goals that tend not to change over a period of time. Educational goals are derived to establish clearly the mission of the total educational enterprise within the community. Pupil services goals must be compatible with the broader purposes of education. Having a knowledge and an understanding of the educational goals, the pupil services manager can extend or elaborate them to create pupil services goals. Each of these goals can be redefined as subgoals for the five pupil services. Goals become mission-oriented. They do not state when and how personnel will accomplish them or how it will be known that they have been accomplished and by how much. To do this, it is important to go beyond generalities to specifics. Objectives provide the vehicle for this next step.

OBJECTIVES

It was said that goals provide direction. Such statements tell little of what pupil services personnel will do specifically, when and how they will do it, and how they will know when they have done it. Written objectives must describe specific outcomes that can be measured in some meaningful way. "An OBJECTIVE is a measurable desired accomplishment whose attainment within a given time frame and under specifiable conditions can be evaluated. The attainment of the objective advances the system toward corresponding goals."[19] If a pupil services team has identified a set of goals, the team must restate, clarify, quantify, or define the goals. It is at this point

51

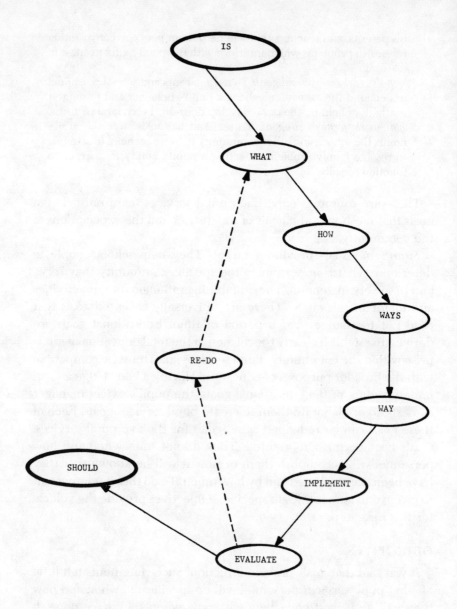

Fig. 2.2.   Problem-solving model for goal-to-objective activity.

that many people reach an impasse. To focus on a general, timeless target is one thing, but to detail it with criteria indicators and milestones is another. Kaufman presented an approach to this goal-to-objective activity by suggesting a six-step problem-solving model.[20] Perhaps at the risk of another oversimplification, it can be portrayed (Figure 2.2) as a linear process with a closed-loop feedback mechanism.

The most important aspect of this model is the clear identification of the "is-should" relationship. The "should" is elaborated by asking the question, "What should be?" What specific activity or behavior is desired by the community, the school, or the pupil services team? This is the goal. The "is" should describe precisely what is occurring at the moment. At the time something is stated as a "should," it implies that it is not now and therefore it is possible to state a condition or situation that needs to be changed. "A NEED is . . . the discrepancy between *what is* and *what is required*—(what should be) —a definition that indicates that a need is a measurable difference or distance between a present state or condition and what is required to be accomplished."[21] Once the team knows where they are and where they want to go, they can proceed to describe how they will get there. But, first, consider a tangential thought. Suppose they do not know where they want to go and they are unhappy with what is? It may be necessary to conduct a *needs assessment.* Such an activity moves them back into the goal-defining realm, and time and energy is needed to work with the total community to determine what should be.

Kaufman continued by saying that "a problem is defined as the requirement to reduce or eliminate a discrepancy between *what is* and *what is required* to a specified level."[22] The "what" segment of the model is a specific statement of what the manager would expect to observe when the "should" has been reached. As Mager points out, goal analysis must be performed so that "having identified a goal that you consider important to achieve, be able to describe the performances that represent your meaning of the goal. In other words, be able to describe specific outcomes that, if achieved, will cause you to agree that the goal is also achieved."[23] In other words, how does the manager know a goal when he sees one?

A task force of California pupil services educators and managers came together in 1970 and again in 1971 to create a process guide for the development of objectives. They recognized that objectives could come from several sources: from the current program of activi-

ties, from a needs assessment procedure, or from external sources. The task force developed a format for providing a complete statement of an objective. The format has been used extensively and represents one approach to be used by a pupil services team that is intent upon becoming accountable through management by objectives. The basic format, hereafter called SPOP, is as follows:

1. SITUATION: Where will attainment of the desired outcome be assessed? What are the characteristics of the school and community which affect population or have implications for process outcomes?

2. POPULATION: Who comprises the target group? What are the characteristics of the population?

3. OUTCOME: What is the desired behavior to be acquired by the target group? To what degree is the desired behavior to be achieved and by what percent of the target group?

4. PROCESS: How and when will the target group acquire the desired behavior? That is, what guidance-related activities will be employed to implement the desired outcome?[24]

It is well to point out that one goal may have any number of objectives and an objective may have implications for more than one goal (Figure 2.3.)

The flexibility noted in Figure 2.3 can be found in the SPOP format

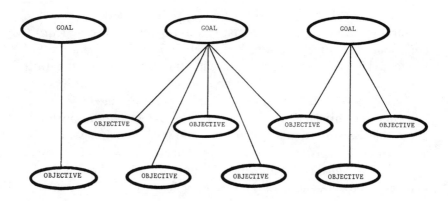

Fig. 2.3. A goal may have a number of objectives, and an objective may relate to more than one goal.

for developing objectives. A SITUATION statement may be used for any number of population, outcome, and process statements. A POPULATION statement may be followed by any number of outcomes and process statements. An OUTCOME statement may be accomplished by any number of processes. If a desired outcome is not met by one process, change the process and try again. Referring to Kaufman's problem-solving model, there are many alternatives to getting what is required. If one approach does not work, try another (redo if necessary).

This flexibility also works in reverse. A process may develop any number of outcomes. An outcome may be desirable for any number of populations, and so forth. It is important to recognize that SPOP as a format is a guide and should be used by the pupil services team only as a tool. The team cannot afford to make the format an end unto itself and forget the primary purpose of assisting young people to reduce their needs.

Examples. In order to continue the logical progression begun in an earlier section, some examples of the SPOP approach are offered. Recall that the goal statement was: TO ASSIST EACH PUPIL, HIS TEACHER, AND HIS PARENTS TO AGREE GENERALLY ON THE ACHIEVEMENTS AND BEHAVIOR TO BE EXPECTED OF HIM. From this statement, a subgoal was derived for each of the five pupil services. Following each pupil services subgoal is an example of an objective written in the SPOP format.

Attendance service subgoal: To resolve problems that interfere with a pupil's school progress resulting from nonattending behavior.

1. SITUATION: A small neighborhood elementary school (K-6) located in a low socio-economic section of a large metropolitan area, where parental attitudes toward school tend to be negative.

2. POPULATION: The parents or guardians of those pupils whose attendance pattern is irregular or whose nonattendance patterns have exceeded twenty-five percent of the days school was in session.

3. OUTCOME: To reduce nonattending behavior by ten percent by the end of the first semester.

4. PROCESS: The district shall employ a community aide to work under the supervision of the district child welfare and attendance officer. Upon receiving the names of the target population, the community aide will go into the homes at a time when the entire family is available to discuss the nonattend-

55

ing behavior of the child. Emphasis shall be on listening to the family rather than threatening the family with legal action. The community aide shall act as liaison between the family and the child's behavior. He shall report his findings to appropriate school personnel.

Guidance services subgoal: To help each pupil to understand himself in relation to the social and psychological world in which in lives.

1. SITUATION: A school of approximately two hundred students, grades 9-12, located in a rural, economically marginal, farm community.

2. POPULATION: Fifty-five ninth grade boys and girls.

3. OUTCOME: By the end of the ninth grade, each student shall be able to identify five major strengths he has and to write an essay describing how his strengths might contribute to the social and psychological climate of the community.

4. PROCESS: All entering freshmen will be assigned to a career orientation course offered twice a week for one year. The content of the course shall be centered on the individual as a dynamic, developing adolescent in a changing society. The counselor shall teach the course, using a group guidance approach. The class will be limited to a maximum of thirty students.

Health services subgoal: To provide health counseling to each pupil, his parents, and teachers, in order to help them plan corrective action for health problems interfering with the pupil's effectiveness in learning.

1. SITUATION: A suburban junior high school located in an affluent community.

2. POPULATION: Twenty boys who have been identified as having muscular coordination problems in physical education.

3. OUTCOME: All twenty students will have either corrected their problem or have begun appropriate therapy for correction by the end of the first semester.

4. PROCESS: The school nurse shall plan for and hold individual conferences with each of the students, their parents, and the physical education teacher. Following the conference, the parents shall work with their own family physician in planning for the physical correction. The nurse shall coordinate the project with the physical education teacher, the parents, and the family physicians.

Psychological services subgoal: To help parents and school personnel understand the causes underlying a pupil's behavior and to suggest methods of helping the pupil develop desirable behavioral patterns.

56

1.	SITUATION:	An elementary school located in a midwestern small town.
2.	POPULATION:	Five fourth-grade boys whose overt behavior is disruptive to the classroom learning process.
3.	OUTCOME:	A reduction of the disruptive behavior by eighty percent within twenty school days.
4.	PROCESS:	Using appropriate behavior modification techniques, the school psychologist shall meet with each boy once a day to discuss his behavior and prescribe activities to improve it. The psychologist will consult with appropriate teachers and the parents of the boys to observe the psychological environment surrounding the boys and to suggest activities, compatible with the activities prescribed for each boy, to reinforce the positive behavior of the boys.

Social work services subgoal. To serve as liaison between a pupil's home, the school, and other community helping agencies in an effort to resolve family problems affecting a pupil's ability to learn or to function socially.

1.	SITUATION:	An overcrowded senior high school located in an inner-city ghetto area.
2.	POPULATION:	Ten girls requesting permission to withdraw from school to assist their mothers in the home.
3.	OUTCOME:	Within one school month, family problems are to be reduced sufficiently to allow each girl to remain in school without further pressure to seek another withdrawal.
4.	PROCESS:	The school social worker will interview each girl to learn of the reasons the girls are needed at home. A home visit and conference with the parents will verify the girl's statements. Working with appropriate community agencies (welfare department, local employment office, other social agencies), a coordinated effort will be initiated to reduce or resolve the family problems. The school social worker will consult with each girl's counselor and teachers to rearrange the student's course program as needed.

One difficulty in presenting examples such as these is the natural tendency to criticize the specifics and overlook the concepts. No attempt was made in these illustrations to offer them as models; rather, emphasis was placed on the components needed in developing operational objectives.

The pupil services manager, in cooperation with his team, must develop his own objectives from broad goals. The objectives place a time perspective and a quantitative value on the results to be obtained. Each objective identifies where, by whom, what, how and when an activity will be accomplished. It is reasonable to assume that a goal may have from one to many objectives. It is also possible that one objective may contribute to more than one goal. Considerable flexibility is available, but caution should be used in attempting to communicate this flexibility to the administration and to the community because of the multiplicity of unique combinations of goals and objectives that can be obtained.

What has been said so far can be considered as the thinking or planning stage. No recommendations for definite action have been offered—only sets of possibilities. In moving from the drawing board to the completion of the activity, it is necessary to bring in the third component—programs.

PROGRAMS

The term "program" is familiar to all school personnel. There is the English program, the guidance program, the athletic program, the maintenance program, and so forth. "A program is a group of interdependent, closely related activities or services contributing to or progressing toward a common objective or set of similar objectives."[25] Critical elements of a program include personnel, facilities, equipment, and supplies. Programs are usually constrained by the financial, legal, and ethical considerations of the organization. Thus, when one talks about the English program, he is encompassing teachers, students, books, supplies, the classroom, the financial support, the activities carried on within the classroom, and other parts that make up the whole. The primary purpose of a program is to provide a vehicle for the accomplishment of the objectives. A program is the process component of the objective. Many programs can be created—as many as there are objectives (Figure 2.4).

Each objective must have a program or programs. It is of no value to write an objective and not develop a program to accomplish it. Programs can be very simple or complex and of short duration or continuously operating over a period of years.

Each program is made up of one or more specific components—personnel, facilities, and equipment and supplies. It is possible to have a program without equipment and supplies. A program may not have any special facilities. But no program can survive without personnel. After all, it was said that a target population exists in all

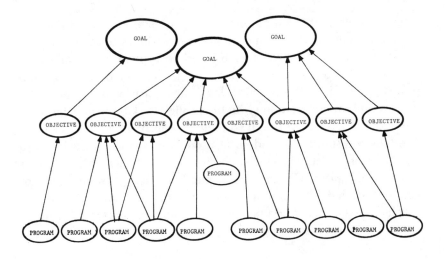

Fig. 2.4. Goals, objectives, and programs.

operational objectives and someone, or several people, needs to be identified as working with the target population.

Personnel

The most crucial component in a program is the people who make it operate. Since pupil services teams are providing services to, for, and with pupils, it is not necessary to dwell on the need to have pupils as part of the personnel of a program. That is a given requisite and will be accepted. That population has been identified in the operational objective.

The personnel of concern here are the members of the pupil services team—the professionals, the paraprofessionals, the clerical staff, and other people who are involved in the pupil services enterprise. Two concepts are important to keep foremost in mind when thinking of the people needed to operate pupil services programs. The first is the concept of *professionalism*. The term "professional" is an oft-used term that has many connotations. The term "real pro" means a person who is well-trained, experienced, and approaches his tasks in a deliberate, competent manner, recognizing that his worth is measured on what he can produce or contribute to the total team effort.[26] In this sense, professional could be applied to all staff members. It can also mean that a person is a member of a recognized profession, such as the medical, legal, or educational profession. A profession is an association of highly proficient, knowledgeable people with a deep commitment to their chosen practice. It has a code of ethics and standards of identification. A profession contributes to the good of society through a service to society which recognizes professional status. Unfortunately, pupil services personnel are not yet professional—they are in the process of becoming. Counselors, psychologists, social workers, nurses, attendance officers have many of the attributes attributed to a profession, but as Armor comments about counselors:

> One of the major arguments that can be made against considering counseling as a profession is the very location of its practice. Unlike many other professionals, almost all guidance counselors are located in institutional settings controlled by persons who are not in the same profession. This is a potential threat to professional autonomy, and autonomy has traditionally been viewed as one of the most crucial aspects of a profession.[27]

Pupil services personnel must become more involved in their own destiny. They need a voice in the selection, recruitment, training, licensing, and evaluation of those coming into and working in the field. Pupil services as a "becoming" profession is still influenced by too many external sources.

The second concept about personnel is the *team approach*. Counselors, nurses, and others tend to operate in isolation. Occasionally, two or three people may discuss a student common to all, but there seems to be no planned activity for mutual efforts on behalf of all students. If, as it has been said, the goals of the organization have been clearly stated, and objectives have been determined, then one should expect some programs to be designed to draw upon the expertise of the total team—the limitations of one member augmented by the talents of another. No one person can be all things to all students effectively. The recognition of mutual support is essential. The acceptance of the team concept is dependent upon the ego strength of each team member. An effective program built around a highly proficient team has no place for jurisdictional disputes over who is to do what and when. A well-designed program will not allow such disputes to arise.

There are some other aspects regarding personnel to be considered—training, selection, continuing education, and evaluation of people. A manager's responsibility and his total effectiveness is predicated on how he responds to these four areas.

Training. Although it is not the manager's primary responsibility to train pupil services personnel, he should have a major interest in recognized training programs. From such programs he will get his staff. The quality of his staff is dependent upon the quality of its training. Pupil services educators are concerned that what they include in their curriculum is what personnel in the field need to know and use. The relationship between educator and supervisor must be a close reciprocating one of shared information and experiences. Every effort must be made to involve the manager in the formal education program and for pupil services educators to extend their assistance, following completion of an individual's training, into the field for effective placement and follow-up information.

Selection. If competent personnel are employed, many potential problems will be dissipated. The selection process should involve not only the manager, but other staff personnel and, where feasible, students. Assuming that prospective employees meet district-stated criteria for employment, the crucial element of the process is the determination among several candidates who can contribute the most to the total program. Several key areas might be used to identify the right person for the position:

1. Does the person exhibit ego-strength—that characteristic within the individual which enables him to differentiate between what he does and who he is?
2. Does the person exhibit a tolerance for frustration?
3. Can the person articulate a personal philosophical position that signifies a strong professional commitment?
4. Does the person exhibit a profound affection for young people?
5. Does he transmit that he is open, accepting, the kind of person who comes across as one you would like to have working with your own children?

Although it is difficult to respond to these questions in a short, or even a long interview, a skillful manager, with the help of staff and students, can get some impressions and will make a decision. The appropriateness of the decision will be tested later. Because it is a team, each candidate must be evaluated according to how he fits into the team. His strengths and weaknesses must be weighed against the strengths and weaknesses of the rest of the staff in order to find the best match.

Continuing Education. A person's personal and professional growth does not end following training and employment. Continuing provision for growth activities must be provided. It is well to employ the best qualified person available, but the manager must insure that he does not stagnate. Each member of the team is responsible for his own personal growth, but the manager must provide the environment for professional growth to occur. A well-functioning team will strive to grow together. Periodic exposure to programs in other districts, in-service programs within the district, and opportunities to attend professional meetings and conferences are essential elements of the continuing professional development of the staff.

Evaluation. One of the manager's most difficult tasks will be to evaluate his personnel. Evaluation always begins as a personal look at ourselves. "We evaluate ourselves continuously while we work," states Coney.[28] As a guide to performance evaluation, Coney suggests six rules:

Rule 1: In performance evaluation, we evaluate the job a person does, not the person himself nor the method he uses.

Rule 2: In order to evaluate performance, we have to define that performance.

Rule 3: Setting objectives cooperatively with those to be evaluated is the best means of assuring that there will be agreement on what are the objectives of the organization.

Rule 4: Performance evaluation should be made upon the basis of mutually agreed upon and cooperatively developed standards of performance which specify what is to be done and the means for measuring satisfactory completion.

Rule 5: We must provide those whose performance we are going to evaluate with all reasonable assistance to help them achieve success.

Rule 6: Performance evaluation gives each member of the team an opportunity to improve, and that's what evaluation is all about.[29]

Facilities

Programs must take place somewhere. Facilities must be provided, if called for in the objective. An objective may ask for nothing more than the opportunity for two people to encounter each other. In this instance, open space is all that is needed and should be provided. It is the manager's duty to see that such space is available. Normally, facilities refer to housing of staff and the necessary furnishings contained therein. Regardless of what may be written in the objective, facilities must be provided so as to promote a sound psychological atmosphere among the people involved. Facilities can be sterile or they can be warm spaces for people to relate one to another. Whatever the team believes about human relationships must be reflected in the architecture of the program. Creativity can be used to convert existing spaces into desirable places for operating programs.

Equipment and Supplies

Many programs may not need equipment or supplies, but where such items are called for in the objectives, they should be available. One cannot expect a program requiring extensive data gathering to function if appropriate machinery is not available. Realistic planning must take place. Wherever possible, thought should be given to modern techniques for processing data. Computers have been the core of many jokes and some people would say that they dehumanize the individual; but, as a *tool,* the computer and its peripheral equipment can bring new dimensions to the pupil services program.

Constraints

In each category above, the essential elements of a program have been identified. All of them cost money. Finances are a very realistic matter. Most school districts are facing financially difficult times. Monies are not available—or if they are, then highest priority is usually given to classroom activities. Lack of financial support should not be given as an excuse for not providing sound programs. It does mean that alternative programs must be found for the accomplishment of the objectives that have been set. If an objective cannot be reached through a specific program due to financial limitations, look to another approach to meeting the objective. If all alternatives have been exhausted, then it is time to question the priority of the objective. Either the school or the community values the objective enough to fund it properly, or it does not. Either the manager can convince them, or he cannot. If he cannot, then it is best to work on those items of value not only to him but to the school and the community.

Two other constraints, in addition to finances, must be recognized —legal and ethical matters. Laws cannot be violated no matter what and how crucial the problem. Laws can be changed, if needed. Programs cannot be illegal. Why jeopardize the entire operation due to the infringement of some illegal activity within one of a manager's programs? The manager must make sure he is aware of the laws of his state governing his operation. He must also make sure his staff is aware of them. Ethics are mainly a personal matter, but they become a concern to the staff when one member performs in an unethical way. It has been suggested that performance counts. What methods a person uses to achieve results is mainly that person's responsibility —unless he is unethical in the method he uses. A manager must be aware of such activity and be ready to intervene if need be.

Summary. It has been stated that a program is the unique combination of people, places, and things brought together to accomplish common objectives. Each program is interdependent with other programs and with the educational system. The implementation of programs, however, does not guarantee that an objective will be accomplished. It is essential to build into the program(s), as determined by the objectives, a method of assessing the results. Evaluation is an essential component of a statement of an objective and of an objective-based pupil services program.

EVALUATION

The basic purpose of the endeavors of pupil services managers is to provide the necessary organizational environment, under skillful management, that will allow his staff to assist young people to mature and to take their place in a dynamic and changing society. This is done by identifying valued goals and then by setting out to accomplish them. Goals are timeless and immeasurable entities. One really cannot be sure when goals have been reached. How does one know an accomplished goal when he sees one? By developing objectives, the goals are restated, clarified, quantified, or redefined. When a manager has developed appropriate indicators describing the kind of behavior he wishes a population to exhibit upon completion of some prescribed activity, he can measure how well he is doing. A statement of the objective provides the manager with the opportunity to look at his goals and to know how well he is accomplishing them within a specific time frame.

Through specific programs, the manager is committing his best resources to accomplish that which he and his team values. In order to know if they are moving in the right direction, they need to measure or to assess their progress from time to time. In essence, they will be evaluating not only their product (terminal behavior) but their process (interim behavior). "The purpose of evaluation is *not* to prove but to improve."[30] One can always improve. That which people are doing cannot, and should not, remain the same over a period of time. There IS a better way of doing things. In a changing society, a manager needs to re-examine current procedures to insure that he is meeting current *and* future needs. It is important to eliminate the "but-we've-always-done-it-this-way" syndrome.

"Evaluation is the process of delineating, obtaining, and providing useful information for judging decision alternatives."[31] People are constantly evaluating. Every waking moment is spent in assimilating information to be used in making decisions, either consciously or unconsciously. A person will get up in the morning, look outside to observe the weather, and decide what to wear. On entering a room, his eyes tell him if the degree of darkness or lightness warrants a change in lighting. He cannot escape evaluation. One needs to recognize its importance in context to daily activities and to use it for the betterment of man.

The term evaluation often raises semantic problems—what is evaluation and what is research? O'Hare and Lasser discussed this problem and offered an evaluation-research continuum (see Figure 2.5) that might be useful for managers in determining what type of measurement procedures they may want to use with their pupil services programs.[32]

There are other terms that may be used interchangably with evaluation, but for the purpose of this discussion the term evaluation will be used. Evaluation is defined as:

> . . . a process of determining the attainment of objectives in terms of standards. Evaluation is concerned with those persons and factors involved in furthering the guidance function for the stated purposes. . . . Evaluation is making judgments of guidance (pupil services) functions in terms of their values, ideas, solutions, methods, and products. The judgments may be either qualitative or quantitative.[33]

Critical Concepts

Several concepts associated with evaluation need to be stressed. The four that will be mentioned here are formative and summative evaluations (process-product), norm-referenced (NRM), and criterion-referenced (CRM) measurements. Each of these concepts has

65

Informal Evaluations Based On Opinion, Intuition

Data Counting, Administrative Reporting, Reporting Environmental Characteristics

Statement of Observable Behavioral Outcomes— Subjective Evaluation of Outcome Attainment

Statement of Observable Behavioral Outcomes— Assessment of Outcome Attainment

Longitudinal Studies— Assessment of Outcome Attainment

Evaluative Research (e.g., National Study of Guidance and Studies Relating Environment, Pupil, and Behavior Change)

Figure 2.5. An evaluation-research continuum. Robert W. O'Hare and Barbara Lasser, *Evaluating Pupil Personnel Programs* (Fullerton, Calif.: California Personnel and Guidance Association, 1971), p. 21.

been treated extensively in other documents, so only a brief word will be said about them.

Formative Evaluation. There is much to be said about evaluation through time as one moves toward a terminal point. Such evaluation, or feedback, provides managers with the opportunity to adjust their activities—when it is obvious that such adjustment is necessary—before they reach the end product and find that they could not accomplish what they set out to do. Feedback is an extremely important part of everyone's life. It helps man to be adaptive. Formative evaluation provides people with periodic feedback. It helps managers be more efficient and economical in their efforts to see that what ought to work, works. Keirsey and Bates consider this activity as the assessing-monitoring stage of a result systems management program.[34]

In planning pupil services activities for the year, milestones should be identified, at which time the manager will evaluate progress. Such evaluation need not be formal, but all participants need to know what is happening and why. Progress can be measured. This means that some indication of where the program started must be known. For example, if a person sets out to go to New York City and he is in Chicago, it makes a difference if he started from Honolulu or from Washington, D.C. Did he expect to be in Chicago at this time or did he expect to be in Pittsburgh? If he expected to be in Pittsburgh, having come from Honolulu, it appears obvious that he is behind schedule. He may have been too optimistic. He may need to redesign his objective, since it appears that he will not reach New York when he said he would.

If he left from Washington, D.C., bound for New York and finds himself in Chicago, it may be that he is off course. Any continuation of his direct flight without course corrections will not get him where he wanted to go. If he is insistent about getting to New York, he must modify his activity and make the necessary corrections. If he feels that New York is no longer his destination, he continues his present course but he will have to change his objective. This analogy is another oversimplification of a process crucial to a manager's work, but the idea of what is involved and why formative evaluation is important.

Summative Evaluation. Managers must accept this concept as the crux of their activity. This tells them if what they said they were going to do has been done and how well. They are evaluating the product of their activity. In this case, it makes little difference knowing the point of departure as long as they know where they are at the moment. If a person said he would be in New York City by a given date and he is in New York on time, then whether or not he began in Honolulu or Washington, D.C., is irrelevant. Product evaluation is that last step of an objective that tells the manager how he will know if he accomplished the goal he wished to achieve. Either he has reached it or he has not. If he has not, then through product evaluation, he will know how far off he is, and this becomes input data for decision making. If he has not, he must raise some questions regarding the various components of what he did. The goal may have been out of reach. The objective set may have been unrealistic. More may have been expected from the population than it could deliver. Unknown variables may have intervened. The program set may not have been apropos for the population or the situation. Whatever the cause, summative evaluation data is available that will help the manager to determine his next course of action.

Both formative and summative evaluation can and should be used. Managers and their staffs must decide how and when to use the two procedures. A program that effectively encompasses both approaches allows the manager to know where he is at any specified point of time and how well he did at the end of the activity. He is in a position to report his effectiveness and to make decisions regarding future program development and improvement.

Norm-Referenced and Criterion-Referenced Measurement. A manager has now established a schedule for evaluation. He is faced with the task of determining the most effective measuring instrument. Whatever device he chooses must be considered only as a tool and not as an end in itself. Two means of measurement are available. Traditionally, educators become accustomed to the commonly called "standardized tests." It would be better to call them norm-referenced measurement (NRM) instruments. This means that a person is measured on some activity and his efforts are compared with others—theoretically a national sample of like persons—who also were measured with the same instrument. A person is judged on his relationship to a so-called normal distribution of people across the country. A manager may wish to compare the relationship of his program with that of another. A tool to use to judge the differences would be a NRM instrument. There are some advantages to these tools but also some distinct disadvantages.

Criterion-referenced measurement (CRM) compensates for some of the disadvantages of NRM. By CRM it is meant those instruments "used to compare an individual's attainment of desired outcomes with a prespecified performance standard. Minimal acceptable levels of performance, called criterion levels, are generally established for each set of outcomes."[35] When operational objectives are established, stating specific outcomes, provision is made for CRM. Managers are not concerned with how well their program compares with another, but rather whether or not their program has met predetermined expectations.

Within the broad design of the evaluation process, there is a place for both formative and summative evaluation, as well as a place for both NRM and CRM instruments. Once again refer to the examples cited earlier. Looking only at the outcome statements decide whether it is a formative or summative evaluation and the type of instruments to be used.

Attendance Service Objective Outcome:
    To reduce nonattending behavior by ten percent by the end of the first semester

Formative _____
Summative _____
NRM _____
CRM _____

Right! It is summative evaluation using CRM. It is possible to build in a formative evaluation stage by checking the attendance pattern of the group at the end of each school month

Guidance Service Objective Outcome:
    By the end of the ninth grade, each student shall be able to identify five major strengths he has and to write an essay describing how his strengths might contribute to the social and psychological climate of the community.

Formative _____
Summative _____
NRM _____
CRM _____

Once again it is summative and CRM. Consider for the moment how a manager might reword the outcome statement to provide for a formative evaluation phase and using NRM tools.

Health Services Objective Outcome:
    All twenty students will have either corrected their problem or have begun appropriate therapy for correction by the end of the first semester.

Formative _____
Summative _____
NRM _____
CRM _____

69

Be careful! This is tricky. It is *both* formative and summative. But only CRM is used. In this case there is no possibility of using NRM. The objective is too personal.

Psychological Services Objective Outcome: A reduction of the disruptive behavior by eighty percent within twenty school days.	Formative _____ Summative _____ NRM _____ CRM _____

The possibility exists for both formative and summative evaluation, although it is not clearly stated. How would this outcome be rewritten to provide for both approaches?

Social Work Services Objective Outcome: Within one school month family problems are to be reduced sufficiently to allow each girl to remain in school without further pressure to seek another withdrawal.	Formative _____ Summative _____ NRM _____ CRM _____

By now it should be apparent what is happening. Operational objectives tend to be measured by CRM. They can and should be both formative and summative methods of evaluation.

It is important to build in an evaluation design in any program a manager develops. A part of that design must include a reporting procedure. The outcome of a manager's evaluation needs to be reported to appropriate personnel—teachers, administrators, and the community. Anyone who is involved in the decision-making process must be aware of the effectiveness of the manager's efforts. Priorities are determined from such data. In this way, managers can be accountable over that which they have had some control, and the services to pupils can continue to be of quality nature.

SUMMARY

Four components of a model for managing pupil services—goals, objectives, programs, and evaluation—have been considered. Each component has been analyzed in order to understand the system. By looking at the whole, the synthesis of the model can be observed. It can best be summarized by having each person ask these three questions:

> Where am I going?
> By what means will I get there?
> How will I know when I arrive?

1. Joint Committee on Educational Goals and Evaluation, *The Way to Relevance and Accountability in Education* (Sacramento, Calif.: California Legislature, 1970): Subcommittee on Goals to the Governor's Committee on Public School Education, *Goals for Public Education in Texas* (Reproduced through the Courtesy of the State of Texas by OPERATION PEP: A State-Wide Project to Prepare Educational Planners for California, San Mateo, Calif.: San Mateo County Superintendent of Schools, 1968).
2. State Department of Education, *An Educational Planning and Evaluation Guide for California School Districts: A Program Planning and Budgeting System*, 3rd prelim. ed. (Sacramento, Calif.: California State Dept. of Education, n.d.), p. II–4.
3. Subcommittee on Goals to the Governor's Committee on Public School Education, *Goals for Public Education in Texas*, p. 3.
4. National Conference of Pupil Personnel Services, "Report" (Lake Wilderness, Wash., June 12–20, 1971, mimeographed), p. 3.
5. American Association of School Administrators, *Imperatives in Education* (Washington, D.C., n.d.), p. 164
6. Ibid., p. 3.
7. Max Rafferty, "Education Hasn't Only One Purpose, Sir . . . It Has Five," copyright *Los Angeles Times*, June 26, 1967, reprinted with permission.
8. John W. Gardner, "Beyond Vietnam: What Has Science to Say to Man?" Copyright by Saturday Review Co. First appeared in *Saturday Review*, July 1, 1967. Used with permission.
9. Roger A. Kaufman, Robert E. Corrigan, and Donald W. Johnson, "Towards Educational Responsiveness to Society's Needs: A Tentative Utility Model" (mimeographed, n.d.), p. 3.
10. John W. Gardner, "The Ever-Renewing Society," *Saturday Review,* Jan. 5, 1963, p. 94.
11. Ibid., p. 95.
12. Donald G. Hays, "Fullerton Union High School District Framework for Guidance and Counseling Services" (Fullerton, Calif., 1972, dittoed).
13. National Association of Pupil Personnel Administrators, Robert W. Stoughton, chairman, *Pupil Personnel Services: A Position Statement* (1969), p. 3.
14. Frank E. Wellman, *Criterion Variables for the Evaluation of Guidance Practices: A Taxonomy of Guidance Objectives*, Contract OEG-3-6-001147–1147 (Columbia, Mo.: University of Missouri, 1967).
15. Ibid., p. 1.
16. Ibid., p. 2.
17. Ibid., p. 2.
18. Henry Heydt, "Objectives of Pupil Personnel Services" (Sacramento, Calif.: State Dept. of Education, 1970, typewritten).
19. State Department of Education, *An Educational Planning and Evaluation Guide for California School Districts: A Program Planning and Budgeting System*, 3rd prelim. ed., p. II–6.
20. Roger A. Kaufman, "A System Approach to Education: Derivation and Definition," *AV Communication Review* (Winter 1968), 16:415–25.
21. Ibid., p. 415.

22. Ibid., p. 416.
23. Robert F. Mager, *Goal Analysis* (Belmont, Calif.: Fearon Publishers, 1972), p. 11.
24. Howard J. Sullivan and Robert W. O'Hare, eds., *Accountability in Pupil Personnel Services: A Process Guide for the Development of Objectives* (Fullerton, Calif.: California Personnel and Guidance Association, 1971), p. 17.
25. State Department of Education, *An Educational Planning and Evaluation Guide for California School Districts*, p. II-9.
26. Donald G. Hays, "Counselor—What Are You Worth?" *The School Counselor* (May 1972), 19:309–12.
27. David J. Armor, *The American School Counselor: A Case Study in the Sociology of Professions* (New York: Russell Sage Foundation, 1969), p. 5, © 1969 by Russell Sage Foundation.
28. Robert C. Coney, "Performance Evaluation," *Thrust* (Oct. 1972), 2:11.
29. Ibid., pp. 11–13.
30. PDK National Study Committee on Evaluation, Daniel L. Stufflebeam, chairman, *Education Evaluation and Decision Making* (Itasca, Ill.: F. E. Peacock Publishers, Inc., 1971), p. v.
31. Ibid., p. xxv.
32. Robert W. O'Hare and Barbara Lasser, *Evaluating Pupil Personnel Programs* (Fullerton, Calif.: California Personnel and Guidance Association, 1971), pp. 20–21.
33. William E. Hopke, ed., *Dictionary of Personnel and Guidance Terms* (Chicago, Ill.: J. G. Ferguson Publishing Co., 1968), p. 131.
34. David Keirsey and Marilyn Bates, *Result Systems Management: The Human Side of Accountability* (Fullerton, Calif.: California Personnel and Guidance Association, 1972), p. 37.
35. O'Hare and Lasser, op. cit., p. 30

SELECTED REFERENCES

Keirsey, David, and Bates, Marilyn. *Result Systems Management: The Human Side of Accountability.* Fullerton, Calif.: California Personnel and Guidance Association, 1972.

Mager, Robert F. *Goal Analysis.* Belmont, Calif.: Fearon Publishers, 1972.

McGregor, Douglas. *The Human Side of Enterprise,* chaps. 1–4. New York: McGraw-Hill Book Company, Inc., 1960.

Mitchell, Anita M., and Saum, James A., eds. *A Master Plan for Pupil Services.* Fullerton, Calif.: California Personnel and Guidance Association, 1972.

O'Hare, Robert W., and Lasser, Barbara. *Evaluating Pupil Personnel Programs.* Fullerton, Calif.: California Personnel and Guidance Association, 1971.

Sullivan, Howard J., and O'Hare, Robert W. *Accountability in Pupil Personnel Services: A Process Guide for the Development of Objectives.* Fullerton, Calif.: California Personnel and Guidance Association, 1971.

CHAPTER 3

Ethical and Legal Aspects of Pupil Personnel Work

JOHN F. BANCROFT

THE Hippocratic oath written approximately 400 B.C. is most likely the antecedent of a plethora of contemporary codes of ethical standards for various professional disciplines. A review of literature does not provide much enlightenment regarding the effect of codes of ethical standards upon the quality of professional services, but studious observation causes one to speculate that such statements tend to serve more as professional façades or as public relations rhetoric than as viable, functional guides for practitioners. It seems incumbent upon pupil personnel workers, as behavioral specialists, to provide leadership to reverse this situation. This task demands not only greater wisdom in the preparation of ethical codes, but more importantly the development of professionals with a genuine commitment to ethical standards, and consequently more concern for the welfare of their clients and the integrity of the related professions. Such a commitment implies the capacity to risk personal and professional ostracism and possibly legal penalties.

Legal limitations and protections related to the practices of pupil personnel workers have been established largely through the efforts of two groups—state legislative bodies and professional associations with membership comprised primarily of pupil personnel workers. The efforts of these two groups have sometimes been cooperative, but in many instances they have been oppositional. Legislators have acted from stated goals of protecting clients and assuring appropriate services from professionals. The avowed purpose of the related efforts of pupil personnel workers has been the upgrading of services, and the not-so-openly stated objectives have been the establishment of highly favorable conditions for practitioners and the increased prestige which would likely result.

Relatively few court cases have involved pupil personnel workers. There have been some, however, that have provided some generally accepted legal guidelines, and others have implications for duties performed by such professionals.

There is considerable interdependence between ethical standards and legal guidelines. Clearly, the goal must be the establishment of laws and judicial precedents which not only permit but tend to in-sure commendable ethical practices. There is greater likelihood that this objective will be attained if the efforts of both legislators and pupil personnel workers are guided primarily by concern for the benefits of students.

HISTORICAL DEVELOPMENT OF ETHICAL AND LEGAL PRACTICES FOR PUPIL PERSONNEL WORKERS

Ethical Standards

In a presidential address before the Division of Counseling and Guidance of the American Psychological Association in September 1951, Wrenn included a brief but fairly comprehensive historical review of codes of ethical standards that have relevance for pupil personnel workers.[1] On ethics in counseling specifically, he stated that it was a sad commentary on the maturity of our profession that published literature on ethics in counseling could be discussed quite briefly.

The National Education Association prepared and adopted a code in 1930 which was apparently the first one that had relevance for pupil personnel workers. In 1946 Bixler and Seaman published an article in which they made an urgent plea for the establishment of a code for psychologists. They also suggested three headings for the guidelines, which were responsibility to the individual, to related professions, and to society. Two statements of ethical standards were published in 1951. One was a report prepared by an American Psychological Association Committee on Ethical Standards and the other was developed by a Committee on Ethical Practices of the National Vocational Guidance Association. The former included a statement of ethics in clinical and consulting relationships and was

75

later adopted as the official code of APA.[2] The latter served as a published statement and working standards regarding the counseling done in vocational guidance agencies.

The statement of standards that serves as a code for a majority of pupil personnel workers was prepared in 1961 by a Committee on Ethics of the American Personnel and Guidance Association.[3] This code of ethical standards has remained in effect without revision up to the present time.[4]

In recent years, statements of ethical standards have been prepared by various state and local organizations, as well as by affiliates of national organizations. There have also been guidelines developed for special situations or activities related to the performance of pupil personnel work. The California School Counselor Association adopted a code of ethical standards in February 1966.[5] The results of a recent survey conducted by the author showed that fifteen additional state counselor associations have developed such codes. The American School Counselor Association (ASCA) published a proposed code of ethics in the spring of 1972.[6] Late in 1970 ASCA published a model statement regarding the principles of confidentiality and practical guidelines concerning confidentiality and the school counselor.[7] In an article on the topic of professional issues in group work, Gazda, Duncan, and Sisson stated that associations which have many members involved with group work should define these practices and set up standards and ethics for group practitioners within their own membership.[8] They listed six features which are unique to group practices and therefore should receive special attention in any set of standards or code of ethics. Olsen prepared a statement of ethical standards for and more directly applicable to working with groups for use by students in a counselor education program.[9] APA has recently published "Ethical Standards for Research with Human Subjects."[10]

Although pupil personnel workers continue to refer to and claim allegiance to the general, comprehensive codes adopted by APGA and APA, the trend certainly seems to be toward principles and standards of a narrower and more specific nature.

Legal Guidelines

There appears to be rather common agreement among persons who have made a serious study of legal guidelines for pupil personnel workers that there are relatively few court cases and statutes that are specifically applicable to these areas of professional services. Huck-

76

ins,[11] Wagner,[12] and Killian[13] have included statements to this effect in their treatises of this subject. Those three references plus an article by Pardue, Whichard, and Johnson[14] contain the most thorough historical data on this topic known to the author. A review of these references reveals a sufficient number of statutes, court cases, and rulings to cause one to question the concern expressed by the three authors. These expressions are undoubtedly justified when one compares the number of legal bases for pupil personnel work to those for other professionals. In addition, the study of the legal items listed indicates possible contradictions, as well as a lack of clarity in some cases.

Legal guidelines existing for pupil personnel workers can be grouped into four categories. These include two types of confidentiality in professional relations, namely, privileged communication and qualified privileged. The other major category relates to pupil records. There is one case which alleges malpractice.

In 1941 Wigmore, one of the foremost authorities on evidence, described the criteria under which privilege arises as follows:

> A privilege exists, for persons making or receiving a communication not to disclose the communication, whenever (1) The communication originated in mutual confidence that it would not be disclosed; and (2) The confidentiality of such communications, by securing freedom of consultation, is essential to the efficient maintenance of some intimate relationship between those persons; and (3) The relation is one deemed by the community to need to be thus indirectly fostered; and (4) The injury to that relation, caused by risk of the disclosure of the communication, would be more serious than the injury to justice caused by the option of its suppression.[15]

Huckins indicated that privileged communication refers to the right of the clients of professional persons to prevent these persons from revealing in legal proceedings any information given in confidence as a result of the professional relationship. He further stated that the privilege is designed to protect the client's right to privacy and rests upon the same point of view that promoted the freedom from self-incrimination of the fifth amendment of the Constitution.[16] A court case in 1904, which resulted in a ruling in favor of physicians having privileged communication, appears to be the precedent for this legal status among professionals other than attorneys and clergymen. The latter two professions had been accorded this status for many years prior to that time.[17] Laws have been passed in a few states which

77

extend privileged communication to at least some pupil personnel workers. In 1948 a law was passed in Michigan which provides privileged communication for all professional school employees. Huckins indicated that privileged communication was extended to counselors in Iowa in 1962,[18] but Pardue, Whichard, and Johnson stated that codes of Iowa, Nebraska, and Tennessee, where the term counselor follows the term attorney, the reference is probably not made to counselors in education but rather to licensed attorneys.[19] In 1965 the Indiana legislature passed a law that provided privileged communication for counselors only. The statute adopted in Indiana is rather concise and reads in the following manner:

> Any counselor duly appointed or designated a counselor for the school system by its proper officers and for the purpose of counseling pupils in such school systems shall be immune from disclosing any privileged or confidential communication made to such counselor as such by any such pupil herein referred to. Such matters shall be privileged and protected against disclosure.[20]

Similar statutes were passed in Wisconsin in 1968 and North Dakota in 1969.[21] The author has recently conducted a survey of state consultants for pupil personnel services to determine the status of privileged communication for pupil personnel workers. The information received for Wisconsin is somewhat contradictory to that just reported. It shows that only psychologists have the right of privileged communication and that the law providing this status became effective in 1967. Forty-six of the fifty consultants returned surveys. The information provided regarding the status of privileged communication for pupil personnel workers indicated the adoption of laws affording this privilege since 1969 as follows: psychologists, nine states; counselors, seven states; and social workers, two states. In many of the states the change was made for only one of those three pupil personnel areas. In Hawaii, Idaho, and Montana privileged communication was accorded to both counselors and psychologists. The statute passed in Colorado accorded privileged communication for both psychologists and social workers, but strangely it did not apply to counselors.

Huckins stated that qualified privilege is a facet of the law of libel and slander and safeguards the making of socially necessary communications. Primarily, this status is a safeguard for practitioners in litigation involving charges of libel or slander. In a case not related to school personnel, which was heard in Kentucky in 1910 *(Tanner* v. *Stevenson)*, the court established a basic principle concerning qualified privilege. Essentially, this established the guideline that when communications are conditionally privileged because of the professional or socially necessary character or the relationship in which the questionable information is transmitted, burden of proving the existence of malice as a condition for establishing libel rests with the plaintiff.[22] The first school related case of this nature *(Everest* v. *McKinney)* was heard in Michigan in 1917. Other such cases were *Kenny* v. *Gurley* (Ala., 1923) and *Iverson* v. *Frandsen* (Utah, 1956).[23] In these three cases libel charges were brought against a president of a state normal school, a dean of students, and a school psychologist, respectively. In each case the existence of malice was not established, and the allegations were not sustained.

Most of the legal precedents related to student records could be categorized as relating to the matter of access. Two of them, however, dealt with the matter of the type of record which constitutes a public record and therefore would be available for inspection to any person who had an interest in reviewing them. A widely quoted case dealing with the subject of what type of record constitutes a public record was conducted in South Dakota in 1928 *(State* v. *Ewert)*. The court stated:

> Whenever a written record of transactions of a public officer and his office is a convenient and appropriate method of discharging duties of office, and is kept by him as such, whether required by express provision of the law or not, such a record is a public record.[24]

This case established the principle that records to be public must be prepared and kept by a public officer; however, later cases, in contrast to the finding of this case, stressed that records must also be required by statute to be classified as public. In a Louisiana case *(Wagner* v. *Redman,* 1960) a member of a school board was able to obtain lists of pupil names and addresses maintained by school superintendents.[25] All except one of the other cases related to records were suits brought by parents and a student to gain access to student record information. The exception was a case in New Mexico in 1961, in which newspaper reporters requested the right to examine school records for the purpose of determining whether or not preferential treatment had been accorded athletes. The Attorney General's opinion in this case has considerable value for pupil personnel workers since, although he ruled in favor of the newspaper reporters, he did indicate that personal notes were not public records and therefore not available to any interested person. His ruling stated that:

> The right to public inspection extending to any citizen of this state to inspect school records held by a public officer includes the right of any publisher or reporter to inspect such records for the purposes of his business. However, such right to examination and access does not extend to data or memoranda prepared or gathered by school officials or teachers regarding students or a student's background, for use in teaching such student, and which may be of a confidential or delicate nature, or of a type which is not permanent in character.[26]

Of the other cases in which access was requested by parents and a student, two were held in New York state in 1961: *Johnson* v. *Board of Education, City of New York*[27] and *Van Allen* v. *McCleary*.[28] A case involving college admission records at Bates College was heard in Maine in 1968.[29] In all three cases the judgment was in favor of the plaintiffs. In the two New York cases the records were the regular student cumulative folders, and in the Bates College case, as previously indicated, they were records maintained in the college Admissions Office. This latter case has significance in that reference statements prepared by high school personnel were made available to the student.

The case alleging malpractice was brought against a director of student personnel services at a college in Wisconsin in 1958. Three acts of negligence were charged by parents of a female student who committed suicide following counseling provided by the director. The charges were not sustained.[30]

This historical review does show that legal guidelines for pupil personnel services are indeed very limited in scope and far from inclusive. One factor seems to stand out. There is considerable variation in such standards among the states. As the practitioners performing these fledgling services establish more definite and accepted identities in a society with both self-protective and questioning tendencies, it is rather easy to conclude we have been experiencing the lull before the storm with regard to lawsuits.

CODES OF ETHICAL STANDARDS AND PRACTICES

Statement of Standards

In a presentation a little more than twenty years ago, Wrenn expressed concern over the paucity of literature related to ethics.[31]

Approximately a decade later Flanagan and McGrew indicated that a perusal of the literature clearly emphasized the lack of writing on the subject of ethics in counseling.[32] They noted that this void existed in both available books and journal articles. This trend has clearly been reversed in the past few years, as the many sources referenced for this chapter indicate.

In the brief historical review of codes of ethics previously referred to in this chapter, the most publicized statements of standards for pupil personnel workers were listed.[33] In reviewing the literature related to ethics in pupil personnel work, the author found the Ethical Standards of APGA to be the most frequently referenced code. However, Ethical Standards of Psychologists adopted by APA is referred to almost as frequently. The NEA Code of Ethics of the Education Profession is also discussed in several articles.[34] It seems likely that the proposed ASCA Code of Ethics, if it is adopted by members of that association, will be the one most used in the future by school counselors.

The APA, APGA, ASCA, and NEA Codes of Ethical Standards all include an introductory statement which expresses allegiance to the concept of the dignity and worth of individuals. The APGA and ASCA guidelines also include introductory statements regarding the characteristics of a professional. The format and structure of the statements vary considerably, but as one would expect the principles and guidelines have considerable commonality. Each expresses primary commitment and responsibility to the pupil or client. Guidelines are also contained in the four codes related to responsibilities to colleagues, community, self, and profession. As might be expected, the statements in the proposed code of ethics for school counselors is somewhat more specific than those in the other three codes. It also contains a section dealing with responsibilities to parents, which is not included in the other statements.

It is commonly understood that codes of ethics have been developed primarily to insure the quality of professional services. This concept is made explicit in the APGA Ethical Standards by the following statement:

> The introduction of such standards will inevitably stimulate greater concern by members for practice and preparation for practice.[35]

McGowan and Schmidt looked at the purpose of such codes from a different perspective but seemed to express essentially the same viewpoint when they listed the values counselors might derive from them.

1. They provide a position on standards of practice to assist each member of the profession in deciding what he should do when situations of conflict arise in his work.
2. They help clarify the counselor's responsibilities to the client and protect the client from the counselor's violation of, or his failure to fulfill, these responsibilities.
3. They give the profession some assurance that the practices of members will not be detrimental to its general functions and purposes.
4. They give society some guarantee that the services of the counselor will demonstrate a sensible regard for the social codes and moral expectations of the community in which he works.
5. They offer the counselor some grounds for safeguarding his own privacy and integrity.[36]

Additionally, adherence to ethical principles is generally accepted as a necessary characteristic of professionals. Adams stated that one of the marks of the professional status of counseling is an increasing concern with ethical problems.[37] Flanagan and McGrew commented that one of the most distinguishing marks of a profession should be the concern of its members for their own ethical conduct.[38] In the introduction to this chapter the author indicated that although it is almost impossible to assess the contribution which ethical standards have made with regard to the quality of the performances of pupil personnel workers, subjective evaluation leads him to conclude that it has been quite limited. In a previous article the author of this chapter stated that simply establishing a code of ethics does not guarantee a change in the ways that counselors function.[39] If such a conclusion is justified, then pupil personnel service workers need to give considerable attention to strategies for the implementation of these principles and guidelines.

Implementation of Ethical Codes

When one studies the principles and guidelines in the principal codes of ethics, it becomes most apparent that implementation requires personnel workers who possess particular personal characteristics and skills. Therefore, the primary means of insuring ethical practices would appear to be closely related to selection, preservice training, and the continuing in-service development of all persons so employed. Arsenian, who served as chairman of the APGA Committee that developed that organization's code of ethics, supported this concept by stating that "in the final analysis a code of ethics is as good as the private conscience and the idealism of the individual members of this association".[40] Some members of such committees have apparently believed that it is necessary to have procedures for the enforcement of ethical practices to effect desired behavior of personnel workers. Most of the codes adopted have incorporated statements or provisions for this purpose which range from admonitions to structured procedures.

The APGA Code contains two rather specific statements related to implementation of its provisions. The first deals with a member's responsibility with regard to his relations to his employing institution. That statement reads:

> Within the member's own work setting, if, despite his efforts, he cannot reach agreement as to acceptable ethical standards of conduct with his superiors, he should end his affiliation with them.

The other section deals with a member's responsibility with regard to the ethical behavior of his professional associates. That statement is as follows:

> He is obligated, in situations where he possesses information raising serious doubts as to the ethical behavior of other members, to attempt to rectify such conditions. The member is obligated to concern himself with the degree to which the personnel functions of nonmembers with whose work he is acquainted represent competent and ethical performance. Where his information raises serious doubt as to the ethical behavior of such persons, it is his responsibility to attempt to rectify such conditions.[41]

The APA Ethical Standards of Psychologists includes two statements related to implementation also. With respect to professional competence the following provision is included:

> When a psychologist or a person identifying himself as a psychologist violates ethical standards, psychologists who know first-hand of such activities attempt to rectify the situation. When such a situation cannot be dealt with informally, it is called to the attention of the appropriate local, state, or national committee on professional ethics, standards, and practices.

The second such statement has reference to the matter of misrepresentation of professional qualifications and affiliations. It reads as follows:

> The psychologist is responsible for correcting others who misrepresent his professional qualifications or affiliations.[42]

The above references for these two major codes contain the phrase "attempt to rectify" in three different places. The second provision from the APA Code includes the only directed requirement with the words "is responsible for correcting." None of these statements contains provisions for penalties against members or nonmembers, although that possibility may be implied if a member does refer a situation related to competency to an APA committee on professional ethics, standards, and practices.

By-laws proposed for ASCA in 1968 provided for specific action against a member in the form of severance of membership. It reads:

> A member may be dropped from membership for any conduct that tends to injure the association or to affect adversely its reputation, or that violates principles stated in APGA or ASCA by-laws and code of ethics. Any member charged with engaging in such conduct shall be given the opportunity to present evidence in his behalf through witnesses or otherwise shall be given the opportunity to confront witnesses against him, and shall have the right to appeal and have a hearing before the ASCA governing board, whose decision shall be final. A Committee on Ethics shall consider any charges made over the signature of two ASCA members in good standing and shall have the power to determine whether the charges shall be dropped, whether the accused shall be permitted to resign, or whether the charges are true, subject however to the right of any accused member to appeal to the ASCA governing board from any final decision of the Committee on Ethics.[43]

Apparently these were not adopted as they were not published in issues of *The School Counselor* subsequent to the annual convention, as was the case when the by-laws were revised in 1963[44] and 1965.[45] The recently proposed ASCA Code of Ethics does not contain any statements or provisions for actions in cases of unethical practices either.[46] The implication would seem to be that members of ASCA constitutional or ethical committees with one exception have not viewed either generalized admonitions or specified penalties to be effective methods of encouraging or causing counselors to apply ethical standards. Beymer lends credence to this position by stating that "If there ever has been a case in which a counselor was censured by either APGA or one of its branches for unethical conduct, it has been very well concealed".[47] The author of this chapter presented essentially the same conclusion in a report prepared for the ASCA Ethics Committee, following a review of correspondence to that committee over a period of two years by stating that no member had requested the committee to review allegations of unethical practices during that period of time.[48]

In direct contrast to enforcement patterns just reviewed, the code of ethics adopted by the members of the California School Counselor Association contains quite specific and structured procedures for implementation of its guidelines in the form of a grievance procedure. It reads as follows:

Proper ethical relations should exist between the counselor and his professional associates or supervisors. If the counselor cannot reach agreement with his supervisors as to acceptable ethical standards of conduct as stated by the CSCA Code of Ethics, he may seek support of CSCA in resolving the problem(s). The following grievance procedure should be taken:

a. Place in writing the details of the case stating issues, incidences, methods of attempted resolution, etc.
b. Discuss problem with the immediate superior or principal or superintendent to work for a solution.
c. If no solution of the problem results, present the case to your local, regional, or county level Counseling Ethics and Professional Standards Committee Chairman if one exists.
d. If the local committee is unable to resolve the matter or if there is no local committee, the problem should be referred to the state CSCA Ethics and Professional Standards Committee for review and action.
e. The Chairman of the CSCA Ethics and Professional Preparations and Standards Committee shall contact the district superintendent to indicate that CSCA will conduct an investigation of the situation.
f. After investigation is made, the CSCA Ethics and Professional Preparations and Standards Committee shall make its recommendation to the CSCA Executive Council.
g. The CSCA Executive Council shall review the recommendations of the CSCA Ethics and Professional Preparations and Standards Committee. The CSCA Executive Council shall make known its decision to all parties involved.

CSCA Executive Council shall normally take one or more of the following actions:

(1) Recommend that local school administration correct the problem(s) with a specific time factor (maximum) to accomplish the resolution of the problem.

or

(2) Recommend counselors no longer work in that school or district.

or

(3) Recommend no new counselors work in that district.

or

(4) Recommend dismissal of the case. Further, recommend that the counselor accept the situation and stay on the job. Clear the district or local school of any further CSCA action on this specific case.

or

(5) Recommend other action as deemed necessary.[49]

Following the adoption of this code in February 1969, there have been few attempts to employ the grievance procedure. It seems reasonable to question the value of specific enforcement procedures over mild admonitions with respect to the implementation of ethical practices.

Factors Impeding Implementation

The general nature of statements in the major ethical codes that are relevant to pupil personnel work quite probably interferes with extensive application of them. Such ambiguity leaves personnel workers with doubts as to what really is ethical behavior in specific situations. They also make it necessary for practitioners to study the statements much more carefully than if they were presented more in the form of commandments. It seems safe to conjecture that few have been motivated to give the codes the attention this would require.

It was noted earlier that the personal characteristics and skills of personnel workers significantly effect the degree to which ethical guidelines are implemented. Statements by both Schmidt and Schmid seem to amplify that viewpoint. Schmidt has said, ". . . . but in the last analysis such codes are always subject to the interpretation of each individual counselor. That interpretation, in turn, is a function of the individual's personal needs, values, attitudes, and past experiences".[50] Schmid's comment is as follows:

Such questions as legal authority, licensing, competence in diagnosis, differences in qualification standards, and strong differences in theoretical orientation have made it difficult, if not relatively impossible, to set up a code of ethics that would have the same meaning to all counselors.[51]

Clearly the nature of the persons employed in pupil personnel positions have a great effect on the nature and extent to which provisions of codes of ethics are fulfilled.

A conflict in expectations or loyalties appears to be another important factor interfering with the implementation of ethical practices. Indeed most of the codes contain sections which describe several professional responsibilities or commitments. Wrenn expressed concern over this matter more than two decades ago, when he stated that there is a conflict between a counselor's loyalties to his client and his corresponding loyalties to his society, his employing institution, his profession, and himself. More specifically he indicated:

> I believe that for many school, college, or institutionally employed counselors there is greatest danger of unethical conduct in communicating officially to one's superior what is confidential and in discussing case information too freely and casually with colleagues. . . . and it is as sharp an issue ethically when a colleague asks us for information that should not be shared as it would be if we were under oath in a witness chair. . . . It takes more courage and strength of conviction to stand to protect the client than it does to make a decision to protect the employer.[52]

In a rather recent article Patterson considered the question, "Are Ethics Different in Different Settings"?[53] He concluded that among counselors in rehabilitation, employment, and schools, the school counselor is in the most difficult position. He supported this by stating that administrators and teachers put tremendous pressures on counselors to violate confidentiality. Ladd emphasized the plight of school counselors with respect to confidentiality with the following comments:

> It is a common illusion that the typical school official expects guidance counselors to work primarily in helping students to deal with their personal problems. But in fact counselors are expected to help these clients only insofar as it can be done in ways that also contribute to the effective operation and good reputation of the school. . . . It may be discourteous to say so in the pages of this journal, which has such high ideals for counseling, but too often counselors are really tools for administrators."[54]

87

A statement by Clark seems to bring the counselor's dilemma in the matter of loyalties between counselees and the institution into even sharper focus.

> The degree of professional authority granted to the counselor by the official spokesman (the administrator) of the sponsoring unit (the school) is the determinant of the amount of confidentiality delegated to the counselor in regard to information received in the counseling interview. . . . If a rare instance should occur when the interests of the school and the pupil are in an irreconcilable conflict and the counselor must choose between them, the interest of the schools should usually be given precedence.[55]

Such a statement tends to substantiate a conclusion that statements of ethical standards do not significantly affect the behavior of pupil personnel workers. Clark's comment seems to be in direct opposition to the principle in each code referenced that the personnel worker's first commitment is to the student. Adams reviewed some of the results of a study conducted by Smith in which she surveyed 1,225 professional members of the National Vocational Guidance Association (NVGA) regarding the degree to which they would favor revealing confidential information to some authorized agency or person. Public school counselors expressed greater loyalty to society than to counselees in contrast to the views expressed by the other professional members of NVGA who responded to this survey. The results of that survey also showed that the greater the amount of public school teaching experience the respondent had, the greater was his degree of loyalty to society, and the lesser was his feeling of loyalty to the counselee.[56] This final statement is even more disconcerting when one considers that up until very recently there has been an almost universal requirement for school counselors to have experience as a teacher. Although the statements just presented have implications for conflicts of loyalties existing for all professionals performing pupil personnel services, it appears that such conflicts are experienced much more extensively by school counselors. During the past several years as an instructor in theories of counseling and supervised field work, the author has become acutely aware of the allegiance which teachers who are preparing to be school counselors have for their teaching colleagues. They frequently expressed feelings which indicated that they have a strong sense of responsibility to teachers and that one who would do otherwise is a traitor to the teaching fraternity. They presented elaborate rationalizations to justify their positions on this matter. All the information just presented certainly supports the position that conflicts of loyalties and expectations interfere with the implementation of the commonly expressed ethical principle that the primary commitment and responsibility of pupil personnel workers is to the counselee or client.

Several additional factors have also impeded the implementation of ethical principles, but to a much lesser degree than those already presented. There is little evidence to indicate that sufficient study of ethical codes has been incorporated in training programs for pupil personnel workers. Flanagan and McGrew have stated that there was a notable lack of information on this matter contained in books.[57] The author's experience with various counselor education programs causes him to conclude also that instruction on this matter is sketchy and casual at best. Nugent conducted a survey of practices and policies of college counseling centers and found that forty percent released student information without student permission. He decried this serious lapse in ethical practices. In his discussion of means for remedying this situation, he concluded that there is something faulty in the education of counselors and that certainly a seminar on ethics and professional problems should be mandatory, and issues of this sort should permeate the total training program.[58]

Changes in the nature of providing services have caused problems in implementing ethical practices. Gazda, Duncan, and Sisson have pointed out that the explosion of interest in the practice of group work has created a lag between the development of both standards for training and practice and of a code of ethical behavior or practice. Their conclusions were based in part on information obtained by surveying members of an APGA Interest Group on Procedures regarding the extent of problems of ethical practice in group work. Respondents reported twenty violations of ethical practice or behavior. Gazda, Duncan, and Sisson listed seven features which are unique to group practice and therefore should receive special attention in any set of standards or code of ethics.[59] Zimpfer reviewed several ethical issues arising from groups. He concluded that the present APGA Ethical Standards statement is deficient in several respects regarding group work.[60]

The use of paraprofessionals, counselor assistants, and counselor aides in pupil personnel work raises additional ethical questions. Sansbury posed several questions related to the use of a trained undergraduate student (companion) in behavior modification techniques. Questions arise such as how much information about the client ethically can be divulged to the companion and should the reports of the feelings and behaviors of the companion be treated as confidential when talking with the client.[61] Beck considered some of the same matters in a review of emerging issues in counseling and guidance.[62] He stated that ethical practice implies far more than simply profiting from past mistakes of the profession. In urging practitioners to look ahead he posed a series of questions. There were two related to paraprofessionals: How and to what degree shall paraprofessionals be used? What safeguards can be established to insure their ethical behavior in their duties?

Another concept receiving greater interest is the function of school counselors as advocates for students. The possibility of such a counselor function raises most critically the issue of conflicts of loyalties for pupil personnel workers.

Inadequate definition of roles or functions of pupil personnel workers, especially school counselors, is a factor that is sometimes given as causing confusion as to what is appropriate ethical behavior. Again this is most pronounced in the area of conflicting loyalties, and it is quite easy to deduce that the primary commitment could be quite different in a situation where a counselor functions largely as a neo-administrator from one in which he spends most of his time assisting students with educational, career, and personal concerns. It was anticipated that the Statement of Policy for Secondary School Counselors and Guidelines for Implementation adopted by the governing board of ASCA in 1964 would largely eliminate much of the confusion which existed with regard to counselor role and function.[63] The implementation of ethical practices should be enhanced to the extent that this statement made clearer to counselors and their supervisors what tasks counselors should perform.

The facilities in which pupil personnel workers perform their services certainly have an effect upon the degree to which the ethical requirements of confidentiality are maintained. Anyone who has visited several schools has observed many makeshift spaces in which personnel workers are expected to perform their duties. These include small former janitorial closets in which air flow is so poor that the doors must remain open, poorly partitioned spaces where many persons must attempt to provide services to students, and space between shelves in libraries. Although it is clearly unethical to consider highly personal matters in such facilities, it is quite likely that the extent to which confidentiality is abridged in such so-called offices is somewhat limited by the fact that clients or students will not openly share concerns under such conditions. Without question, however, inadequate facilities have and can seriously deter the implementation of a very important ethical principle.

A final factor which may lead to unethical behavior on the part of a few counselors is the matter of the offer of fees for identification of students for educational institutions. This possibility was called to the attention of ASCA members in a recent issue of the *ASCA Newsletter*. A brief information statement read as follows:

> John Shafer, Past President of Florida SCA, brought to the attention of ASCA Headquarters a situation which violates counselor ethics. Counselors in Florida have been offered a monetary bonus by a placement service for securing the highest number of applications from students. This unethical practice could become a nationwide effort, and counselors across the country should be aware of it.[64]

A few months ago the author received an announcement from the president of a university regarding a bachelor degree program for external students. It was addressed to junior and community college counselors and was obviously designed to enlist their assistance in enrollment of students in the program. The letter indicated that it would be impossible to provide such service (without such counselor assistance) on a broad scale without increasing cost to students and stated a $50 fee would be paid for each student so assisted upon his completion of registration and payment of tuition for the first quarter. Also included was a statement that the university did not ask a counselor to violate the ethics of his profession by serving as a recruiter for that particular institution but it was willing to pay for time spent by a counselor outside of the regular work schedule to provide such a service. Such activities by a counselor would certainly seem to be in contravention to ethical concepts indicating that it is inappropriate to accept fees for services provided to one's students.

There are undoubtedly many other factors which have mitigated against fulfillment of ethical principles by pupil personnel workers. The several factors reviewed should be sufficient to suggest why progress toward implementation of ethical guidelines has been so limited. Furthermore, it becomes apparent as one analyzes these matters that the responsibility for effecting ethical behavior lies squarely upon each pupil personnel worker. Our downfall in this regard might well be expressed by a well-known Pogo quotation: "We have met the enemy and he is us."

91

Actions Related to Questionable Practices
by Individual Pupil Personnel Workers

The lack of action regarding questionable practices by individual pupil personnel workers has been documented earlier in this chapter. Our inactivity in this respect indicates among other things a lack of professional maturity on the part of pupil personnel workers and a gross disregard for ethical principles contained in both the APA and APGA Codes of Ethics. These provisions were quoted and briefly discussed previously. The lack of such action surely cannot be the result of universal exemplary practices by personnel workers. Who among us, in all honesty, has not been aware of numerous questionable practices by persons assigned duties as pupil personnel workers? Our disdain for intervening in these instances certainly has been tempered by realizations of almost certain repercussions from some colleagues and possible legal actions. However, our timidity in this respect has most likely been detrimental to the establishment of professional status for pupil personnel work and has certainly established a credibility gap between espoused ethical guidelines and actual behavior. Apropos to this observation are comments by Huckins. He stated:

> Among the salient characteristics of a profession are its concern for the conduct of its members, and its pledge of self-regulation and creditable member practice to society. . . . A regulation which is not enforced spawns disrespect, not only for the code from which it comes, but for the organization which thus fails to support its stated convictions.[65]

Without question, pupil personnel workers by virtue of their inactivity with respect to questionable behavior of colleagues have deterred the implementation of related ethical guidelines.

Cases Involving Both School Systems and Individual Schools

As bleak as the progress toward application of principles of ethics seems to be generally, there have been a few cases in which action based at least partially on such guidelines have improved pupil personnel services. During the school year 1970–71 members of the San Diego Personnel and Guidance Association passed a resolution supporting the employment of full-time counselors in place of noncredentialed advisers employed on a part-time basis. The latter practice had been in effect in the San Diego City Schools quite extensively for some years. The Association held that the assignment of noncreden-

tialed advisers was in effect an unethical practice since it circum-
vented the intentions and provisions of the California Education
Code. The approach of the Association was primarily informational
in nature. Throughout the year, they sponsored nine "living room
discussions," which were attended by students, parents, administrators, counselors, community members, employers, and members of
the Board of Education.[66] As a result of the resolution and the subsequent discussions, additional full-time counselors were employed beginning with the 1971–72 school year to replace many of the part-
time noncredentialed advisers.

In at least one instance the provisions of the grievance procedure
of the California School Counselor Association statement of counselor ethics have been employed to maintain counseling services at
an established level. Recently counselors at Fullerton High School
were assigned attendance duties, which included working at attendance windows. The CSCA Counselors Ethics contains a provision
which states that counselors have a responsibility to the profession to
discuss with professional associates (counselors, teachers, administrators) practices which appear to result in inferior services, in lowering
of standards, or in unsatisfactory conditions of employment.[67] The
counselors believed the attendance assignment lowered the standards of service and discussed this matter with their supervisor without success. Both the staff of the California Personnel Guidance Association and the CSCA Chairman of the CPGA Negotiations
Commission assisted the counselors from Fullerton High School with
supportive data. Their combined efforts were successful.

Suggestions for Activating Ethical Guidelines

The actions or procedures to be followed for the implementation
of ethical guidelines with respect to the various factors which have
been listed as impeding such progress have been either implied or
alluded to in the discussion of these matters. It seems that little
additional elaboration on this matter is required. Statements or revisions of statements which provide clear and more specific definition
of the roles and functions of pupil personnel workers should be prepared regularly through the cooperative efforts of all persons concerned with these services. They should certainly reflect changing
cultural conditions and needs, improved professional qualifications of
personnel workers and changing practices in providing pupil personnel services. Although there may be minor differences in agreement
as to the specific design of facilities, the general requirements for

93

them are well-known, and pupil personnel workers should take most affirmative action to see that satisfactory offices or facilities are provided for them. In the matter of accepting fees for identification, placement, and enrollment of students in other institutional programs, such activity certainly constitutes a conflict of interest and unacceptable ethical practice. The increasing interest and concomitant literature related to ethics certainly should do much to bring about more extensive consideration of such standards both during training and subsequent to employment. It has been noted earlier that there is a definite trend toward the preparation and adoption of more specific codes of ethics. The very general nature of the statements prepared by NEA, APA, and APGA has certainly contributed to extensive variations in interpretation and application. Even at the risk of omissions it seems advisable that codes should be revised or replaced to provide much more specific statements. These need to provide guidelines for emerging services for which existing codes are either inadequate or inappropriate. With respect to factors related to personal characteristics and conflicts of loyalty, it seems imperative that selection, training, and in-service growth center around development of each personnel worker in areas of personal awareness and self-assurance. Such characteristics should permit a pupil personnel worker to function in a sensitive and fairly independent manner.

It is the author's view that the processes of selection and training represent the most significant means of effecting commendable ethical practices. Further elaboration of this viewpoint seems advisable. The author has long felt that educators of pupil personnel workers have been strangely hesitant to apply selection procedures which they deem appropriate, and frequently assist in applying, in the selection of persons for other professional programs. As an example, for some time a temperament inventory has been utilized to assist with the selection of students for the nursing program at the college where the author is employed. There are numerous instruments which have wide usage and general acceptance that could and should be employed in the process of selecting students for training in pupil personnel programs. In addition to improved initial selection procedures, educators of personnel workers have a responsibility to do more than academic screening of such students throughout the period of the training program. Beck has spoken rather precisely to this matter in the following statement:

94

There will be, as every counselor educator knows, candidates who will be so rigid, so personally threatened, or so ingenious that a counselor's certificate in their hands would negate all that we deemed essential. It is perhaps the greatest ethical obligation of the counselor educator either to steer these persons out of the field, or to delay their entry until they show more openness or breadth of life experiences, because one who has not been able to cope with change in his own life seems a poor risk to understand or to adjust to the vast changes in society which will impinge on his prospective clients.[68]

There is also a need for more emphasis on personal development in training programs. Much of the course work completed by pupil personnel workers can serve as a ready vehicle for such growth. A professor who teaches a course covering the psychology of personality at the college where the author is employed continuously requires his students to consider and describe the application of concepts studied to their own lives. Certainly, quality group membership experiences can help persons both during training and following employment in the areas of improved awareness and skills in interpersonal relations. Support for these concepts was provided in the Standards for Preparation of Secondary School Counselors prepared by the Association for Counselor Education and Supervision in 1967.[69] This statement indicates that such a program should provide opportunities for self-evaluation and further development of self-understanding. Specifically, it states that opportunities for improvement of interpersonal relationships should be provided through small group activities, and counseling services by persons other than the counselor education staff should be available to students in counselor education. There is a further factor which should be clearly stated relating to selection and training, and that is, simply, personal growth must not be neglected following employment. Professional associations, as well as training programs, provide many opportunities for such development, and pupil personnel workers should avail themselves of these opportunities.

LAWS AND COURT DECISIONS GOVERNING PUPIL PERSONNEL WORK

Pupil personnel workers quite possibly have less understanding of legal matters related to their services than they do of the ethical standards. There seem to be several factors which have contributed to this naiveté. The emphasis in most law courses related to pupil personnel services is upon those that have applicability to children

95

and child welfare. As has been mentioned before, there have been relatively few laws, court cases, and legal rulings directly related to these services. Not only does this limit the base for such instruction but minimizes publicity which would focus the attention of personnel workers on the matter. Although legal problems have not been common for personnel workers, Schmidt believes there is a wide variety of potential problems in the legal area. He expressed this by stating:

> It would seem that counselors might benefit from having more information about laws that affect them and more knowledge about legal procedures. . . . Counselors might want to know what legal basis there is for their work, what have been the legal influences in the development of their profession, what legal rights and obligations are associated with their services, and what to do if they become involved in a lawsuit or other legal matter.[70]

The emphasis in Schmidt's statement is primarily with the safeguarding of the pupil personnel worker. It would seem that personnel workers should be equally, if not more concerned, with legal provisions designed to protect students' rights. At least two factors seem to suggest that the need is ever-increasing for pupil personnel workers to have a good understanding of legal provisions related to their services. There has certainly been a change in the nature of services performed by such personnel. There has been a pronounced shifting from an almost total emphasis upon educational and career concerns to considerable attention to personal adjustment matters. Suits alleging libel, malpractice, or invasion of privacy are much more likely with services of the latter nature. The simple fact that there are more pupil personnel workers than at any time in the past is bound to increase the legal activity related to this field of work. In the area of confidentiality, much concern is now being expressed over both the extensiveness and accessibility of pupil records maintained with modern electronic processing equipment. Huckins believes such factors definitely increase the vulnerability of school counselors with respect to involvement in litigation.

> It is inherent in the personal and confidential nature of the information and material which counselors handle, speculate about, and sometimes transmit, and in the legal status of the employing school district. Although there now may be a contrary trend, school districts have traditionally been held by the courts to be immune from liability on the

theory that the state is sovereign and cannot be sued without its consent. . . . Furthermore, school counselors can exercise no choice regarding the type of client or counselee they will serve.[71]

There appears to be some reason to question one idea expressed by Huckins, namely, that allegations will normally be brought against individual pupil personnel workers rather than the school. The cases reviewed which involved access to student records were brought against the boards of education or trustees rather than individual employees.

General Areas of Legal Concern—Privileged Communication
In the section of this chapter in which the historical development of legal guidelines for pupil personnel work was reviewed, it was noted that privileged communication is the privilege of the client. Wagner has provided a more precise legal definition as follows:

> Privileged communication, as used in the law of evidence, pertains to the protection afforded a person who discloses in confidence information about himself or others to another person, and the further disclosure of such information by the second party as evidence in a judicial proceeding, except by permission of the person who first gave the information.[72]

We have also noted previously that this status is accorded to pupil personnel workers and their clients in very few states. Many pupil personnel workers express considerable concern that they are unable to maintain confidentiality of information regarding their students or clients because the status of privileged communication has not been extended to them by law or court precedent. Others do not view this as being particularly threatening to the maintenance of confidentiality, as they express the position that such workers do not have to or should not reveal confidential information except under oath. Huckins has stated this as follows:

> Just as recorded confidential information need not and should not be released without a court order neither should counselors feel obligated to give such information verbally to any official unless they are in court under oath.[73]

It would seem, however, that most of the personnel workers believe that privileged communication is desirable. One of the resolutions adopted by the APGA Senate in 1967 reflected this viewpoint.

> Be it resolved, that APGA be urged to take every possible step in collaboration with state branches to promote enactment of privileged communication legislation at the state level without delay . . .[74]

Wrenn supported this concept also by stating that counselors and clinical psychologists should seek privileged communication the same as that afforded lawyers, physicians, and ministers in most states.[75] An opposite viewpoint was expressed by Goldman. He questioned the wisdom of counselor attempts to gain the right of privileged communication through legislation and further expressed the point of view that we should be directing our energies more toward the rights of students, especially the right of privacy. He supported this concept with a comment that the individual's privacy today is more threatened by the schools than by the courts.[76] There is value for pupil personnel workers to have the right of privileged communication. Without doubt, it would enhance the professional status of these workers. It may well be, however, that the energy and efforts required to obtain such legislation at this time would exceed the value to clients and personnel workers. We may be according far too much importance to this particular legal factor. Comments by Bangs supports this latter viewpoint. He stated:

> This restricted legal confidentiality of the courtroom is a minute stitch in the total texture of ethical confidentiality. . . . Since a privileged communication rule, moreover, does not apply to the prelegal or non-legal setting, how much client protection is really afforded? . . . Protection of the client's rights is assured best through a dedicated adherence to the already existing codes of ethics that afford a much broader personal safeguard than the very narrow circumstances of the courtroom. . . . It seems that more prestige and sense of professionalism could accrue to the counseling profession through ethical standards than through legal prescription.[77]

The author believes that too much emphasis has been placed upon obtaining privileged communication for pupil personnel workers. There is some value to being accorded such status, but that it will come about gradually as a concomitant of increased professionalization of these services.

Conditions for Utilization of Student Record Information

The secondary school has assumed the dubious distinction of serving society as an important and unique repository of student records containing twelve or more years of a student's life summarized in a cumulative record folder according to Heayn and Jacobs.[78] Furthermore, increasing amounts of intimate information is being placed in folders, along with such familiar information as grades and test results. According to them, the cumulative record folder is much more than an academic record—it is a human document. This factor provides a sound and pervading basis for the increased concern expressed by many pupil personnel services workers that greater study be given to both the determination of what should be in student records and under what conditions that information should be used. Goldman believes that counselors and their institutions must perform this function and that they are entitled to collect whatever information is specifically and vitally necessary. But, in addition, he believes they must be prepared to document the necessity for the information placed in student records with evidence or at least strong logic.[79]

A fairly large proportion of the legal guidelines relating to pupil personnel work have dealt with pupil records. It would seem, therefore, that there should be reasonable clarity from a legal standpoint as to how personnel workers should prepare and use student information. The three court cases reviewed in the historical section of the chapter in which parents and a student had requested access to cumulative records provided some basis for concluding that such information must be made available to parents or students when requested. Additionally, a few states have passed legislation which specifies to whom student record information may be provided.

The practice of qualified privilege for pupil personnel workers who face suit for alleged libelous statements has been fairly well established by court cases. In the case of *Iverson* v. *Frandsen,* the court affirmed that, "where a psychologist, as a public official, made a professional report on plaintiff's mental level as being that of a high-grade moron, in good faith, and as representing his best judgment, such report was free from actionable malice and was not libelous." Wagner concluded that there was little question that legal protection would be afforded pupil personnel workers who were reporting or recording their observations of students, provided the oral or written reports were made without malice or malicious intent.[80]

There has been considerable discussion regarding what constitutes public records. This concern stems from the fact that, at common law, public records are available for inspection to any person who has sufficient interest to request access to them. There seems to be fairly common agreement that records are public which are made or kept by a public officer and which are required by statute. In the case of *Wagner* v. *Redman* heard in 1960 in Louisiana, a superintendent was compelled to furnish a school board member the names and addresses of pupils enrolled at certain schools. This ruling was based upon the conclusion that the superintendent was a public official and that a state statute specified that each parish superintendent was to keep such records. Similar rulings have been made in at least one other court case and an Attorney General's opinion. One of the biggest questions regarding public records is the definition of a public officer. In the case heard in Louisiana, the superintendent was considered to be a public officer. In the Attorney General ruling, in which newspaper reporters had requested to examine the pupil records of athletes, it was stated that the term "officer" did not apply to school teachers, school nurses, or other school employees.[81] Although he did not cite a particular court ruling, Foley indicated that permanent student records in general meet the criteria set for public records and therefore fall under the jurisdiction of common law. The first of these criteria is, "The records are under the care of a public officer." Parenthetically, Foley also stated, "It is of interest that, legally, teachers and principals are not public officers: they are employees, while superintendents and school board members are public officers." He concludes however, that when the permanent record information of a pupil is mandated by an official body, such as a school board, it meets the criteria of public records.[82] These contrasting statements suggest that even though pupil personnel workers would not normally be considered as public officers, the records they prepare may so be classified because they are mandated by the school board.

One of the features of cumulative records which distinguishes them from personal notes kept by pupil personnel workers is that they tend to be permanent in nature. It has been pointed out previously that the Attorney General ruled in the New Mexico case that the right to public inspection did not extend to the examination of notes by teachers of a confidential or delicate nature or of a type which is not permanent in character. Because of this opinion many writers suggest that pupil personnel workers keep a separate file of any personal student information they wish to keep on a temporary basis. Pardue, Whichard, and Johnson's recommendation in this regard is as follows:

100

Any additional temporary memoranda or worksheets which reflect disciplinary, psychiatric, or other highly personal information, and which might be easily misconstrued by third persons or outsiders, should be kept to a minimum and retained by and for the counselor himself only for his work in assisting his client. Such notes or temporary jottings should be destroyed as soon as they are no longer needed in such capacity.[83]

Such statements provide some assurance that pupil personnel workers will not be required to make personal file information available as public records. Provided they can substantiate that the information contained is highly personal and that they do not keep such information on a permanent basis.

Although there does not appear to be any legal basis for the recommendation, Huckins believes that it is essential that the manner in which student records are to be handled is a matter of school policy. He believes that such a policy should be officially adopted by the board of education and should include how and to whom information will be released.[84] Since the board of education does represent the law-making body at the local level, it would seem that a policy adopted by them would provide a considerable source of support in any informal or formal action regarding access to student record information. Problems related to such a procedure could be the development of cumbersome or overly restrictive policies. Such a recommendation would seem to imply that local pupil personnel workers must do their homework and be actively involved in drawing up such guidelines. They should be guided by both legal standards and accepted ethical practices.

Another area of legal concern for pupil personnel workers is in the area of providing information in court cases. One concern faced by all pupil personnel workers from time to time has to do with their legal and ethical responsibility whenever a counselee tells them of some illegal act. Many are fearful that they may be subject to prosecution if they have such information and do not convey it to law enforcement officials. Sources reviewed did not stipulate legal requirements to do so. Some comments indicated that situations of this nature were more of an ethical problem than a legal one. In any event, information presented in court regarding statements students have made describing incidences may well be hearsay. On the basis of court rulings evidence has been defined as hearsay when its probative force depends upon the competency and creditability of some person other than the witness. Furthermore, it has been legally established that, subject to certain exceptions, the court will not receive testimony of a witness as to what some other person told him as evidence of the existence of a fact asserted. Huckins stated that, "Counselor records dealing with anything which a client has said in a counseling interview might also be considered as inadmissible as evidence in the same manner that the testimony of a counselor concerning a happening or situation described to him by a counselee would be objectionable."[85] In his article dealing with the law, the counselor, and student records, Killian concluded with the statement, "I have yet to mention the most important thing. This is simply that counselors have little to fear from the law if they perform in a professional and ethical manner."[86] Even though pupil personnel workers might feel there would be considerable value in having clear legal bases for matters such as confidentiality, the maintenance and utilization of student records, and the legal implications of providing information conveyed to them by students in court cases, the author shares with Killian the idea that the strict adherence to accepted ethical practices should obviate most of our concerns in the legal area.

Unique Factors Related to Minor Clients

Several authors have expressed concern about the fact that in many respects minors are not accorded the full rights of citizens but are rather given second-rate status. There appears to be a tendency for pupil personnel workers to function from this frame of reference. The younger the child the less is the concern for maintaining confidentiality. Many personnel workers discuss intimate personal information of very young students with almost no concern as to their right to privacy. Ware expressed the belief that there is reason to practice a higher standard for dealing fairly and in good faith with younger clients. She believes this is necessary because of the fact that counselors and students are not equals.[87] Patterson discussed the special issue of the right of confidentiality of the client against the parent faced by pupil personnel workers in their relationships with minor students. He indicated that in many instances students are involved in a counseling relationship without the knowledge of their parents and frequently with the desire that this fact be withheld from their parents. This raises questions such as: Does a student have a right to enter a continuing counseling relationship without the knowledge of his parents if he desires to do so? Should the counselor feel ethically obligated to respect a student's right of confidentiality

102

from the parents? If a counselor becomes aware that a student's parents are opposed to counseling, should the counselor discontinue the relationship? The court cases in which parents have requested and gained access to information in student records would tend to indicate that the law does not provide a child with a right to withhold information from his parents. Because of the limited confidentiality in working with minors, it is frequently suggested that students be informed of this matter at the beginning of the counseling relationship. Patterson believes that such a practice would lead to the undermining of counseling in the school. He takes a very strong stand favoring full rights for students with the following comments:

> There is too little respect for the rights of children in our society and in our schools. They are not full citizens nor are they even treated as persons. . . . The only ethical position that a school counselor can take is that confidentiality for the communication of a child in counseling must be maintained against the prying of his parents as against that of anyone else, including teachers and administrators.

He further expressed the concern that minors have been deprived of their rights far too long, but that this situation is changing. He cited a case involving students wearing arm bands in protest against the war in Vietnam in which the ruling by the Supreme Court held that students are "persons" under the Constitution.[88] The author obtained information from his survey which also tends to suggest increased status for students. The state of Delaware enacted legislation in 1970 related to disclosure of pupils' school records which included a provision that pupils who have reached the age of fourteen may sign requests for the release of their record information to other schools, a prospective employer, or a licensed physician. The law specifically indicates that a minor having reached the age of fourteen shall be considered an adult for the purposes prescribed by the law.

The preceding information certainly does not provide a sound legal base for the practice of pupil personnel workers with respect to the rights of minors. Without doubt there are many who hold and strongly defend quite different points of view on this matter. Ladd certainly does not agree with according full rights to minors. He suggested that a graded system might be used which increases young persons' civil liberties as they grow older and as they earn recognition from their elders.[89] It seems to the author that immaturity does not provide a reasonable basis for withholding personal rights; therefore, it would appear appropriate and advisable that personnel workers provide open support for the establishment of legal guidelines which will provide minors full civil rights.

Restrictions Related to Student Appraisal

For a little more than a decade considerable concern has been expressed regarding the use of testing in the schools. Huckins believes that pupil personnel workers may have infringed upon student privacy through the use of psychological tests. This is especially true of tests and inventories designed to measure personality characteristics. Not only do they attempt to elicit very personal information, but in many cases their effectiveness depends upon disguising the intent of the items so that the student is unaware of the possible implications of his answers. The author did not find references to legal regulations which apply to testing and the student's right to privacy, but there are reports of actions taken by National Congressmen which have relevance. A U.S. senator has offered an amendment to the National Defense Education Act for the purpose of prohibiting psychological testing in projects conducted with such funding, and congressional hearings have been conducted in which questions relating to psychological testing figured prominently.[90] Goldman emphasized his concern in this matter by stating that, "Schools and colleges have, in fact, badly invaded the privacy of their students. They have probed, questionnaired, inventoried, and surveyed—usually without giving the student a real choice as to whether he will respond."[91] His statement contains at least two messages. Much more data is obtained about students than is reasonable and necessary, and students should be given some option in the matter of providing information. The author strongly supports these concepts. Short of impelling reasons for requiring the completion of any test or inventory, and especially those which deal with more intimate factors, pupil personnel workers should certainly discuss with students the possible value of the information to be gained. The final decision to complete such instruments should usually be left to the student.

INTERDEPENDENCE OF ETHICAL STANDARDS AND LEGAL GUIDELINES

Upon careful study of ethical standards and legal guidelines for pupil personnel work, one observes an obvious complementary and interdependent relationship. Where the two areas are in accord, the results are a greater likelihood of optimum services to pupils and desirable working conditions for personnel workers. In instances where the two provisions are not complementary, personnel workers find themselves in a dilemma. Huckins observed that:

> Although both the law and codes of ethics have in mind the assurance of moral and equitable behavior, they sometimes are at variance as to how this can best be achieved. The practitioner to whom such codes apply sometimes may find himself caught between forces which are in seeming opposition. The collective conscience of his profession and his own moral convictions as a counselor may not always be in accord with legal dictates.[92]

Some of the more common interdependent relationships are: confidentiality and privileged communication, collection and use of student information and right of privacy, research with human subjects and infringement of individual rights, and professional behavior and malpractice. Some of the concerns, implications, and means of negotiating these situations will be discussed briefly.

Confidentiality Versus Privileged Communication

Privileged communication has previously been defined as the right of the client against release of confidential information without his consent. However, pupil personnel workers should know that a judge may waive this privilege if he believes a case warrants that action. The meaning of confidentiality is not quite so clear-cut, but in common usage by pupil personnel workers it certainly connotes that communication between a worker and a student is private and will not be shared with others. It seems highly probable that pupil personnel workers have conveyed this concept either quite explicitly or in implied ways to their clients throughout the years. Most personnel workers can readily recall many times when they have assured an anxious, insecure student that what is discussed will be held in strict confidence. In the light of existing legal provisions, it appears that such positive statements may well be foolish and possibly somewhat dishonest except in the few states where pupil personnel workers are accorded privileged communication status.

Various writers take positions related to confidentiality which are quite different and frequently almost in direct opposition. Some appear to be overly concerned with the lack of legal protection for pupil personnel workers and make very definite suggestions that such practitioners inform students at the outset of all conditions in which they may not be able to maintain confidentiality. These writ-

105

ers seem to imply that it may even be unethical not to make such conditions known to students. Ladd authored one of the strongest statements expressing this viewpoint by declaring, "Counselors should be required to make it completely clear to counselees what information about them may be made available to other persons, who those other persons may be, and in what form the information may reach them."[93] Others have concluded that such an approach would be most detrimental to establishing and maintaining effective counseling relationships, especially with students who have serious personal concerns. Furthermore, they believe that short of making rather lengthy statements to cover every eventuality it is often difficult to determine in advance if anything may be revealed which cannot be maintained in confidence. There are others who believe that it is the personnel worker's responsibility to interject comments expressing the fact that confidence may not be maintained any time a student appears to be likely to present information in this category. The latter of these two positions is more palatable for the author; however, he would take the stand that either practice has a high probability of interfering with the establishment and maintenance of effective relationships between student and worker. The author's position is more in accord with Patterson when he asked, "What student would ever talk to a counselor about personal problems involving sex or drugs under such a condition?"

In the final analysis, it seems that pupil personnel workers must determine which is the greater need—optimum conditions for maintaining helping relations with clients or safety from the standpoint of possible legal action. Patterson presented a viewpoint which seems worthy of much reflection when he was writing about the advisability of informing students beforehand of conditions in which it might be impossible to maintain confidentiality by stating: "The client must not be betrayed, say the writers. Under such a condition the problem of betrayal will never occur. But what a cost to assure counselor tranquility."[94]

Much concern has been expressed over the fact that ethical standards clearly require confidentiality, while the probability that this can usually be fulfilled exists only when privileged communication is accorded. This is a conflict and dilemma faced by most pupil personnel workers. Most practitioners believe this can be resolved only when they are accorded the right of privileged communication. This may well be a reasonable goal, but it would appear such status will be difficult to attain on a wide scale until pupil personnel workers are viewed with higher professional esteem. In the meantime, it seems wise to re-emphasize that the portion of confidentiality related to privileged communication is minuscule.

Collection and Use of Student Information Versus Right of Privacy

Concern that pupil personnel workers may invade privacy of students has been expressed by various authors. They hold that such workers may acquire information rather easily since they have a captive audience, their clients are younger and therefore in a sense weaker than they are, and they have considerable freedom to administer various tests. Assuming the validity of these views, unless considerable discretion is employed in the matter of collecting data about students it seems likely that information may be obtained which could constitute invasion of privacy. Additionally, the author of this chapter believes pupil personnel workers find many reasons, and are subjected to much pressure, to share the information collected. These reasons are usually couched in terms which indicate that the information is being shared for the welfare of the student. Serious reflection may reveal that some reasons for giving out information are, at least in part, rationalizations based upon power or ego needs of pupil personnel workers. Frequently, disclosures to others are the result of a pupil personnel worker's inability to withstand pressures from colleagues. Even worse, in some cases it appears that both the collection and dissemination of pupil information borders on what might be referred to as highly unethical psychological voyeurism.

Certainly, the previous negative comments should not stand without additional statements indicating the clearly beneficial aspects of obtaining and sharing appropriate student information. All pupil personnel workers, parents, and students are aware of many instances when accurate information professionally obtained, shared, and used has been most beneficial. It also seems reasonable for colleagues who have referred students to pupil personnel workers to expect some feedback. Furthermore, contemporary behavioral specialists regularly express interest in the development of open trusting relationships in all associations. It should be possible to fulfill the latter two conditions without conveying factual information that should be held confidential by commenting in a general manner.

Another factor which has created considerable concern in the area of record keeping and dissemination is the extensive development of electronic means of processing data. In the past, privacy has been

107

protected somewhat because the methods of data storage, retrieval, and report preparation were slow and cumbersome. The technology is now available to reverse this situation completely. This factor presents a new reason for careful professional study in determining the information which should be contained in student files. It also requires the development of highly secure file protection systems.

The right to privacy is based upon provisions of the fourth amendment to the United States Constitution. The actual meaning of this concept as it relates to pupil personnel work is somewhat confusing and not well-established. Comments by Ware related to this matter are as follows:

> The emerging right to privacy is a legal concept stating that persons should have the right to sue for damages if their individual privacy has been invaded. . . . The courts have been dealing with the right to privacy only in this century and, to say the least, the law is in flux.[95]

Court rulings have previously been reviewed which indicated some precedent for access to record information by parents and students as well as to other interested persons. Two additional guidelines related to accessibility to pupil records have been fairly well-established by legal opinions. Personal notes of pupil personnel workers should be kept separate from cumulative records and they should be destroyed as soon as they are no longer of value to the person who recorded them. When such practices are followed, it seems likely that they will not be made available to parents, students, or other interested persons by court order.

The author believes that the apparent dilemma which exists with respect to student record information can be pretty much resolved by following two simple guidelines. Very little, if any, information should be maintained which is not known to the student. To a much greater degree, student record information should be released only with the consent of a student.

Record Information Release and Preparation of References Versus Slander or Libel

Frequently, record information or reference statements are submitted to prospective employers or admissions officers at the request of a student. Whenever such material contains information which is not beneficial or possibly detrimental from the standpoint of the purpose for which it was requested, the possibility of a suit of defama-

108

tion exists. There are practical and ethical procedures which pupil personnel workers could follow in such instances that should essentially eliminate being subjected to legal action. In instances in which students request record information forwarded which contains material of questionable value to them, they should be so informed prior to fulfilling the requests. Whenever a pupil personnel worker is unable to give a student a positive reference, he should make this fact known to the student before forwarding such a statement. In each case, the student should clearly have the option to withdraw the request for the sharing of the information. Another procedure, which merits serious consideration, is requiring a student to sign a release statement prior to providing the requested information. Employing these three suggestions provides almost total protection to pupil personnel workers when performing these activities.

Research with Human Subjects Versus Infringement of Individual Rights

The ethical codes adopted by APGA, APA, and CSCA all contain specific statements with regard to research with human subjects. Each clearly has the purpose of requiring researchers to refrain from practices which may infringe upon individual rights. This concept is concisely stated in the APGA Ethical Standards as follows, "In the performance of any research on human subjects the member must avoid causing any injurious effects or aftereffects of the experiment upon his subjects."[96] The APA guidelines contained in the Ethical Standards of Psychologists is not quite so delimiting with regard to research which may be injurious. When the possibility of physical or psychological injury exists, it does require that human research subjects be thoroughly informed of the nature of the research and possible consequences before agreeing to participate.

No legal cases or judicial opinions related to this specific conflict situation were reported in the literature reviewed by the author. Quite recently, however, there has been reported through mass news media an experiment which most blatantly ignored the concept of the human dignity of the participants. This was a forty-year federal experiment in which a group of two hundred prisoners were denied proper medical treatment for venereal disease. The experiment was designed to determine through autopsies what damage untreated syphilis does to the human body.[97] Certainly, the abrogation of individual rights should not have to be anywhere near that gross to make researchers aware of the need for strict adherence to

109

ethical guidelines for research with human subjects, but reports of such should remove any vestiges of lethargy in this matter. The recently proposed ethical standards for research with human subjects developed by APA indicates the careful concern members of that association have given to the subject. In addition to ten proposed ethical principles the fairly voluminous draft extensively considers numerous problems and incidents related to the principles.[98] The adoption and implementation of specific ethical principles for research with human subjects should be a matter of high priority for pupil personnel workers.

Professional Behavior Versus Malpractice

Although only one case involving an allegation of malpractice against a pupil personnel worker has been reported in contemporary professional literature, cognizance of the almost exponential increase in malpractice suits against medical practitioners would suggest that pupil personnel workers should realistically expect to be the subject of more suits of this nature also. Huckins indicated that, "Malpractice generally refers to any professional misconduct, carelessness, or lack of skill in the performance of an established and socially imposed duty."[99] Beymer expressed the belief that a charge of malpractice will be made against a counselor in the near future and suggested the charges will be, "That the counselor behaved in a careless, negligent, or stupid manner; that he could have and should have known better."[100] Beymer's thesis is that the primary protection against malpractice suits is knowledge and performance in a presently accepted professional manner.

In the one malpractice case against a pupil personnel worker, a director of student services for a college was charged with malpractice after a counselee committed suicide. The complaint alleged that the director with responsibility for maintenance of a counseling and testing center should have recognized the emotional condition of this counselee. The decision was in favor of the defendant but hardly on grounds that would enhance the professional status of pupil personnel workers. The court ruled, "To hold that a teacher who has no training, education, or experience in medical fields is required to recognize in a student a condition and diagnosis of which is in a specialized technical medical field, would require a duty beyond reason."[101] Huckins commented upon this decision as follows, "If the degree of professional competence claimed for counselors in the professional literature had been accepted as the standard of reasonable proficiency, however, a difference in action on the demurrer might have been expected."

There appear to be two valid suggestions for pupil personnel workers to minimize the possibility of facing a malpractice suit. These are careful adherence to ethical practices and continuing in-service growth in order to be able to perform in a presently accepted professional manner.

SUMMARY COMMENTS AND RECOMMENDATIONS

The information presented in this chapter suggests to the author that much still needs to be done by pupil personnel workers with regard to ethical standards.

In addition to the increased emphasis upon ethical concepts in pupil personnel training programs, there is a pronounced need for supportive professional organizations to plan more effective means of insuring adherence to ethical practices. The California School Counselor Association has established a service which has considerable potential for helping individual counselors or the counselors in a given school or community with problems related to the nature and quality of counseling services. Area Assistance Teams have been constituted in each of the nine Association regions in the state to conduct in-depth study of issues involved in a CSCA member's or group's request for professional assistance in resolving grievances.[102] Members of the teams have special knowlege about ethical standards, legal guidelines, administration of counseling, and counselor roles. They make on-site visitations, and their approach is one of informed cooperation and sensitive communication. Initial experiences of the teams indicate that such a service will enhance local counseling programs and concomitantly ethical standards.

There are two glaring voids in current codes of ethics for emerging pupil personnel practices, namely, group activities and the use of paraprofessionals. The extensive use of group work suggests that the development of a separate code would be appropriate. At a minimum, the existing major codes should be revised to include a section on ethics in group work. In the meantime, pupil personnel workers who are involved with group work would do well to study and apply the concepts and suggested code included in articles by Gazda, Duncan, and Sisson[103] and Olsen,[104] which have been reviewed earlier.

Ethical concepts and legal guidelines are virtually nonexistent for paraprofessionals in pupil personnel work. The rapidly increasing

111

employment of students and other persons with limited professional preparation to assist personnel workers demands serious consideration of the concomitant ethical and legal implications. Several recommendations seem to be in order until professional committees and authorities have established more formalized guidelines in the use of paraprofessionals. A carefully planned selection procedure should be employed, which includes the use of instruments designed to assess personality characteristics. Persons selected need to have considerable self-awareness, a sensitivity to the needs of others, and the capacity to relate effectively with others. A structured pre-service and in-service training program should be developed and implemented. Such a program should emphasize desired ethical standards and related legal concerns. A comprehensive job description should be prepared, with attention given to restricting activities to those clearly within accepted ethical practices. Finally, each paraprofessional should be under the direct supervision of a professional pupil personnel worker.

It is generally accepted that the enactment of "friendly" or supportive legislation is the preferred method of establishing legal guidelines. Representatives of professional associations usually have much more opportunity to proffer professional information and direction in the legislative process than is possible in court cases or legal opinions. The enactment of legislation thought to be desirable by pupil personnel workers usually requires considerable effective actions by key members of a professional organization. One of the most important is the establishment and maintenance of a cooperative relationship with legislators who have a sincere interest in services related to proposed legislation. During the past year, representatives of the California Personnel and Guidance Association worked cooperatively with legislators over a five-month period to get a counseling identification bill passed. This legislation introduced a definition of counseling into the California Education Code and described the role and functions of counselors. The primary activities related to the passage of the bill have been reported in the association newsletter and may be of considerable interest and value to members of other pupil personnel organizations.[105] Of course, there is also a need for professional associations to develop structures and procedures to assist members involved in court cases that clearly have implications for affecting standards of services. Ethics or professional preparation and standards committees frequently assume this responsibility.

Pupil personnel workers who find themselves involved in a court action as a witness will undoubtedly face the prospect with some trepidation. Killian has made suggestions which should be of value as follows:

> The one thing I have tried to make clear in discussing testimony in judicial proceedings is that the witness—the counselor—can discuss his problems of confidentiality, relevance, and possible harm to the student with the judge and often with counsel. If in doubt about any point, he should do just that.[106]

Several additional conclusions seem warranted to the author as a result of this study and analysis of ethical and legal aspects of pupil personnel work. Ethical standards are not understood nor applied by pupil personnel workers at a commendable level. There is a credibility gap between stated ethical standards and actual practice. Although there is value to clients and personnel workers when ethical guidelines and legal provisions closely parallel one another, the absence of legal provisions such as privileged communication is not as delimiting as expressions by many professionals indicate. As legislation is developed, both legislators and pupil personnel workers need to be primarily concerned with the welfare of students. Most importantly, the improvement of pupil personnel services centers essentially in the selection and training of capable pupil personnel workers. Practitioners with excellent personal adjustment and courageous commitment to ethical standards, especially that of primary responsibility to the student, are essential.

1. C. Gilbert Wrenn, "The Ethics of Counseling," in *Guidance Readings for Counselors*, Gail F. Farwell and Herman J. Peters, eds. (Chicago: Rand McNally & Co., 1960), pp. 420–24.
2. American Psychological Association, "Ethical Standards of Psychologists," *American Psychologist* (May 1968), 23:357–61.
3. Seth Arsenian, "The APGA Code of Ethics," *The Personnel and Guidance Journal* (Oct. 1961), 40:204–5.
4. American Personnel and Guidance Association, "Ethical Standards," *The Personnel and Guidance Journal* (Oct. 1961), 40:206–9.
5. John F. Bancroft, "Activating a Code of Ethics," *The Personnel and Guidance Journal* (Dec. 1971), 50:260.
6. American School Counselor Association, "Code of Ethics Proposed," *ASCA Newsletter* (Post-Convention 1972), pp. 9–10.
7. American School Counselor Association, "Principles of Confidentiality," *ASCA Newsletter* (Dec. 1970), 8:4.
8. G. M. Gazda, J. A. Duncan, and P. J. Sisson, "Professional Issues in Group Work," *The Personnel and Guidance Journal* (April 1971), 54:637–43.
9. Leroy C. Olsen, "Ethical Standards for Group Leaders," *The Personnel and Guidance Journal* (Dec. 1971), 50:288.
10. American Psychological Association, "Ethical Standards for Research with Human Subjects," *APA Monitor* (May 1972), 3:I–XIV.
11. Wesley Huckins, *Ethical and Legal Considerations in Guidance* (Boston: Houghton Mifflin Co., 1968), p. 1
12. Elmer E. Wagner, *Legal Implications of Duties Performed by Pupil Personnel Workers Employed in California Public Schools* (Los Angeles: Los Angeles County Superintendent of Schools Office, 1966), p. 2.
13. John D. Killian, "The Law, The Counselor, and Student Records," *The Personnel and Guidance Journal* (Feb. 1970), 42:14–20.
14. Jerry Pardue, Willis Whichard, and Elizabeth Johnson, "Limiting Confidential Information in Counseling," *The Personnel and Guidance Journal* (Sept. 1970), 49:14–20.
15. Huckins, op cit., p. 32.
16. Ibid., pp. 30, 31.
17. Ibid., p. 32
18. Ibid., p. 35.
19. Pardue, Whichard, and Johnson, op. cit., p. 15.
20. Killian, op. cit., p. 430.
21. Pardue, Whichard, and Johnson, loc. cit.
22. Huckins, op. cit., p. 50.
23. Ibid., p. 51.
24. Ibid., p. 25.
25. Loc. cit.
26. Ibid., pp. 28, 29.
27. Killian, op. cit., pp. 26, 27.
28. Ibid., p. 27.

29. Martha L. Ware, "The Law and Counselor Ethics," *The Personnel and Guidance Journal* (Dec. 1971), 50:305–10.
30. Huckins, op. cit., pp. 42, 43.
31. Wrenn, op. cit., p. 20.
32. Mary Margaret Flanagan and David R. McGrew, "A Suggested Code of Ethics for School Counselors," *The School Counselor* (May 1961), 8:136–41.
33. Wrenn, op. cit., pp. 20–24.
34. National Education Association, *NEA Handbook* 1970–71 (Washington, D.C., 1970).
35. American Personnel and Guidance Association, op. cit., p. 206.
36. Lyle D. Schmidt, "Some Ethical, Professional, and Legal Considerations for School Counselors," *The Personnel and Guidance Journal* (Dec. 1965), 44:-376–82.
37. James F. Adams, "Ethical Responsibilities of the Counselor," *The School Counselor* (May 1965), 12:197–205.
38. Flanagan and McGrew, loc. cit.
39. Bancroft, loc cit.
40. Arsenian, op. cit., p. 205.
41. American Personnel and Guidance Association, op. cit., pp. 206, 207.
42. American Psychological Association, "Ethical Standards of Psychologists," op. cit., pp. 357, 358.
43. "Proposed By-laws of the American School Counselor Association" (Washington, D.C.: American School Counselor Association, 1968).
44. American School Counselor Association, "ASCA Constitutional Revisions," *The School Counselor* (May 1963), 10:169–77.
45. American School Counselor Association, "Revised Constitution of the American School Counselor Association," *The School Counselor* (March 1966), 13:-163–72.
46. American School Counselor Association, "Code of Ethics," loc. cit.
47. Lawrence Beymer, "Who Killed George Washington?", *The Personnel and Guidance Journal* (Dec. 1971), 50:249–53.
48. John F. Bancroft, "Ethical Practices," *ASCA Newsletter* (May 1969), 6:3.
49. California School Counselor Association, *Counselor Ethics* (Fullerton, Calif., 1969).
50. Schmidt, op. cit., p. 381.
51. Curt Schmid, "Code of Ethics for Counselors," *The School Counselor* (Sept. 1967), 15:64–67.
52. Wrenn, op. cit., p. 427.
53. C. H. Patterson, "Are Ethics Different in Different Settings?", *The Personnel and Guidance Journal* (Dec. 1971), 50:254–59.
54. Edward T. Ladd, "Counselors, Confidences, and the Civil Liberties of Clients," *The Personnel and Guidance Journal* (Dec. 1971) 50:261–68.
55. Charles M. Clark, "Confidentiality and the School Counselor," *The Personnel and Guidance Journal* (Jan. 1965), 43:482–84.
56. Adams, op. cit., p. 203.
57. Flanagan and McGrew, op. cit., p. 137.
58. Frank A. Nugent, "Confidentiality in the College Counseling Center," *The Personnel and Guidance Journal* (May 1969), 48:72–77.
59. Gazda, Duncan, and Sisson, op. cit., p. 637.
60. David Zimpfer, "Needed: Professional Ethics for Working with Groups," *The Personnel and Guidance Journal* (Dec. 1971), 50:280–87.

115

61. David L. Sansbury, "Emerging Ethical Concerns of the Counseling Center Psychologist," *The Personnel and Guidance Journal* (Dec. 1971), 50:318–19.
62. Carlton E. Beck, "Ethical Practice: Foundations and Emerging Issues," *The Personnel and Guidance Journal* (Dec. 1971), 50:320–25.
63. American School Counselor Association, "The Role of the Secondary School Counselor" (Washington, D.C., n.d.).
64. American School Counselor Association, *ASCA Newsletter* (Sept. 1972), 10:9.
65. Huckins, op. cit. p. 53.
66. California Personnel and Guidance Association, *Compass* (Summer 1971), 3:6.
67. California School Counselor Association, op. cit.
68. Carlton E. Beck, "Ethical Aspects of Change in Counselor Education," *Counselor Education and Supervision* (Spring 1967), 6:216–21.
69. Association for Counselor Education and Supervision, *Standards for the Preparation of Secondary School Counselors,* 1967 ed. (Washington, D.C., 1967).
70. Schmidt, op. cit., p. 378.
71. Huckins, op. cit., p. 2.
72. Wagner, op. cit., pp. 7, 8.
73. Huckins, op. cit., p. 33.
74. American Personnel and Guidance Association, "Resolutions Adopted by 1967 APGA Senate," *Guidepost* (May 1967), 9:11.
75. Wrenn, op. cit., p. 419.
76. Leo Goldman, "Privilege or Privacy: I," *The Personnel and Guidance Journal* (Oct. 1969), 48:88.
77. Arthur J. Bangs, "Privelege and the Counseling Profession," *The Personnel and Guidance Journal* (Dec. 1971), 50:270–75.
78. Maurice H. Heayn and Howard L. Jacobs, "Safeguarding Student Records," *The Personnel and Guidance Journal* (Sept. 1967), 46:63–67.
79. Leo Goldman, "Privilege or Privacy: II," *The Personnel and Guidance Journal* (Nov. 1969), 48:184.
80. Wagner, op. cit., p. 23.
81. Huckins, op. cit., pp. 25–29.
82. Walter J. Foley, "It's Time to Re-examine Confidentiality of Pupil Records," *The School Counselor* (Nov. 1967), 14:92–96.
83. Pardue, Whichard, and Johnson, op. cit., p. 19.
84. Huckins, op. cit., p. 24.
85. Ibid., p. 38.
86. Killian, op. cit., p. 432.
87. Ware, op. cit., p. 307.
88. Patterson, op. cit., pp. 257, 258.
89. Ladd, op. cit., p. 267.
90. Huckins, op. cit., p. 19.
91. Goldman, "Privilege or Privacy: I," loc cit.
92. Huckins, op. cit., p. 13.
93. Ladd, op. cit., pp. 265, 266.
94. Patterson, op. cit., p. 258.
95. Ware, op. cit., pp. 306, 309.
96. American Personnel and Guidance Association, "Ethical Standards," p. 208.
97. Associated Press, by-line Jean Heller, Washington D.C., July-Sept. 1972.
98. American Psychological Association, "Ethical Standards for Research with Human Subjects," op. cit., pp. i–xix.
99. Huckins, op. cit., p. 41.
100. Beymer, op. cit., p. 252.
101. Huckins, op. cit., pp. 42–45.

102. California School Counselor Association, *CSCA Info* (Dec. 1971), 11:1.
103. Gazda, Duncan, and Sisson, op. cit., pp. 637–43.
104. Olsen, loc. cit.
105. California School Counselor Association, *CSCA Info* (Oct. 1971), 11:2–4.
106. Killian, op. cit., p. 432.

SELECTED REFERENCES

American Personnel and Guidance Association. "Ethical Standards," *The Personnel and Guidance Journal* (Oct. 1961):40:206–9
———, "Ethical Practice: Preserving Human Dignity," *The Personnel and Guidance Journal* (Dec. 1971), 50:252, 255–59, 288, 305–9.
Huckins, Wesley. *Ethical and Legal Considerations in Guidance*, pp. 24–40, 42–45, 48–51. Boston: Houghton Mifflin Company, 1968.
Wagner, Elmer E. *Legal Implications of Duties Performed by Pupil Personnel Workers Employed in California Public Schools*, pp. 1–3, 5–9, 11–22. Los Angeles: Los Angeles County Superintendent of Schools Office, 1966.
Wrenn, C. Gilbert. "The Ethics of Counseling" in *Guidance Reading for Counselors*, pp. 420–30, edited by Gail F. Farwell and Herman J. Peters. Chicago: Rand McNally & Co., 1960.

CHAPTER 4

Technology in Pupil Personnel Services

ROBERT W. O'HARE

ALTHOUGH technology has had and will continue to have a dramatic effect on society, the word *technology* still evokes a variety of interpretations and feelings. In relationship to educational programs the inference is often negative, primarily because some educators tend to associate technology exclusively with equipment and hardware. Schutz states that technology has been "equated with mechanization, borrowing on the heavy use of equipment in industry. It is often equated with the aversive consequences attributed to the use of such equipment and machinery, as in technological unemployment and technological pollution."[1] Komoski says that "our present understanding of 'technology' itself is still so influenced by the machine-centered, mass-producing, man-reducing technology of the first industrial revolution that most talk about the 'impact of technology on education' still precipitates an emotionally charged atmosphere, inhospitable to effective communication."[2] Technology should not be equated solely with machinery and equipment, since hardware might or might not be an important part of technology. A recent report of The Brookings Institute defines technological knowledge as

> a set of techniques, each defined as a set of actions and decision rules guiding their sequential application that man has learned will generally lead to a predictable (and sometimes desirable) outcome under certain specified circumstances.[3]

118

Wiesner states that it is wrong to equate technology and science because, "Science is the quest for more or less abstract knowledge, whereas technology is the application of organized knowledge to help solve problems in our society."[4] Ofiesh defines educational technology as the "application of scientific knowledge, including learning theory, to the solution of problems in education. . . ."[5] Although disclaiming it as an attempt at definition, Komoski states that "technology refers to any man-made device, process or logical technique designed to systematically produce a reproducible effect."[6] Silverman distinguishes between technology as method and technology as application:

> Technology as method is an approach to problem solving and to the creation of new programs, methods and machines that is rational and orderly. . . . Technology as application uses the results of technology as method.[7]

All the above definitions have elements of commonality and are useful in providing a framework or perspective for the discussion of technology in pupil personnel. A point which is not clear, however, is whether these definitions are limited to the application of existing processes and hardware to education or whether they are sufficiently expansive to include the development of what Komoski terms "indigenous educational technology."[8] It is important to be concerned with the application of existing technologies to education but even more important to be concerned with the development of technology intrinsic to education which concentrates on a thorough understanding of the learning process. Such a technology would permit more appropriate uses of existing hardware and procedures but, more important, would provide the necessary data for the development of a new generation of hardware and procedures.

Although equipment and hardware are discussed throughout this chapter, the emphasis is on attaining an understanding of the scope and potential of technology in education.

SYSTEMS TECHNOLOGY IN GUIDANCE

A discussion of systems is an appropriate starting point in the consideration of technology. The notion of systems, which was introduced to educational administration during the early 1950s,[9] has by now gained considerable popularity among educators.

Corrigan and Kaufman define system as

A closed-loop analytic and developmental process which can be utilized to continuously: (1) assess the results of performance; (2) maintain sensitivity to performance requirements; and (3) provide for the self-correction of performance in order that the specified objectives can be achieved.[10]

More simply, a system can be defined as a "set of elements organized to satisfy a definable user requirement";[11] as the "organization of an orderly whole, clearly showing the interrelationship of the parts to each other and to the whole itself";[12] or as the "selection of elements, relationships, and procedures to achieve a specific purpose."[13]

Unfortunately, like technology, systems concepts are frequently misunderstood, and may be associated exclusively with complicated charts and diagrams. Excessive time may be devoted to such trappings with little time remaining to achieve stated outcomes. Some offices do not need paint, since the walls are papered with charts that are hailed as simplified plans. On the other hand, as Silvern states, "the systems approach is *not* common sense rigorously applied."[14] Somewhere between these two extreme positions one can develop useful and practical planning procedures.

One of the chief advantages in using some form of systems thinking is the increased probability of achieving desired outcomes or objectives. The design and operation of a complex system requires the statement of precise outcomes, the designation of activities to implement each outcome, and assessment of the degree to which each outcome is attained.

Campbell and others indicate that the systems procedures are outcome-oriented.

Systems models show relationships and flow from start to finish and facilitate the management and monitoring of a program. Problems and impediments to achieving the goal can be spotted, modifications installed, resources shifted, and deadlines adjusted. The systems approach identifies alternative methods for achieving a goal, creates a searching attitude, insures "backup" plans if the primary plan breaks down, and has procedures for determining the success of the program built into the system. Through trial installation, monitoring, and feedback, a program is continuously assessed to determine the degree to which it is achieving its initial goal.[15]

Systems theory is used in a variety of forms in different fields of endeavor. Silvern, however, identifies four characteristics which are common to all systems applications.[16] These characteristics are usually implemented in the following sequence:

1. Analysis—identifying the problem, existing elements, and interrelations.
2. Synthesis—combining unrelated elements and relationships into a new whole.
3. Models—predicting effectiveness without implementing system.
4. Simulation—evaluation of alternate solutions through the study of math or symbolic models.

Corrigan and Kaufman have defined the basic steps in any problem-solving model.[17] The steps are shown in Figure 4.1.

Mitchell has used this technique in the Culver City (California) schools with the objective of studying the dropout problem and increasing the school's holding power (Figure 4.2).[18]

Another application of systems concepts in guidance has been proposed recently at the Center for Vocational and Technical Education.[19] The application includes four basic components: (1) specifying program objectives, (2) generating alternate methods, (3) designing program evaluation, (4) implementing planned changes.

These four components are used as a basis for developing a ten-phase procedural model: (1) context evaluation, (2) assigning pro-

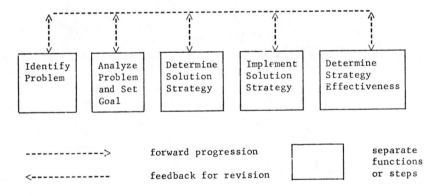

Fig. 4.1.   Basic steps in problem-solving model.

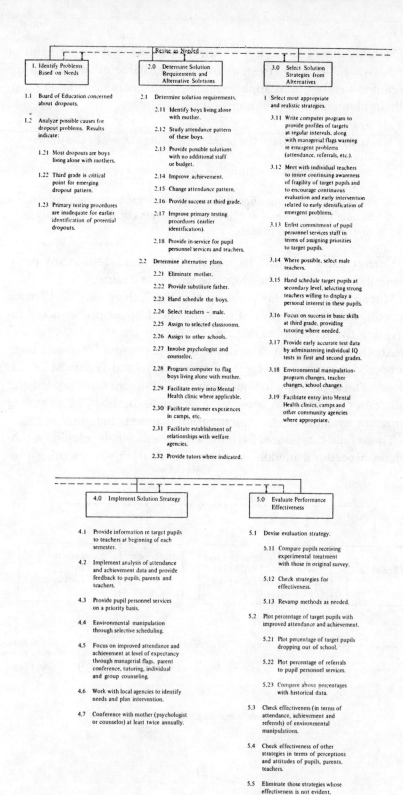

1. Identify Problems Based on Needs	2.0 Determine Solution Requirements and Alternative Solutions	3.0 Select Solution Strategies from Alternatives

1.1 Board of Education concerned about dropouts.

1.2 Analyze possible causes for dropout problems. Results indicate:

1.21 Most dropouts are boys living alone with mothers.

1.22 Third grade is critical point for emerging dropout pattern.

1.23 Primary testing procedures are inadequate for earlier identification of potential dropouts.

2.1 Determine solution requirements.

2.11 Identify boys living alone with mother.

2.12 Study attendance pattern of these boys.

2.13 Provide possible solutions with no additional staff or budget.

2.14 Improve achievement.

2.15 Change attendance pattern.

2.16 Provide success at third grade.

2.17 Improve primary testing procedures (earlier identification).

2.18 Provide in-service for pupil personnel services and teachers.

2.2 Determine alternative plans.

2.21 Eliminate mother.

2.22 Provide substitute father.

2.23 Hand schedule the boys.

2.24 Select teachers – male.

2.25 Assign to selected classrooms.

2.26 Assign to other schools.

2.27 Involve psychologist and counselor.

2.28 Program computer to flag boys living alone with mother.

2.29 Facilitate entry into Mental Health clinic where applicable.

2.30 Facilitate summer experiences in camps, etc.

2.31 Facilitate establishment of relationships with welfare agencies.

2.32 Provide tutors where indicated.

1 Select most appropriate and realistic strategies.

3.11 Write computer program to provide profiles of targets at regular intervals, along with managerial flags warning re emergent problems (attendance, referrals, etc.).

3.12 Meet with individual teachers to insure continuing awareness of fragility of target pupils and to encourage continuous evaluation and early intervention related to early identification of emergent problems.

3.13 Enlist commitment of pupil personnel services staff in terms of assigning priorities to target pupils.

3.14 Where possible, select male teachers.

3.15 Hand schedule target pupils at secondary level, selecting strong teachers willing to display a personal interest in these pupils.

3.16 Focus on success in basic skills at third grade, providing tutoring where needed.

3.17 Provide early accurate test data by administering individual IQ tests in first and second grades.

3.18 Environmental manipulation- program changes, teacher changes, school changes.

3.19 Facilitate entry into Mental Health clinics, camps and other community agencies where appropriate.

4.0 Implement Solution Strategy	5.0 Evaluate Performance Effectiveness

4.1 Provide information re target pupils to teachers at beginning of each semester.

4.2 Implement analysis of attendance and achievement data and provide feedback to pupils, parents and teachers.

4.3 Provide pupil personnel services on a priority basis.

4.4 Environmental manipulation through selective scheduling.

4.5 Focus on improved attendance and achievement at level of expectancy through managerial flags, parent conference, tutoring, individual and group counseling.

4.6 Work with local agencies to identify needs and plan intervention.

4.7 Conference with mother (psychologist or counselor) at least twice annually.

5.1 Devise evaluation strategy.

5.11 Compare pupils receiving experimental treatment with those in original survey.

5.12 Check strategies for effectiveness.

5.13 Revamp methods as needed.

5.2 Plot percentage of target pupils with improved attendance and achievement.

5.21 Plot percentage of target pupils dropping out of school.

5.22 Plot percentage of referrals to pupil personnel services.

5.23 Compare above percentages with historical data.

5.3 Check effectiveness (in terms of attendance, achievement and referrals) of environmental manipulations.

5.4 Check effectiveness of other strategies in terms of perceptions and attitudes of pupils, parents, teachers.

5.5 Eliminate those strategies whose effectiveness is not evident.

Fig. 4.2. Culver City Unified School District (California). Problem: need to increase the school's holding power.

gram goal priorities, (3) translation of goals to student behavioral objectives, (4) input evaluation: method selection, (5) input evaluation: selection of techniques, (6) diffusion: trial implementation, (7) process evaluation, (8) product evaluation, (9) adoption, (10) recycling.

Ryan has proposed a general system for school counseling programs (Fig. 4.3).[20] She describes this as a model in which there is an exchange between the system and its environment, a degree of orderliness and organization, identification of component parts, and relationships among parts and between parts and the whole, and where the functioning takes place in relation to the accomplishment of goals.

Less complex procedures have been proposed by Sullivan and O'Hare based on program management procedures that have proved useful at SWRL.[21] Recognizing the importance of planning, implementing, and monitoring guidance programs, a system was suggested that can be utilized effectively at any level of responsibility (e.g., board of education, administration, counselor). The system in-

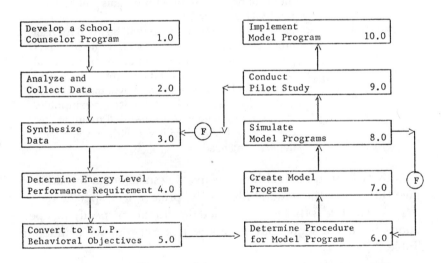

Fig. 4.3.   Flow chart model of school counseling program, process model

123

cludes a written Activity Description and Task Schedules. The Activity Description can be used to: (1) clarify initial planning, (2) provide a basis for review and approval, and (3) specify resources, general objectives and constraints. Here is a sample Activity Description.[22]

PROBLEM: The current guidance programs in many district schools were developed several years ago. These programs either do not have specific pupil objectives or may be based on objectives that are now outdated.

OBJECTIVE: To develop statements of specific objectives in the SPOP (Situation, Population, Outcome, Process) format for the guidance program in each district school.

PLAN OF ATTACK: The guidance department at each district school will be responsible for development of objectives for their school. Prior to the development of objectives, the district guidance director will meet with all guidance personnel to provide training in procedures for developing objectives. Final statements of objectives for all programs will be written by December 15.

RESOURCES: Each guidance staff member will be freed from all other guidance duties for one and one-half days per week during October to develop the initial statement of objectives and for a total of two days during the last two weeks in November to revise and finalize the initial statements. Responsibility for arranging schedules to free staff members for the specified period will rest with the guidance department head.

Activity Descriptions, although conveying sufficient information to give the reader the general idea of the project, lack specific detail. A Task Schedule is the recommended document for specifying operations and event sequences. A sample Task Schedule is included in Table 2.

Cooley and Hummel state that most research projects have not resulted in modification of guidance practices because they have not used an appropriate systems approach.[24] They have not been accompanied by: (1) statements of specific objectives for guidance, (2) identification of necessary information, (3) definition of appropriate procedures, (4) evaluation of those procedures, (5) packaging of results, and (6) dissemination of developed programs to the schools.

TABLE 2

SAMPLE TASK SCHEDULE

PROGRAM: *Development of Objectives for Guidance Program in Each District School*

RESPONSIBILITY: *Director of Guidance* (actual name of person should be used)

	Event	Start Date	Completion Date	Responsibility
1.	Develop draft of plan to develop objectives for district guidance programs	6/01	9/01	Guidance Director
2.	Review plan	9/01	9/15	Assistant Superintendent
3.	Revise plan based upon review	9/15	9/22	Guidance Director
4.	Approve final plan	9/22	9/29	Assistant Superintendent
5.	Conduct training for developing objectives	9/29	10/05	Guidance Director
6.	Submit plan for development, implementation and analysis of needs survey	10/01	11/01	Guidance Department Heads
7.	Submit to Dept. Head objectives derived from NSG	10/01	11/01	School Guidance Staff
8.	Submit to Dept. Head objectives derived from current guidance program	10/01	11/01	School Guidance Staff
9.	Submit to Dept. Head objectives derived from all other sources	10/01	11/01	School Guidance Staff
10.	Write final list of objectives for school and submit to District Director	11/01	11/08	Department Heads
11.	Review lists of objectives for each school	11/08	11/15	Guidance Director
12.	Revise plans based on review	11/15	12/01	Department Heads and School Staffs
13.	Approve final plans	12/01	12/15	Guidance Director

A strong plea for the use of systems technology in guidance is made by Youst.[25] He indicates that until a systems approach is utilized, new developments (procedures and equipment) in guidance will never be more than attachments to existing programs. The new sensational developments may even divert attention from the more critical guidance problems if systems approaches are not used.

Although there is much concern about the pros and cons of systems technology, there is little doubt that planning, implementation, and monitoring are necessary and desirable. The specific approach— complex charts or less complex Activity Descriptions and Task

Schedules—depends on the user. Each approach, properly implemented, can be effective. One needs to determine, however, the resources required by each.

Oettinger presents an adequate summary of systems technology:

> The myth of systems analysis holds that the educational salvation lies in applying to education the planning and control techniques commonly believed to have been successful in the defense and aerospace industries. Advocating systems analysis as a panacea ranks with making the world safe for democracy, unconditional surrender, and massive retaliation as an experiment in delusion for political ends. Yet, not to believe in the usefulness of systems analysis is to deny the value of reason, common sense, and, indeed, the scientific method.
>
> Systems analysis cannot be dismissed as modern gadgetry. Its best formulations are undistinguishable from descriptions of the scientific method and thus have roots reaching back through Roger Bacon to Aristotle and not, as some believe, just to the RAND Corporation. At its best, therefore, the systems approach can be used in conjunction with well-developed and reliable research designs to solve problems far more satisfactorily than naked intuition.
>
> . . . But there is far less validity than wishful thinking in claims for the success of the systems approach in the design, management, and control of entire space and military systems, in spite of the repeated citations of these enterprises as paradigms for educational and other social systems. It is also easily demonstrable that the educational system is much more complicated than any system yet devised by the military and that we have much less understanding of the former's component parts.
>
> . . . In any case, asking *how* or *how well* is silly unless we know what. The "systems" label should therefore not be given too much significance: it can produce no miracles; you can't just feed it to the computer. Neither should it be ignored. Despite its limitations, taking the systems viewpoint—namely, agreeing in principle that it is better to think about a problem in its whole context than not—is the best available attitude toward any subject . . .[26]

Guidance personnel need to consider the application of some type of planning procedures on a day-to-day as well as long-range basis. Application of such planning procedures to the use of media in guidance is critical.

MEDIA IN GUIDANCE

Audiovisual materials and equipment have been in educational use for decades. Their widespread acceptance is evidenced by the fact that "5,000 new films, filmstrips, tapes, recordings, models, and graphic materials become available each year."[27] It is natural that this usage and acceptance has spread to guidance.

Media Classification

Many media classification systems have been reported.[28] The following classification conveniently identifies major categories of equipment or procedures. Printed media have been omitted. Computers are discussed later in the chapter.

Nonprojected Materials
> chalkboards, bulletin boards, felt and flannel boards, magnetic board, maps, globes, charts, posters, models, objects, specimens, flashcards

Projected Materials (sight or sight and sound)
> slides; slide/tape; filmstrips; filmstrip/tape; transparencies; transparency/tape; 8mm, super 8mm and 16mm films (sound or silent), motion or stop action, color or black and white; projectors (slide, filmstrip, 8mm, super 8mm, 16mm, opaque, overhead); tachistoscopes (controlled readers, microfilm, microfiche); microprojectors; television (black and white or color; open or closed circuit; microwave, 2500 megacycles, VHF, UHF, ETV, ITV, network); cartridge TV (video tape recorder); computer graphics

Audio Materials
> disc and tape recordings, record players, audio tape playback devices, radio

Independent Study Materials
> teaching machines, computer-assisted instruction programmed texts; electronic learning laboratory (used for foreign language teaching, etc.); dial access systems.

Media Research

Voluminous research has been reported regarding the use of media for instruction, but there is a dearth of inquiry regarding media uses in guidance. Assuming that the reasons for using media in instruction are to improve cognitive learning or to improve attitudes, interest, and attention, or to solve logistical and personnel problems (e.g., shortages of key personnel), then one might conclude that most of the same reasons would apply to the use of media in guidance.

Selected examples of media research will be discussed in this section from which a general picture of the state-of-the-art should emerge. Most reported studies result in the finding of "no significant differences" (NSD). Some researchers cite such results as proof that the usage is effective—that as much or more learning occurs by using media. Others interpret the NSD findings negatively for media, inferring that since the media did not make any difference, one should not spend the extra money necessary to implement the program. It is unfortunate that this media comparison type of research represents the majority of media research completed. More penetrating research is required.

Rather than relying on comparisons, research needs to be conducted which will permit the discovery of "the unique attributes of instructional media and their relationships to the performance of particular psychological functions with different kinds of learners. The study of this three-way interaction of stimulus, task and learner is extremely complex, but some evidence is building up that could lead to a more precise understanding of the place of media in the instructional process."[29]

Allen lists five contributions of early media research:[30]

1. attention was focused on instructional media as legitimate and viable and confirmed their effectiveness;
2. a base of suppositions and hypotheses was provided regarding the unique attributes of instructional media which can be studied under controlled experimental conditions;
3. the richness and diversity of media was revealed;
4. a body of measurement, audience-learner analysis, and content analysis techniques evolved;
5. a beginning was made toward the understanding of the persuasive and motivational aspects of communications.

Twyford reports that it can be concluded from media comparison studies that "instruction making extensive use of communications materials and media is at least as effective as conventional instruction."[31] He also indicates that "media often contributes to the learning of outcomes not included in tests." Carpenter and Greenhill in their study of the use of teaching machines, programmed texts, filmstrips, and closed-circuit television reported that each medium could be used without adversely affecting achievement.[32]

The application of television to the current educational system has been described by Komoski as the most outstanding example of a mistake in trying to apply media to education without examining the total learning process and developing a technology indigenous to education.[33] Gerard states that instructional television has failed in this country.[34] In his review of over two hundred fifty studies comparing the use of instructional television with direct instruction,

Stickell classified two hundred seventeen as uninterpretable, twenty-three as partially interpretable, and ten as interpretable. All of the ten resulted in "no significant differences."[35] However, several studies point out that as much or more learning results from the use of television when compared to traditional instruction.[36]

Results similar to those reported for instructional television are also found for research in other media such as films, language laboratories, and programmed instruction.[37]

Media Applications in Guidance

Previous discussion suggests that many questions remain unanswered regarding the effective use of media. Important research questions have been ignored or attacked less than successfully. However, the overwhelming majority of research reported to date indicates that as much or more learning occurs when media are used. It would appear, therefore, that in many situations media applications in guidance are appropriate. A discussion relative to the evaluation and selection of media follows later in the chapter.

Many guidance functions performed by a counselor relate to a teaching role. Kagan states that this includes the presentation of "certain fundamental concepts in test construction and interpretation, an overview of the school's curricular offerings, information about the function and availability of school services including guidance and counseling, student government, students' rights and obligations, and the location and structure of occupational information libraries."[38]

Obviously, the counselor is interested in research results regarding the effectiveness of media for his particular uses. However, when the result of a comparison evaluation is NSD, then the counselor will need to be concerned with purported advantages of a logistical nature. If media can provide logistical help by presenting the basic, routine information in an interesting and accurate manner thus releasing the counselor to perform other guidance functions which require human interaction, then it would appear that the use of media is appropriate.

DeKieffer states that a review of media research during the past fifty years indicates that the major advantages resulting from the use of media are: (1) effectiveness in presenting factual information; (2) clarity in meaning by using visuals as well as audio; (3) permanence of learning by re-creating lifelike situations and involving pupils in the learning process; (4) effectiveness in improving attitudes, emotions, and other behavioral responses; (5) gaining and holding attention.[39]

Media have been used in the guidance function for many years, and new uses are regularly introduced. Following is a listing and discussion of some of the common and unique applications of media in guidance.

Microfilm. Microfilm, a photographic film containing a miniature image, holds several promising uses for education and guidance. The state-of-the-art in microfilming has improved dramatically in the last decade, especially through applications resulting from the space program. For example, complete operation, maintenance, and repair manuals for spacecraft are carried on board in the form of super microfiche. The weight and volume of these manuals made it impossible to include them in their hard copy format. The need to have this information aboard spacecrafts is obvious. To give another example, the entire Bible—1,245 pages—can be reproduced on the surface of a two-inch square of plastic. It can be read with the use of a special viewer which magnifies the pages 50,000 times.[40]

Use of microfilm not only reduces floor space, storage equipment, and maintenance requirements, but also improves the retrievability and usefulness of the information microfilmed. Microfilm is available in many forms, including roll, cartridge, fiche, jacket, aperture card, and computer output microfilm (COM). All forms serve many useful applications. COM has the potential of revolutionizing many aspects of information processing, since it is capable of producing computer-generated microfilm records and data with no intervening paper copy. The information is displayed on a cathode ray tube, and the microfilm record is produced by photographing this display.

The question of whether or not a school district can afford microfilming must be answered by each district after a careful study of costs, estimated uses, utility and usefulness, and the alternatives to microfilming. A microfilming system could be shared within a school district by pupil personnel services and business and instructional divisions. While it might be desirable for a medium-sized or large school district to purchase equipment necessary for film processing, it is also possible to contract with outside agencies for this service. Almost any school district can afford to purchase the equipment required for reading microfilm.

To date, primary guidance-related uses of microfilm have involved record keeping and career or vocational guidance. There is considerable debate regarding the amount of record keeping counselors should do, and this is not to suggest that large amounts of record keeping need be a counselor responsibility. If counselors or pupil personnel administrators are responsible for certain record keeping functions, however, the potential contribution of microfilm should be considered.[41] It has been stated that the "collection, evaluation, and dissemination of occupational information has long been one of the most poorly organized and chaotic aspects of the school counselor's daily work. Although career information in a variety of media is becoming increasingly more available its uses within guidance programs tend to be erratic and inconsistent. The basic reason for the problem is the difficulty of effectively organizing what is essentially an amorphous, uncoordinated mass of facts and data regarding occupational opportunities."[42]

To overcome these shortcomings, two programs which utilize microfilm in career education have been developed: the VIEW (Vocational Information for Education and Work) program designed by personnel in the San Diego County Department of Education, and Project VOGUE (Vocational Guidance for Education) developed by the New York State Education Department and the New York Employment Services.

In the VIEW system accurate and updated information on specific jobs is made available to students on VIEW scripts containing an aperture card which includes a 35mm microfilm frame. A microfilm reader is used to view the occupational brief. Advantages of the VIEW system include the ease with which information can be updated and the use of information relative to local jobs. Subsequent to the development of VIEW in San Diego, the system has been adopted by school districts in a number of states. It is reported that VIEW is used in every high school in Colorado.[43]

A similar project, VOGUE, uses printed descriptions in loose-leaf binders in addition to aperture cards. Studies of this system indicate considerable use of both formats.

Other Media
Audio Recording. With the large increase in use of more sophisticated equipment such as video tape recorders, it would be unfortunate if audio recordings were not fully utilized. The state-of-the-art for audio recordings has improved dramatically. Costs have been reduced; equipment has been miniaturized and is readily available. The intended audiences for guidance, pupils at all educational levels, do not lack access to cassette tape recorders and players. Tapes can

be used to record critical job and career information, college and other educational data, and instructional sequences relative to guidance, such as selected test interpretation information. Tapes have also been used to help students develop job-interview techniques.[44]

In addition, pre-service and in-service counselors have found the tape recorder a useful tool for evaluation and improvement of their counseling skills.

Video Tape Recording (VTR). VTR has been used extensively in counselor education. Forrest reports several studies and lists colleges and universities using VTR.[45] Results have been favorable, and equipment and material costs continue to decrease as use increases.

Kagan has allowed the counselee to view the VTR as a means of facilitating client self-study and awareness and for effecting client experimentation with new behavior. He has also reported the use of VTR to facilitate therapeutic counseling for emotionally disturbed children.[46]

Salinger and Wright report the development of VTR's containing career information and on-the-job interviews.[47] Results of their study and suggested uses of video tapes are included in the report.

Television and Films. Television and film equipment and materials are readily available in the school and home. Information can be presented on either medium depending on available equipment. Cartridge television is now available for the home.

The Georgia Department of Education has produced occupational information films for use on television. Other examples of the use of television include projects in the Atlanta (Georgia) Public Schools, the Delaware Department of Education, the School System of Washington County in Maryland, and "Project You" in Dade County, Florida.

Filmstrips and Slides. Slides and filmstrips have been used widely in guidance programs for several years. Slides are used in many local productions because they are fairly easy to make and provide much flexibility. Many sets of slides and filmstrips with and without accompanying sound are available free of charge from various organizations or available for purchase or rental from commercial organizations. The Ohio Vocational Educational Division and Ohio State University have produced several useful guidance-related filmstrips.

Multimedia Approach. The Rochester Career Guidance Project was developed as a cooperative effort by the New York State Education Department, the Rochester City School District, the Eastman Kodak Company, and the New York State Employment Service. The project is designed to facilitate student exploration of career alternatives. Existing and newly developed career information has been displayed in various media including printed format, microfilm, slide-audio tape, and filmstrip-audio tape.[48]

COMPUTERS

An important aspect of most discussions of education or technology in education is the use of computers. Following is a brief discussion of their historical development and an explanation of computer functioning; uses of computers in education are then explored with emphasis on interactive systems for guidance. A discussion of considerations regarding computer-assisted guidance concludes the chapter.

Historical Development of Computers

The discussion included here on the development of computers is presented in a brief, linear fashion. Although this distorts the history of this development, it does list the major milestones. In his review of the early history of computers Smith states:

> Both historically and logically, computers owe their existence to many prior traditions. Among these are counting and reckoning, writing and the written record, the concept of quantity, the engineering tradition, and many more. Before there were computers there were calculators, before calculators there were adders, and before adders there were counters. Before all of these there occurred to men whose names are lost to history notions of quantity.[49]

According to Smith milestones in the history of computers include the development of:[50]

1. Writing in the fourth millennium B.C.
2. Arithmetic and geometric techniques of dealing with quantities over 5,000 years ago.
3. Counting during the second millennium B.C.
4. Enumeration recording techniques by a number of civilizations including a sophisticated technique practiced by Babylonian scribes in 1800 B.C.
5. Egyptian and Greek reckoning techniques in the fifth century B.C. involving the systematic movement of pebbles on boards.
6. The suanpan (the abacus still in use today) in the twelfth century A.D. in China.
7. An adder consisting of a train of pegged counterwheels used to total up sums by Blaise Pascal in the seventeenth century. (How-

133

ever, credit for the development of the odometer which incorporates the counterwheel principle should be given to Heron of Alexandria in Roman times.)

8. Thirty years later by Leibnitz an adder that would multiply. (Several others, such as Morland, Mohon, Roth, Leupold, Gersten, and Hahn, should also be given credit. The progress of the engineering and machine tool industry of the nineteenth century dramatically forwarded the emergence of calculators.)

9. Plans for a complicated adder by Babbage in the nineteenth century. (Babbage did not complete the adder, or his analytical engine, which would have calculated and obtained results that it could have stored on fresh cards for reuse. However, planning for both machines was instrumental in the development of later machines.)

10. The differential analyzer by Vannevar Bush at the Massachusetts Institute of Technology in the 1930s.

11. The digital ENIAC (Electronic Numeric Integrator and Automatic Computer) using vacuum tubes and electronic circuits.

Huskey states that since the introduction of ENIAC in Philadelphia in 1946, computers have passed through three generations:[51] the first (1953) utilizing vacuum tubes; the second (1958) using crystal diodes and transistors; and the third (1965) introducing combinations of diodes and transistors. The fourth generation has not been officially labeled, but already diodes and transistors are being replaced by integrated circuits on silicon wafers.

How a Computer Functions

The typical counselor or pupil personnel worker needs to have a basic understanding of computer functioning, but knowledge of computer circuitry is best left to the computer specialists, who will presumably maintain and operate the computer. However, the counselor *does* need an understanding of computer capabilities and its potential for the enhancement of student opportunities.

The computer is a piece of hardware consisting of electronic and, to a lesser degree, mechanical gear. The computer and its peripheral devices make up a computer installation or system.

There are two basic types of computers: the analog and the digital. The analog computer makes analogies between mathematical model and physical reality. It has no memory and measures rather than counts. The analog computer processes information continuously, rather than step-by-step, and the results produced are continuous curves or scales instead of discrete numbers. Analog computers are used in situations where physical reality must be approximated, such as testing in wind tunnel simulations. They are less precise than digital computers but are, for appropriate applications, easier to operate, faster, and less expensive.

The digital computer counts rather than measures and manipulates data that can be expressed in separate or discrete units. It has a memory for storing both the data to be manipulated and the instructions which the computer must execute. Results may be presented as discrete numbers. The digital computer is used commonly in business and scientific applications.

Other types of computers include the hybrid analog computer and the hybrid digital computer. The basic characteristics of the analog and digital computers are combined in the hybrids.

The five basic operations performed by most digital computer systems are:

1. *Input.* Two basic types of information are used as input: data to be processed and instructions which indicate to the computer how the data are to be processed. The several input modes include the punched card, punched paper tape, magnetic tape, magnetic disks, mark sense sheets, magnetic ink, and embossed cards such as credit cards. It is possible to input directly from the printed page, but this procedure has not been perfected and currently the reliability is low except for a few special purposes. It is also possible to input by a "light pen" on the surface of a cathode ray display.

The punched card is commonly used as input data. A human machine operator transforms written data into a coded pattern by punching holes (rectangular or circular, depending on make of equipment) in a card. When a hole is punched, an electric circuit can be completed through the hole. The electric circuit activates equipment to initiate the inputting and processing of data.

2. *Storage.* An advantage of the digital computer is its ability to store information. The first storage devices consisted of small iron cores. Since that time, film, magnetic tape, magnetic drum, magnetic disk, and other devices have been developed for storage purposes. Storage can be either internal or external to the computer. Data to be processed and computer instructions can both be stored.

3. *Processing.* Processing is the main function of the computer and takes place in the central processing unit (CPU). Processing consists of manipulating data (calculating and comparing) according to the instructions programmed into the computer.

4. *Control.* Every computer must have a control device to assure

135

the appropriate manipulation of data. A set of instructions—a computer program—provides the control. Various program languages such as PLANIT, FORTRAN, and COBOL have been developed to facilitate the coding of data in a manner which can be interpreted by the computer.

5. *Output.* After data have been processed, the computer is able to report in a variety of modes including printed sheets of paper, punched cards, magnetic tape, cathode ray tube, and audio devices.

Computers in Education

As education becomes more complex, educators begin to realize that the capability of the computer to manipulate voluminous amounts of data may be the solution to some of their data management problems. School personnel have always been responsible for supplying reports to a variety of audiences, including teachers, parents, boards of education, and governmental agencies. Often, however, they have had difficulty in collecting and assembling the necessary data. With the use of computers, educators can meet their report deadlines and still have sufficient time to use the data generated by the report as a basis for establishing a management information system. Planning and decisions can be executed based on appropriate, current data.

Most educational support areas have already utilized the computer. In the business office applications have included budgeting and accounting, payroll, purchasing, supplies and inventory, accounts payable and receivable, and maintenance. Personnel offices have used computers for predicting numbers and types of job vacancies so that additional hiring could be accomplished in advance of resignations, and maintaining personnel records, including data on certification status, leave and attendance records, credits and degrees, and salary. Although salary negotiations might be conducted otherwise, the computer can calculate very rapidly the effect of a dollar or percentage salary increase on the total school budget. Other educational users of computers include administrators, and instructional, research, and pupil services personnel.

The following categorization is arbitrary and is included only to exemplify school district computer use. In practice, each district has its own procedures for assigning tasks to various departments. For example, some of the tasks assigned below to administration might be assigned to pupil personnel services in certain school districts.

Often routine reporting activities are assigned to pupil personnel services when they are more appropriate to administration. But regardless of task assignments, it is important for counselors to understand the computer processes involved and to be able to use the resulting data in their guidance duties. The various educational uses of computers include:

I. Administration

1. Information on students (name, birthdate, sex, address, parent's occupation, handicaps, attendance, schools attended, grades, test results, etc.).
2. Summary reports (attendance, class size, grade enrollment, grade summaries by class, subject, and teacher, test data by subject area, dropout experience, college attendance, etc.).
3. Reports required by governmental agencies.
4. Projection reports (enrollment, use of facilities, budget, etc.).

II. Instruction

1. Courses in computer technology (teaching all aspects of a computer system including keypunching, programming, maintenance, etc.).
2. Computer-Managed Instruction (a classroom instructional management system to provide various audiences with timely, accurate information concerning the progress of students in achieving instructional outcomes, and to provide suggestions for overcoming deficiencies).
3. Computer-Displayed Instruction (the presentation of instructional sequences on cathode ray tubes or other output devices).
4. Computer-Generated Instruction (the presentation of instructional stimuli created by the computer, utilizing constraining statements which prescribe the bounds of a stimulus domain of interest).

III. Research

In some school districts, research activities are limited to the collection and dissemination of data on census, budget, salary, and bond issues. Other districts are more directly involved in research and study instructional effectiveness, test data, and effectiveness of various guidance procedures. The computer helps to facilitate these research activities.

IV. Pupil Personnel and Guidance

Counselors will have occasion to use many of the computer-generated reports mentioned previously. Often they will assume research responsibilities in such areas as guidance effectiveness, predictive and expectancy studies, uses of test data, and college admission studies as well.

Another area of particular concern to the counselor is computer-managed instruction (CMI). Through the use of CMI, the learning process is divided into its component parts in a manner which assists teachers and counselors in identifying learning problems before they can become learning deficiencies. When used properly, CMI is a powerful tool, and educators need to learn to take full advantage of it.

Educators have made considerable use of the computer in scheduling activities. The computer has been used to develop the master schedule for a school as well as schedules for individual students. If the school operates a traditional schedule with fixed class time patterns and sizes the computer simply reduces the logistical problems. The computer is capable of developing more complex schedules, such as flexible schedules with varying time patterns and class sizes.

Advances have been made in applying the computer to various other guidance functions, such as providing a convenient and effective means of interpreting results of the Minnesota Multiphasic Personality Inventory and the California Personality Inventory, developing a screening technique utilizing multi-trait factor analysis, and studying factors related to performance through trend analysis.

An additional role of the computer in guidance provides the opportunity for counselee and computer interaction, through the use of computer information systems. The availability of federal funds in the early 1960s for vocational education encouraged the development of several computer information systems for guidance. The first project of this type is generally credited to System Development Corporation in Santa Monica (Hallworth;[52] Heddesheimer[53]). Development has been stopped on most of the early projects because of lack of continued funding. Consequently, few systems are available for use today. A notable exception, which is discussed subsequently, is the Computerized Vocational Information System (CVIS) developed at Willowbrook High School in Villa Park, Illinois. Examples of other computer guidance systems include a Computer-Based Automated Counseling Simulation System for Vocational Decisions (ISVD), developed at Harvard University by Tiedeman and others;

138

the Computer-Assisted Career Exploration system (CACE), developed at Pennsylvania State University by Impelliterri and others; the Experimental Education and Career Exploration System (ECES), developed at IBM by Minor and others; the Comprehensive Vocational Guidance System, developed at the American Institutes for Research by Flanagan and others; the Total Guidance Information Support System (TGISS), developed at the Bartlesville (Oklahoma) Public School System, and the Counseling Information System (CIS) 9/10, developed by Follett Publishing Company. In the following section, a few of these projects are discussed in detail.

V. Vocational Counseling System (System Development Corporation)

This computer-based vocational guidance system was developed by System Development Corporation under the direction of Harry Silberman.[54] Work on the project was not completed because of funding cuts. The system is reported because it is an important contribution to the state-of-the-art. Tryout and development took place at a Los Angeles high school, with 5,000 students and ten counselors, and at a Los Angeles junior high school, with 1,800 students and five counselors.

The overall purpose of the system was to automate selected information-processing guidance functions, which a computer could expedite as well or better than a human counselor, and to free the counselor for tasks which did require human interaction and judgment. The system utilized group guidance techniques to strengthen its humanistic aspects. The computerized functions included provision for educational and vocational information, student program-planning information based on probability studies previously undertaken as part of the project, and selected clerical tasks, such as the generation of student report cards.

Information about the student, probability statements, and educational and vocational information was stored in the computer. The system was programmed to perform a variety of functions, including three types of interviews: for high school program planning, for post high school educational planning, and for vocational planning. A user language (PLANIT) was developed to allow the computer to query the user. The query had to be answered by the user selecting one of the answers suggested by the computer, except in the case when the computer asked an open-ended question and the user replied in conversational format. In this case the reply was irrelevant, as the

139

computer gave only a generalized reply. In the sample interview which follows,[55] replies of the counselee are preceded by four stars. The stars are used to indicate that the computer has finished a statement and it is time for the counselee to respond. The counselee uses the CR key to indicate that he has completed his statement. The CR is not displayed on the printout.

SAMPLE INTERVIEW

Is your name Debora Anderson?

**** Yes

According to my records this is how you did last semester.

CODE	COURSE	GRADE
1	P.E.	A
2	English 1	A
3	General Science	A
4	European History	C
5	Algebra	B
6	School Service	A

Is this correct? If so, type Yes; if not, type No.

**** Yes

Are you having any problems with any of these courses? Please type yes or no.

**** Yes

Type the number of each course that is giving you trouble. Type CR after each number. When you are all through, type / and CR.

**** 4/

What kind of problem do you have with European history? Please type in the nature of the problem. A few words will be O.K. When you are all finished, type / and CR.

**** I don't turn my work in on time./

I see . . . If you would like to discuss this problem further, make an appointment to see your counselor.

140

Would you like to continue with this interview at this time, or would you like to discuss your problems with your counselor before you continue? Type Go if you'd like to continue. Type Stop if you'd like to stop.

**** Go

Do you plan to continue your formal education beyond high school?

**** Yes

Which of the following is most like the school you plan to attend?

1 Ivy league college
2 Other college or university
3 California state college
4 Junior college
5 Business or vocational school
6 I have not yet decided

Type the appropriate code.

**** 3

Do you intend to major in engineering or one of the sciences? Please type yes or no.

**** Yes

Here are some areas of science and some examples

CODE	AREA	EXAMPLES
1	Physical Sciences	Physics, chemistry, geology, etc.
2	Biological sciences	Biology, pre-med, pre-nursing, etc.
3	Social sciences	Psychology, sociology, anthropology, etc.
4	Mathematics	Math, statistics, computer programming, etc.
5	Engineering	Architecture, drafting, electronics, etc.

Please type the code number of the kind of science you intend to major in.

**** 3

All right. Let's see if we can pinpoint your area.

1 Psychology
2 Sociology
3 Anthropology
4 Social Work

Type the appropriate code.

**** 1

O.K. . . . The grades you get in high school largely determine the type of college you will be able to attend. Let's just take a look at your projected high school grades based on your present performance. Students who got grades like yours in junior high did as follows at Cubberley—

70 percent earned A or B
20 percent earned C+
10 percent earned C

On the basis of your projected grades, your present college choice indicates that you are thinking pretty realistically about your future life.

Now that we've got some idea of what you'd like to do after high school, let's look at your high school course plans. In the 10th grade, the required courses are—

English 2
Contemporary world history and geography
Physical education

What other courses would you like to take next year? Look at the list of courses. When you have decided what courses you want to take, type Yes. If you can't make up your mind at all type No.

**** Yes

Good. Type the code number of each course you want to take. Type CR after each number. When you are all through, type / and CR.

**** 70

**** 93

**** 111

**** /

OK, here is the program you have proposed:

142

English 2
Contemporary world history and geography
Physical education

French 1
Math M 1
Biology 1

Are you satisfied with this program? If so, type Yes; if you would like
to change it, type Change.

**** Yes

VI. Information System for Vocational Decisions (ISVD)

ISVD has been a cooperative developmental effort by Harvard
Graduate School of Education, New England Education Data Systems, and the Newton (Massachusetts) Public School System. Principal developers included: David V. Tiedeman, Robert P. O'Hara,
Russell G. Davis, Allan B. Ellis, Edward Landy, Richard M. Durstine,
Wallace J. Fletcher and Michael J. Wilson. The project has been
reported by Tiedeman and others,[56] and voluminous documentation
is available elsewhere. Funding for the project has been terminated,
and development has stopped, at least temporarily.

ISVD has been characterized as the most complex of the computer-assisted guidance projects. It not only provided a broader scope
but also allowed much flexibility as the student interacted directly
with the computer using natural language.

ISVD attempted to facilitate decision making by students by providing materials and procedures which lead to an understanding of
the decision-making process, psychology of career choice, alternatives and consequences of specific decisions, personal characteristics,
and of the responsibilities resulting from decisions. All of this was
provided through the computer, with the counselor providing the
opportunity for additional supervised practice in decision making.

Data stored in the computer consisted of five major files: occupational, educational, military, personal and family living, and student
characteristics. Students accessed the data files through the use of
three computer routines: *exploration* which facilitates the identification of preferred alternatives, *clarification* which clarifies by query-
ing the student on his knowledge of selected alternatives, and *review*
which permits the student to compare earlier decision statements
with later action.

143

Training in decision making was available through computer-assisted instructional (CAI) sequences and through simulated games.

Following is a sample interview,[57] with the computer output in upper case and the student input in lower case. Notice that the counselee responds in natural language. The computer was programmed to interpret the conversational response with additional comments and queries.

WHAT WOULD YOU LIKE TO DO TODAY?

I want to think about colleges to apply to next year.

SINCE WE KNOW THAT YOU HAVE NOT EXPLORED YOUR COLLEGE CHOICE WITH THE SYSTEM BEFORE, THE FIRST THING WE WOULD LIKE TO FIND OUT IS IF YOU HAVE THOUGHT ABOUT THIS CHOICE ENOUGH TO HAVE SOME ALTERNATIVES IN MIND. IF YOU DO, TYPE THE NAMES OF EACH OF THE ALTERNATIVE COLLEGES. IF NOT, TYPE IN THE WORD NO.

Harvard University, Boston College, and Berkeley.

GOOD. WHAT KINDS OF THINGS DID YOU DO IN EXPLORING COLLEGE CHOICE? DID YOU READ ANY COLLEGE CATALOGUES OR TALK WITH YOUR GUIDANCE COUNSELOR? MAKE AS COMPLETE A STATEMENT AS POSSIBLE.

I read the catalogue for Harvard and Boston College. I talked with my guidance counselor, and had a couple of interviews with the Dean at Harvard. My father went to Berkeley, so that's why I'm interested in going there.

THESE ARE THE ACTIVITIES THE MACHINE HAS RECOGNIZED OR ANALYZED FROM YOUR STATEMENT. YOU HAVE DISCUSSED THE MATTER WITH MEMBERS OF THE FAMILY, SPOKEN WITH A GUIDANCE COUNSELOR, READ SOME COLLEGE CATALOGUES, SPOKEN WITH COLLEGE OFFICIALS.

HERE ARE SOME OTHER THINGS THAT MAY BE A GOOD IDEA TO DO IF YOU HAVEN'T ALREADY. YOU COULD HAVE DISCUSSED THE MATTER WITH A TEACHER. NOW THEN LOOK AT THE LIST OF EXPLORATION ACTIVITIES THAT YOU PERFORMED OUTSIDE OF THE SYSTEM. HERE IS THE LIST OF YOUR PRESENT ALTERNATIVES. HARVARD UNIVERSITY, BOSTON COLLEGE, AND BERKELEY. NOW TYPE IN THE ACTIVITIES THAT YOU FEEL HELPED YOU MOST IN MAKING UP YOUR MIND OR GAVE YOU SOME ALTERNATIVE COLLEGES TO THINK ABOUT. PLEASE TYPE THEM IN ORDER OF IMPORTANCE.

144

The interviews and talking with my Dad.

GOOD. BEFORE WE GO ON TO EXPLORE COLLEGE CHOICE, WHAT ARE THE FACTORS THAT YOU THINK ARE IMPORTANT IN CONSIDERING WHICH COLLEGES TO APPLY TO?

Grades, class rank.

ANYTHING ELSE?

Tuition costs, test scores.

HERE ARE SOME OF THE FACTORS THAT OTHER STUDENTS FOUND IMPORTANT: (1) CURRICULUM CHOICE, (2) COURSE SELECTION (HIGH SCHOOL SUBJECTS), (3) GRADES, (4) CLASS RANK, (5) TEST SCORES (PSAT, SAT, CEEB, ACT), (6) EXTRACURRICULAR ACTIVITIES, (7) FUTURE VOCA-TIONAL PLANS, (8) GOAL IN GOING TO COLLEGE (9) POST COLLEGE EDUCATION AND/OR TRAINING.

HERE IS YOUR LIST. GRADES, CLASS RANK, TUITION COSTS, TEST SCORES. LOOK AT BOTH LISTS AND THEN TYPE IN ALL FACTORS FROM BOTH LISTS THAT YOU CONSIDER IMPORTANT IN THINKING ABOUT COLLEGE CHOICE.

High school courses, grades, class rank, test scores, tuition costs, future vocational plans.

FINE. THERE ARE SEVERAL WAYS THAT YOU CAN GO ABOUT THINKING ABOUT COLLEGE CHOICE WITHIN THE ISVD SYSTEM.

YOU CAN GO THROUGH SOME CONCEPT SCRIPTS WHICH ARE DESIGNED TO GIVE YOU SOME FACTS ON TOPICS RELEVANT TO COLLEGE CHOICE. OR YOU CAN PLAY THE LIFE CAREER GAME. USING THE DATA OF A MAKE-BELIEVE STUDENT WHO IS LIKE YOU IN SOME WAYS, YOU GO THROUGH THE PROCESS OF SELECTING A COLLEGE FOR HIM.

IF YOU HAVE SPECIFIC COLLEGES IN MIND, YOU CAN GET DATA ON THEM BY ACCESSING THE EDUCATION DATA FILE.

IF YOU LIKE, YOU CAN LET THE SYSTEM GUIDE YOU THROUGH A STATE-MENT OF PREFERENCES TO COME UP WITH A LIST OF COLLEGES THAT MOST NEARLY MATCHES YOUR PREFERENCES. OR YOU CAN ELECT TO FIRST GO THROUGH A UNIT ON DECISION MAKING, A UNIT THAT TRIES TO HELP YOU UNDERSTAND YOURSELF AND OTHERS IN RELATION TO MAKING DECISIONS. WHAT WOULD YOU LIKE TO DO?

Access the education data file.

YOU HAVE ACCESSED THE EDUCATION DATA FILE. FOR DEMONSTRA-
TION PURPOSES ONLY, THE FOLLOWING SCHOOLS HAVE BEEN IMPLE-
MENTED. HARVARD COLLEGE (MEN), GOUCHER COLLEGE (WOMEN),
BERKELEY UNIVERSITY (LARGE STATE-SUPPORTED SCHOOL), BOSTON
COLLEGE (RELIGIOUSLY AFFILIATED), AND CARNEGIE INSTITUTE
(TECHNICAL TRAINING SCHOOL).

THE FOLLOWING VARIABLES HAVE BEEN IMPLEMENTED . . . COSTS
(INCLUDING TUITION, ROOM AND BOARD, AND OTHER FEES), REQUIRED
ENTRANCE EXAMS, CRITERIA USED IN SELECTING STUDENTS, AND RE-
QUIRED HIGH SCHOOL COURSES. NOW THEN YOU CAN QUERY THIS
MICRO DATA BASE IN ANY WAY THAT YOU WANT. PLEASE DO NOT USE
QUESTION MARKS. IF YOU WISH TO STOP AT ANY TIME, TYPE IN THE
WORD STOP.

YOU MAY BEGIN.

How much does it cost to go to Harvard.

TUITION AT HARVARD IS 2000 PER YEAR INCLUDING LAB AND HEALTH
FEES. ROOM AND BOARD IS 1170 DOLLARS. NONRESIDENT STUDENT
FEE IS 25 DOLLARS. BOOKS AND SUPPLIES ABOUT 70 PER YEAR. PER-
SONAL EXPENSES ABOUT 375 DOLLARS, INCLUDING ROOM SUPPLIES,
CLOTHING, CLEANING AND LAUNDRY, RECREATION, AND OTHER PER-
SONAL EXPENSES (EXCEPT TRAVEL).

What high school courses should I take for Boston College.

NO SPECIFIC NUMBER OF UNITS IS REQUIRED HOWEVER THE FOLLOW-
ING MINIMUM IS REQUIRED . . . ENGLISH (4), ALGEBRA (2), PLANE
GEOMETRY (1), FOREIGN LANGUAGE (2), TRIGONOMETRY (FOR STU-
DENTS PLANNING TO MAJOR IN MATH, BIOLOGY, CHEMISTRY OR PHYS-
ICS) (2), (FOR STUDENTS PLANNING TO MAJOR IN THE ABOVE SCIENCES
AND FOR APPLICANTS TO THE SCHOOL OF NURSING), ACADEMIC ELEC-
TIVES (5).

What specific entrance exams are required.

BOSTON COLLEGE REQUIRES THE SAT AND THREE ACHIEVEMENT
TESTS. ENGLISH, LEVEL OR II MATHEMATICS, AND ONE OF THE CAN-
DIDATE'S CHOICE.

Does Berkeley require the SAT.

APPLICANTS WHO ARE INELIGIBLE, DUE TO GRADE AVERAGE, OR TO
UNIT OR DISTRIBUTION DEFICIENCIES, OR WHO HAVE GRADUATED
FROM AN UNACCREDITED SECONDARY SCHOOL, MAY QUALIFY FOR

146

ADMISSION BY CEEB EXAMINATIONS. THE THREE ACHIEVEMENT TESTS REQUIRED FOR THOSE APPLYING FOR ADMISSION ARE . . . ENGLISH, ONE TEST IN SOCIAL STUDIES OR FOREIGN LANGUAGE, ONE TEST IN MATHEMATICS OR A SCIENCE. REQUIREMENTS FOR CALIFORNIA RESIDENTS . . . TOTAL SAT SCORE OF AT LEAST 1000, AND TOTAL SCORE ON THREE ACH OF AT LEAST 1650 WITH NO SINGLE ACH LESS THAN 500.0. REQUIREMENTS FOR OUT-OF-STATE RESIDENTS . . . TOTAL SAT SCORE OF AT LEAST 1100 AND TOTAL SCORE ON THREE ACT OF AT LEAST 1725.0.

What are the costs there.

TUITION AT BERKELEY IS 980 DOLLARS PER YEAR OF THREE QUARTERS FOR OUT-OF-STATE STUDENTS. NO TUITION FOR CALIFORNIA RESIDENTS. ROOM AND BOARD VARIES BETWEEN 600 AND 940 DOLLARS. INCIDENTAL FEE OF 242 DOLLARS. ASSOCIATED STUDENTS MEMBERSHIP FEE 11 DOLLARS. BOOKS AND SUPPLIES ABOUT 80 TO 110 DOLLARS.

How do they choose their students.

BERKELEY SELECTS ITS CANDIDATES ON THE BASIS OF A CANDIDATE'S SECONDARY SCHOOL RECORD AND CEEB SCORES. ALUMNI RELATIONSHIP AND GEOGRAPHICAL DISTRIBUTION NOT RELEVANT.

How about Harvard.

HARVARD CHOOSES ITS CANDIDATES ON THE FOLLOWING CRITERIA. SECONDARY SCHOOL RECORD, SCHOOL'S RECOMMENDATION, AND CEEB SCORES. ALSO, CHARACTER, PERSONALITY, AND EXTRACURRICULAR PARTICIPATION ARE STRONGLY EMPHASIZED. SPECIAL TALENTS AND INTERESTS ALSO CONSIDERED.

How much does it cost to go to Goucher.

THERE IS A COMPREHENSIVE FEE OF 2950 DOLLARS PER YEAR, INCLUDING TUITION, ROOM AND BOARD, AND LAB FEES. STUDENT ACTIVITY FEE OF 13 DOLLARS, HEALTH FEE 50 DOLLARS, AND GYMNASIUM OUTFIT 27 DOLLARS. OTHER COSTS INCLUDE BOOKS AND SUPPLIES ABOUT 100 DOLLARS.

What kinds of courses should I take.

16 UNITS REQUIRED, THE FOLLOWING RECOMMENDED. . . . ENGLISH (4), MATHEMATICS (3), (2 IN ALGEBRA, 1 IN GEOMETRY), ONE FOREIGN LANGUAGE (3), HISTORY (2), LABORATORY SCIENCE (1). THE

147

COMMITTEE ON ADMISSIONS MAY ALLOW ENTRANCE CREDIT FOR
WORK IN ELECTIVE SUBJECTS NOT LISTED.

How do they pick their students.

GOUCHER COLLEGE BASES ITS CANDIDATE'S SELECTION ON THE SEC-
ONDARY SCHOOL RECORD, THE SCHOOL'S RECOMMENDATION, AND
TEST SCORES. OTHER IMPORTANT FACTORS ARE PERSONAL CHARAC-
TERISTICS, EXTRACURRICULAR PARTICIPATION, AND INDIVIDUAL IN-
TERESTS. ALUMNAE RELATIONSHIPS AND GEOGRAPHICAL DISTRIBU-
TION CONSIDERED.

I think that I would like to stop now.

WOULD YOU LIKE A SUMMARY OF YOUR EXPLORATION OF THE EDUCA-
TION DATA FILE.

Yes.

VII. Computerized Vocational Information System (CVIS)

This computer-assisted guidance project was developed by staff
(JoAnn Harris and others) at Willowbrook High School at Villa Park,
Illinois, under a grant from the Illinois State Board of Vocational
Education. The system has been in operation since 1968 and is avail-
able at low cost from Project CVIS. The project has been reported
by Harris and others.[58]

The main function of the computer in this project is to make
appropriate vocational and educational information available to students and to automate selected administrative tasks such as scheduling and attendance reporting. All queries made by the computer are
answered by the student selecting from multiple choices presented.
The system operates at three levels: junior high school, secondary,
and community college.

At the junior high level the student enters the system by responding to thirty multiple choice items designed to assist him in thinking
about his personality characteristics, values, activities, interests, abilities and school achievement. Input of the student is compared to
Roe's classification system. The student receives output from the
computer, listing in order the types of occupations he may wish to
study. The student completes the study of occupations with the aid
of filmstrips and audio tapes. Following this, the student interacts
with the computer a second time and is allowed to compare his

responses to the thirty multiple choice items presented earlier to responses of an "ideal" for each occupation identified by the student. After additional study, using filmstrips and tapes, the student returns to the computer a third time to receive information about the kind of high school program he will need for the occupation selected. He also receives feedback relative to probability of success in the selected occupation based on achievement and aptitude data previously stored in the computer.

The student at the secondary and community college level uses the system in a similar manner and is permitted exploration in any of seven areas: four year colleges, local community colleges, local technical and specialized schools, local apprenticeships, local jobs, military information, and select-a-course.

CONSIDERATIONS REGARDING COMPUTER-ASSISTED GUIDANCE

Although it is generally accepted that the computer can be helpful in implementing selected aspects of guidance, there is considerable disagreement and debate regarding the degree to which the computer should be used and whether certain functions, such as counseling, should ever be computerized. These concerns can be grouped into three categories: logistical, psychological, and educational.

Logistical Considerations

Logistical considerations center around four topics: man-machine communications, equipment reliability, general applicability and compatibility, and cost.

Regarding communications, man must have a way of communicating with the machine. Some type of language which both the computer and user will understand is essential. The computer must be able to respond appropriately when commanded by a user who understands and is able to use the language. The language selected might be a natural language such as English, a query language such as PLANIT, or an artificial language such as COBOL or FORTRAN. The most convenient and useful language for the user, but the most difficult language to program, is natural language. It is convenient because the user does not need to learn a new language. He can interact with the machine in his natural language. Further, the interaction can be in a *conversational* or *constructed* mode, rather than a *nonconversational* or *selected* mode where communication is restricted to selecting the most appropriate answer from several which have been programmed. The only guidance project which has utilized this to any degree is ISVD.

Query languages are useful in that they are relatively easy for the user to learn and they do facilitate a type of communication between man and machine. Communication is limited, however, to a query or selected mode as described previously.

Artificial languages are useful to programmers but do not readily facilitate communication, because the typical user does not understand the artificial language.

Development of functional computer-assisted guidance projects has been delayed for several reasons, including the man-machine communication problem. The solution to this problem, however, appears to be only time and money. Within this decade, it is likely that computer-assisted guidance functions will result from use of natural language in the audio as well as written mode.

Equipment *reliability* does not appear to be much of an issue. Computers have increased in reliability dramatically in their short lives. Locke and Engler report that as early as 1968 reliability had increased from one failure per 1,000 to one failure per 350,000.[59] When equipment is being developed and tried out, some failures are to be expected. Reducing the number of failures becomes a function of time and money. The outlook is optimistic, since the reliability of equipment may be increased as much as man is willing to increase it.

The issue of general *applicability and compatibility* of computer systems is of concern to many educators. It has been necessary for most school districts interested in purchasing computer systems to justify them on the basis of use in areas such as business, administration, instruction, and pupil personnel. In some cases it is difficult to design computer systems which satisfy the varied user requirements. This becomes less of a problem as new, more sophisticated computer systems are developed and as educators increase the use of computers within each functional area.

Compatibility does remain a concern. Programs are designed for use on specific computer systems, and any change in equipment necessitates programming changes. What might be considered by some as a minor change of updating a single piece of equipment can become a major problem in the system. For example, each new generation of computers has produced new program requirements,

150

since programs written for one generation of equipment have not functioned on a subsequent generation.

Cost is always a critical factor, especially to educators. Funds are necessary not only for the purchase, operation, and maintenance of equipment and programs but also for the development of software. Private industry has funded, and profited from, the development of computer equipment. Similar development of the necessary software has not occurred, however, and funding, for the most part, has come from government, usually federal. Federal funds for such development have declined dramatically recently. Consequently, development in this area will lag until additional funding is made available.

Equipment and operational costs have declined substantially, in general. In early computers, costly vacuum tubes were essential. Great fears were raised as comparisons were made to failure ratio in radio vacuum tubes. Some estimated that repairmen would continuously be replacing tubes. Vacuum tubes improved, of course, and these fears were never realized. Transistors were substituted at a cost of approximately $2 each in 1960. Later, integrated circuits each with a capacity of 50 transistors were used at a cost of $3 per circuit.[60] Today, costs are less than $1 per integrated circuit.

One hundred twenty-five million multiplications could be performed on the ENIAC for $12,800; on the UNIVAC for $1,420; and on the IBM 7030 for $29.[61] Today the cost is significantly less. Margolin and Misch report that in 1956, 100,000 instructions could be executed by the computer for $0.22.[62] By 1970 that cost had decreased to $0.01. Similarly the cost of computer memory has decreased from one and one-half cents per bit of memory to two mills or 2/1000 of a cent per bit.

Savings measured in time might result in financial savings as well. Today computers exist which can execute more than ten million instructions per second. A problem that would have taken an hour to execute on the fastest earlier computers can be executed in only a few seconds today.[63]

Martin and Norman illustrate the decreasing cost of logic circuitry with an investment example.[64] If one were able to invest money at the same growth rate as the decrease in circuitry cost, $1 invested at birth would have increased to over a million dollars by age thirty. The U.S. Gross National Product would have been surpassed by age seventy.

A valid argument for the use of computers in guidance is that counselors will have more time for important human-type functions, such as counseling, because the computer will very effectively perform routine data counting and reporting functions frequently required of the counselor. However, where the counselor finds himself performing as a clerk preparing input for the computer and where students find themselves completing endless forms, it is no surprise that there has been some resistance to computers. Add fouled up computerized student scheduling and noisy teletype machines in a counselor's office, and the basis for a full scale revolution against computers has been formed. Machines, like anything else, can be misused. It is the human who is responsible for the misuse. The most effective medicine will become a poison if taken in inappropriate quantities or if combined incorrectly with other medicines.

Change is threatening to many humans. Change produces uncertainties and, consequently, security is reduced. As a result, some charge that the computer is dehumanizing. If some other device had caused the change, then the charge would have been that the other device was dehumanizing. Nevertheless, computers can perform many data-counting and record-keeping functions much more rapidly, effectively, and at a lower cost than counselors, thus freeing the counselor for more important functions. If the counselor has devoted most of his time to chores of this nature, he will be threatened by the computer. Wrenn states that if the counselor "has been an 'information-dispensing' counselor, then he should shun the computer; it can do a much better job than he can at *this* game, and this superiority may become all too apparent."[65] If, on the other hand, the counselor has not had to depend on the execution of these routine tasks as his "Linus blanket," he will accept the computer as an effective, useful tool, freeing him to perform more important tasks. Walz suggests that the use of the computer is for the hardy, "those prepared to examine and question and in turn to be challenged and confronted. If counselors can't stand the heat in the kitchen, they had better use recipes that use technological ingredients more sparingly."[66]

Despite statements such as "the computer and data are neutral, only humans are biased and prejudiced," and "machines don't cause runarounds, humans do," and "some students would prefer machines to their inept counselors," and "machines are more readily accessible than humans," there is legitimate concern for the study of issues in these areas. A tremendous amount of data—sometimes critical and confidential—could be entrusted to the control of a few persons. Cogswell and others have been concerned to the point of recommending the following:[67]

1. Right of Access
   If a dossier or information file is to be kept on any person, that person should be notified of the existence of the dossier and be allowed access to it at will.
2. Right of Knowledge of Source
   The subject of a dossier shall have the right to know the source of any information included in his file, and that such source be recorded with the information.
3. Right of Review, Refutation, and Appeal
   The subject of a dossier shall be permitted to review and refute any information in the dossier, and that his refutation be included as an integral part of the dossier, and that appeal mechanisms be instituted for the deletion or change of information in the dossier.
4. Right of Approval of Dissemination
   The subject of a dossier shall have the right to approve (or veto) the transfer of information from his file to other agencies, persons, or files.

Educational Considerations

Computer technology will allow educational functions to be completed more effectively and will also permit the attainment of goals previously thought unattainable. Instructionally the potential is great as a result of advancements being made in computer-managed and computer-assisted instruction. In the area of guidance the counselor, freed from routine tasks, will be able to perform more important tasks. In both counseling and instruction greater individualization will be possible. Some fear the contrary, however—that more standardization will occur. Since what constitutes an optimal amount of standardization has not yet been determined, increased standardization can be interpreted as being advantageous or disadvantageous only if a person's point of view and the area involved are considered. But the question that still remains is, will the interaction between machine and counselee become too standardized?

Because of limited experiences with systems such as ISVD which employ natural language, it is difficult to answer the above questions adequately. The potential for such systems appears to be great, and it is hoped that additional funding will be made available for developmental work.

NEED FOR EVALUATION

Pupil personnel workers have a responsibility to determine the effectiveness of equipment and procedures before they implement them on a wide scale. The counselor does not necessarily need to conduct evaluation studies himself, but he should be responsible for reviewing studies completed by others, such as the developers, to ascertain the effectiveness of the equipment or procedure. Generally, commercial developers and publishers do not try out their products in a rigorous manner; if they do, data are not always available.

If counselors themselves need to conduct evaluation studies to determine equipment and product effectiveness it is suggested that criterion-referenced procedures be utilized.[68] What is the objective which should be achieved as a result of using a particular procedure or device? How do you measure the degree to which the objective has been achieved?

After determining the degree of outcome attainment, it is possible to compare the effectiveness of one program or procedure with another and to evaluate factors such as cost, reliability, adaptability.

SUMMARY

This chapter has presented an overview of technology in education and guidance.[69] Recognizing that technology is more than just equipment, emphasis was placed on media, systems, and computer applications in guidance and their ramifications.

There is little question that media can be used effectively to enhance the achievement of outcomes in a guidance program. However, there still exists some tendency in education and in guidance to jump on the bandwagon and use media equipment indiscriminately. Most outcomes can be achieved with or without the use of media. If media save time or money, provide greater flexibility, and are effective in achieving a desired outcome, the counselor should consider implementation. If media use does not provide an advantage, the counselor needs to be very cautious in his decision to use it.

The greatest amount of suspicion and debate exists in the area of computer-assisted guidance. This is a field still in its infancy, and a certain amount of caution is not surprising. It is probably healthy as long as it is remembered that development has just begun and opportunities for expansion and tryout must be provided. There is little question but that the computer is useful in selected fields of guidance. Most would agree that a certain amount of interaction between counselee and machine is acceptable and perhaps desirable. The debate begins with the question of the degree to which the computer is to be used.

1. Richard E. Schutz, "The Nature of Educational Development," *Journal of Research and Development in Education* (Winter 1970), 3:39-64.
2. P. Kenneth Komoski, "The Continuing Confusion About Technology and Education or the Myth-ing Link in Educational Technology," *Educational Technology* (November 1969), pp. 70-74.
3. Richard R. Nelson, Merton J. Peck, and Edward D. Kalachek, *Technology, Economic Growth and Public Policy* (Washington, D.C.: © The Brookings Institution, 1967).
4. Jerome B. Wiesner, "Technology and Innovation," in *Technological Innovation and Society,* edited by Dean Morse and Aaron Warner (New York: Columbia University Press, 1966), pp. 11-16.
5. Gabriel D. Ofiesh, "Educational Technology for a Science of Education," *Educational Technology* (Jan. 1970), pp. 10-14.
6. Komoski, op. cit., p. 74.
7. R. E. Silverman, "Two Kinds of Technology," *Educational Technology* (Jan. 1968), p. 3.
8. Komoski, op. cit., p. 71.
9. Stephen J. Knezevich, ed., "Administrative Technology and the School Executive" (Washington, D.C.: American Association of School Administrators, 1969), p. 17.
10. R. E. Corrigan and R. A. Kaufman, *A System Approach for Solving Educational Problems* [Operation PEP, Office of the San Mateo County (Calif.) Superintendent of Schools, October, 1967].
11. J. F. Keoski, J. P. Crumpler, and J. R. Kinzer, *Criteria for Decision Making* (Autonetics Division of North American Rockwell, March 1968).
12. Henry A. Bern et al., "Reply to Questions About Systems," *Audio-Visual Instruction,* 10(5):367.
13. Van C. Hare, Jr., *Systems Analysis: A Diagnostic Approach* (New York: Harcourt, Brace and World, Inc., 1967).
14. Leonard C. Silvern, "Systems Approach—What Is It?", *Educational Technology* (Aug. 30, 1968), p. 6.
15. Robert E. Campbell, Edward P. Dworkin, Dorothy P. Jackson, Kenneth E. Heoltzel, George E. Parsons and David W. Lacey, *The Systems Approach: An Emerging Behavioral Model for Vocational Guidance* (Center for Vocational and Technical Education, the Ohio State University, Jan. 1971), p. 3.
16. Silvern, op. cit., p. 6.
17. Corrigan and Kaufman, op. cit., pp. 204-231.
18. Howard J. Sullivan and Robert W. O'Hare, editors, *Accountability in Pupil Personnel Services: A Process Guide for the Development of Objectives* (Fullerton, Calif.: California Personnel and Guidance Association, 1971), pp. 112-13.
19. Campbell et al., op. cit.
20. T. Antoinette Ryan, "Systems Techniques for Programs of Counseling and Counselor Education," *Educational Technology* (June 1969), p. 9.
21. Sullivan and O'Hare, op. cit.
22. Ibid., p. 42.

23. Ibid., p. 45.
24. William W. Cooley and Raymond C. Hummel, "Systems Approaches in Guidance," *Review of Educational Research* (1969) 39: 251-62.
25. David B. Youst, "Another Application of Systems Technology" (paper presented at the American Personnel and Guidance Association Convention, March 1970).
26. Anthony G. Oettinger, "The Myths of Educational Technology," Copyright 1968 by Saturday Review Co. First appeared in *Saturday Review*, May 18, 1968. Used with permission.
27. Loran C. Twyford, Jr., "Educational Communications Media" in *Encyclopedia of Educational Research*, (New York: Macmillan Company, 1969) pp. 367-80.
28. The following are some useful writings on media classification: Robert DeKieffer, "Implications of New Educational Media"[in *Planning for Effective Utilization of Technology in Education*, edited by Edgar L. Morphet and David L. Jesser, (New York: Citation Press, 1969)], pp. 263-78; Edgar Dale, *Audio-Visual Methods in Teaching* (New York: Dryden Press, New York, 1946) p. 39; Briggs, Campeau, and Gagne, *Instructional Media: A Procedure for the Design of Multi-Media Instruction*, Chapter 2 (Pittsburgh: American Institute for Research, 1967); Louis Forsdale, *Newsletter of 8mm Film in Education*, Number 1 (Teachers College, Columbia University, 1965); Walter M. Lifton, ed., *Educating for Tomorrow: The Role of Media, Career Development, and Society* (John Wiley and Sons, Inc.: New York, 1970).
29. William H. Allen, "Instructional Media Research: Past, Present, and Future," *AV Communication Review* (Spring 1971), 19:11-12.
30. Ibid., p. 7.
31. Twyford, op. cit., p. 370.
32. C. R. Cayentes and L. P. Greenhill, *Comparative Research on Methods and Media for Presenting Programmed Courses in Mathematics and English* (University Park, Pa.: Pennsylvania State University, 1963).
33. Komoski, op. cit., p. 72.
34. R. W. Gerard, "Shaping the Mind: Computers in Education" (Applied Science and Technological Progress, A Report to the Committee on Science and Astronautics, U. S. House of Representatives, by the National Academy of Sciences).
35. David White Stickell, "A Critical Review of the Methodology and Results of Research Comparing Televised and Face-to-Face Instruction," doctoral thesis (University Park, Pa.: Pennsylvania State University, 1963).
36. For the use of television in instruction see: Presley D. Holmes, Jr., *Television Research in the Teaching-Learning Process* (Detroit: Wayne State University, 1959); Hideya Kumata, *An Inventory of Instructional Television Research* (East Lansing, Mich.: Michigan State University, 1956); Loran C. Twyford, ed., *Instructional Television* Research Reports (U.S. Naval Training Device Center, 1956); C. R. Carpenter and others, *An Investigation of Closed-Circuit Television for Teaching University Courses* (University Park, Pa.: Pennsylvania State University, 1958); Clifford G. Erickson and Hymen M. Chausow, *Chicago's TV College—Final Report of a Three-Year Experiment* (Chicago City Junior College, 1960); William M. Brish, *Washington County Closed-Circuit Television Report* (Hagerstown, Md., 1964); Wilbur Schramm, *Educational Television: The Next Ten Years* (Stanford, Calif.: Stanford University, 1962); Godwin C. Chu and Wilbur Schramm, "Work-Study Conference on New Educational Media for National University Extension Association," *Office of Education Research Reports 1956-65, Resumes* (Washington, D.C.: Government Printing Office, 1967); J. C. Reid and D. W. McLennan, *Research in Instructional Television and Film* (Washing-

157

ton, D. C.: Government Printing Office, 1967); J. H. Kanner, "Future Trends in Television Teaching and Research," *A V Communication Review* (1956), 5:513-27; J. H. Kanner, "Teaching by Television in the Army—an Overview," *A V Communication Review* (1958), 6:172-88; G. L. Gropper and A. A. Lumsdaine, "The Use of Student Response to Improve Instruction: An Overview," Report 7 (Metropolitan Pittsburgh Educational Television Stations and American Institutes for Research, 1961).

37. Readings in other than television media for instructional use are: Charles F. Hoban, Jr., and Edward B. Van Ormer, *Instructional Film Research, 1918-1950.* Technical Report No. SDC-269-7-19 (University Park, Pa.: Pennsylvania State College, December, 1950); Edgar Dale, James D. Finn, and Charles F. Hoban, Jr., "Audio-Visual Materials" in *Encyclopedia of Educational Research,* edited by Walter S. Monroe (New York: Macmillan Co., 1950); H. W. Vander Meer, *Relative Effectiveness of Instruction by: Films Exclusively, Films Plus Study Guides, and Standard Lecture Methods* (U. S. Naval Training Device Center, 1950); W. A. Wittick et al., *The Wisconsin Physics Film Evaluation Project* (Madison: University of Wisconsin, 1959); Sarah W. Lorge, *The Relative Effectiveness of Four Types of Language Laboratory Experiences* (New York City Board of Education, 1963); John B. Carroll, "Research on Teaching Foreign Language," *Handbook of Research on Teaching,* edited by N. L. Gage (Chicago: Rand McNally & Co., 1963) pp. 1060-1100; Emma Birkmaier and Dale Lange, "Foreign Language Instruction," *Review of Educational Research* (April 1968), 37: 186-99; Raymond F. Keating, "A Study of the Effectiveness of Language Laboratories," *A V Communication Review,* (Spring 1964), 12:106-7; Lewis D. Eigen and Kenneth Komoski, *Automated Teaching Project* (Collegiate School, New York City, 1960); Arnold Roe et al., *Automated Teaching Methods Using Linear Programs* (Los Angeles: University of California, 1960); Margaret B. Fisher and Leslie F. Malpass, *A Comparison of Programmed and Standard Textbooks in College Instruction* (University of South Florida, 1963).

38. Norman Kagan, "Multimedia in Guidance and Counseling," *The Personnel and Guidance Journal* (Nov. 1970), 49: 197. Copyright APGA.

39. Robert DeKieffer, "Implications of New Educational Media", Chapter 12 in *Planning for Effective Utilization of Technology in Education,* edited by Edgar L. Morphet and David L. Jesser (New York: Citation Press, 1969)], pp. 263-78.

40. James Martin and Adrian R. D. Norman, *The Computerized Society* (Englewood Cliffs, N. J.: Prentice-Hall, Inc., 1970), p. 28.

41. For further information relative to the use of microfilms in education contact Dick Smith, Grossmont Union High School District, Post Office Box 1043, La Mesa, California 92041.

42. Henry Brito, "Implications of New Technology for Vocational Aspects of Counselor Education," in *Implications of New Technology for Counselor Education,* American Personnel and Guidance Association, March 1969.

43. *Vocational Education: Innovations Revolutionize Career Training* (National School Public Relations Association, 1971).

44. L. B. Kenyon, "Dust Off the Tape Recorder," *Occupations* (1952), 2: 372.

45. Donald V. Forrest, "The Use of Video Tape Recordings (VTR) in Counselor Education," section in *Implications of New Technology for Counselor Education,* a Committee Report of the Association for Counselor Education and Supervision, March 1969.

46. Norman Kagan, op. cit., p. 200.

47. Malcolm Salinger and Wilbert Wright, "Videotape as a Medium for Vocational

Decision-Making Information," *The Personnel and Guidance Journal* (Nov. 1970), 49: 205.

48. For further information refer to Walter M. Lifton, ed., *Educating for Tomorrow: The Role of Media, Career Development, and Society* (New York: John Wiley and Sons, Inc., 1970).

49. Thomas M. Smith, "Some Perspectives on the Early History of Computers," in *Perspectives on the Computer Revolution*, edited by Zenon W. Pylyshyn (Englewood Cliffs, N.J.: Prentice-Hall, Inc., © 1970), p. 8.

50. Ibid., pp. 7-15.

51. Harry D. Huskey, "Computer Technology," chap. 3 in *Annual Review of Information Science and Technology*, edited by Carlos A. Caudra and Ann W. Luke (Chicago: Encyclopaedia Britannica, Inc., 1970), p. 73.

52. H. J. Hallworth et al., "A Computer Assisted Vocational Counseling System" (paper presented at the Canadian Council for Research in Education, Ottawa, Ontario, March 1970).

53. Janet C. Heddesheimer, "A Computer-Based Management and Education Information System for Counselor Education," Doctoral dissertation (Columbus: Ohio State University, 1971).

54. Reporting the computer-based vocational guidance system developed by System Development Corporation are: D. P. Estavan, C. P. Donahoe, and J. W. Boyk, *Implementation of Vocational Counseling System*, TM-4409 (Santa Monica: System Development Corporation, 1969); and J. F. Cogswell, C. P. Donahoe, D. P. Estavan, and B. A. Rosenquist, *The Design of a Man-Machine Counseling System*, SP-2576/001/01 (Santa Monica: System Development Corporation, 1966).

55. Cogswell et al., pp. 11–14.

56. David V. Tiedeman et al., *An Information System for Vocational Decisions, Final Report* (Cambridge, Mass.: Harvard University, 1970).

57. Ibid., pp. 21-26.

58. JoAnn Harris, "Can Computers Counsel?" *Vocational Guidance Quarterly* (March 1970), pp. 162–164.

59. Robert W. Locke and David Engler, *Run, Strawman, Run* (New York: McGraw-Hill Book Company, 1968).

60. Ibid., p. 9.

61. Ibid.

62. Joseph B. Margolin and Marion R. Misch, *Computers in the Classroom* (New York: Spartan Books, 1970), pp. 11–12.

63. Ibid., p. 15.

64. James Martin and Adrian R. D. Norman, *The Computerized Society* (Englewood Cliffs, N.J.: Prentice-Hall, Inc., 1970), p. 11.

65. C. Gilbert Wrenn, "The Danger Within," *The Personnel and Guidance Journal* (Nov. 1970), 49: 183.

66. Garry R. Walz, "Technology in Guidance: A Conceptual Overview," *The Personnel and Guidance Journal* (Nov. 1970), 49: 180. Copyright APGA.

67. J. F. Cogswell, D. P. Estavan, C. P. Donahoe, Jr., and B. H. Rosenquist, *Exploratory Study of Information-Processing Procedures and Computer-Based Technology in Vocational Counseling*, TM-3718 (Santa Monica: System Development Corporation, 1967).

68. Robert W. O'Hare and Barbara Lasser, *Evaluating Pupil Personnel Programs* (Fullerton, Calif.: California Personnel and Guidance Association, 1971).

69. An excellent treatment of technology in guidance and counseling can be found

in special issues of *The Personnel and Guidance Journal* (Nov. 1970); and *Educational Technology* (March 1969).

SELECTED REFERENCES

Association for Counselor Education and Supervision. A Committee Report. *Implications of New Technology for Counselor Education.* March 1969.

Burnham, Robert W., Johnson, Donald H., and Youst, David B. "Some Applications of Educational Media in a Support System for Educational and Career Planning," in *Educating for Tomorrow: The Role of Media, Career Development, and Society,* edited by Walter M. Lifton. New York: John Wiley and Sons, Inc., 1970.

Career Education and the Technology of Career Development (Proceedings of the Eighth Invitational Conference on Systems under Construction in Career Education and Development, Oct. 7–8, 1971). Palo Alto, Calif.: American Institute for Research, 1972.

Computer-Based Vocational Guidance Systems (Summary of papers presented at the Fourth Symposium for Systems under Development for Vocational Guidance). Parts II–III. Washington, D.C.: U. S. Government Printing Office, 1969.

Educational Technology, March 1969, pp. 7–46.

Ellis, Allan B., and Tiedeman, David V. "Can a Machine Counsel?" in *Computer-Assisted Instruction, Testing, and Guidance,* edited by Wayne H. Holtzman. New York: Harper & Row, 1970.

Holtzman, Wayne H. "Computers in Education" in *Computer-Assisted Instruction, Testing, and Guidance,* edited by Wayne H. Holtzman. New York: Harper & Row, 1970.

Huskey, Harry D. "Computer Technology" in *Annual Review of Information Science and Technology,* vol. 5, edited by Carlos A. Cuadra. Chicago: Encyclopaedia Britannica, Inc., 1970.

Knezevich, Stephen J., ed. *Administrative Technology and the School Executive,* chaps. 2–3. Washington, D. C.: American Association of School Administrators, 1969.

Lewis, Stephen L. "The Characteristics of Different Media" in *Educating for Tomorrow: The Role of Media, Career Development, and Society,* edited by Walter M. Lifton. New York: John Wiley and Sons, Inc., 1970.

Magnino, Joseph T., Jr. "Document Retrieval and Dissemination" in *Annual Review of Information Science and Technology,* vol. 6, edited by Carlos A. Cuadra. Chicago: Encyclopaedia Britannica, Inc., 1970.

Martin, James, and Norman, Adrian R. D. *The Computerized Society,* chaps 1, 8, 14–15. Englewood Cliffs, N. J.: Prentice-Hall, Inc., 1970.

Meierhenry, Wesley C. "Computers in Education" in *Computers in the Classroom—An Interdisciplinary View of Trends and Alternatives,* edited by Joseph B. Margolin and Marion R. Misch. New York: Spartan Books, 1970.

Mesthene, Emmanuel E. "Computers and the Purposes of Education" in *Computer-Assisted Instruction, Testing, and Guidance,* edited by Wayne H. Holtzman. New York: Harper & Row, 1970.

Nelson, Carl E. "Microform Technology" in *Annual Review of Information Science and Technology,* vol. 6, edited by Carlos A. Cuadra. Chicago: Encyclopaedia Britannica, Inc., 1970.

O'Hare, Robert W., and Lasser, Barbara. *Evaluating Pupil Personnel Programs,* chaps. 1–5. Fullerton, Calif.: California Personnel and Guidance Association, 1971.

Review of Educational Research, entire issue, April 1968.

Robinson, Louis. "An Orientation to Computer Technology" in *Computers in the Classroom—An Interdisciplinary View of Trends and Alternatives*, edited by Joseph B. Margolin and Marion R. Misch. New York: Spartan Books, 1970.

Simms, R. L., and Fuchs, Edward. "Communications Technology" in *Annual Review of Information Science and Technology*, vol. 5, edited by Carlos A. Cuadra. Chicago: Encyclopaedia Britannica, Inc., 1970.

Sullivan, Howard J., and O'Hare, Robert, eds. *Accountability in Pupil Personnel Services: A Process Guide for the Development of Objectives*, chaps. 1, 5–6. Fullerton, Calif.: California Personnel and Guidance Association, 1971.

Super, Donald E. *Computer-Assisted Counseling.* New York: Teachers College Press, 1970.

Teplitz, Arthur. "Microfilm and Reprography" in *Annual Review of Information Science and Technology*, vol. 5, edited by Carlos A. Cuadra. Chicago: Encyclopaedia Britannica, Inc., 1970.

The Personnel and Guidance Journal, entire issue, Nov. 1970.

CHAPTER 5

Staff Roles and Relationships

KENNETH W. ROLLINS

SCHOOL systems have long tended to look upon the business communities as models of organization. Schools expanded from single teacher red schoolhouses to multiple-teacher buildings with teaching principals, to multiple-building systems with superintendents and full-time principals. It was natural that they took nearby business models for organization as they grew. School board members were often businessmen, bankers, and other organizational-oriented persons. The superintendent who gave the appearance of being a businesslike educator won the plaudits of both his teachers and the businessmen, perhaps because both groups may have felt confidence in his familiar role. Not unexpectedly, it can be seen that school systems within the influence zone of any large organization, will tend to take on some of the characteristics of that body, reflected in tables or organization, titles, personnel policies, relative salary structure, and strategies for change. School jurisdictions within the vicinity of the District of Columbia, for example, harbor, for better or worse, identifiable characteristics of the federal colossus which dominates the environment. Many board of education members who determine policies of these educational enterprises are government employees.

MARK HOPKINS' LOG GOT CROWDED

For the past fifty years or more there has been a growing complexity developing in educational systems. More thoroughly trained teachers, graduate work in subjects, administration, and specialized school services, and programs to provide for students once "pushed

162

out" have been both results of and influences on this growing complexity. The phenomenal increase in the nation's population and the urban-suburban centralization of population have made bigness as much a problem for school systems as for other community services. Small school systems with one high school and two or three elementary schools have suddenly found themselves within a few short years bursting into massive systems. Keeping up with school facility demands, expanding instructional methods and materials, curriculum modifications, personnel selection, supervision, and evaluation, and social pressures have compounded the problems and decisions of school administrators. It was all very well to picture Mark Hopkins on one end of a log and a student on the other as the perfect school when, in the middle of the nineteenth century, there was great selectivity as to the student and the moon was a safely romantic orb. Mark would discover today that the American school superintendency is one of the world's most demanding and sometimes impossible positions. It should attract some of the best minds in the land because of the sheer proclivity and audacity it requires to be an educator-manager-economist-politician-improviser-group leader-tax expert-negotiator-budget officer-businessman, all in one nearly every day.

Changing Influences in Education

Teacher organizations have strengthened to a point of establishing tenure, and more lately to a strategic position of negotiating remuneration and other conditions of employment. Once the public was less skeptical of educators and more willing to assume that they knew best what children ought to learn. Since the curriculum showed little identifiable change, there was community acceptance of the familiar school program, even if it gradually became obsolescent in the changing socio-economic world in which the children lived. The authority of the principal of the school, perhaps to a lesser extent that of the classroom teacher, was seldom open to serious question. Today the public demands, challenges, sues, pressures, and otherwise conveys the idea that the schools are theirs, not the principal's, nor the teacher's, nor the superintendent's, nor even the property of the board of education, the members of which are supposed to be representing them. Sometimes so much energy is consumed in contemporary discussion, research, criticism, and countercriticism regarding the operations of the schools that many administrators and staffs literally find it taxing the system to get the ongoing decisions made and subsequent work done. There almost always is a sometime ben-

163

efit in sincere community study and criticism. There is also a potential deficit in returns when continuing attacks weaken morale within an organization, instead of providing support for healthy improvement.

ORGANIZATION OF PUPIL PERSONNEL STAFF

As succinctly stated by Hatch and Stefflre:

> The personnel function has been defined as that part of the educational process that is specifically planned for each individual student to assist him to become more self-directive and socially integrated. This function is shared with many individuals on the school staff. The administrative problem that must be resolved at this point is how to integrate the primary and secondary functions of all members of a staff in such a manner as to bring about maximum service for the pupils.[1]

Sizes of school systems and their financial support often determine not only the existence of pupil services but to a great extent the roles and relationships of people involved in these services. Small, medium, and large school systems are dominated by administrative organization. Figure 5.1 shows that the counselor as possibly the only pupil personnel specialist in the small system, has neither counterpart nor supervisor to offset any deficiency or bias of the counselor. Guidance services rest with his own professional orientation and the degree to which he is convincing with the principal, the faculty, and the superintendent of schools.

SMALL SCHOOL SYSTEMS

Small systems have few specialists. Since the National Defense Act of 1958, however, it would be a rare system indeed that did not have at least one trained counselor, generally attached to the high school, and sometimes being of consultant help to elementary schools. Some school systems as far back as the 1930s first became aware of the guidance movement, sometimes through early writings of Brewer, Jones, Parsons, Allen, and other pioneers. While few if any teachers had training in counseling, materials and provisions of time were occasionally made to give some assistance to high school students. One new assistant principal in a small Maine town was heard to say in 1941, "One of my responsibilities is *guidance,* whatever that is."

Curiously, the first available pupil service type person outside of the classroom in small systems has been someone who made little pretense of being a counselor or psychologist. It was the school nurse. In small towns the school or public health nurse (category depending upon whether paid by the health department or the school system) was probably the first auxiliary service to the classroom. The nurse screened children for sight and hearing impediments, making contributions which seemed essential to the learning situation. Equally as obvious, in view of living conditions prevalent in poorer areas, were her checks for communicable and infectious conditions, her inspections for pediculosis, and her observations on possible nutritional deficiencies. Some of these energetic, indefatigable, feared-and-

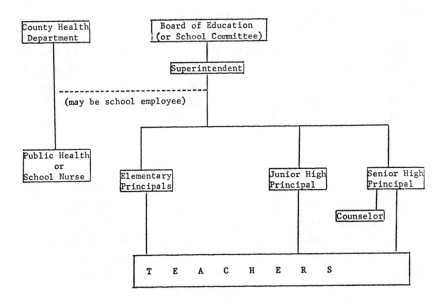

Fig. 5.1. Chart of typical small school system. Counselor assigned to high school staff may have some relationship to junior high school for articulation and orientation purposes.

loved nurses of small communities and counties were and are heroic in their achievements, with few resources at their command, but with strong determinations and a deep dedication to children.

Embellishment of the pupil services in the small system beyond the school counselor and the related resource of the school nurse usually went in the direction of getting someone who could provide the essential psychometric services for screening and placement of exceptional children. Sometimes this was a psychologist, who also would become a valuable referral source and provide direct assistance to teachers and parents. Sometimes the addition was a well-trained guidance counselor with further graduate work in behavioral sciences, including psychometrics. Two or more counselors, one designated "director of guidance," supplemented by the school nurse (who operated parallel to rather than as an integral part of pupil services) thus would become the total guidance or pupil services of the school system. At this juncture, the director of guidance often was assigned to the superintendent's office, rather than to the high school principal, and extended coverage to the whole system. If there was an attendance officer, he or she may then have been assigned to the guidance office, but often as not these primitive operations were also parallel rather than put together, to avoid any "contamination" of the latter's service role, as against the former's compulsory role.

Small Does Not Mean Poor Service

While small school systems have few specialists, if they have any time at all to work on their mission of guidance and counseling, or other ways of meeting the special needs of children, they often do very well. The awareness and the sensitivity of individuals—beginning with teachers in the classrooms and homerooms, the itinerant school nurse, the few but alert school principals, and the skeleton counselor group—constitute the quality of pupil services. These people do what they can to understand learning problems and developing human behavior. If they are good, their services are frequently superior to that which may be available in larger systems, because they have some advantages: small school system *ergo* small towns. They have the knowledge of individual circumstances and community interrelationships to draw upon in working with students and families. The lack of social workers is overcome by knowing people directly and seeing them frequently around the town, at work or play, shopping, or in their homes. There is no reason to assume

166

naiveté or ineffectiveness. Quite often, to the contrary, the few available professionals are looked upon as is the small town doctor—perhaps not the greatest, but exceedingly adequate for most local needs, and generally well regarded. Because of such status, the teacher, nurse, and counselor—as the pupil services general practitioners of small towns—are usually able to muster practical resources for individuals and help them cope with circumstances adequately. Sometimes, of course, there are conditions or underlying etiologies which are obscure to less sophisticated specialists. Diagnostic and remedial resources of larger systems with well-defined pupil personnel services, competent counseling, and special education provisions then have some advantages for students. But they also develop other disadvantages for which there are few easy solutions. These problems will be considered later in this chapter, as larger systems are analyzed.

MODAL SCHOOL SYSTEMS

Some thirty-two percent of the public school systems in the United States have enrollments of from 1,000 to 5,000 pupils. Organizational patterns of pupil personnel services in these modal systems are similar in general, and tend to vary mostly in details that are affected by the wealth of the school district and how much support there may be for specialists in pupil services. Original organization of pupil services in these systems often was influenced by the competence and influence of the people who then occupied key positions and by their perceptions of pupil services. Some of the inappropriate tasks of counselors, for example, came from misconceptions of administrators which brought about expectations that became entrenched. Anachronistic guidance programs are today causing the criticisms of a whole profession, and yet are still being determined outside the profession.

Line-and-Staff Organization Appears

Some educators have assumed that the line-and-staff concept, so apparent in school systems as auxiliary services developed, may have been a spin-off from the military experiences of men and women who became school administrators. Line-and-staff has been totally ingrained in patterns of military organization. However, the organizational plans of business also recognized this model, and there is some evidence that it may have been in existence about the turn of the century. As far back as 1910 Superintendent Blewitt of the St. Louis public schools wrote:

> The line-and-staff conception regards the principal as vested with the immediate responsibility of setting in motion and directing all those forces that must be at work to instruct and to educate the pupils of the school most skillfully. Under this conception the principal makes use of the supervisor as one of his effective means of accomplishing his plans. He does not regard the supervisor as one who filches from him, his office or as one on whom he may unload responsibility that presses too heavily upon his own easy indifference or incapacity.[2]

Services which are not school-based, but which are itinerant or centralized, are organized under one or more staff departments of the superintendent's office. The head of these services answers directly to the superintendent. Thus, the behavioral science practitioners not based in the school are staff. This line-and-staff relationship is seen throughout most school systems. It appears to be based upon a concept that school systems are run from the top down, that there is a direct line of command from superintendent to classroom teacher. Pupil services positions, being "staff" in the organization, are occupied without authority, other than the authority of wisdom, which is not always allowed to prevail. Their supervision comes from the superintendent to a director of pupil services or a director of guidance, whose status is approximately equal to that of the principals, who is a member of the executive staff of the superintendent, and who is qualified himself as a counselor, psychologist, pupil personnel supervisor, or school social worker. Coordination of pupil services with school programs is easily planned and communication maintained through the superintendent's periodic staff meetings, which bring principals and the director together, along with the director of instruction and others who affect the educational provisions for the system. Since the school principals within the system are also members of the superintendent's staff group, the opportunity for communication tends to decrease the number of ambiguities between school administrators and directors of pupil services. The skillful leadership of an effective superintendent brings out areas of agreement to overcome areas of potential conflict. The sometimes pernicious edge of uncertainty between administrative control of in-school pupil services (counselors) and professional influence in the pupil services field is minimized. Whether or not this edge of uncertainty is a threat to the teamwork of principals, director, and counse-

168

lors is often determined by the skills in relationship and intentions of each personality. The essential setting for good relationship, however, is something made possible by the superintendent, and in the modal organization the opportunity is present to some degree as a natural feature of size. Without cooperation and trust in line and staff, some observers see the net effect as "those who have the power lack the knowledge, and those who have the knowledge lack the power." The obvious losers are the students; the less obvious losers are the professionals themselves, who may never know the satisfaction of the highest levels of effectiveness being shared in a cohesive team effort.

Centralized and itinerant services are "staff" as indicated in Figure 5.2. They do not determine but make recommendations regarding administrative decisions, policies, and practices, according to their areas of expertise, or judgments they may have. Traditionally, their roles have been related primarily to understanding, evaluating, and interpreting the behaviors and learning characteristics of pupils. *Only* through their consulting with teachers and principals and their coordinating of programs agreed upon by administrators have they had the opportunities to influence their colleagues. "Only" can be a considerable amount of influence, however, if competence is recognized and relationships are mutually supportive.

Modal May Be Optimal

The school systems with pupil enrollments between 1,000 and 5,000 may have advantages less likely in larger and smaller systems. These systems are small enough so that the superintendent is seen frequently by many teachers, and even more frequently by his principals, directors, and supervisors. The chief spokesman for pupil services is a specialist in his area, not an administrator without special training in guidance or psychology or school social work. He is present when decisions are made concerning his department and the personnel therein. His centralized pupil services staff may include psychologists, social workers, pupil personnel workers, community coordinators, child accounting, research and testing, and the supervisors of these services, if there are any. The larger the system the more division of labor, hence the proliferation of departments and divisions. For example, research in small and modal systems is usually confined to pupil and program appraisal through the system-wide testing program and a few additional surveys or studies. Research in larger systems is often determined by questions raised in meetings

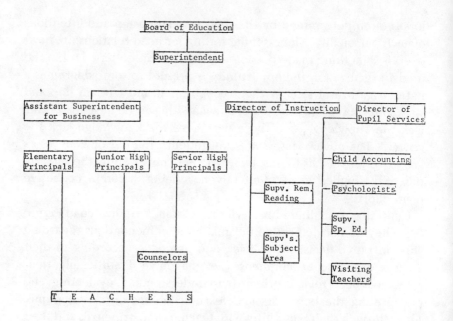

Fig. 5.2.   Modal system organization. System is large enough to have staff specialists, who head departments, and others who work out of these departments.

of the board of education, and covers many studies from learning methods comparisons to surveys of student involvement in "the drug scene." The modal system may be optimal, given good leadership, because: (1) it serves a community small enough to be known well by educators in both social and economic matters; (2) there is a greater opportunity for frequency of contact between key people in the system; (3) community agency personnel are known to pupil services workers, often on a first-name basis, and their cooperation is useful in the interests of children and youth; (4) the understandings and attitudes of counselors and other pupil services people are more effectively diffused among the other professionals who work with students; and (5) parents have the opportunity to know teachers and pupil services personnel.

LARGE SCHOOL SYSTEM ORGANIZATION

In general, line-and-staff organizational patterns in large school systems are similar to those of modal systems; but, with the increase in size, something occurs in organization and communication that changes the course of relationships and often reduces per-unit effectiveness. The top echelons of large school systems are almost exclusively manned by administrators who were advanced along the line from assistant principals to principals to area assistant superintendents, to associates or deputies. Back in their first excursion from the classroom there might have been a short term of being a counselor, with or without certification, but seldom any other experience in the special fields of pupil services. By the time an administrator has reached the executive staff in a large school system, his background of administrative tasks and concerns has given him skills and attitudes which have made him successful along the line at least in that system. Then, through promotions, he may find himself as an assistant superintendent for pupil services, or associate superintendent in charge of several departments, one of which may be pupil services. On the executive staff, he suddenly is spokesman for pupil services, which he may know little about, except having used them. The specialists in psychology, counseling and guidance, school social work, community coordination, and pupil personnel work are below the level of decision making in large system hierarchies. Thus, it is not surprising that, after these services "peak out" in expansions of the system, there tends to be a gradual dilution of support, generally without consciousness on the part of the administration. New programs are often brought in at higher levels. It takes expert knowledge of a field to champion its contributions and status with authority. The nonexpert is unaware of what his compromises may do to a service he supposedly supports. Ginsberg's criticisms of guidance were toward the *results* of the erosion of support and cumulative insertion of nonguidance tasks for counselors.[3] He seldom appeared to address himself to the organizational dynamics that brought about

171

much of the circumstance, leaving an impression of inept counselors instead of sometimes incapacitated counselors.

More Is Less

The large school system has more of everyone: more counselors, more psychologists, more pupil personnel workers or visiting teachers, more clinicians and diagnosticians. But, above all, it has large numbers of students, many complex and interrelated services, and an enormous range of student characteristics in abilities, ethnic and cultural origins, social backgrounds, and economic conditions. The specialized, sophisticated services and personnel are not necessarily more able to provide for students than they are in smaller systems,

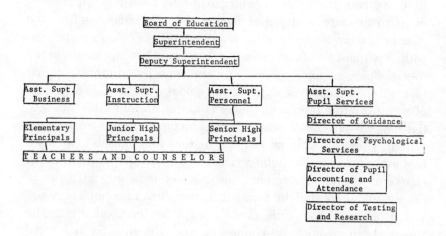

Fig. 5.3.   Large school system organization, showing subordinates to assistant superintendent for pupil services. Sometimes the assistant superintendent is a psychologist or guidance person; more often, he is an administrator.

partly because the proportion of assistance is seldom better and sometimes worse. There are other reasons: complexity of the system tends to reduce efficiency of cooperative efforts; specialists in pupil services are not represented at the executive level by an expert in the field; insufficient supervision is provided for in-school personnel, primarily the counselors; principals tend to see supervision beyond their own as unnecessary for counselors; executive level is wary of creating hostility among organized principals, hence judgments and opinions expressed by their own specialized staff often are less influential than anticipated consensus among principals. Result: decisions concerning pupil services are oriented to the administrative point of view, then they are handed down instead of being worked out on the basis of evidence and judgment available through the behavioral sciences as well as through administrative perceptions.

Thus, as explained by Hart and Prince, "Although the counselor has a professional and research basis for defining his role and function within the school setting, his freedom to implement the role is often limited by the school administrator who has different role expectations for him."[4]

PROFESSIONS IN PUPIL SERVICES

The genesis of positions in pupil services followed the growing perceptions of educators and parents that people with certain understandings were worth having available. It has already been mentioned that the school nurse, not ordinarily thought of as a pupil services functionary, in fact, tended to be the first out-of-classroom person whose first concern was the children. The reason was that people did not want to bring their children together in large groups with the potential of rampant disease being spread because of their forced proximity.

Useful to the public health officials was the realization that the child was a window into the health conditions of his home. They could keep track of these conditions with least effort or invasion by having a nurse in surveillance.

School Nurse

The nurse who serves the school is, in some systems, a direct employee of the school system, and in other systems is under the Department of Public Health. She is responsible for working with personnel in the school or schools to which she is assigned. In some ways, she deals with all aspects of health, including emotional, mental, physical, social, and environmental. She will:

1. Meet with the faculty early in the school year to discuss the program for the health of the school-age child, the identification of deviations from health, the importance of teacher observations, and the types and methods of referrals.

2. Work with the health committee of the PTA to further the health work in the school and participate in PTA meetings on request.

3. Hold planned teacher-nurse conferences for the purpose of reviewing the health status of all children in a classroom. These conferences with teachers are planned through principals and are scheduled at a time satisfactory for teacher and nurse.

4. Have consultations with school personnel. These consultations may be initiated by the school personnel or nurse for the purpose of discussing problems of health and adjustment of an individual or small group of students.

5. Work with the school medical adviser to arrange medical evaluation for children with health problems (see Regulation 525-1).

6. Make home visits when these are indicated to give nursing care (under medical supervision) and help the family plan for providing care.

7. Serve within the school as a resource person in matters of health, health education, and policies of the Department of Public Health. Upon request of the teachers, participate occasionally in classroom activities relating to health.

8. Plan with teachers for handling of minor first aid and screening of health problems for referral to the nurse.

9. Arrange for the care of sick children and give first aid to children who are referred by school personnel while the nurse is in the school.

10. Study school environment to identify elements conducive to accidents and try to eliminate hazards.

11. Teach basic principles of healthful living to individual children and parents.

12. Train and supervise volunteer workers. Help the principal with the recruitment of these workers.

13. Maintain and use health records and explain medical findings and recommendations.

14. Report to parents and teachers on findings of health appraisal and screening and help the family arrange for further investigation or necessary care. Check periodically to insure appropriate follow-up.

15. Confer and plan with the principal regarding children who are absent because of known long-term illness, including children who are receiving home teaching.

174

16. Supervise the health of foster children.
17. Help with nutritional aspects of the school lunch program when called upon.

Decision Making Begat Guidance

Then there were the problems of educational choices, aroused by the observations that high school graduates had difficulties finding jobs, partly because they did not know how or where to look for employment. Further search into the problem of finding jobs or suitable further training brought out the truth that the graduates seldom knew themselves. Nor had they known themselves well enough back in school so that they could choose wisely among the courses of study. Gradually, helping students with choices encompassed not only educational and vocational decisions but personal and social choices and behaviors which affected the potentials and opportunities of the youth. Counseling was born.

The School Counselor

The school counselor, a full-time member of a school staff, is the principal professional worker identified with guidance services and is specifically certified for such work. From elementary school through junior and senior high school, there are both similarities and differences in the work of counselors according to developmental levels of the students served. Each counselor engages in counseling, consulting, and coordinating activities appropriate to the student population served:

1. *Counseling Activities*
   (a). Provides individual and group counseling services for students and others relative to personal, social, educational, and vocational matters.
   (b). Assists students and parents in assessing learning progress and in planning educational programs.
   (c). Helps to identify problems of adjustment which impede learning and assists in overcoming these problems; intervenes to assist students in crisis situations.
   (d). Assists students in gaining an increasing awareness of self through identity development and through discussing the career implications of personal values, interests, and aptitudes.
   (e). Counsels with registering and withdrawing students concerning their options and choices; follows up students who have withdrawn, giving them further assistance and counseling as called upon.

175

2. *Consulting Activities*
   (a). Works with students and other school personnel to provide a psychological climate within the school that will promote learning and satisfying interpersonal relationships.
   (b). Participates in the educational appraisal of pupils and the interpretation of their learning potentials toward modification of instructional programs or placement within current programs.
   (c). Assists teachers, principals, and parents in understanding learning and behavioral problems and in working to develop solutions to such problems.
   (d). Reinforces the personal guidance relationship that teachers have with students.
   (e). Helps to interpret the school program to students and parents in cooperation with teachers and administrators.
   (f). Acts as a resource to the faculty and the principal by interpreting student needs as they relate to curriculum directions and changes.
   (g). Serves as a resource person for information to parents and students concerning available and appropriate out-of-school services which may be helpful; coordinates referrals with pupil services workers when indicated.

3. *Coordinating Activities*
   (a). Participates with school personnel, pupil services personnel, and others in staff meetings concerning the needs of individual pupils, with responsibility for coordinating information and following up on students referred to pupil services, and organizes prescribed actions in cooperation with staff members.
   (b). Provides orientation of students new to the school and to students entering another level of the school program.
   (c). Cooperates with school-community programs that relate to the guidance of children and youth.
   (d). Assists the principal and others in planning programs and activities, which involve parents and school staff toward making the school a resource in meeting relevant community needs.
   (e). Coordinates guidance-related research studies, practical experiences for graduate students in guidance, and other activities which contribute to the counseling profession.

The school principal and the guidance personnel assess the counseling needs of students and parents, the means of increasing availability of counselor, and strategies for delivery of services that may not be within the usual hours or facilities. Such provisions may include continuing counseling and other guidance services during the summer; providing services during evening hours, periodically or as arranged; conducting early morning, daytime, or evening group sessions for parents or students; and contacting students informally outside the guidance office, in neighborhood facilities such as libraries or recreation centers, or in students' homes by arrangement. Principals should encourage such appropriate activities and adjust duty hours accordingly. The emphasis should be upon flexibility of guidance services to provide realistically for local conditions.

The Elementary School Counselor

The elementary school counselor's work centers on understanding and identifying the learning characteristics of children. Working closely with the teachers and the parents, the counselor contributes to an increased understanding of the potentials of children and helps establish a positive psychological climate for learning.

Early identification of any factor which might impede learning is an essential part of the elementary counselor's mission. A further objective of the elementary counselor is to help the child develop awareness about himself and his world in ways that enable him to feel secure and adequate.

The Middle School/Junior High School Counselor

At the junior high school level, students are in the exploratory stages of their school programs. Each teacher assesses student progress in relationship to particular instructional objectives; the counselor evaluates the total educational experiences of the student. He observes the emerging patterns of personality, interests, aptitudes, and values which will be significant in identity formation and career planning. The counselor encourages the student in self-understanding as educational choices become more numerous and occupational awareness increases. Frequently the junior high school counselor interprets the developing potentialities of the student with his parents in the course of reaching program decisions.

The High School Counselor

As high school students grow in independence, the counselor works to foster rational self-management in making personal, social, and vocational decisions. Maturing adolescents develop increased introspection, are more concerned with identity formation, have expanded educational choices, experience greater freedoms in social behaviors, and must make significant decisions regarding their immediate and ultimate careers. The high school counselor handles a

177

large, constantly changing body of information, conducts follow-up studies, assists in job placement, and responds to contacts for continued services by former students.

OTHER PEOPLE WITH GUIDANCE RESPONSIBILITIES

The Teacher

The teacher's contributions to the guidance program can be highly significant to students and their success in school. His first concern is to guide the learning activities of children and youth in such ways that students have success identities. He involves them, motivates them, experiences with them. The teacher is sensitive to the factors that affect behavior in learning. In the development of students' skills, understandings, and knowledges, the teacher is aware that successful, satisfying relationships and experiences motivate learning. The teacher:

1. Recognizes the individuality of each student in order that expectations are reasonable and learning is meaningful to the student.
2. Maintains faith in and rapport with youth and shows genuine concern for their successful school experiences.
3. Provides both planned and incidental opportunities for students to talk with him and respects the confidentiality of any student's information about himself.
4. Uses counselors and other specialists as resources to understand and cope with learning and emotional problems of students.
5. Urges students to seek appropriate assistance through counselors, nurses, and other pupil services, when indicated by severity of problems or needs.
6. Capitalizes on opportunities to show relationship between school subjects and occupational fields as a means of increasing awareness of students, providing additional motivation for learning, and contributing to career planning.
7. Contributes to evaluations of the guidance program and assists in planning for improvements.

The School Principal

The principal is a key person with responsibility for the local guidance program and for the priorities expected of counselors. He uses the resources of area and central office guidance and pupil services staff to plan and provide guidance services for the school jointly with the school guidance staff and guidance advisory committee. He assigns duties to counselors and supporting services personnel in accordance with Board of Education policy and the school's guidance objectives and establishes priorities to assure that counselors are available to meet with students, parents, and teachers. He provides for a periodic review of the guidance program and the dissemination of information concerning counseling services to the school staff and the community. He selects personnel to fill guidance vacancies from available and approved candidates, with the help of area and central office counseling specialists, and is responsible for the periodic evaluation of counselor performance.

Supervisory Staff in Guidance

Guidance supervisors and area guidance coordinators provide professional leadership, supervision, and in-service training in the field of guidance. They participate in the selection and evaluation of counselors and act in an advisory capacity in setting standards for facilities, materials, and other supports for an effective guidance program. They observe economic conditions which may affect educational and career opportunities and social trends which may affect attitudes, motivations, and life styles. They assist counselors individually and in seminar groups to improve their counseling abilities. They coordinate guidance activities with other departments and with agencies and organizations, institutions, technical schools, colleges, and universities. They stimulate the career planning emphasis of guidance services and coordinate guidance program development with career and vocational education and other program efforts.

Guidance Advisory Committee

In schools served by guidance personnel, an advisory committee on guidance, including parents, teachers, and students, is essential in developing a guidance program which is responsive to the needs of students in the school community. The desirable outcomes of a guidance advisory committee are to increase understanding and communication between the guidance personnel and the people they serve, to involve appropriate resource people in guidance efforts, and to maintain the effectiveness of guidance services. Each guidance committee should submit an annual report to the principal of the school, reflecting its views on the status of the guidance program, perceptions of the needs within the school community to which the guidance program should address its efforts, and appropriate suggestions.

179

Paraprofessionals

In science, engineering, medicine, and now in education, there has been a growing awareness that, as a matter of economy, the work of professionally prepared people should be augmented by the use of subprofessional personnel. Many of these paraprofessionals, or aides, have been trained in highly technical skills, such as medical laboratory or X-ray technicians. Some have particular skills in research or data processing. Some meet people, fill out case history forms, retrieve information, or otherwise deal directly and indirectly with the lives of children, youth, or adults. Society pays too much for the services of professionals to indulge in their doing activities which could be done as well or better by much less expensively trained individuals.

The counselor aide, by whatever name he or she may be given in a particular school system, has become a valuable support to the counselors, and by contacts, to students and teachers as well. Assuming the guidance office has secretarial assistance to do those things, generally of a communicative or recording nature, which are done by secretaries, the counselor aide has other tasks. Looking at the noncounseling activities which are still within the realm of guidance, counselor aides, guidance assistants, or paraprofessionals usually have guidelines for this position which cover the following items:

1. Maintains educational and occupational information materials to provide counselors, students, and teachers with recent and accurate data that is important to students, particularly to support decisions.
2. Retrieves such information in a variety of combinations which may be useful to particular students, teachers, or counselors, or to classes.
3. Under the direction of counselors, prepares for and facilitates such events as career and college programs, test administrations, and field trips for occupational and educational information; accompanies such field trips to assist counselors and other adults.
4. Responds to contacts made by students; maintains a caring, friendly attitude; uses judgment on urgency of need for counselor intervention, if priorities have to be recognized because of work load.

While there will be other tasks for counselor aides, the important standard is that these tasks are related to the guidance objectives and efforts of the school, and that they require less than the professional judgment and skills in relationship to competent counselors. In the guidance services, it is the employment and training of paraprofessionals for essential, relevant duties which would constitute the differential staffing, more than specific assignments of counselors. Students should not have to sort out the apparent categories of counselor responsibilities or expertise before seeing a counselor. In doing so, they would have to sort out their problems as they see them. The interrelationship of personal, social, educational, and vocational factors can be confusing enough without the added decision of whom to see in a differentiated nest of counselors. Each student should feel that he can see a counselor whom he knows, whom he trusts, and whom he views as a primary resource. If necessary, the counselor can orchestrate the uses of additional resources. The paraprofessional can be one of the most significant, as his responsibilities back up the work of the counselor, and extend the guidance program.

OTHER POSITIONS IN PUPIL SERVICES

While some further discussion of counseling will be forthcoming in this chapter, it would be presently useful to look at other pupil services positions. These include the school psychologist, pupil personnel worker, and a school social worker. As the schools became more of a place for all children and less elite, the learning characteristics of children, particularly their limitations, became a growing concern. Someone was needed who had studied learning and mental conditions, who could evaluate in some standard way, and help teachers, principals, and parents come to decisions regarding placement of children. The psychologist first tended to be a clinical psychometrist but gradually emerged with particular trainings for school operations.

School Psychologists

Early expectations of school psychologists were centered around identification of exceptional children. Psychometric evaluations and interpretations became the stock in trade of the itinerant psychologist. Sometimes they were paid according to the number of tests given before they became regular members of school system staffs. The testing kit was the replication of the doctor's bag and just as often misunderstood. The kit provided for some standardized samplings of human behavior which could (and still does) furnish the disciplined examiner with evidences of mental functioning: psychomotor, intellectual, social, and emotional responses. Some teach-

181

ers and principals uncritically tended to assume the psychometric sessions were supposed to have healing powers. "The psychologist has worked with this child, and still there has been no appreciable change." One might as well assume that the stethoscope in the doctor's bag or even the more exhaustive medical laboratory tests are in themselves remedial.

Psychologists for some time have turned their work in schools toward a greater involvement in the learning processes, and a more gestalt-oriented interpretation of learners. Generally, there have been improved cumulative records, group testing, health histories, more insightful teacher observations, and better descriptions of learning and social behaviors. There is less need, albeit not elimination of, the testing kit, and more need for intelligent interpretation of the wealth of behavior samplings already gained through the ongoing learning experiences of children. Today the psychologist, while still predominantly evaluating children with learning problems or individual social-adaptive problems, is frequently contributing to curriculum development, human relations sessions, in-service training, and group counseling. The interaction of psychologist with students themselves, with teachers, counselors, pupil personnel workers, principals, and professional study groups, has expanded as the school system and the individual psychologist both learn to use competencies not previously anticipated. Training of school psychologists has altered significantly in the last decade, from clinical, psychometric functioning, to this greater involvement.

The school psychologist is trained to analyze and diagnose problems of school adjustment, behavior, learning, emotional development, and educational disability. Then, together with other people who work directly with children, and sometimes with children themselves, the psychologist develops strategies for solutions of these problems. The critical understandings and skills which the psychologist makes available to the total spectrum of educational concerns:

1. Relationships of principles of human growth and development to the processes of developing personal, social, and vocational adequacy.
2. Application of mental health concepts to educational programming; including psycho-educational diagnosis of educational and emotional disabilities.
3. Prescription of programs to ameliorate educational and emotional difficulties in the classroom.
4. Appraisal of the developmental status of children experiencing

severe educational problems (e.g., emotional, physical, perceptual, and intellectual deficits).

5. Communication of information derived from the science of psychology to educators and ancillary personnel.
6. Application of psychological interventions to the modification of behavior in the educational setting.
7. Expertise in the statistical theory, rationale, and implementation of individual and group assessment techniques.
8. Design and initiation of educational research as it pertains to psychological growth and development in an educational milieu.
9. Application of psychological information to staff development, parent education, and traineeships in school psychology.
10. Consultation to the administration in the provision of psychological knowledge to the complexities of contemporary educational management.

Needs Precede Services

Enlarging school systems, and particularly city systems, were running into all kinds of social problems in trying to get all the children of all the people into school through compulsory attendance laws. At first, enforcement was considered the answer. Truant officers went after them. These truant or attendance officers kept discovering situations with which they did not feel they alone could cope. Family relationships and family socio-economic problems could be seen that were so destructive to children that mere school attendance was hardly the issue. Survival itself could be the child's prime reality. So social workers were trained to give assistance to parents, to enable them to know what resources were available. Social workers come in different dimensions of training and with varying nomenclatures: visiting teachers, school social workers, pupil personnel workers. Therefore, regardless of differences of title, including such relatively new names as "child development specialist," the counselors, psychologists, and pupil personnel workers are the principal recognized functionaries with state certifications or licensing. There are also new positions which are below the graduate level in preparation, some even not requiring a bachelor's degree, known by many names, but all of them in support positions to one or more of the three professionals. Since the counselor is given more coverage later in this chapter, the others are presented further here.

Pupil Personnel Worker

In some states (e.g., Maryland) there is a position explicitly entitled "Pupil Personnel Worker" which is somewhat analogous to the

183

"School Social Worker" (Michigan). The counselor and the "PPW" in Maryland are trained with nearly identical graduate programs. The former has work in educational and occupational choices that balances the latter's work on field case studies. Basic behavioral science backgrounds are similar.

Duties and Responsibilities. The primary duty of the pupil personnel worker is to assure the best possible school program for every individual of school age and to accept the responsibility for determining and authorizing adjustments, programs, and placements to this end. When the regular public school system is unable to meet the needs of the child, the responsibility of the pupil personnel worker extends to decisions affecting out of school placement and for use of private or public resources to meet his educational needs. It shall be the responsibility of the pupil personnel worker to:

1. Be responsible for evaluating and, if appropriate, authorizing modifications or exceptions to the established administrative procedures when they are necessary for individual welfare.
2. Receive and evaluate referrals from school personnel, pupils, parents, public and private agencies and authorize appropriate programs consistent with acceptable procedures.
3. Evaluate referrals through observations, conferences, home visits, analysis of accumulative data and to utilize other school departments and community resources and agencies in determining appropriate direction and program.
4. Evaluate problems and causes of irregular school attendance.
5. Evaluate transfer requests and authorize them if appropriate.
6. Determine public school placement or offer appropriate alternatives for children released from institutions.
7. Review reports on suspensions and withdrawals and work with school administrators in alleviating the causes.
8. Evaluate requests for exclusion and make recommendations for action to the Area Supervisor.
9. Maintain a casework relationship with children who are having continuing problems of adjustment.
10. Counsel with and help develop out-of-school programs for children who have been withdrawn or excluded from school.
11. Coordinate services to effect an appropriate program for children with special needs.
12. Assist local school administration with articulation and orientation programs with particular emphasis on pupils with special needs.
13. Assist parents and agencies in nonpublic school placement of pupils.

184

14. Coordinate the case management process between school, board of education, juvenile court, health department, welfare, and other community agencies.
15. Interpret the services of public and private agencies to parents and the local school.
16. Make home visits in order to develop a cooperative home-school program and afford continuing parent counseling where necessary.
17. Consult with administrators, counselors, and teachers regarding the recognition of behavior and learning problems.
18. Serve as resource people as requested in the parent and teacher Child-Study programs.
19. Plan with school personnel and community agencies in organizing study groups and workshops pertaining to mental health and social behavior.

Similarities between these areas of responsibility and the following position guidelines for school social worker are evident.

School Social Worker

Duties and Responsibilities. The school social worker upon referral by pupil personnel, provides intensive casework service for a limited number of children who have social and emotional problems which seriously affect their ability to learn and adjust to the school program.

It is the responsibility of the social worker to:

1. Counsel with parents in helping them to understand and provide for the emotional and social needs of their children, particularly as they relate to the learning process.
2. Assist parents who are economically and socially deprived to better understand the public school system, including its opportunities and procedures and its demands for certain kinds of behavior.
3. Provide principals, teachers, and pupil personnel workers with information regarding the individual needs of children referred and suggest recommendations for meeting them.
4. Know and interpret to parents and school personnel the services of public and private agencies.
5. Serve as a resource person to faculties and parent-teacher associations in the areas of mental health and social adjustment.
6. Extend services to small groups of students or parents who need it.
7. Maintain an efficient system of case records and other activities.
8. Perform other duties as assigned.

185

Attendance Workers

There are many patterns of provisions for enforcing pupil attendance laws. The truant officer as such is an anachronism in today's school systems. Certain visiting teachers and pupil personnel workers are assigned the responsibility of enforcing attendance laws. Their energies tend to be directed more obviously toward causation and solution than punishment. They turn to an ultimate legal confrontation only if no other way has worked to bring about a pupil's attendance in school. There is a tendency toward ambiguity in relationship on the part of pupil personnel workers or similar people whose responsibilities include enforcing attendance and school placement. On the one hand, they understandably wish to be seen as friends and resources to the errant pupil and his family. It is a reasonable assumption that such concern and interest should generate a more positive regard for school-related persons who are trying to help one. Lurking behind this friendliness, however, is a realization on the part of the disguised attendance officer that "who doth not answer to the rudder shall answer to the rock." Skillfully handled, the enforced accountability can be as much evidence of sincerely caring as any kindness would be. The family involved actually can develop a higher self-regard and discover that they and their children are seen by the school as significant members of the community. Abandonment of children with poor attendance whenever it occurs may well be one of the most destructive omissions in pupil services practice, for the self-concepts of both the child and his family.

However, the essential functions of pupil personnel workers are to use all the resources at their command to have students in school or school-related programs. These resources include first of all their own understandings and skills, their caring, and their commitment. After these characteristics come familiarity with community agencies, court personnel, variations in school programs within the system, and whatever other knowledges and provisions that may be needed to assist students to have positive educational experiences and move toward responsible adulthood.

ISSUES IN PUPIL SERVICES

Issues have arisen with the development of multiple roles in school personnel services. Some of the expansion may have occurred as the result of the development of guidance counselor as a profession.

Counselors, with greater understanding through their own graduate study of the uses of behavioral science in learning and school situations, turned to psychologists for yet more resources. Some of them went on to becoming bona fide psychologists themselves. But more of them demanded more sophisticated interpretations and services from psychologists, thereby influencing the expansion of the school psychologist's role within the system. The visiting teacher, the school social worker, the pupil personnel worker, the school nurse, and educational diagnosticians developed areas of functioning. While all these services stimulated each other, they also created territoriality problems, and still do. Today there is a greater overlap than ever in what practitioners in these different positions profess to have as their own viable objectives in working with children and youth. Generalized, the objectives sound the same. Specific tasks and settings still vary somewhat, but all of them tend to include "counseling" as one of their tasks, including the school nurse. Yet specific training in counseling has not necessarily been a part of the graduate work of some of these practitioners. Counselors, counseling psychologists, psychiatric social workers, and pupil personnel workers are supposed to have critically supervised training in counseling techniques. Many people feel that, because they can create friendship, establish confidence, and carry on an intimate conversation, these skills constitute all that is necessary in counseling. Obviously, they are essential, but counseling goes much further, taking a client through a process of assessment and evaluation that is considerably more than a casual conversation. Counseling moves through discovery of options, consideration of values, establishing priorities, toward resolutions of problems and making decisions.

One of the issues then, is the yet-unsettled question of how many people get into the counseling process. At the same time that there is one movement toward more professionals in behavioral sciences getting into counseling, there is another movement toward getting teachers and student peers into caring relationships with more children and youth. Counselors certainly are not opposed to such relationships, which should be a part of any good school climate. They do, however, feel that there should be some understanding delicacy about calling these contacts the same as counseling. There is some sort of irony in an apparent assumption that anybody can counsel, but if a counselor does, he has to have graduate training and be certified by his state department of education to do so.

CLIMATE FOR CHANGE

The sum of the parts of social change and its impact upon education today suggest organizational evolution not yet perceived by many school officials. Authority is far from absolute today, if indeed it ever were for long. Having "authority" today increases vulnerability instead of security. The notion that a superintendent is the *head* of the school system, subject only to the blessings of his board of education, is dimmed by countless realities. Teachers have increased collective security to the extent that they raise serious questions about management and supervision without the potential threat that once may have made them more cautious. Students have worked for emancipation as bona fide citizens. They have pushed board members to adopt a series of policies which recognize their rights and encourage their involvement in planning and decision-making within the school, to an extent once not seriously considered. Repressive rules have been dropped or at least have been modified significantly. Students have pressed administrators and teachers into defensive postures when attempts to enforce codification of dress and hair styles have been made. School attendance is no longer viewed by some people as the critical criterion of student reliability it once was. Instead, work experience or productivity in independent study have made reliability an essential characteristic toward achieving the student's own objectives. It is more of a self-induced factor which, when it works, results in a more mature personality.

The changing times is illustrated by quoting a statement made ten years ago by Zeran and Riccio, which at that time was considered a harmless truism of education, and particularly guidance:

> Research has indicated that post-high-school aspirations and the problems of the reluctant learner and the drop-out are keyed directly to the attitudes of the community in which the boys and girls are growing.[5]

Today we know that the attitude of the parents in many communities is strongly favorable toward continuing education for their children. Whereas the high school and college drop-outs or step-outs are confounding their education-oriented parents with identity-before-goal behaviors.

People within the school system have viewed changes in relationships and educational methods as evidence that organizational patterns might also be modified. The line-and-staff concept, as function-

188

ing in most systems, leaves much to be desired in actual human experiences, and consequently in real efficiency.

The most frequent evidence of dissatisfaction in working relationships within larger school systems is the alienation, distrust, and defensiveness sometimes articulated within the local schools in reference to the perceived seat of power. "Central-office-itis" is a sort of emotional viral infection common to school systems (and other organizations), the severity of which is in direct proportion to the psychological distance felt between the individual in the local school and the superintendent and staff "up there" or "downtown," or wherever their offices may be. Communication in large systems is so much a problem that mutual regard and common belief in the rationality of colleagues are hard pressed, operational at best within the least threatened, most mature personalities. And even these personalities have constantly changing "barometric readings" according to the flow of events, and inroads on their territoriality.

Vulnerability of Counselors

Of all the pupil services, the position of counselor is most susceptible to distortion from its conceptual origins and objectives. The reasons are legion. The principal can perceive a counselor as two more hands and one more good head to get done many things which are important to him in running his school. Actual counseling time can get compressed into minuscule proportions of the total time a counselor puts into this "multijob." In the aftermath of the 1970 White House Conference on Children and Youth, Eckerson stated:

The roles of counselors may soon bury them. Even now, counselors may be sinking into a coma, soon to be followed by death. The coroner's report may succinctly state the case: strict adherence to traditional roles and functions. A diagnosis of the disease that is infecting guidance in general reveals many contributing factors: faith in the objectivity of test results and grades; limitation to the one-to-one relationship in counseling; preoccupation with techniques; observance of outmoded certification requirements; disregard of nonacademic talents; overinvolvement with college-bound students; and inability to comprehend and deal with the dynamics of the social revolution that is shaping diverse cultures within the country. If standardization leads to the obsolescence of guidance, a new profession will surely emerge to fill an obvious void. Human development specialists may fall heir to a new role designed to humanize learning and living for all people. Whether or not counselors will move into the role will depend upon

189

their ability to adopt new ideas now being advanced in the literature of guidance and other behavioral and social sciences.[6]

Thus, the call for change. Yet the school has fastened the counselor into certain inexorable tasks often that nobody else wishes to do. These tasks sometimes might have enough affinity to decision making on educational programs so that the counselor's involvement is rationalized much of the time and real the rest of the time.

Feingold addressed the need to make better use of personnel:

> Most counselors now recognize the need for utilizing nonprofessional and support personnel for carrying out clerical and other routine activities. This will accelerate in the decades ahead, enabling professional workers to maximize the utilization of their professional skills and training. A recommended ratio of one professional to three counseling aides may well emerge.[7]

The litmus test of guidance responsibilities is seldom given by administrators alone, without the urging of supervisory personnel: "If something has to be done to run the school, *even if there were no guidance services*, then it is not a guidance function." That test would throw out much of the record-keeping, report card processing, research information retrieving, group testing, scheduling and rescheduling which impedes real counseling activities. It is possible that the busiest counselors could be some of the least productive in terms of the objectives of helping students in their own rational self-management and making appropriate decisions. A curious observation, however, has been that some of the most effective counselors, who really counsel, tend to have the least administrative expectations for doing other things. Principals do not intentionally stand in the way of counselor relationships that are obviously of benefit to children and youth. Autonomy is a function of competence for counselors and all others who have to use judgment often and well. Constant, effective work is seldom blocked.

The counselor's publics are people with whom he has contacts. They include students, teachers, parents, administrators, other pupil services workers, and corrective agency personnel. A counselor will have over five thousand meaningful contacts with others in his publics each year. Most of his responsibility during these contacts has something to do with understanding and interpreting the student, his learning characteristics, his options, his decisions, and the outcomes of such decisions. It is not difficult to see that when one person

190

contacts the counselor, there is a *want* instigating the contact. Maybe the *want* is a true expression of *need;* maybe it is not the need at all. Maybe it is in conflict with another person, who also contacts the counselor and expresses another *want.* At this juncture of cross-purposes, the counselor is at his greatest level of vulnerability. He simply cannot please everybody, or be all things to all people. Yet his publics can press him, often in their personal or familial frustrations, to try to be so. Then they become critical if he does not alleviate their own disequilibrium. (It is noted in passing that counselor training programs seldom provide for practice in working with adults—the teachers and parents of students.)

Fortunately, out of the some five thousand contacts per year, the well-trained counselor is generally effective in being somewhere between an adequate to outstanding resource. To see the real "pros" in action, is to behold some of the finest artists in human relations operating in contemporary society. Their daily orchestration of counseling, consulting, and coordinating draws constantly upon skills and understandings of incredible scope. Yet where do these masters in human engineering stand in the prestige hierarchy of a school system? According to one study, they are eighth, behind the high school department chairman, the school psychologist, elementary school principal, director of guidance, supervisor of instruction, high school principal, and superintendent.[8] They are ahead of the high school teacher, elementary school teacher, school social worker, librarian, nurse, and head custodian.

Cook reminds us,

> One of the things we are discovering in this age of historical crises is that professionalism alone is not the answer to all our needs. Responsible human beings who are willing to take risks on behalf of others is what is finally needed, which means that we have to remain aware of our freedom *not* to be a professional.[9]

Lately the students and parents appear to be the prime movers in attempting to extricate the counselors from the deadlines of paperwork and into more accessibility. They are looking for teachers and counselors both who can "read" and respond to youth in a culture shock setting, and in whom youth can have trust. The "humane school" is a plea from the youth. The suburban affluent family with its values for achievement has pressed upon the children themselves and the schools they attend. The "hippie" and the drug "freak" are

191

to a great extent the reactions to the pressures of affluence in the midst of a world which is making slow progress at best in a caring social awareness with practical, constructive commitment to people with needs.

Main street has gone. The schools and the shopping centers somehow seem similar, both of them offering endless choices but lacking something in human contacts unless it can be engineered deliberately into the use of space and movement of people toward each other in a common humanity. Older thinkers and young people who read their writings are again in the forefront of creating acceptance of differences between people with divergent cultural backgrounds and values. Suddenly with integrated schools and a jet world, man has to acknowledge, appreciate, and explore differences, rather than be apprehensive about them. Now youths seem to sense that if they are to have the opportunity to expand their universe of human relationships, it has to start in small units: the home, the neighborhood, and the classroom. Or there may well be no future to experience. Groups of youth in discussing the future eventually express this awareness, not necessarily with morbidity, but as a fact of life—or of annihilation. Somehow the school must be geared to both *relevant competencies* and *identity development* in ways that enable students to face the future with confidence.

PROJECTIONS IN STAFF ROLES AND RELATIONSHIPS

In the setting described above, the challenge of change demands recognition of the potential for improving the climate for learning. Few school administrators have seriously employed a philosophical model for thinking why organization is the way they have inherited it, or made it. Organization, it has been seen, is based upon an assumption of authority and responsibility that goes in a direct line from the superintendent down to all others in a school system. The hierarchy model dominates. Even in the staff side of the line-and-staff organization, there are "pecking orders" of positions and disciplines. Thus, a psychologist is seen to have greater status than counselor, school social worker or pupil personnel worker, perhaps even if they were all to be roughly on the same salary basis.

Trends in organizational patterns will be slow to appear, because of the mind sets of present administrators. However, the social forces which have been apparent since the 1950s are already making inroads on the thinking of some educators who are curious enough to study their effects. Suddenly one is reminded of the Prophet's words on children, ". . . You may strive to be like them, but seek not to make them like you. For life goes not backward nor tarries with yesterday . . ."[10] We are in an age in which older people are following examples of youth to an unprecedented extent. Witness styles of dress, hair, and political thought. School boards, once actually remote from the children for whose education they provide, are listening in open meetings to petitions for more humane education, more involvement, greater flexibility of course requirements, students' rights, and students' evaluations of teachers and administrators.

Open school programs, innovations in facilities and schedules, and other modification at the school level between the students and teachers cannot be expected to thrive and continue to change under an umbrella of archaic hierarchy above the local school. The students have gone directly to the board of education to make change happen. The local school has already modified many previous expectations and relationships in response to the students. In few cases have the results been disastrous, regardless of predictions of shocked elders. It may be that where things did not work out well either the principal and dominant members of the faculty were hostile to change, or they went along to "keep the natives quiet," without intelligent and responsible commitment on the part of both students and faculty. Between the local school and the board of education is a matrix of established organization which has grown, been reorganized, grown some more, been reorganized again, sometimes with little more logic than the propitiations of power figures; often under the guise of consultant studies.

The Identity Culture

One has to comprehend what really is happening in society to project change in staff roles and relationships in school systems or other institutions. Glasser postulates that we are in the midst of a movement which started in the 1950s and is likely to change just about everything:

> Recently something new has happened, that is the struggle for a goal —a profession, a diploma, a home, a family—has been superseded by the struggle to find oneself as a human being, to become aware of and enjoy the pleasures implicit in our own humanity. Unlike goals, which vary widely, role, or as I prefer to call it, identity, is about the same for all people: everyone aspires to a happy, successful, pleasurable belief

in himself. Role, or identity, is now so important that it must be achieved before we set out to find a goal. We can no longer afford to ignore this new priority in human motivation. Institutions that ignore the new motivational sequence—role before goal—will fail. An example is our schools which continue to be goal-directed and unresponsive to role needs even though few students are willing to work toward school goals before gaining self-recognition. As a result, our schools are burdened with failing students.[11]

And again, Glasser points out:

> The need for role to precede goal must be new or we would never have evolved our present institutions, all of which serve goal-directed functions. We have all changed toward role precedence more than we realize; the young more than the old, but everyone to some extent. Unless we can understand a great deal about this change, we will be unable to solve the social problems that it is producing.[12]

A potential fallacy of the "Career Education" program, for example, being emphasized by the U.S. Office of Education, could lie in an assumption of goal-before-role, which Glasser contends is fast becoming an anachronism. The survival society is being superseded by the identity society, with *role* dominant in the guidance of youth. The question is: Will the school board members, administrators, and staff people working with the program understand the identity society and interpret the thrust of education in light of the trend? The temptation to opt for hardware, early decisions, and hard-core skill programs regardless of the identity problems of youth may drown the efforts in a simplistic orientation to life. Identity formation can be a slow process. Interim learnings should allow for exploration without premature commitments.

Effecting Changes in Staff Relationships

The kind of school and the sorts of relationships within that school and with the community in a free society, an identity-oriented society, are in for some retooling. That is, unless we are to assume that we are actually educating children for a controlled, goal-oriented society which is to serve the state. Therefore, a consideration of change in staff roles and relationships begins nearest to the students, hopefully extending throughout the system with some consistency. These factors are relevant:

1. The colleague relationship between teacher and student should be the dominant relationship. Teachers and students, after all,

are engaged together in an enterprise with objectives of increasing both general and specific adequacies of children and youth through education. They are *colleagues* in the learning process, not masters and slaves. While the accent is upon the learning experiences of the students, certainly the teachers' involvements with the students during the process provide the opportunities for stimulating colleague relationships, psychological identifications, and transference relationships, all developmental contributions to maturing students. The dynamics, furthermore, are mutually beneficial, with the students and the teachers both growing in skills of communication, cooperative endeavors, and increments of satisfaction. The identity role is strengthened in the colleague climate because there tends to be greater respect for the individual and support for his self-awareness.

2. *Extending the colleague climate* to the present hierarchy of school systems would humanize the system and facilitate planning and processing. Small systems may be saved by their size, with a great amount of give-and-take on a colleague basis between everybody who desires to participate. Larger systems, however, find administrators and specialists talking about how to make something work more frequently than unhurriedly considering why they should, or what the effect upon learning and growing may be. The "big decisions" are too often made behind executive doors, the specialists having to accommodate themselves and their program to predetermined conditions without prior input. The rule of thumb should be, "Colleague over hierarchy until somebody has to make a decision, *and* be accountable for that decision."

3. *Consensus on objectives* and identification of desired outcomes bring administrators and staff specialists together. Their concerns become mutual in how to plan and program for appropriate use of human and material resources toward meeting the objectives. Consensus on objectives requires input from the experiences of students and faculties, administrators *and* supervisory staff, who are the "quality control" guardians of services. Cultural and economic changes that affect students and, in turn, the school program are not always easily discerned. Even when they are identified, there is no automatic consensus regarding relative significance of social phenomena or what should be done about such changes. A social studies council of teachers, students, parents, and whatever specialists or expert consultants might be

195

available could help the system "read" the changing times. Consensus is often impossible because people's perspectives are at variance. Consensus is sometimes the victim of expediency. Consensus has to be foregone if there is a justifiable urgency in decision and action. In general, however, the identification of desired outcomes and the commitment of involved people toward such outcomes are essential components of the educational enterprise.

4. *Facilitating* roles of administrators and supervisors should supersede *authority* roles. The professional competencies in guidance or other pupil services are enhanced by supportive action to desirable programs.

Policies to Reorganize Roles

Many school systems support guidance programs without having adopted and occasionally reviewed an official policy of the board of education which clearly states objectives and directs the ways in which programs are to be facilitated. The vulnerability of some pupil services programs in times of economic stress for the school system is often in direct relation to the degrees of being understood and being effective. One school system, wrestling with roles and relationships as they affect the guidance program, recently had a cooperative committee of counselors, teachers, supervisors, and administrators evolve a policy statement through study sessions over several months. An ad hoc committee of the board of education then met with counselors and supervisory personnel to analyze what the larger committee had done, and to modify the policy statement. The statement addressed purposes, basic rationale, accountability, responsibilities of counselors, teachers, administrators, supervisors, and guidance advisory committees. In this school system there had been counselors since 1934. Thirty-nine years passed before the board of education adopted a policy formally stating the goals of guidance services.[13] These goals were stated as follows:

The Board of Education supports a strong program of counseling and of guidance services because of the benefits it can provide to students, parents, and faculty. The program must be staffed with persons highly skilled in counseling on personal, social, educational, and career matters. These individuals must be supported by personnel and strategies for providing a full array of guidance services. The proposed program shall have the following objectives:
1. The students should become increasingly proficient in analyzing

196

his learning patterns, identifying and developing his potential, and planning his educational experiences.

2. The student should know that there is within the school community an adult who, upon request, will act as his advocate in any reasonable cause.
3. The student should have access to a counselor of his choice or any other member of the school staff to discuss personal and social concerns, with confidentiality respected.
4. The student should be encouraged to utilize counseling services for assistance with personal and social problems which have an effect on learning, motivation, and personal development.
5. The student should be helped to understand his abilities, interests, and values as factors in making educational choices and to use logical processes to his decision making.
6. The student should have increased self-awareness and a positive sense of identity.
7. The student who needs special attention should be identified and should be provided with modifications to the regular curriculum or program alternatives, to motivate him and make his school years productive.
8. The student should have increased awareness of the world of work and of the options open to him for employment or future education.

Perhaps more significant for organizational purposes were the provisions for implementation of certain strategies stated in the policy. The implementations relieve principals from positions of sole arbiters in determining all the facets of the guidance services in the schools. A committee of counselors prescribes the advocacy role and its utility within the school setting. An advisory committee including students, parents, counselors, and administrators will propose selection, training, and evaluation procedures. A third group will work on new position guidelines or job descriptions for counselors. This group will include the superintendent or his designee, working with counselors and supervisory staff. Each school shall have an advisory committee for guidance which shall make a report to the principal, with recommendations regarding changes which should more nearly insure that the objectives of the services are being met. The board of education is departing from the concept that each school principal is responsible for everything that goes on in his school and, therefore, should determine, in this instance, how counselors are utilized. Committees and study groups, including representatives of all parties affected by the existence of guidance services, should be able to contribute significantly to understandings and objectives.

197

Ideally a whole school faculty is responsible and accountable regarding the educational experiences of youth as provided within the schools. Certainly the counselors are the prime group to be accountable for the guidance services. However, each principal is expected to broaden involvement in planning, execution, and assessment of guidance services to include not only the staff but the students and parents who are clients of the services. Such involvement increases the total sensitivity of the school to the objectives of the guidance program, and should tend to keep the services relevant to the needs of youth. Clearly, the principal's role of facilitator in a colleague climate is more pronounced than his traditional role of ultimate authority within a school which, after all, is no more "his" than everyone else's.

THE STUDENT IN THE PROCESS

In the illustration of relationships, using guidance as the example, the guidance responsibilities of counselors, teachers, administrators, and supervisory staff have been given. Students are not just objects of services. If they were it would be like putting clothes on a mannequin. They may be beautiful clothes, but the mannequin cannot respond to them. The identity-seeking youth is very much alive, experiencing, responding, and making choices. His quest for greater involvement in determination of things which he is going to experience, educationally and otherwise, should be respected as much in pupil services as in the classroom. The objective of guidance and other pupil services, succinctly stated, is that students move toward rational self-management. Training for self-management comes through involvement in decisions, plans, and actions which affect the student in some way. Classroom teachers have increasingly found ways to bring students into partnership relationships for a new learning climate. Guidance in particular, of all pupil services, should do the same, inasmuch as guidance services touch all students in one or many ways during each school year.

Students should not only be involved they should be seen as valuable resources for counselors and teachers. They obviously are most aware of student opinions, dissents, and enthusiasms. They are best able to discern what is happening to other students. They can open the way for some students who are hesitant to turn to guidance

198

services. Their ideas and innovations are often sound and relevant to the needs of others. Their awareness of each other's human conditions establishes an authenticity to their views. Student representatives are essential members on a school guidance advisory committee. Their full membership makes it more evident that the adult members including counselors, teachers, and parents as well, recognize their identity and respect their contributions. Working *with* students is significant as opposed to working *for* students. In this way, their self-management is enhanced.

SUMMARY

Tracing the development of school system organizations, we have seen that small, modal, and large systems have both similar and unique dynamics operating in them. The line-and-staff concept is still dominant, but it is possible that social changes will alter the effectiveness of line-and-staff and bring about something else. Pupil services in large systems are particularly vulnerable to administrative controls, which neutralize their advocacy roles. Supervisory staff can effect change and improve services through their involvement with counselors and other pupil services personnel in selection, in-service support, evaluation and assessment. Administrators and supervisory staff must share unequivocally the accountability for provisions of services, the limitations placed upon services, and the reporting of accomplishments and needs of the services and personnel. Roles and relationships were analyzed, particularly with the illustration of the school-based counselor and significant others in the guidance program.

Large systems and static school programs are serious hazards to the relevance of learning for the children of the times. The large systems, in particular, tend to dilute the effectiveness of pupil services. Suggested remedies first stressed the colleague relationships totally within the educational enterprise, from superintendent to student, and mostly between the student and the teacher. Hierarchy is acidifying the enthusiasm and innovative efforts of many people in school systems, as communications move through a bureaucratic digestive tract. When large systems attempt to organize into smaller units more responsive to area communities, too many decisions still are guarded jealously at the top, nullifying much of the proposed gain. Executive staffs cling to the power posture, rather than that of existing to facilitate the educational experiences of youth, as guided by professional and support personnel who are in daily contact with students.

Another remedy to renew the vitality of guidance and other pupil services is to bring students and parents into working advisory committees, along with teachers and counselors. Out of the insights and understandings of these people should come valid directions for guidance services and greater appreciation of the work of counselors and others in providing such services. Perhaps the realistic provisions for accountability of principals and supervisory staff in selection and evaluation of personnel, and support of a viable program in each school are the final steps that bring services more in line with a change of culture and student needs in the next decade.

1. Raymond N. Hatch and Buford Stefflre, *Administration of Guidance Services* (Englewood Cliffs, N.J.: Prentice-Hall, Inc., 2nd ed., © 1965), p. 87. Reprinted by permission of Prentice-Hall, Inc.
2. Harold Spears, *Improving the Supervision of Instruction* (Englewood Cliffs, N.J.: Prentice-Hall, Inc., © 1953), quoted from Fifty-sixth Report of the Board of Education (St. Louis, 1910), p. 26. Reprinted by permission of Prentice-Hall Inc.
3. Eli Ginsberg, *Counseling and Guidance in the Schools* (New York: McGraw-Hill, 1971), pp. 213-34.
4. Darrell H. Hart and Donald J. Prince, "Role Conflict for School Counselors: Training Versus Job Demand," *The Personnel and Guidance Journal*, Jan. 1970, pp. 374-79.
5. Franklin R. Zeran and Anthony C. Riccio, *Organization and Administration of Guidance Services* (Chicago: Rand McNally & Co., 1962), p. 202.
6. Louise O. Eckerson, "The White House Conference: Tips or Taps for Counselors," *The Personnel and Guidance Journal*, Nov. 1971.
7. S. Norman Feingold, *A Counselor's Handbook* (Cranston, R.I.: Carroll Press, 1972), p. 117. Reprinted by permission of Carroll Press.
8. C. Winfield Scott and Mary Monroe Cherlain, "Occupational Status of the High School Counselor," *Vocational Guidance Quarterly*, Sept. 1971.
9. David R. Cook, *Guidance for Education in Revolution* (Boston: Allyn and Bacon, 1971), p. 554.
10. Kahlil Gibran, *The Prophet* (New York: Alfred A. Knopf, 1964).
11. William Glasser, *The Identity Society* (New York: Harper & Row, 1971), p. 8.
12. Ibid., p. 9.
13. Policy Statement on Guidance Services, Montgomery County Public Schools, Rockville, Md., 1973.

CHAPTER 6

Role of the Instructional Staff

JANE A. BONNELL

EMPHASES in the role of the school in educating the child have multiplied with time. The first widely accepted emphasis was on "skills," which was fitted to an era when initial literacy was a prime demand. A second widely accepted emphasis was that of passing on the cultural heritage, thus stressing the need for a civilizing and socially unifying role of the school.

Today many educational emphases are identified. Among them is personal growth, an emphasis fitted to an era in which students use education for scrutinizing and bringing things into order and meaning—meaning for them. This emphasis necessitates contact with individual students in environments where children are taught in ways that facilitate them and their development.

The guidance commitment to the preservation of the dignity and individuality of students parallels the current emphasis. Thus, the teacher who facilitates the learning of the child or student plays an important part in furthering the purposes of guidance work. Giving emphasis to the guidance role of the teacher recognizes: (1) that the teacher spends more time with the child than any other professional, (2) that the relationship existing between the teacher and the student is critical, and (3) that the classroom is the only place where certain kinds of guidance processes occur.

CLASSROOMS OF TODAY'S SCHOOLS

As adult roles in the schools and classrooms of today become more diverse, student exposure to adult attention differs. Opportunity for a variety and depth of relationships grows for each student, as does opportunity for effective guidance of each pupil. It is critical that planning be done for the guidance processes which can go on in the classroom.

The following descriptions of classrooms in various schools illustrate the settings in which boys and girls and adults have opportunity to experience critical relationships.

The Open-Space School

This type of innovative school emphasizes team teaching and continuous progress; it also features open-space construction. The first two, continuous progress and team teaching, are educational aspects which facilitate individualized instruction. The third, open-space construction, is a utilization of space to promote and facilitate learning and instruction.

Team teaching requires that pupils be grouped and regrouped for learning. Placement in groups is subject to change, depending upon pupil progress in each area of school work. The teacher team plans and directs the education of the pupils assigned to each group.

Continuous progress is a plan of school organization in which children progress at their own rate. Learning is continuous based upon attainment of objectives.

Open-space construction creates large classrooms of one hundred to one hundred and fifty children and four or five adults. Areas of instruction are separated by a core of space which provides for a learning materials center. Adjacent space is available for physical education. Teacher planning centers adjoin each classroom.

The House High School

Each "house" has its own student body, its own teaching staff, its own counselors and principal. There are no classrooms, as such, in the "house"; but, there is a place for everything that is usually done in a classroom. Lecture, recitation, and individual study are placed in areas designed for these activities.

Each "house" contains a large group room, a number of seminar rooms, some small group study rooms, and plenty of space to study independently. In addition, there is a library or resource center on every floor with study materials in immediate reach of both the teacher and the student. A planning center is located in the resource area so that students may obtain the teacher's help frequently and easily.

HOW CHANGES AFFECT THE TEACHER'S GUIDANCE TASK

Teachers cannot remain static. Trying new books, new programs, and finding new approaches are changes being demanded. The climate of experimentation is generating alternative curricular offerings. As teacher roles change, teacher emotions, needs, and attitudes change also. The teen-age expression, "let them all hang out," referring to exposing old feelings and attitudes as a prelude to taking on new ones, is cognizant of the challenge to old and static ways.

Exerpts from newsletters published by various schools illustrate ways in which changes are being initiated in school programs.

What Is A.I.S.?

At least forty students can answer that question, but they may do so in forty different ways. A.I.S. (Advanced Independent Study) is a new educational program designed to fit each student in a highly individualized way.

The program is as varied as the interests of the students themselves. Classes of study may range from research in mythology to actually building and learning to play the guitar. One student intends to get her credit in a government course by serving as a congressional page; another plans to undertake a study in the culture of the American Indian.

Experimental Resource Rooms in Elementary Schools

Each resource room has a classroom program specifically designed to meet the individual needs of children through the use of specially trained teachers and aides. Using materials and equipment not usually available in the regular classroom, teachers provide special help to youngsters with learning disabilities or school adjustment problems. The resource rooms also provide services to talented students who can profit from an individualized enrichment program in basic academic areas.

Teachers need to look for sensibility and feeling in their pupils as well as abilities to perform intellectual tasks. Pupils' efforts to understand themselves and the things around them demand no less.

Teachers are under great pressure to teach the basic skills, skills of thinking and learning as well as those skills necessary for a job. Chil-

204

dren must become literate thinking people who can sustain themselves in adult work. Teachers teach the basic skills. But beyond these skills are factors that affect the thinking process—emotions, needs, attitudes, and habits—those factors termed by David H. Russell, in *Children's Thinking*, the "motives of thinking". A "Schema for Thinking" is provided by Lee Bennett Hopkins in *Let Them Be Themselves*.[1]

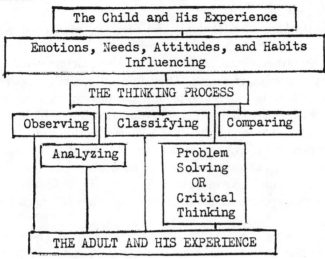

Fig. 6.1. Schema for thinking.

Learning about "motives," so integral a part of The Child and His Experience and so much a part of The Adult and His Experience, is a recognized and legitimate learner activity. The teacher plays a critical role in teaching about these things. The time spent in the classroom with students, the relationships developed there, play a vital role in the adaptation of children to learning, to each other and later, to the world of work. Guidance is concerned with the learning, with the personal development, the social relationships and the emotional adaptations of children in school.

Curriculums developed either nationally or by the classroom teacher vary considerably in the extent to which they foster or permit teachers to practice guidance in the classroom and school. Curriculums also vary considerably in their approaches to teaching, learning and guiding pupils. Joyce, Weil, and Wald[2] have organized curricular approaches into four families which represent different orientations toward man and his universe, toward the teaching-guiding task. The four are: (1) those oriented toward social relations and

205

toward the relation between man and his culture, and which draw upon social sources, (2) those which depend on information-processing systems and descriptions of human capacity for processing information, (3) those which emphasize personality development, the processes of personal construction of reality, and the capacity to function as an integrated personality as the major source, (4) those developed from an analysis of the processes by which human behavior is shaped and reinforced.

These authors, like Hopkins, find teaching concerned with the context within which the teacher studies and teaches about motives; i.e., the emotions, needs, attitudes, and habits, factors that affect the thinking processes of pupils. They find all teaching models concerned with social relationships and the development of an integrated personality. Their discussion of models of teaching and their mastery by teachers suggests that a large repertoire of approaches may be present in any one teacher or any one staff. Teachers who define their own situations and know their own approaches can explore channels and have more time for individual children, for establishing needed relationships, and for pursuing needed guidance practices.

Role of the Instructional Staff in Contributing to the Guidance Program

The awareness that students seek to find personal significance in successful learning experiences of all kinds in school is a compelling force in teaching today. Changes in the way the learning process is viewed are resulting in changes in the atmosphere of the total school experience. Teachers and administrators are both "curriculum committed" and "student committed." Teachers' attempts to incorporate into the teaching task the ideas of Skinner, Glasser, and others have brought more specification of the learning process and definition of the teaching task. Objectives that assess students' entering abilities have been developed in most subject matter areas. Evaluation of these objectives has related teaching activity specifically to the learning needs of students. Teachers who set sequential learning tasks are fostering "independent learners," students who are aware of their "content needs," who participate in setting their own objectives, and who use assessment as a measure of progress toward mastery. Mastery, in its turn, is stated, known, and measureable.

Strategies to teach factors which affect the thinking process—i.e., emotions, needs, and habits—like the content strategies, are based upon the cognitive, social-emotional, relationship needs of the learner. Attempts to teach these "hidden curricula" are helping to elaborate the guidance work of the teacher, giving it new meaning and focus. In the words of Dinkmeyer and Caldwell:

> It is the conviction of the authors that any realistic examination of the role of counseling and guidance in the school, viewed in terms of the totality of the educational experience, must be built upon a comprehensive, research oriented, functional approach to the developmental needs of today's children and youth. This premise would necessitate projecting a program that would begin at the elementary school level. Such a basic approach, employing principles that apply to all educational levels, could also provide a basis for the implementation and adaptation of other additional programs in a more unified, consistent pattern.[3]

Just as the new strategies of teaching for content and emotional growth are being linked to stated objectives and, hence, are altering the teacher's role in the classroom and creating a new atmosphere for learning, the traditional guidance roles of the teacher are being restated in more operational terms. Particularly in city schools, adult supporting roles have proliferated, so that teachers are coordinating the instructional and guidance work of specialists, paraprofessionals, students-in-training, volunteers and parents. This activity is changing the uses of the traditional personnel services, the psychological, social work, health, and guidance services. At the same time, teachers are working with the psychologist, social worker, nurse, and counselor to establish good referral practices, to develop meaningful student records, and to identify special needs, talents, and deficiencies. They are consulting about many areas of instructional and guidance work including those of concern to other professionals within and without the school; some of the work involves the home, agencies, and parents.

Much of what teachers do in relation to those who perform the major personnel service functions are indirect services. Educating and guiding students in academic planning, vocational choice, in matters of self-worth and self-discipline and personal adjustment, require skills teachers and workers seek to acquire because they are essential to their discipline and professional competence. The "human relations" curricula of the schools whether direct activities with competency based procedures or objectives and responsibilities in the role definitions of the professional staff, demand the skills of: (1)

207

talking—oral and pictorial; (2) listening—observing and record keeping; (3) acting and interacting—sociometrics, role-playing, and group work; (4) consulting—with school personnel, auxiliary personnel, and parents; (5) identifying needs; (6) meeting needs.

A brief presentation of each of these skills indicates the potential of each for use by teachers in contributing to the guidance program. Their use by personnel workers in the school setting is regarded as essential if the goals of the work are to be assured.

Following the discussion of the skills, accounts of the work of teachers and personnel staff workers are presented. In these accounts, new roles for educators emerge, and the work of guidance in the schools assumes new significance.

THE TEACHING-LEARNING PSYCHO-SOCIAL SKILLS

It is recognized that the skills discussed here are not presented in completeness or necessarily in the aspects specifically used by teachers in contributing to the guidance program or by counselors in the school setting. The competency required of each category of worker is peculiar in some respects and in some degree to his role, function, and situation, as well as to his personal orientation.

Talking—Oral and Pictorial. Talking with students is a consciously developed skill of the educator, teacher, and personnel worker. It is a highly personal activity, one often related to a situation or event. To participate orally in an effective way in conferences, interviews, therapy, in guiding decision making, teachers and counselors need to know a variety of techniques. Dinkmeyer and Caldwell discuss "Tell Me," "Contact," and "Silence" techniques in talking. They focus on the elementary school in their discussions of a "mirroring" approach and "probing" and "questioning" responses. Pictorial techniques are projective approaches using pictures, drawings, and color and shape stimuli. Cues for understanding pupils can be taken from these sources and can be used to help students make decisions about matters relevant to them.

The talking-discussing which goes on in the classroom or school may itself serve as therapy. Teachers and counselors who help students know their value systems and draw conclusions about the various forms of their own behavior are doing this through talking.

Listening—Observing and Record Keeping. Elaboration of these skills has been a concern of counselor and teacher training. For counselors, these skills have been operationally defined and taught

208

as interview techniques. In the classroom, teachers are currently teaching listening skills as strategies of cognitive growth in math, science, reading, and language arts. Task oriented group work, as well as sensitivity and confrontation group approaches to learning, have a goal of improving, expanding, and using these abilities to the fullest. Listening closely to what students say helps teachers and counselors know feelings and sense underlying attitudes.

Acting and Interacting—Sociometrics, Role-playing, and Group Work. Studies of individuals in groups and of group responses through psychodrama, field force study, group dynamics, role-playing, T-groups, encounter experiences, sensitivity training, and behavior-shaping strategies have contributed insights useful to educators and counselors. Those who have acquired knowledge of these approaches can act and interact using their insights to pursue needed guidance practices. Increasing the kinds of adult roles in schools is also increasing the range of activity and ways of acting; adults who work in school classrooms act and interact in an increasing variety of patterns. The opportunity for students to experience new ways of interacting and reacting has grown. In addition, the development and use of behaviorally stated objectives, use of the concepts of learning modules and mastery tests, and of contingency management techniques have contributed to the focus, definition, and explicitness of the teaching-guiding-learning interaction.

Consulting—School Personnel, Auxiliary Personnel, and Parents. The consulting role of teachers and counselors is based upon understandings and observations they have of the overt and covert systems of the school, their knowledges of the complex norms, processes, and social patterns which shape and direct the energies of students and staff. They need to understand relationships in the system as well as organizational features. When they achieve clear, mutual objectives and establish joint priorities, communication is likely to be freer and less obstructed. Through consultation, their goals are shaped and reached because they introduce better information, use creativity and expertise. Consulting demands that they scrutinize a variety of elements in each situation, as well as the procedures which go on. They must interchange ideas and reactions in order to foster goal setting, decision making, and actions to achieve purposes.

Identifying Needs. Needs assessment of cognitive and affective elements for individuals and groups precedes effective intervention. To do this, teachers and counselors need human relations skills, training in developing educational diagnoses and alternatives, and techniques to evaluate responses. Collection of information for affective needs study is a systematic, programmed procedure. This particularized data must be related, made meaningful, and reported well to be useful in guiding youth in their decision making.

Meeting Needs. Cognitive curricular programs along with psychological and vocational curricular programs are needed by "curriculum-committed," "student-committed" teachers and counselors. Providing all of these is a recognized task of educators. To know these channels, to explore them in pursuit of adequate education for children is the goal of those who seek to educate. To meet these comprehensive needs, educators are working toward adequate curricula based on research and conceptual frameworks.

What are the ways in which pupil personnel specialists function with the classroom teacher?

What do today's teachers do which contributes to the guidance work in the schools? What activities of teachers are guiding pupils in significant new ways?

THE TEACHER AND THE COUNSELOR

The counselor in school seeks to further the goal of the preservation of the dignity and individuality of each student. He strives to shape the educational system so that it responds more humanely to all individuals. Counselors focus on the efforts of students to get along in the school and, less directly, in the community. While recognizing the conservative nature of the school, counselors try to reflect the movement of the times toward change and to introduce modification into the institution of the school. In order to help to create alternatives and practices to fit new values, new realities and new insights, counselors ascribe to the generally accepted goals of psychological education: (1) to promote the humane psycho-social aims of education; (2) to teach processes which are useful to students in reaching the goals they choose; (3) to increase positive mental health; and (4) to foster normative development.[4]

Students need the guidance of teachers and counselors in relation to the number of personal decisions they must make. Involvement with drugs, teen-age pregnancy, venereal disease, truancy, and family problems are on the increase. Teachers in contact with students about their cognitive and affective learnings must study student decisions and attitudes and values. They talk with counselors who, in turn, talk with students in order to add insights to those of the teachers. In this way, teachers contribute indirectly to the counseling work. Teachers make direct referral of students to counselors for: (1) confirmation (of teacher knowledges) and assistance in planning, (2) further intensive study of problems, (3) crisis attention, (4) support and encouragement, (5) self study, (6) relationship concerns and activity. Teachers' observations, notes on behavior, and experiences with students are indirect helps which contribute to the work of counselors with students.

Curricular programs in skills and occupational training centers and in innovative educational arrangements have multiplied. Teachers in these specialized areas acquaint counselors with their program requirements and opportunities so that counselors can serve students more effectively. Teachers facilitate counselors' having accurate program data.

A teacher who participates in a survey of needs such as the following is helping to determine the focus of the counselor service and is a direct and indirect influence on the functions of the counselor in the school.

An Elementary School Need Survey was conducted to assess the extent to which elementary teachers felt they were receiving the assistance they felt they required for maximizing their effectiveness as teachers. A list of functions and services (admittedly incomplete) was used and teachers were asked to estimate the importance of each service on a five-point scale of "essential" to "don't want it." The extent to which each function and service was being provided was rated on a four-point scale "very adequate" to "no service at all." In addition, the position of the person who most often provided the service mentioned was to be indicated using nine categories: principal, assistant principal, other teacher, counselor, psychologist, supervising teacher, social worker, nurse, and (other). Forty-six items were presented. The purposes of the survey were presented to teachers: (1) helping to reveal the need for the program; (2) indicating the extent the need has been fulfilled as a result of the presence of elementary counselors; and (3) indicating future directions for future counselor role and function. The survey was carried out in a number of elementary schools, some where there were counselors and some where there were none.

A relevant summary statement from the report on the survey is as follows:

The teachers who have taught at a school with counselors and then were without counselors overwhelmingly judged services better with counselors in the school. From the teachers' perspective, counselors seemed to be most effective in those areas related to individual services as opposed to affecting school organization.

Teachers participate in the follow-up planning for such counselor activity as:

1. Helping teachers understand the effect of parent behavior on children.
2. Explaining and interpreting pupil behavior in and outside the classroom to teachers.
3. Acquiring for teachers, and helping them put into use, materials which will help children develop realistic concepts of themselves and their environment.
4. Helping teachers know the impact of curricular experiences and materials on the children's concepts of themselves.
5. Working with teachers to mobilize the resources of the school to aid the development of individual pupils.
6. Taking referral of groups of children to counsel.
7. Taking referral on individual pupils to counsel when it may be helpful to them.
8. Arranging with teachers to counsel with parents to find new ways to help a child.
9. Accepting teachers' requests to intervene in crises.
10. Facilitating teachers' referrals of children with serious problems to appropriate agencies.

THE TEACHER AND THE SCHOOL PSYCHOLOGIST

Teachers no longer view the work of the school personnel specialist who is trained in psychology as that of magical curing of "problems." Together, teachers and school psychologists engage in activity in schools (and less directly in communities) in order to make plans to assist in the growth of individual children. Their work with behavior in the classroom is currently based upon a psychosocial model:

> The psychosocial model, in contrast, assumes that behavior is a function of both the individual's past learning (i.e., personality) and the particular stimuli faced in a given situation. The individual's past learning includes not only behavioral skills, but his expectancies, attitudes, values, and other affective attributes. The given situation is defined both by its psychosocial and interpersonal characteristics . . .[5]

A good example of this new approach is summarized in a May 1972 news release which announces a screening program for preschool and kindergarten. Teachers who receive the services of the school psychologist are alerted and prepared to deal with children in individualized ways.

> The service goes farther than the medical examination children receive before enrollment. . . . It alerts first grade teachers to potential learning problems and equips them with specific recommendations for adjusting the child's program accordingly. . . . The program is designed to catch potential learning barriers early, rather than wait to react to those that appear after the child is well into his lessons.

Through the psychological screening and follow-up program, teachers also identify children who show a potential for being academically talented. Another objective of the program is that of helping teachers involve and cooperate with parents. The October 1972 *Progress Report* of this activity, known as *Project Intercept,* states:

> Orientation meetings have been held with the various staffs to be involved in the second phase of the screening, that is, the diagnostic "team" involvement. This includes the school psychologist, school social workers, speech therapists, physical education consultants and school nurses. Support and cooperation from these staffs and their supervisors have been most encouraging.

Teachers work with school psychologists to implement the program, to know the program's purposes, and to learn the basic instruments to be used in the initial screening phases of the work. Teachers cooperate with psychologists in meeting the needs of all the children in the elementary program as is reported in the planning:

> The diagnostic team of experts should also be able to work with any new student who moves into the district who through a screening procedure appears to need the service; his age and grade level would not be a factor in his being seen or not being seen for thorough diagnostic analysis. Further follow-up diagnostic evaluations on students already seen, but for whom the teacher needs new diagnostic evaluation will be done.

Teachers participate in making prescriptive remedial suggestions in educational planning meetings with the team of learning experts involved in the project. They participate in professional growth courses projected for project personnel.

> Remedial techniques will be explained and class discussion will hopefully clear up questions. Materials handed out will also be given to any teacher who may not have enrolled in the class but whose students are involved in the project. On another evening, literature and techniques related to the academically talented will be the major topic. A spin-off of such in-service is greater awareness and esprit de corps of the teacher group.

THE TEACHER AND THE SCHOOL SOCIAL WORKER

Teachers, at the request of school social workers, are participating in efforts to redesign the school social work service so that the delivery system is more responsive to their needs and to those of children. By making their expectations known, teachers are helping to create new roles for social workers, are contributing to the accomplishment of new emphases in the classroom.

In an innovative school social work service especially designed for pre-kindergarten, teachers have helped to define the role. They selected the functions of the social work program by choosing from ten possible ones listed for the program and adding those functions they would like to see the worker perform. The activities listed were:

1. working with individual children
2. working with the teacher
3. mobilizing community resources
4. interpreting the home to school
5. working with individual parents with particular problems
6. doing educational work with parents in groups
7. helping plan classroom management
8. interpreting a child's behavior to teachers
9. consulting with teachers on mental health needs of children and how to include these needs in the pre-kindergarten program.

In another new emphasis, the worker and the teacher worked out ways of getting parents to be teacher-helpers in a first grade classroom. The proposal for this program describes the following activity:

> Each mother will be trained by the classroom teacher and myself to act as a teacher assistant. The teacher and I (social worker) will reinforce the mother's involvement by offering her tangible rewards that are carefully selected to improve her self-concept and identity.

214

The teacher will benefit from the aid extended her by using the extra time afforded her for more individualized attention to children.

In another activity, teachers worked with a school social worker in a series of demonstrations on group management. Using the series, "Transactional Analysis for Everybody," by Alvyn M. Freed, lessons with transparencies for use with a class group were developed to teach the concepts of transactional analysis. Demonstrations with children provided live examples for the understanding and discussions of all those participating in the work. Teachers observed the worker's participation with groups of children to learn about growth in insights about causes of behavior as well as understandings-of-self responses.

In some schools "social adjustment" rooms have replaced the rooms formerly known as classrooms for emotionally disturbed children. A greater degree of social work service has been made available to help these children and teachers. Teachers work with social services to insure that: (1) each child placed in a school adjustment room will have a treatment program planned for him; (2) consultation is available; (3) crisis situations have adequate attention; (4) work with parents—individually and in groups—is afforded frequently; (5) assistance is given to planning and carrying out integration with the regular classrooms in the buildings.

Teachers will evaluate the "enriched" service, by using a questionnaire about the work, by review of records, by recording parent contacts, and by studying oral and written evaluations of parent groups. A count of children "integrated" into regular classrooms, and review of difficulties encountered in the activity, is also to be done.

THE TEACHER AND THE SCHOOL NURSE

Teachers have recognized that there is nothing which contributes so significantly to the achievement of educational potential as good health. They have advocated that schools should provide comprehensive and articulated health services for children. When outside funding became available for disadvantaged children, and teachers were involved in the planning for spending of funds, the nursing service in schools was one means teachers chose to supplement the school program. Teachers welcomed the health screening programs and nursing services provided on a part or full-time basis in new preschool and other innovative instructional programs.

Teachers, like children and parents, have viewed the services of

215

registered professional nurses, many of whom have had experience in public health nursing, as one of the most appropriate adjuncts of the educational program. The areas of concern of the nurse in the school relate closely to the lives of students in the classroom: (1) healthful school living or environmental health, (2) health services, and (3) health instruction.

The school programs in which teachers and nurses work sometimes create somewhat different roles and emphases from which they view the health services and health instruction. Both are much concerned with environmental health teaching about the school, the home, and the community.

Teachers are involved to a more or less degree with the coordinating, appraisal, informational, follow-through, maintenance, recording, treating and emergency health activities of the nurse as they affect some or all of the students in their classes or the school. Teachers plan with the nurse to bring information to students on such concerns as: venereal disease programs, sickle cell anemia control programs, alcohol and drug education, and color vision screening.

Teachers deal with these areas of health education by planning with the nurse for classroom time, by follow-up discussion and instruction for individual students and for groups and parents. Teachers do supportive health follow-up on weight control, dental care, and nutrition needs of students. Frequently, teachers communicate with nurses on dangers to health of students such as injury of late pregnancies in the school. They foster nurses' efforts to provide more service of physicians to children, keep track of changes in health regulations and make these known to students and parents.

The duties of the teacher in regard to the health needs of students supplement those which the nurse carries out in the areas of health service, instruction, and environment. Examples of these are:

Health Services

Participating in the health activities within the school setting.
Making general appraisal of the health status of children in the classroom as an on-going procedure.
Helping in the distribution and collection of health forms.
Supplementing the work of the nurse if needed in following up health recommendations of physicians and dentists.
Participating in health screening procedures through the management of pupils and program adjustment.

216

Supporting the need for adequate first aid facilities and facilitating treatment.
Working to secure accurate and complete growth records, weight, and measurement of each child.

Health Instruction

Participating in health instruction in appropriate ways.
Utilizing professional training in growth and development, emotions, behavior, nutrition, and disease to teach and inform.
Participating with the nurse and other school personnel in health instructional programs of special concern, such as sex education, mental health, safety prevention, school safety, home safety, traffic safety (street crossing), playground safety, fire prevention.
Teaching and counseling children regarding personal health problems, such as cleanliness, personal care, good nutrition, rest.
Counseling with pupils, parents, teachers, counselors, special teachers, diagnosticians, physical education teachers regarding appraisal findings and recommendations.

Environmental Health

Assisting in maintaining a safe, clean, and healthful environment.
Environmental health factors of concern to include: lighting, ventilation, heating, seating, toilet facilities, drinking fountains, playground equipment.

Teachers learn nurse visit schedules in schools and help set referral procedures. They use health resource personnel, such as nutritionists, health educators, sanitarians, dental hygienists, and vision technicians, in health instructional programs in the classrooms and within the school.

THE TEACHER'S ROLE IN THE GUIDANCE PROGRAM

Today many children come to school with a great diversity of experience in living in different cities, states, and countries. Many have attended several schools, and some have adjusted to living in family groups changed by divorce, mishap, or disaster. In most schools there exists, or circumstances are creating, a diversity of culture, language, and beliefs in the classrooms. These differences can pose problems and opportunities for teachers, problems which need study, planning and follow-up; opportunities to teach new information, insights, and understandings. Teachers who engage in study of pupil problems and differences use techniques such as case study, individual and group analysis. Autobiographical essays and sociometric studies are helpful to teachers and counselors in understanding and motivating learners. Field trips and films are appropriately used particularly at the elementary level in career guidance. Testing is a source of data for the teacher as well as for the counselor.

Test Interpretation. It is said that thirty million tests were given to students in American schools in 1960. The current pressure upon teachers to be accountable for the achievement of pupils in specific content areas has encouraged the use of measures of achievement in greater quantity than ever before.

Undoubtedly, tests can be effective tools of diagnosis and, when they are used in conjunction with other evidence, for self-study and planning for the future. Since the most favorable conditions of testing are sought, most group tests are given by teachers who know the pupils best. The use of criterion-referenced measures has tied teaching activity to diagnostic test performance and item mastery. Teachers look at post-test performance for evidence of gain or growth.

Another current emphasis for which testing and test interpretation are needed is that of vocational guidance. The testing of large numbers of students usually requires teacher participation in the administration and interpretation of the interest and aptitude inventories used in the preprogramming and prevocation counseling.

Career Education. Career selection is a difficult task, but schools are undertaking more education at earlier levels so that choices can be made a little easier. Many types of comprehensive and involved interpretation and information-giving processes involving teachers, guidance personnel and parents are being undertaken in schools. An example of a typical career information program is one reported in a school newsletter:

> More than 50 adults actively involved in various careers participated in the PTSA program. They met with interested students to discuss opportunities in their vocations, and to explain the necessary training requirements. . . . Most of the resource people for the program represented occupations students had expressed a preference for through the use of questionnaires . . .

Teachers participate in the planning and execution of such comprehensive occupational information-giving programs.

A greater emphasis on community education is fostering more

teacher preparation and participation in helping people know their interests, abilities, and values and how these might relate to career planning.

At the elementary level, teachers are helping their pupils know themselves and the relationship between schooling and work, factors important to occupational choice. Teachers try to help students mature so that they are aware of other people and the roles they play in their lives, aware of jobs in their futures as involving and prolonged activity in which other people are an important influence.

Parent-Teacher Conferences. Parents' involvement and interest in schools is increasing in a variety of ways. In response, many schools have extended scheduled parent-teacher reporting programs upward from the elementary schools into the middle school, junior high, and high schools. Teachers are better prepared to report the individual progress of students in curricular materials having specified goals and measurement. Computerized data techniques are providing information to report the progress of individuals and groups.

Some advantages of parent-teacher conferences are: (1) they provide a closer working relationship; (2) parents feel that they have a part in the schooling of their child; (3) it is possible to be more specific about achievement; (4) teachers get a wider perspective on the child; (5) they are a meeting ground for problems; (6) they foster good public relations.

Teacher contributions to the conference may be: (1) the progress made in classroom work; (2) work habits in school; (3) social adjustment—relationships with other children; (4) interests, aptitudes, abilities; (5) relationships with teachers; (6) health and emotional problems; (7) evidences of initiative, originality and responsibility in school situations; (8) response to school rules, regulations, and procedures.

Conducting a good interview with parents follows the rules of good interview procedure. In-service work for teachers helps them expand their skills in interviewing. These are an important aspect of a developing parent-teachers conference program.

Support for Curriculum Building.
The teaching-curriculum activities and the guidance-pupil-personnel services have a very important juncture at the point where the student becomes an active learner. To the extent that his learning will be augmented or reduced because of human relations in the interactions and activities in which he must engage, the guidance services have a

direct contribution. Beyond this, on a supporting level, the guidance services can make major contributions by advising curriculum specialists on unique characteristics of children for which special programs must be designed.[6]

Traditionally there have been two sources of data for teachers; and counselors' use in determining the needs of pupils. They are the failure reports and the attendance records. Now alternative school programs are being designed to accommodate special learning needs. Teachers contribute information and help design the ongoing programs. Many school systems now have the capacity to process much pupil and program data so that they can describe a pupil group and look at the relationships which exist between data on the pupil and the program. As knowledge about the teaching-curriculum-guiding activity in classrooms, programs, schools, and school systems accrues in this process, changes will be initiated.

In-service Education. The teacher collaborates with the guidance worker in areas of in-service education such as: (1) human development, (2) determinants of learning, (3) career information, (4) test interpretation, (5) conferencing with parents, (6) pupil records. For example, the many uses of tests might be reviewed: (1) using tests to evaluate pupil differences and aptitudes; (2) finding the variety of abilities probed by tests; (3) sharing with students, teachers, and parents the results indicated by tests; (4) using test results as an aid to decision making.

CONCLUSION

Educators are aware that changing and multiplying emphases have brought new perspectives to education and to the roles of the teacher and counselor. Strong forces are pushing greater recognition of the duality of cognitive and psychological orientations of students. The curriculum-committed, student-committed school is reviewing instructional roles, planning new guidance activities, incorporating changing values and innovative ideas, finding new perspectives and purposes.

The role of the instructional staff in contributing to the guidance program is a role of both direct and indirect service.

High level skills are needed by both educational and guidance personnel—skills of talking, listening, acting and interacting, consulting, need identification, and strategies for meeting needs.

Activities in schools illustrative of programs in which the instructional staff participate in the guidance program and contribute to the guidance program demonstrate the emerging trends in teaching for content mastery and the concomitant need for teaching psychological balance to the students in today's schools.

1. Lee Bennett Hopkins, *Let Them Be Themselves* (New York: Citation Press, 1969), p. 166.
2. Bruce R. Joyce, Marsha Weil, and Rhoada Wald, "The Training of Educators: A Structure for Pluralism," *Teachers College Record* (Feb. 1972), 73(3):371-91.
3. Don C. Dinkmeyer and Charles E. Caldwell, *Developmental Counseling and Guidance: A Comprehensive School Approach* (New York: McGraw-Hill Book Company, 1970), Preface, pp. v-vi.
4. Alfred S. Alschuler and Allen Ivey, "The Human Side of Competency-Based Education," *Educational Technology* (Nov. 1972), 12(11):53-55.
5. Russell M. Grieger, "Psychosocial Assessment: A Model for the School Community Psychologist," *Psychology in the Schools* (April 1972), 9(2):112-13.
6. Gerold T. Kowitz and Norma Giess Kowitz, *Operating Guidance Services for the Modern School* (New York: Holt, Rinehart & Winston, Inc., 1968), p. 245.

SELECTED REFERENCES

Dinkmeyer, Don C., and Caldwell, Charles E. *Developmental Counseling and Guidance*, pp. 1-492. New York: McGraw-Hill Book Company, 1970.

Fullmer, Daniel W., and Bernard, Harold W. *The School Counselor-Consultant*, chap. 1:2-28. Boston: Houghton Mifflin Company, 1972.

Hansen, Donald A. *Explorations in Sociology and Counseling*, chap. 7:200-36. Boston: Houghton Mifflin Company, 1969.

Hopkins, Lee Bennett. *Let Them Be Themselves*, pp. 1-205. New York: Citation Press, 1969.

Kowitz, Gerold T., and Kowitz, Norma Giess, *Operating Guidance Services for the Modern School*, chap. 13:239-54. New York: Holt, Rinehart & Winston, Inc., 1968.

Moffett, James. *A Student-Centered Language Arts Curriculum, Grades K-6: A Handbook for Teachers*, chaps. 1-6:1-97. Boston: Houghton Mifflin Company, 1968.

CHAPTER 7

Pupil Personnel Services in San Diego County

GLEN N. PIERSON

THE COMMUNITY SETTING

SAN DIEGO COUNTY is 4,258 square miles in area, extending seventy miles from San Clemente in the north to the Mexican border in the south, and eighty miles from the Pacific Ocean east to Imperial County. The diversified topography of San Diego County includes mountains, intermontane valleys, deserts, and the Pacific coastline. The economic community encompasses a missile and aircraft complex, diversified agriculture, tourist-connected business, military installations, and highly developed research facilities and industries.

The county population in 1970 was estimated at 1,358,500, which is approximately seven percent of the estimated total 1970 California population of 19,715,490. The area has experienced rapid growth in the postwar years, as evidenced by the 1950 population of 556,808 and the 1960 population figure of 1,049,000.[1]

This rapid growth in general population has resulted in dramatic increases in public school enrollment. The 1950 fall enrollment in grades K-12 in San Diego County was 86,634. By the fall of 1960 this enrollment had increased to 217,091, and in the fall of 1970 enrollment was 305,143.[2] An examination of these figures indicates that the public school enrollment had increased at a faster rate than the general population.

This twenty-year period of rapid growth has placed heavy burdens on local taxpayers to provide the capital outlay for school buildings and other public service facilities. While the state has provided school construction funds to local districts when their bonded indebt-

223

edness reached a fixed percentage of assessed valuation, the local taxpayer has repeatedly been asked to approve bonds for school construction and tax rate increases for increased operating costs.

San Diego County is rapidly becoming a hub of activity for education and research. Three universities (plus a university extension division), one state university, and seven junior colleges enrolled more than 55,000 full-time students during the fall term of 1971. California State University, San Diego, enrolling approximately 20,000 full-time students, has gained a reputation for both academic training and community service. The new University of California at San Diego, including the world-famed Scripps Institution of Oceanography and a new University Medical School, will enroll 27,500 students by 1995.

Two private universities—United States International University and the University of San Diego—offer a wide variety of undergraduate and graduate studies. United States International University in recent years developed a doctoral level program in human behavior, and a number of school personnel in this area have completed, or are enrolled, in that program.

The seven public-supported junior colleges in the county have grown rapidly in the past few years, and had a total full-time and part-time enrollment of almost 52,000 students in the fall of 1971.

Nonpublic education at the elementary and secondary level includes a variety of church-affiliated schools, as well as independent schools and military academies, along with a number of proprietary vocational and special schools. It is estimated that approximately six to eight percent of the elementary and secondary pupils attend nonpublic schools.[3]

Cultural facilities and activities offer exceptional opportunities for the adult and child population in this area. The Museum of Man, the Natural History Museum, the Serra Museum, the San Diego Aero-Space Museum, and the Palomar Observatory offer displays and educational programs spanning a wide range of cultural interests.

The San Diego Zoo offers the community an outstanding animal and plant collection for study and observation, enhanced by the three-quarter million dollar Elmer C. Otto Education Center on the Zoo grounds and the new Wild Animal Park at San Pasqual, where animals live in near natural habitat.

The Fine Arts Gallery housing the Putman Collection in the new Timken Wing, the LaJolla Museum of Art, and many smaller galleries exhibit permanent and traveling collections of fine art in all mediums.

The San Diego Public Library offers a modern library program. It has 640,000 volumes, eighteen branches, and three bookmobiles offering services in all areas of the city. The San Diego County Library serves the rural areas with twenty-seven branches, ten stations, and one bookmobile. Each incorporated city in the county also has its own library facilities and services.

When reviewing the educational and cultural facilities of the county, a few additional items should be included. The warm, dry, all-year climate of most of the county has important effects on education. It makes it possible to utilize buildings with minimal weather interference, to avoid close confinement to inside classrooms, and to implement structural and architectural innovations that would be impractical elsewhere. The heavy reliance of Southern California on the automobile and the lack of adequate fast public transportation create traffic and parking problems, particularly at secondary schools and colleges, that require careful planning and control. A third item relates to the increased demand for adult education. With a growing percentage of retired persons, with persons with more leisure time and more education, and greater availability of a variety of courses, seminars, institutes, workshops and weekend trips, adult education may well become the fastest growing segment of the educational enterprise.[4]

In recent years, a number of studies have been made to determine public attitude to the educational systems in San Diego County. These studies have generally indicated a very stable set of public attitudes, with between seventy and eighty percent of the respondents indicating they feel the school systems are either "very good" or "satisfactory."[5] Ideas for improvements in education, expressed by persons polled, include better trained teachers and administrators, more discipline, greater utilization of school buildings, and improved curricular offerings. It is the overall impression of this author that the educational programs of San Diego County compare quite favorably with school systems throughout the country. This is not meant to imply that the area does not face a number of pressing concerns relating to education.

Concerns with education which merit discussion include financial problems, disenchantment with formal education, student-centered problems, and community pressures.[6] Since the focus of this chapter is on pupil personnel services, the discussion of these concerns and their ramifications will be brief.

The financial concerns are closely related to the rapid growth of the county. This growth has resulted in a demand for "buildings, bodies, and books." The proportion of funds from the state level has been steadily declining, and this has placed a heavier burden on local property taxpayers.

The disenchantment with formal education involves the need for schools to change as social needs change. School districts are responding to this concern by involving staffs and lay citizen groups in the definition of clearly defined goals and objectives that may be presented to governing boards for adoption. A later section of this chapter will discuss the development and implementation of goals and objectives for pupil personnel services.

Another concern involves student conduct, as well as student goals and aspirations. With regard to conduct, there have been widely publicized riots, demonstrations, and other incidents on school campuses, as well as the problems of drug abuse and vandalism. Deeper concerns are evoked by the mood of frustration and alienation that affects a substantial number of students. Even though it appears that school districts in the county have suffered from much less student unrest than many other areas, the difficulties have been serious. Many observers feel the waning public financial support of education is attributable in part to student unrest. Pupil personnel programs can play a major role in solving these problems of student unrest.

Community pressures include the demand for greater equality of opportunity in education by minority and underprivileged groups and the call for neighborhood input into the operation of schools. Progress on these concerns is being made through compensatory education programs and citizen advisory councils. The role of a pupil personnel program in the solution of these concerns should not be minimized.

THE SCHOOLS

A review of a few statistics will reveal that the magnitude of the educational systems in San Diego County is substantial. In May 1971, when civilian employment in the county totaled 444,200, there were over 48,000 persons employed in various facets of education. This figure is over ten percent of civilian employment, and, for comparison, it equals the total combined employment in contract construction and aerospace. It is estimated that about twenty-five percent of the educational employment is in the field of higher education.[7]

During the school year 1971–72 there were 422 public schools serving students in grades K-12. These schools ranged in size from a one-room country school, enrolling fourteen students, to a large urban school with an enrollment of 3,500 students. The fall 1971 enrollment in grades K-12 in all school districts in the county was 311,294, which is approximately twenty-three percent of the total county population.[8]

Educational facilities of the school districts are generally operating above capacity. While a few buildings could handle increased enrollments, they are usually in areas where the supply of students has diminished, due to population shifts. In many instances, school facilities are overcrowded, and relocatable buildings are required. In an effort to increase the use of school facilities, several districts in the county have instituted year-round schools. The most prevalent plan is the 45–15 plan. Under this program, the school population is divided into four groups, and each group attends a nine-week school session, followed by a three-week vacation. By controlling the starting time for each group, it is possible to increase facility use by about twenty-five percent.

A substantial portion of the county's population is concentrated in the narrow coastal strip that comprises about twenty percent of the county's land area. This coastal zone is experiencing increasing pressure for development and urbanization, and it is expected that the current intense need for the development of new schools will continue.

Within the county are twenty-eight elementary districts, six high districts and nine unified districts. Each of these districts is governed by an elected board of from three to seven members, and each board selects the chief administrative officer for that district. State legislation has mandated that each county have a committee that develops plans for district organizations that would place the education of children in grades K-12 under a single district.[9] These plans require the approval of the state board of education and are then submitted to the voters of the area. District reorganization plans have been developed on a specified schedule in all portions of the county not served by a unified district, but only two unified districts have been approved by the voters in the past eight years.

In California, education is a function of the state, which establishes general requirements and provides basic financial support. Immedi-

227

ate control and responsibility for operating the schools rests with the local school district.

Between the state and local levels is the intermediate unit administered by the County Superintendent of Schools. San Diego County's intermediate unit, the Department of Education, San Diego County, provides leadership and coordination for improvement of educational programs in all school districts of the county. In addition, the department contributes to regional and statewide activities. Accomplishment of its goals often involves it in coordinating the activities of other educational institutions—colleges, universities, research centers—and business, industry, and public agencies. Since the concept of regional intermediate units is being implemented in numerous areas of the country, a brief overview of the department is provided.

The department is housed in its own separate facility of five buildings, containing 77,000 square feet that were built in 1961. Employed by the department are 96 certificated and 244 classified employees.

The County Superintendent of Schools, appointed by an elected five-member County Board of Education, is the department's chief administrative officer. The administrative structure includes three divisions, each headed by an assistant superintendent. The Business Services Division includes a Field Services Section that assists school districts to improve school business procedures and provides budget and financial advising. The Data Processing Section computes payrolls and writes salary warrants for the school districts and also provides, on a contract basis, a pupil personnel data processing package that includes test scoring, attendance accounting, student records, and class scheduling. Additional services from this division include schoolhouse planning, legal interpretations, financial and statistical reporting, and internal accounting and purchasing.

The Special Services Division includes a Credentials Section that registers credentials for all certificated school employees in the county, and a Reports Section that assists districts in attendance accounting procedures and processes reports, including textbook requisitions, to the State Department of Education. The Production Section performs duplicating and printing services for the department. This division administers educational programs for pupils in juvenile halls and rehabilitation centers operated by the County Probation Department and operates classes for mentally retarded

228

pupils residing in small school districts. Another major responsibility of this division includes communication and cooperation with school boards and professional and lay organizations involved in the educational process. The Personnel Section handles recruitment and selection of staff and provides an advisory placement service for all school districts in the county.

The Curricular Services Division is composed of six sections. The staff of the Curriculum Coordination Section includes specialists in various curricular areas who provide coordination, leadership, and service to the local school districts. Staff activities include the planning and leading of workshops and other staff development projects and the development of instructional materials. The Community Educational Resources Section brings newly discovered knowledge and information into the classroom in the form of multimedia instructional materials. The staff selects and retrieves information and materials from cooperating agencies and adapts and develops the materials to serve curricular needs of the schools. The Occupational Education Section works to strengthen and expand vocational education programs in local school districts and also administers the Regional Occupational Program. This program, supported by a county-wide tax, provides financial support for vocational and technical courses that are open to students, out-of-school youth, and adults without fee even though the courses are outside their district of residence. This concept of regional programs prevents duplication of expensive facilities and equipment and has markedly increased enrollment in vocational and technical programs in the county. The School Library Section includes a contract library service for elementary schools, a curriculum library available to the department staff and all school personnel in the county, and consultant services to school libraries in all districts. The Audio-Visual Services Section offers school districts a contract service for films and related materials and has the production capabilities of a photographer, graphic artist, mobile videotape, and color television cameras and recorders. The Pupil Personnel Service Section, also included in the Curricular Services Division, will be described in more detail in the following portion of this chapter.

Pupil Personnel Services
Although the relative size of the district, as well as the grade levels served, does affect the quantity and type of pupil personnel services

provided, most districts provide the typical range of services. These services include: guidance, psychological, special education, nursing, child welfare and attendance, and social work.

Included within guidance services are the usual functions of counseling, appraisal, information, consultation, evaluation, and follow-up. The secondary schools in the county maintain a pupil/counselor ratio of approximately 500 to 1 and virtually all the counselors serve on a full-time basis. Counseling clerks or secretaries are provided in the approximate ratio of one clerk per three counselors. California certification requirements provide that persons serving more than half-time in a counseling assignment must possess either the General Pupil Personnel Services Credential or the Designated Services Credential with a specialization in counseling.[10] Ten years ago the larger districts in the county had a number of persons serving on a part-time basis who did not possess a counseling credential. In recent years these districts have adopted the practice of making full-time counseling assignments to individuals possessing the required credentials.

Title V of the National Defense Education Act had a marked impact on guidance services in San Diego County. California State University, San Diego, conducted a number of summer and year-long institutes, and a substantial number of local counselors initiated or completed a counselor education program under the Part B provisions of this act. The Bureau of Pupil Personnel Services in the California State Department of Education administered Part A funds of this act by permitting districts to submit applications on a competitive basis. Districts were required to maintain a specified pupil/counselor ratio to be eligible for project funds, and were required to improve the ratio each year to continue their eligibility for project approval. While the type of projects approved covered a wide range of topics, the basic intent of a substantial number of them was to initiate or add to the counseling staffs in local schools and to provide clerical assistance to counselors. Within the county, it is possible to identify a number of counseling positions that were initiated with NDEA Title V-A funds and continued with local funding based upon favorable evaluation results of the project.

The typical counselor job description specifies services to: students; teachers, and other certificated staff members; administrative staff; parents and the community; and self and department. The job description for counselors in the Santana High School in the Grossmont Union High School District is included for review. (See Appen-

230

dix A-1.) Job descriptions for all certificated staff members have recently been reviewed by all districts in California. Legislation enacted in 1971 mandated the evaluation of all probationary employees on an annual basis and all tenured employees at least every two years.[11] Guidelines for implementing this legislation call for the employee and his supervisor to reach agreement on reasonable goals and objectives based upon the job description, and the degree to which the goals and objectives are achieved is the substance of the evaluation.[12]

Direct supervision of building counselors is usually performed by the principal or vice-principal. Large high schools often staff a head counselor position. The individual in this position supervises other counselors, and his supervisor is the principal or vice-principal. Staff supervision and in-service training for counselors is usually a responsibility of the district level director of pupil personnel.

Physical facilities for school counselors are adequate to very satisfactory in secondary schools constructed in the last decade in San Diego County. The inclusion of career centers, attractive waiting and reception areas, and space for ancillary personnel are common features in the newer buildings. (See Figs. 7.1 and 7.2.) A majority of the recently constructed schools have followed the recommended practice of preparing educational specifications for the guidance functions as a step in architectural planning and have incorporated recommendations from the literature regarding location and design of facilities.[13]

The contract year for counselors is usually ten to twenty days beyond the teaching year. This additional time is used for orientation programs, registration and scheduling of students, and development of materials and reports. Salaries for counselors in most districts are in a ratio of from 1.04 to 1.20 of experience and preparation placement on the teacher schedule.

Most counseling vacancies or new positions in districts in the county are filled by individuals with prior teaching experience in the district. Exceptions are made if a qualified person is not available from within the district, if a member of a specific minority is being recruited, or if an individual with specific skill or experience, as in group work, is desired. The three largest districts in the county maintain an eligibility list from which counselor vacancies are filled. In addition to a written exam, individuals are rated by an interview team composed of counselors, administrators, and students. Building

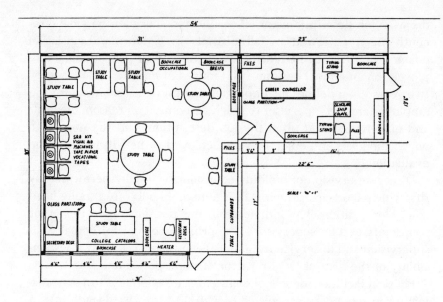

Fig. 7.1. Career Counseling Center, Crawford High School, San Diego, California.

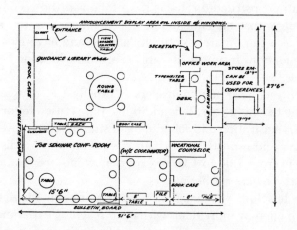

Fig. 7.2. Career Development Center, Mount Miguel High School, Spring Valley, California.

principals or other supervisors of counselors at the building level make their selection after interviews with the top candidates on the eligibility list.

An innovative use of paraprofessionals for the junior high level guidance program was initiated in the fall of 1971 by the San Diego Unified School District. Under provisions of the federally funded Public Employment Program, a career aide was selected for each of the eighteen junior high schools in the district. The aides, unemployed at the time of selection, ranged in age from early twenties to mid-fifties, with the median age being in the late twenties. Eight of the group had bachelors' degrees, and all but one of the remainder had completed a two-year community college program. A career counselor was given the responsibility for coordination of the in-service and orientation program for the aides and to provide continuing staff supervision. A career center was established in each junior high, and this center served as home base for the aides.[14] The center contained a rich collection of materials and equipment related to career information and decision-making skills. The head counselor at each school had supervision responsibility for the career aide. During the orientation program, the role of the aides and their relationship to counselors was carefully developed. Job duties included keeping the materials in the center in order and helping students locate pertinent materials, arranging field trips, and making classroom presentations on career information topics. Response to the career aide program by pupils, faculty, and administration has been most favorable, and the program will be continued. The program is an illustration of the career-ladder concept in that one aide has resigned to enter a full-time counselor education program and several others are enrolled in part-time counselor education programs.[15] (See Figs. 7.3 and 7.4.)

Guidance services at the elementary level are still at the development stages in San Diego County. A number of districts initiated elementary counseling positions on a pilot basis under the provisions of Title I or III of the Elementary and Secondary Education Act or Title V-A of the National Defense Education Act. Approximately twenty-five positions were established, and, although some of these funding sources have been reduced or eliminated, the author is not aware of any position that has not been continued with local funding. However, the financial squeeze on local district budgets has prevented the establishment of additional positions. The elementary counseling positions established by districts placed emphasis on con-

233

Fig. 7.3.   The Career Guidance Center at Horace Mann Junior High School in the San Diego Unified School District has a VIEW reader and a rich collection of printed career information material. (Photo credit: Dept. of Education, San Diego County.)

Fig. 7.4.   Students browsing in the college corner of the Career Guidance Center at Montgomery Junior High School, San Diego Unified School District. (Photo credit: Dept. of Education, San Diego County.)

sultation services to teachers and parents. A majority of the counselors devoted about two-thirds of their time to these functions, with the remaining time being spent in group and individual work with students.

The provision of psychological services by districts is historically linked to the California legal requirements that school districts operate programs for a number of categories of handicapped children. Children must be examined and certified by a school psychologist before they are eligible for placement in these programs. This function of identification of special education pupils has developed into a rather restrictive role in some instances and has led to the "kit-carrying psychologist" label. School psychologists, through their local and state professional organization, have been working for an expanded role that includes more services to typical children, and they are meeting with success in these endeavors. The social problems of drug abuse, venereal disease, and unwed mothers, as well as the "hang-ups" of typical students, represent areas where the services of school psychologists may be effectively utilized. The job description for school psychologist in the San Diego Unified School District (See Appendix A-2.) is considered representative of this position in most districts in the county. An examination of the staffing ratios for school psychologists in the school districts of the county indicate that the recommended ratio of one psychologist per 1,500 is rarely met. Although the ratios vary among districts, the staffing of one psychologist per 3,000 pupils would reasonably represent typical practice.

California credential requirements for school psychologists include one academic year of training beyond the masters' degree with field work and practicum requirements. The usual work year is two to four weeks beyond the teaching year. Typical salary would be a ratio of 1.10 to 1.30 of experience and preparation placement on the teacher schedule.

The usual administrative practice is to base the school psychologist at the district office. The psychologist is responsible to the director of pupil personnel services, or in larger districts, to a supervising psychologist. Typically, the psychologist has an assignment covering two to four schools, the exact number depending on the size of the schools and the staffing ratio of the district. Although the immediate supervisor of the school psychologist is usually based at the district office, they do have a staff role with the site administrators and are encouraged and expected to develop effective working relationships with each site administrator.

Attention should be drawn to the trend of decentralizing psychological and related central office services. A local illustration of this trend was the decision of the Grossmont Union High School District to base one psychologist at each of the eight high schools in the district.[16] This change, implemented in September 1971, was made to provide greater visibility to the school psychologists and to identify them as members of the school pupil personnel team. Each psychologist is responsible to the building principal, while the district director of pupil personnel services provides staff supervision. At the inception of the program, the assistant superintendent for instruction and the director of pupil personnel services met with each building principal and psychologist to clarify roles and relationships and to reach agreement on the type of service to be provided by the psychologist. After one year of operation under this plan, the district director of pupil personnel services reported that it was being well received by principals, building staffs, and the psychologists. The psychologists reported that they were providing a different type of service, with less emphasis on testing and more parent and staff conferences and many self-referrals by students. They felt they had not been "misused" by principals and that the teaching staff had a clearer conception of their role and considered them valuable members of the school team.

School districts in San Diego County provide a wide range of special education programs. California law requires school districts to provide programs for physically handicapped and mentally retarded minors. An exception is made for small school districts, and in these instances the office of the county superintendent of schools is responsible for the education of the handicapped children. The programs provided by the Department of Education, San Diego County, will be discussed in the next section of this chapter.

In addition to the state-mandated programs for physically handicapped and mentally retarded children, most districts also operate programs for educationally handicapped and mentally gifted minors. Two of the larger districts, San Diego Unified and Chula Vista City, also operate developmental centers for severely handicapped minors.

Included in the physically handicapped category are blind and visually impaired, deaf and hard-of-hearing, orthopedic handicapped, speech impaired, and other health impaired, including coronary cases and children requiring home instruction. In most of these categories, the severity of the handicap requires the children to be

236

in special classes where special equipment and materials are available.

Programs are provided for educable and trainable retarded children. Traditionally, most educable retarded children have been placed in special classes of from twelve to eighteen pupils, with a teacher having a special credential for teaching the retarded. However, in recent years, the trend has been to integrate these children into the regular program for a portion of the day and provide individualized or small group instruction in the basic subjects for the remainder of the day. Charges that minority children have been misplaced in programs for the retarded have resulted in state regulations that carefully detail the procedures to follow when considering a child for placement in programs for the retarded.

Specialized counseling and work experience programs for the retarded have been emphasized by school districts. The three largest districts in the county operate sheltered workshops, and the San Diego Association for the Retarded operates a workshop for retarded adults. However, additional sheltered workshop facilities are needed in both the metropolitan and the rapidly growing north county areas.

Programs for educationally handicapped minors are the most rapidly increasing programs in this county. Authorized by the legislature in 1965, they permit enrollment of children with neurological handicaps, emotional disturbances, behavior disorders, and severe learning problems, but not children who are mentally retarded. The enrollment limit for this program is two percent of district enrollment, and program options include special day classes or learning disability groups. Since placement in programs for the educationally handicapped does not carry the social stigma often associated with placement in special education, a number of districts have reached the two percent enrollment limit. This limit, imposed by the state to restrict the financial obligation for this program, does not permit service to all pupils with these handicaps, which many authorities estimate at approximately ten percent of the school population.

Developmental centers permit enrollment of severely handicapped children at three years of age. Through these centers, many children who would otherwise require institutionalization or custodial care are able to remain with their families. Many children are on waiting lists for the two existing programs in this county, and additional centers need to be developed in the east and north portions of the county. However, state funds have not been available for development of these programs.

Minors scoring two standard deviations above the mean on individual intelligence tests are eligible for placement in gifted programs. Types of programs include special classes, enrichment activities in regular program, seminar and correspondence courses, and special counseling programs. In some districts, the responsibility for the curricular aspects is placed in instructional services; in other districts, this function is the responsibility of pupil personnel services. In all instances, however, the pupil personnel services staff has responsibility for the identification of gifted minors.

Since the functions of school nurses include services to pupils, as well as instructional services with regard to health education, nursing services in some districts are under the supervision of the pupil personnel services unit, while in other districts the nurses are in the instructional unit. Many districts are establishing health clerk positions to perform height and weight checks and record-keeping functions. In these districts, the nurse serves in a consultant role to monitor health history data, and serves on admission committees for special class placement. In many instances, nurses are working closely with teachers on such health education topics as nutrition, sex education, venereal disease, and drug abuse.

Positions with sole responsibility for child welfare and attendance are staffed by only two districts in the county. In other districts, the child welfare and attendance functions are assigned to counselors, social workers, psychologists, or vice-principals.

The staffing for social work also varies among the districts. The largest district in the county, San Diego Unified School District, uses the title of district counselor for the fifty-five individuals performing this function. California State University, San Diego, has a well-developed School of Social Work, and a number of students from the program complete their supervised field experience in districts near the campus. In other districts, the social work function is performed by other members of the pupil personnel team.

The administrative responsibility for pupil personnel programs is naturally determined in part by the enrollment of the district. Within San Diego County, there are seventeen districts enrolling less than 1,000 pupils each. Most of the pupil personnel functions for these districts are performed by the Department of Education, San Diego County, in a manner that will be described in the following section. Districts in the 1,000 to 4,000 enrollment size, of which there are eleven in the county, typically employ a school psychologist on a full or part-time basis and a school counselor. The school superintendent or assistant superintendent in districts of this size usually has administrative responsibility for the program.

San Diego County has fourteen districts in the 4,000 to 20,000 enrollment size. The typical pattern in these districts is to employ a director of pupil personnel services, whose salary range and level is at or slightly above that of a school principal. The director typically is responsible to the assistant superintendent for instructional services. The larger districts in this range usually employ supervisors for special education and psychological services, who report to the director of pupil personnel services. A substantial number of the directors have a background in school psychology, since this is often the first pupil personnel position established in a small district; it is not uncommon for an individual to move from that position into the director position as the district grows.

The one district above the 20,000 size in San Diego County serving pupils at the K-12 range is San Diego Unified, with a pupil enrollment of approximately 130,000. This district employs an assistant superintendent for pupil personnel services. In addition, there are central office-based directors for each of the usual pupil personnel functions and a number of supervisors for subfunctions.

A review of the 1970-71 budget category "Total Current Expenses for Education" revealed that the total dollar figure for the forty-three districts serving grades K-12 was $254,424,199. The total average daily attendance for these districts was 317,767. This yields a per pupil expenditure of approximately $800. Isolation of total expenses for pupil personnel services would be quite involved, since they appear in more than one budget category. Perhaps the best estimate would be obtained by considering the budget category "Other Certificated Salaries of Instruction." While this category would include a few salaries not related to pupil personnel services, this would be offset by such items as psychologists' salaries for special education pupil identification that are reported in other budget categories. With this qualification, the total expenditure for this budget category for the above-mentioned ADA was $12,569,264. This yields a per pupil expenditure of approximately $39. This suggests that approximately 4.9 percent of the current expenses for education in San Diego County are devoted to pupil personnel services.[17] This compares quite closely with the 4.2 percent reported in a study of 227 school systems conducted in 1965-66 by the Interprofessional Research Commission on Pupil Personnel Services. It should be noted that both percentages are below the frequently recommended allocation of 5 to 8 percent of operational funds for pupil personnel services.[18]

UNIQUE CHARACTERISTICS OF THE PUPIL PERSONNEL SERVICES

The provisions for services from an intermediate unit between the local school districts and the state department of education are extensive in California and a few of the other states. There is a trend toward expansion of this type of service. A brief overview of services provided by the Department of Education, San Diego County, was provided earlier in this chapter. The following discussion will provide a more detailed description of pupil personnel services provided by the Department and describe how these services interface with programs in local school districts.

Included in the Pupil Personnel Services Section are ten guidance coordinators, four special education coordinators, two career development counselors, and the director. The classified staff members number fourteen.

The major long-range objective of the Pupil Personnel Services Section is the strengthening of pupil personnel programs in local school districts. The services provided from the intermediate level are necessarily different from the services provided by district personnel. Moreover, the program of services provided by the section is constantly shifting emphasis in response to the changing needs of individual school districts.

To achieve the long-range objectives, the staff of the section undertakes a broad range of activities in the various schools and districts including: conferences with administrators, counselors, and teachers regarding guidance programs; staff development programs centering around testing and counseling; program development in special education; planning and conducting workshops and seminars specifically designed for administrators, counselors, and teachers on such topics as child growth and development, career development theories, and program evaluation; coordination of research projects designed to improve courses of study and the placement of students in appropriate learning situations, developing and field testing materials for use by counselors and teachers; direct psychological services in small school districts; presentations to boards of trustees apprising them of the need for specific services; participation of district and interdistrict committees dealing with pupil personnel topics; reviewing and recommending professional library materials for use by dis-

240

trict personnel; and cooperation with various community agencies in the implementation of their programs.

In the last section, reference was made to the provision of direct pupil personnel services to small school districts by the Department. Elementary districts with less than 900 average daily attendance (ADA), high school districts with less than 300 ADA, and unified districts with less than 1,500 ADA receive guidance and psychological services from the Department. State funds are provided to the department for this service. Five guidance coordinators have geographic assignments to school districts, and the provision of these direct services to small districts in their assigned area is one of their responsibilities. While the Pupil Personnel Services Section does have a professional commitment and the legal responsibility for the provision of direct services to small school districts, their major thrust is program development and coordination services in all school districts.

An illustration of the program development function would be Project VIEW (Vital Information for Education and Work). Initial work on project VIEW began in 1965 in response to the following identified needs: (1) the training of school counselors in the area of career planning was generally inadequate; (2) many school counselors were not able to keep abreast of current occupational information; and, (3) much of the occupational literature being used in the schools did not communicate to the students. Four years of pilot, developmental, and demonstration efforts resulted in a model system to collect, abstract, synthesize, produce, store, and disseminate career information that was specific to those criteria which local consumers—students and counselors—had established. Project VIEW is well documented in the literature, and the program has been modified and adapted in over thirty other counties in California and in twenty-six other states.[19]

The recognition that other services beyond the provision of occupational information were needed in local schools led to the establishment of the Career Information Center. Services of the Center, in addition to Project VIEW, include a mobile counseling program, a Dial-A-Career Program, in-service education programs, and the development of vocational materials.

The mobile counseling program, composed of two twenty-seven-foot vans, each staffed with a career counselor and a counselor aide, provide job training information, as well as counseling, testing, and referral services to adults and out-of-school youth throughout San

241

Fig. 7.5. One of the two mobile counseling vans operated by the Department of Education, San Diego County. (Photo credit: Dept. of Education, San Diego County.)

Fig. 7.6. The mobile counseling vans bring career information and career counseling to clients at shopping centers, adult schools, and community agencies. (Photo credit: Dept. of Education, San Diego County.)

Diego County. In cooperation with local public schools, the mobile program, equipped with extensive vocational materials and various multimedia equipment, assists community citizens in obtaining data on educational and vocational training programs. Extensive use of community agencies is made in serving the needs of citizens. Schedules listing the hours and locations of the mobile units are published and distributed throughout San Diego County. (See Figs. 7.5 and 7.6.)

The Dial-A-Career program is a service designed to enable youth and adults to obtain both verbal and written career information in English or Spanish. A personal, bilingual daytime telephone service is available to residents of San Diego County concerning questions they have regarding education and vocational training opportunities and job information. A bilingual nighttime answering service to record requests for such information is also available. These calls are answered within twenty-four hours.

The county-wide administration and use of a vocational interest survey is coordinated through the Center. This survey instrument is administered annually to over 23,000 students, and the staff has developed materials for local schools to use when interpreting the results to students, faculties, and the community.

To assist local school district staffs to keep abreast of the rapidly changing career guidance field, a regular program of in-service training is provided. Such assistance includes the use of nationally recognized specialists in various aspects of career guidance, as well as of locally prepared career development materials. As needs arise and are identified within the community, various other materials are prepared and distributed to assist the career guidance efforts throughout San Diego County. The brochure "Looking for a Career," listing all vocational training available in the community colleges in the county, is one example. The "Career Information Directory" which lists career assistance in the form of speakers, tours, and printed materials available to schools from over one hundred fifty San Diego businesses or industries is also an example of the materials available from the Career Information Center.

Three examples will be provided to illustrate the coordination function of guidance services within San Diego County by the Pupil Personnel Services Section. The Guidance Directors' Council was organized in 1970 by one of the guidance coordinators to provide leadership to district directors of pupil personnel services and other individuals with administrative responsibilities for guidance, special

243

education, and related functions. The Council, which has no officers or dues, meets on a monthly basis during the school year. A guidance coordinator chairs the meeting and has responsibility for planning the programs. Attendance has always been above ninety percent of the forty members, and ratings for each meeting have been in the two highest categories—"very worthwhile" and "worthwhile." A majority of the members have accepted the responsibility of presenting a topic or program to the group. Programs during the 1971-72 school year covered topics such as: career guidance objectives; performance objectives, job performance, and the guidance director; some ideas and some instruments for evaluating guidance programs; and accountability and evaluation in pupil personnel services.[20]

A second coordination effort is represented by an informal organization with a smaller, yet more diverse, membership. The Guidance Round Table brings together counselor educators, counselor supervisors, line counselors, and school administrators. The primary purpose of this organization is to facilitate communication between the individuals. Ancillary purposes are to provide ideas for program modification and improvement and to discuss common problems experienced by the members in their work. The membership of the Guidance Round Table is limited to eighteen so that it is possible to conduct meetings in an informal atmosphere and have an open exchange of ideas and information. The membership of the group is structured to insure that all regions of the county are represented. Each of the five branches of the San Diego Personnel and Guidance Association elect two members. One member from each branch is a practicing counselor, while the other is a school administrator. There are four ex-officio members as follows: Executive Secretary of the San Diego Personnel and Guidance Association; Chairman of the Department of Counselor Education at California State University, San Diego; Director of In-school Counseling in the San Diego Unified School District; and the Director of Pupil Personnel Service at the Department of Education, San Diego County. This group of fourteen elects four additional members. Care is exercised in the election of these individuals to insure representation by guidance personnel from all levels, including community colleges and other counselor education programs in the area.

One member of the Round Table has responsibility for the program each month. The prepared remarks by the presenters are limited to about thirty minutes to provide ample time for discussion at each meeting. The group meets once each month at 7:30 A.M. for breakfast and at 8 A.M., the planned program begins. The meetings close promptly at 9 A.M. so that the members may attend this meeting without a major conflict to their daily work schedule. Attendance at these early morning meetings has been quite high, and this suggests that the Round Table is providing a valued service in facilitating communication between practicing school counselors, school administrators, and counselor educators and supervisors.

The third example of coordination services is the support provided to the San Diego Personnel and Guidance Association (S.D.P.G.A.), an affiliate of the California branch of the American Personnel and Guidance Association. The Pupil Personnel Section was chiefly responsible for the formation of the S.D.P.G.A. in 1961. A guidance coordinator serves as the executive secretary of the group, and clerical services are provided by the section. The association provides a number of valuable in-service training programs for the nearly four hundred members each year. An innovative program sponsored by the association was the living room discussion groups. Counselors from all parts of the county were encouraged to invite a group of about fifteen people into their home for an evening. The groups were structured to include parents, students, school board members, teachers, and counselors. Purposes of the groups were to: create an awareness in the community of guidance services available; develop an awareness of unmet needs of counselors, students, and parents; change or modify perceptions; and develop new directions or thrusts. An evaluation of the program suggested that the expected outcomes were realized, and the living room discussion groups will be continued.

Special education services are also provided by the Pupil Personnel Service Section of the Department. California law places responsibility upon the County Superintendent of Schools for the education of physically handicapped and trainable mentally retarded children in districts of less than 8,000 ADA. The superintendent may permit the district to operate programs, contract with larger districts, or directly operate programs to serve these children. In any instance, authorization is provided to levy a tax over the area served to raise the difference between program costs and state support for the programs.[21] Within San Diego County, contracts are developed with larger districts in each geographic region for the education of these children. Special education coordinators from the Section facilitate the enrollment and transportation of children to these programs and provide monitoring and consultant services to the program.

The Section also provides program development and coordination services to all special education programs in the county. Two projects are being conducted with funding under the provisions of Title VI-B of Education of the Handicapped Act. One project, a mobile resource center, provides a 27-foot van staffed with a resource teacher and an intern for in-service training of teachers of educationally handicapped children. The van is equipped with an extensive collection of curricular materials and audio-visual equipment. When the van is scheduled at a school, a teacher of educationally handicapped children may bring a small group of children to the van for diagnostic and prescriptive work with the resource teacher, while the intern works with the rest of the students in the class. The resource teacher and intern also conduct regularly scheduled regional in-service training programs regarding diagnostic and remediation techniques.

The second project in special education has two components. One component, SEARCH (System for Educational Accounting and Recording Children with Handicaps), involves the development of a data processing system for registering children by type of handicap, area of residence, age and race, and also records the educational program they are receiving or require. SEARCH has potential for becoming a state-wide system for management data regarding special education program and services. The second component, CBRU (Computer Based Resource Units), provides curriculum resource units for special education teachers. The units, developed through the Instructional Materials Center at the State University of New York at Buffalo, include large group and individual learner objectives with suggested activities, materials required, and suggested evaluation procedures. This data is coded to a number of learner characteristics and stored on computer tape. The Regional Data Processing Center at the Department of Education, San Diego County, has a library of these tapes, and a special education teacher may specify learner characteristics of the children in the class and receive resource units with objectives and the related activities, materials required, and evaluation procedures for each child.

Coordinators in the Pupil Personnel Section plan and conduct a number of in-service training programs each year for school psychologists, social workers, and nurses. The section coordinates the issuance of work permits for minors and also coordinates the state-mandated testing program. The requests for services and district evaluation of office services suggests the programs and services pro-

246

vided by the Pupil Personnel Section are well received by the consumers.

ISSUES AND ALTERNATIVES AND PROGRAM EVALUATION

A thoughtful consideration of pupil personnel programs in San Diego County leads one to conclude that many of the issues currently identified in the literature are relevant to this region. These issues would include: the philosophical basis for pupil personnel services; ethical considerations such as privileged communication and confidentiality of information; role and function of various staff positions; and professional training and selection of staff. Since these and related issues are competently treated in current material[22], three program needs identified by this author will be considered. While it is unlikely that the program needs would be refuted by many persons employed in the pupil personnel field, the alternatives selected to resolve these needs could lead to consideration of a number of issues.

The first need to be considered is to foster improvement in school programs and practices. Pupils, parents, and professional educators all speak to the need for making schools more relevant, less bureaucratic, and more person-oriented. The issue involved is the role of pupil personnel workers as change agents. As a profession, we value the uniqueness of individuals and, by name, our services are pupil-oriented. Yet we are all painfully aware of institutional practices that are counter to a pupil-oriented program. As pupil personnel workers, we need to identify those institutional practices and propose alternative practices that are pupil-oriented. The means employed to bring about these improvements in public education must be open to discussion and examination, professionally motivated, and endorsed by the governing body of the institution.

A second and somewhat related need is to expand the sphere of influence of pupil personnel programs. Since our focus is on pupils, we sometimes neglect to consider the services that should be provided to parents and faculties, and our relationships with other governmental and social agencies. The current emphasis on career education appears to be an effort to expand the sphere of influence regarding occupational preparation.[23] The role of pupils, parents, teachers, and the community with respect to career education is being identified and members of each group can see that they are an important element. In like manner, pupil personnel programs should

247

increase efforts to involve these groups in the attainment of program goals.

The third need is related to program goals and involves the need for clearly identified program objectives. This need is highlighted by the current emphasis on program accountability and cost-benefit analysis. From the pupil personnel administrator's point of view, program objectives are helpful since they facilitate both program planning and evaluation.

To aid in the development of pupil personnel objectives, a task force assembled by the Bureau of Pupil Personnel Services of the California State Department of Education produced a process guide. An edited version of this guide was prepared for publication by the California Personnel and Guidance Association.[24] This guide follows the conceptual framework proposed by Wellman as an outgrowth of the National Study of Guidance.[25] This framework provides for the classification of objectives in the educational, social, and vocational domains.

It is the point of view of this author that the current emphasis on accountability and evaluation will lead to the strengthening of pupil personnel programs. Further, we will have data available to answer the question, "Do pupil personnel services really make any difference in the lives of the children and youth we serve?"

1. *Population Trends: San Diego County* (San Diego: County Planning Dept., 1970).
2. *Enrollment by Grades, San Diego County* (San Diego: County Dept. of Education, Jan. 1972).
3. *Background Material on Educational Services and Facilities* (San Diego: Comprehensive Planning Organization, Feb. 1972), p. 1.
4. Ibid., p. 21.
5. Ibid., p. 5.
6. Ibid., p. 8
7. Ibid., p. 1
8. *Enrollment by Grades, San Diego County,* op. cit.
9. *Education Code* (Sacramento: California State Dept. of Education, 1969), Sections 3141–3306.
10. *California Guidance Newsletter* (Sacramento: California State Dept. of Education, Sept. 1970), 25(1):3.
11. *Education Code,* op. cit., Sections 13485–13489.
12. *Guidelines for School Districts to Use in Developing Procedures for Evaluating Certificated Personnel* (Sacramento: California State Board of Education, March 1972).
13. Kenneth H. Parker, "Location of Guidance Facilities Within the School Plant," *The Personnel and Guidance Journal* (Dec. 1957), pp. 251–54; *Physical Facilities for Pupil Personnel Services* (Sacramento: California State Dept. of Education, Bureau of Pupil Personnel Services, April 1971).
14. Thomas L. Jacobson, "Career Guidance Centers," *The Personnel and Guidance Journal* (March 1972), 50:599–604.
15. Thomas L. Jacobson and Eugene K. Journey, "The Career Center: Career Education Delivery System for the Junior High School" (San Diego County Dept. of Education, 1972, mimeographed).
16. Nicholas S. Mallek, "Memo to Governing Board," Grossmont Union High School District, July 26, 1971.
17. *Annual Report of Financial Transactions of the School Districts of San Diego County* (San Diego: County Dept. of Education, Nov. 1971).
18. John R. Gaskins, "A Research Report on Pupil Personnel Services," in *California Guidance Newsletter* (Sacramento: California State Dept. of Education, Sept. 1968), 23(1):7.
19. Glen N. Pierson, Richard Hoover, and Edwin A. Whitfield, "A Regional Career Information Center: Development and Process," *Vocational Guidance Quarterly* (1967), 15:162–70; Edwin A. Whitfield and George A. Glaeser, "Microfilm Approach to Disseminating Vocational Information; An Evaluation: Project VIEW," *Vocational Guidance Quarterly* (1969), 18:82–86.
20. P. Marvin Barbula, "Bulletin to Chief Administrative Offices" (San Diego: County Dept. of Education, 31, no. 271, June 22, 1971).
21. *Education Code,* op. cit., Sections 894–5.
22. Ruth Barry and Beverly Wolf, *Modern Issues in Guidance—Personal Work* (New York: Bureau of Publications, Teachers College, Columbia University, 1957); Bruce Shertzer and Shelley C. Stone, *Fundamentals of Guidance* (Boston: Houghton Mifflin Company, 1966).

23. Sidney P. Marland, "Career Education Now," an address delivered at the Convention of the National Association of Secondary School Principals, in Houston, Texas, Jan. 23, 1971.

24. *Accountability in Pupil Personnel Services: A Process Guide for the Development of Objectives,* (Fullerton, Calif.: California Personnel and Guidance Association, monograph no. 3, 1971).

25. Frank T. Wellman, "A Conceptual Framework for the Derivation of Guidance Objectives and Outcome Criteria," ERIC Document no. ED 012 470.

CHAPTER 8

Pupil Personnel Services in Denver City Schools

JAMES M. O'HARA

THE COMMUNITY SETTING

THE Denver Public School District, officially designated as School District No. 1 in the City and County of Denver in the State of Colorado, is located on the high plains east of the front range of the Rockies. Its 1970 population of 514,678 lived in the heart of a metropolitan area of 1,229,798, which comprised the Denver standard metropolitan statistical area. In the last twenty-five years this region has grown at a rate greater than other regions in Colorado. In fact, the growth rate surpasses that of virtually all other urban areas in the country. This trend is expected to continue at least through the current decade.

According to the 1970 census, the median family income in Denver was $9,654. The population includes approximately seventeen percent Hispano, nine percent Negro, seventy-two percent Anglo, one-half percent Indian, with the remainder being Asian or of other ethnic origins. Females outnumber the males by approximately 30,000 in Denver.

Historically, the Denver Public Schools has benefited from strong financial and other kinds of community support for its educational activities. State law allows the board of education to increase its budget, within limits, on its own initiative. The board may levy a tax of up to four mills a year for a capital reserve fund and also may increase its general fund budget by up to six percent on its own initiative. Beyond these limits, there must be approval of the registered qualified electorate in the school district. Generally, when voter approval has been sought, it has been given.

A normal range of community supportive services in urban settings is available in the Denver community. Social, welfare, mental health, and other pupil-serving agencies have a good working relationship with the school system, primarily through the school social work program. However, there is increasing concern about services for children and families not able to afford needed services. Some assistance has become available for such children through special federal projects, such as Model Cities, but the need still exceeds available resources.

What would be identified as major community needs would largely be a function of who was doing the identifying. The Denver Chamber of Commerce and its affiliates developed the following "Metro Goals for Greatness," in 1969, reflecting their views of problems in need of attention.

1. Stapleton International and Regional Airports
2. Higher Education—Public and Private
3. Platte River Development
4. Urban Renewal and Model Cities
5. Metropolitan Public Schools
6. Water and Flood Control
7. Ground Transportation
8. Health (Includes Air and Water Polution)
9. Recreation and Culture
10. Governmental efficiency.[1]

Others would subscribe to the following account:

Denver City and County has witnessed the traditional pattern of problems faced by core metropolitan cities across the nation. These include: dispersal of retail and service businesses to outer city and suburban locations; development of major new employers and older expanding employers into peripheral and suburban sites or beyond; the tendency for higher and middle income citizens to move or locate in newer or suburban communities; concentration of ethnic and racial minorities in the core city; constantly rising cost of physical improvements and maintenance of public facilities such as streets, etc.

The list of core city problems is almost endless. Many problems are shared by the entire metro area—transportation, air and water pollution, flood and storm drainage control, water distribution, and sewage disposal.

Other problems are uniquely the core city of Denver's problems: e.g., taxes, school integration, welfare programs, Model Cities, urban renewal, and others. Occasionally, the solution to one core city problem may be applied successfully to the solution of a suburban problem.[2]

Still other citizens would identify other major problems.

In viewing these problems, it is safe to assume that the school system alone will not solve all these problems. However, it also seems safe to assume that without an effective school system, none of these problems will be solved.

The Schools

The overall organizational and administrative structure of the Denver Public Schools can be identified as a typical line and staff organizational pattern. Under the general direction of the Superintendent of Schools, there is an assistant superintendent in charge of each of the following four major divisions: Education, Administrative Services, Facility Planning and Engineering, and General Administration. Figure 8.1 shows the departmental organization plan within the Division of Education.

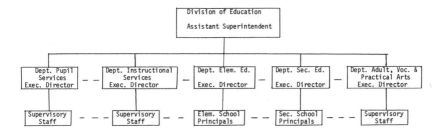

Fig. 8.1. Departmental organization of Denver Division of Education.

The functions of the various departments within the Division of Education are evident in the titles of the departments which are as follows: Pupil Services, Instructional Services, Elementary Education, Secondary Education, and Adult, Vocational and Practical Arts. Each of these departments is headed by an executive director. As is evident in the chart, the Executive Director of Elementary Education has a line relationship with elementary school principals, and the Executive Director of Secondary Education has a line relationship

253

with secondary school principals. Other executive directors and staff members in their departments serve in a staff/consultant relationship to school principals except in limited areas of activity.

A Department of Health Services, which includes physicians, nurses, a dental hygenist, and other health personnel, is a part of the Division of General Administration.

The numbers of schools and enrollments, K through 12, in regular schools in April 1972 was as follows:

LEVEL	NUMBER OF SCHOOLS	ENROLLMENT
Elementary	92	50,881
Junior High School	18	21,197
Senior High School	9	17,541
TOTAL	119	89,619

The peak enrollment year was 1968–69 at approximately 96,000 pupils, and since then enrollment has declined annually.

The organizational pattern in elementary schools varies considerably in relation to the educational needs of the pupils. At one extreme is a small suburban elementary school staffed by teachers and a school principal, with some pupil services available on call and a minimal school nurse service. At the other end of the continuum is a large inner-city school with a principal, assistant principal, teachers, a full-time social worker, a full-time counselor, a full-time nurse, part-time psychologist, and additional teacher specialists and aides. Other schools, organizationally, would fall between these extremes.

At the junior high school level and the senior high school level, the typical organizational plan for the professional staff is as shown in Figure 8.2.

In this plan, which is typical for junior high schools (minus athletics) and senior high schools, the principal has three administrative assistants, one of whom is identified as the vice principal and the other two are identified as assistant principals. One of these staff members is in charge of administrative services, another is in charge of instructional services, and the third is in charge of pupil services. The term vice principal is used to identify the person who is in charge of the school in the absence of the principal. This staff member's regular assignment may be in the instructional area, in the administrative area, or in the pupil services area. In relation to needs at the local school level, each of these administrators in turn may

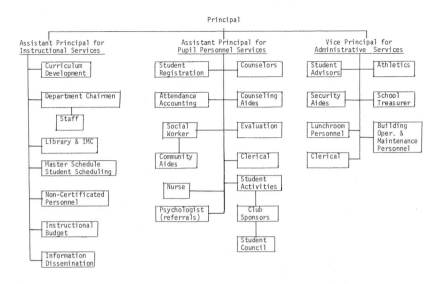

Figure 8.2. Typical organization of Denver secondary schools.

have staff members who assist them in carrying out their responsibilities. The person in charge of administrative services, for example, may have one or more assistants assigned primarily to work in the area of pupil discipline. The person responsible for instructional services usually has departmental chairmen in the various academic areas with whom he works. The person in charge of pupil services may have a guidance chairman or head counselor to help coordinate activities within the guidance area and, on occasion, within the pupil services area.

As set forth in the chart, the administrator in charge of pupil services does have a line relationship with the pupil services workers, the nurse, and other staff members working in the pupil services area.

Typical responsibilities for this administrator, under the direction of the school principal, are as follows:

1. To provide leadership in the overall organization and administration of a program of pupil services.

255

2. To coordinate and direct the services of pupil services staff members assigned to the school, including the counselors, psychologist, social worker, nurse, and others as assigned.
3. To participate in the selections and assignment of pupil services staff members.
4. To evaluate the effectiveness of the overall and the various components of the pupil services program.
5. To insure that adequate staff development activities are provided for staff members in the interest of improving the effectiveness of the services.
6. To initiate activities as needed to improve the cooperation among pupil services staff members and other staff members involved in instructional services and administrative services in the school.
7. To keep the principal apprised of needs in the pupil services areas.
8. To make recommendations relative to budget and to administer the pupil services budget for the school.
9. To serve as liaison with pupil services supervisors and consultants in the school system in the interest of best utilizing their services in maintaining an effective program of pupil services in the school.

In smaller secondary schools, this staff member may have other responsibilities than those usually associated with the administration of the pupil services program.

Except for counselors and other staff members involved in guidance services at the local school level, budget and manpower allocations to various schools is the responsibility of the staff members in the various offices in the Department of Pupil Services. Nurse allocations are the responsibility of the Department of Health Services. Counselors and other guidance staff members are allocated to the secondary schools by the Department of Secondary Education. However, school principals do have the prerogative of utilizing these allocations and teacher allocations in ways they consider most consistent with the needs of the schools. In most secondary schools, one or more teacher allocations are converted to counselor assignments in order to provide high priority services to the pupils.

In senior high schools, specialists, identified as "college and scholarship counselor" and "career counselor," are available in addition to the "general counselor." The specialists conduct informational activities for all pupils and assist individual pupils on a referral basis —self-referral or otherwise. More descriptive data about these positions are presented later in this chapter.

PUPIL PERSONNEL SERVICES

Several factors which should be helpful in understanding the organization and administration of pupil services in the Denver Public Schools are as follows:

1. The term pupil services is used instead of pupil personnel services.
2. A broad range of pupil-related activities beyond that usually identified as pupil services is part of the responsibility of the Department of Pupil Services.
3. The responsibilities of staff members in the Department of Pupil Services are essentially staff-consultant-resource type responsibilities, with limited administrative-line responsibilities.
4. Health services are not a part of the Department of Pupil Services, but a close working relationship exists between the staffs in both departments.
5. Budget for school counselors and other guidance personnel in the schools is a responsibility of the Department of Elementary Education and the Department of Secondary Education.

Figure 8.3 shows the organization within the Department of Pupil Services and relationship to school principals and other departments.

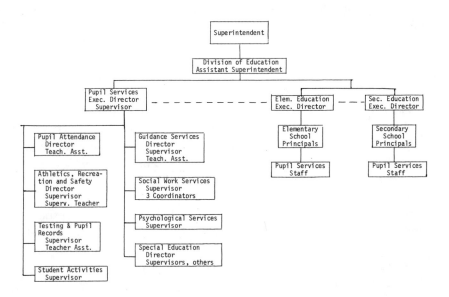

Fig. 8.3. Organization of Denver Department of Pupil Services.

As is shown in Figure 8.3, there are eight offices in the Department of Pupil Services. Two of these offices usually are not identified as part of pupil services in other school systems: Athletics, Recreation and Safety and Student Activities. Special Education in many school systems is a part of the Department of Pupil Services, as it is in Denver. The other five offices in the department, in almost all instances, are joined together in the Department of Pupil Services: Guidance Services, Social Work Services, Psychological Services, Pupil Attendance, and Testing and Pupil Records. The staff members assigned to the five offices as shown in Figure 8.3 are as follows:

Guidance Services: Director, Supervisor, Counselor Assistant
Psychological Services: Supervisor
Social Work Services: Supervisor, three Coordinators
Pupil Attendance: Director, Teacher Assistant
Testing and Pupil Records: Supervisor, Teacher Assistant

These staff members are certificated, and their services are supplemented by some noncertificated employees, including clerical staff members assigned to their offices.

Figure 8.3 also shows the relationship between the Department of Pupil Services and the Department of Elementary Education and the Department of Secondary Education. The relationships are essentially "staff" relationships, as are the relationships between the staff members in the various offices in the Department of Pupil Services and the principals in the elementary schools and the secondary schools. The chart also clearly sets forth the fact that pupil services staff members in a school work under the direction of the school principal while the staff members are in the schools. The directors, supervisors, and others in the Department of Pupil Services serve as resource people and consultants to the school principals and the staffs in the schools.

Budgets for social workers and for psychologists are the responsibilities respectively of the Supervisor of Social Work Services and the Supervisor of Psychological Services. These staff members and those assisting them work closely with school principals and their staffs in determining needs for these services in the schools and in determining allocations for each school. To help insure appropriate use of social workers and psychologists, a negotiations-type process takes place involving the worker, the principal or his designee, and

258

the supervisor or his designee. Ideally, their understandings are put in writing and given to all parties involved in this process.

Position descriptions are available for the various staff members assigned to the offices in the Department of Pupil Services. Generally, these require that the staff members be responsible for providing professional leadership, insuring coordination of services, providing needed services to schools, planning and conducting staff development activities, and assisting in evaluation of services.

Approved job descriptions are on file in the Department of Personnel Services for pupil services workers assigned to the school.

School Social Worker:
POSITION TITLE: School Social Worker, M.S.W.
REPORTS TO: Supervisor, Social Work Services

Basic Function
To utilize social work training and skill in providing direct service to parents and their children whose behavior, attitudes, and circumstances are such that they need specialized individual attention and help in order to fully utilize educational opportunities; to provide consultation to school staffs as part of a problem-solving process; to utilize community organization skills in understanding and meeting the needs of the larger school community; to coordinate social work activities with school objectives.

Major Responsibilities
1. Assist with educational problems
    - where academic performance is not in keeping with expectancy, especially where there is such possible causation as emotional factors and problems in interpersonal relationships
    - where there is possible need for special education
    - as a consultant in mental health aspects of curriculum planning
    - by assisting teachers in incorporating mental health aspects into classroom procedure
    - by making recommendations for specific children regarding class placement.
2. Provide direct assistance when behavior indicates emotional maladjustment, i.e., when the child
    - has difficulty getting along with others
    - is disruptive and overly aggressive
    - is excessively shy, withdrawn, fearful
    - displays disproportionate attention seeking and/or inability to accept authority
    - displays bizarre behavior
    - displays unsocial behavior related to limited ability.
3. Provide direct service to children and parents through

259

- individual casework to alleviate conditions and feelings which interfere with the child's use of learning opportunities
- group work when it is indicated that this method can provide mutual self-help through the group process
- family interviewing when the presenting problems suggest that family members can best be helped through assistance to the total family as a unit.
- other techniques, such as behavior modification, crisis intervention, when these methods seem indicated.

4. Provide direct help to families
- when the family's personal problems are affecting the child's adjustment to school
- by referring parents to appropriate community agencies which can offer them help for their problems
- by serving, when appropriate, as a liaison between school and home.

5. Assist in providing service to the school community by
- developing understanding of the larger school community—its unique aspects and needs
- utilizing social work methods (including community organization skills) in helping meet these needs
- collaborating with other school "team members," community, and agency personnel in identifying gaps in service and in coordinating efforts and resources.

6. Serve as a consultant to school personnel
The consultation role is identified in social work training as a specific technique for use in the problem-solving process. The social worker serves as a consultant to the school personnel
- when he can effect broader change than he could through direct service
- when there are indications that the child's problems can best be resolved by direct service from other school personnel utilizing consultation from the social worker.

7. Provide help with problems of pupils' irregular attendance
- when the nonattendance and/or truancy indicate serious personal-social-academic problems
- when the attendance problems at a particular school are too few to warrant the assignment of a social work assistant.

8. Provide help with pupils' economic problems
- when economic assistance (car fare to school, lunches, books, clothing, etc.) is part of the comprehensive social work service being offered to the family
- when the economic problems at a particular school are too few in number to warrant the assignment of a social work assistant.

9. Assume the primary liaison role with community agencies when
- the child's school or home problems suggest referral to a community agency

- coordination of effort and information between schools and agencies is needed
- gaps in services suggest the need for school and agency to utilize community organizational skills in developing more adequate services.

10. Supervise social work assistants and community aides
    - as assigned.
11. Provide field work (internship) experience for graduate social work students and other students from local colleges and universities.
    - as assigned.

School Psychologist:
POSITION TITLE: School Psychologist
REPORTS TO: Supervisor, Psychological Services

Basic Function
Apply psychological knowledge and expertise in the schools, with special attention focused on the child as he interacts within the school and/or learning environment.

Major Responsibilities:
1. Serve as a resource person and through primarily consultative efforts establish a sharing relationship to better enable school personnel to:
   - understand a child's individual strength and deficit areas
   - assist in the appropriate modification of learning, curriculum, and classroom management procedures
   - develop ways to facilitate learning and the adjustment of children, individually as well as in groups
   - suggest improvements for the learning climate or atmosphere of individual classrooms.
2. Assist school personnel in enriching the experiences, mental health, and overall growth of children.
3. Serve as a resource person to school personnel in identifying or recognizing exceptional children and recommend suitable measures for working with them.
4. Conduct in-service programs in assigned schools in order to extend knowledge and understanding of behavior, learning, child growth and development and/or mental health.
5. Work with local school unit parent groups and others concerned with the learning processes and behavior of students.
6. Work closely with other ancillary services personnel in an effort to evaluate existing services and to recommend appropriate change as well as ongoing local school unit in-service needs.
7. Serve as an aid in the appropriate referral of children to other community agencies, such as the John F. Kennedy Center, Univer-

261

sity of Colorado Day Care Center, Children's Hospital Evaluation and Treatment Center, etc.

8. Assist Special Education and Health Services personnel re: the appropriate assignment of children to Denver Public Schools Special Education programs.

9. Perform psychological evaluations for pupils referred by teachers, principals, parents, and other school personnel. Psychological evaluation may entail observation, consultation, review of pertinent data and/or the administration of individual psychometrics. Types of individual psychological tests which the psychologist may administer are: (a) projective or personality, (b) intelligence, (c) perceptual-motor and/or visual-perceptual, (d) achievement, (e) learning methods, (f) attitudinal, (g) language development.

General Counselor

POSITION TITLE: General Counselor (High School)
REPORTS TO: Principal or his designee

Basic Function

Help to provide effective guidance and counseling services in his school under the direction of the building principal or his designee with professional supervision and assistance from the Office of Guidance Services, in accordance with the objectives and policies of the Board of Education.

Major Responsibilities

1. Counsel with individual pupils and with groups of pupils.
2. Provide pupils, teachers, and parents with specific information and help as needs are identified.
3. Provide specialized skills in the areas of counseling, adolescent growth and development, and human relations.
4. Aid pupils in their development of a positive self-image and effective personal-social relationships.
5. Encourage and help pupils to explore a variety of factors and alternatives involved in developing educational and vocational plans.
6. Assist pupils in selecting course offerings to meet high school graduation requirements and other educational and vocational objectives; assist in scheduling pupils into selected courses.
7. Help pupils examine and increase their knowledge and understanding of various occupational fields in the broad area of the "world of work."
8. Provide pupils with information related to education and training opportunities beyond high school.
9. Help teachers identify specific individual pupil strengths and weaknesses and assist them in planning appropriate educational activities to meet identified needs.

262

10. Work in a cooperative relationship with other members of the pupil services team.
11. Make referrals to appropriate school resources for specific additional help from the social worker, school nurse, school psychologist, or other specialized personnel.
12. Make recommendations, when appropriate, for changes and additions to the school curriculum to better meet the needs of the pupils and/or staff.
13. Keep accurate records on assigned counselees and guidance activities and make periodic reports to the principal.
14. Help plan and conduct orientation activities for pupils new to the school.
15. Interpret test scores to pupils and parents.
16. Assist pupils to learn how to make decisions and solve developmental problems they face in their growth to maturity.
17. Monitor the progress of each pupil in adjusting to the scholastic, social, and personal demands of his/her school life.
18. Keep the principal informed of major problems and developments regarding the guidance program in his school.

Career Counselor (Senior High School)
POSITION TITLE: Career Counselor
REPORTS TO: Principal or his designee

Basic Function:
Provide effective career guidance and counseling service in his school under the direction of the building principal or his designee, with technical assistance and consultation from the Office of Guidance Services, in accordance with the objectives and policies of the Board of Education.·

Major Responsibilities:
1. Plan and coordinate vocational guidance and counseling activities for high school pupils.
2. Work closely with Youth Opportunity Center personnel to provide job placement services for in-school youth and graduating high school seniors.
3. Coordinate and/or conduct programs and activities to prepare youth with effective techniques and methods for finding employment.
4. Assist pupils in the employment seeking process for part-time and summer work and for permanent work following graduation.
5. Work cooperatively with Cooperative Occupation Education teacher-coordinators to develop work training stations for Cooperative Occupation Education pupils.
6. Plan activities such as career days and excursions to places of

business and industry to increase pupil knowledge and understanding of entry level jobs and career opportunities.

7. Serve as a resource person by assisting general counselors and other school staff members to work with pupils in career planning activities.

8. Keep teachers informed of career guidance resource materials which relate to their subject areas.

9. On a referral basis, counsel pupils with special needs concerning educational and vocational goals and employment opportunities.

10. Work with the librarian in establishing and maintaining files of current occupational information.

11. Maintain files and catalogs of information about post high school programs of vocational education and training.

12. Provide pupils, counselors, parents, and teachers with specific information about jobs and careers as needed.

13. Establish and maintain contacts in the business/industry community to keep career counseling information current and to develop and locate employment opportunities for pupils.

14. Assist in administering and interpreting aptitude tests and interest inventories.

15. Keep counselors and pupils informed about vocational training opportunities that are available through high school vocational courses, Cooperative Occupation Education (C.O.E.) programs, and the high school extension program at Emily Griffith Opportunity School.

16. Register pupils for high school extension programs at Emily Griffith Opportunity School and provide the liaison service between Opportunity School and the home high school.

17. Act as liaison between the high school and outside agencies such as the National Alliance of Businessmen, Neighborhood Youth Corp., and Youth Opportunity Center.

18. Arrange for group meetings as needed for students planning post-secondary vocational or technical education.

19. Keep accurate records and make periodic reports to the Office of Guidance Services.

20. Keep the principal or his designee informed of all major problems and developments concerning the preparation of young people to progress from school to paid employment and/or post high school vocational training.

College and Scholarship Counselor—Senior High School
POSITION TITLE: College and Scholarship Counselor
REPORTS TO: Principal or his designee

Basic Function
Administer an effective program of college planning activities for his school under the direction of the building principal or his designee, with technical assistance and consultation from the Office of Guidance

Services, in accordance with the objectives and policies of the Board of Education.

Major Responsibilities
1. Plan, conduct, and coordinate college counseling activities for pupils at the high school level.
2. Maintain and update college and scholarship informational materials and catalogs in cooperation with the school librarian.
3. Counsel pupils concerning scholarships and other financial aid programs.
4. Provide pupils and parents with specific information, help, and encouragement in the area of college planning.
5. Serve as a resource person by assisting all counseling personnel and other school staff members to work with pupils in their college planning needs.
6. Help pupils examine and increase their knowledge and understanding of various post-secondary educational opportunities.
7. Work in a cooperative relationship with general counselors and others of the Pupil Services team.
8. Work with agencies, organizations, foundations, and colleges concerning financial aid opportunities, visitations, and "College Night" programs.
9. Assist in administering and interpreting aptitude tests, achievement tests, and interest inventories that deal with college planning.
10. Keep accurate records on college-bound pupils and make periodic reports to the Office of Guidance Services.
11. Conduct group guidance meetings for all college-bound pupils at each grade level.
12. Work closely with other staff members in planning for college admission tests.
13. Conduct follow-up studies to provide information about pupils who apply for college admission and/or enter college.
14. Develop procedures to insure that potentially capable and interested pupils from minority or underprivileged groups are given special encouragement and aid in securing admission to colleges or universities.
15. Coordinate the preparation of recommendations for pupils applying for college admission.
16. Serve as a resource person to contributing elementary and junior high schools concerning college guidance activities.
17. Work closely with colleges, organizations, and foundations on financial aid programs and problems.
18. Participate on college guidance advisory committees.
19. Participate in visits to collegiate institutions.
20. Keep the Office of Guidance Services and the principal or his designee informed of all major problems and developments regarding college counseling activities in his school.

Other Pupil Personnel Services Positions

Although no formal position description is on file for the eleven counselors assigned to elementary schools, this program has been described as follows: A major purpose of counseling services in an elementary school is to bring the full impact of the school into the best possible focus upon the unique needs of the individual child. One function of the counselor may be viewed as constituting an attempt to systematize and insure proper facilitation of certain functions that commonly get performed only incidentally. The elementary school counselor makes a significant contribution in the process of identifying and providing for the developmental needs of children. The counselor's primary task is to help the pupil to learn about himself, his relationship with others, his environment, and to relate this information to his decisions. Through working with the counselor, the pupil learns to make decisions more independently.

The program is designed to provide pupils with:

1. additional help in recognizing and resolving problems that interfere with their learning or personal relationships;
2. additional specialized assistance by the professional staff in diagnosing individual difficulties and weaknesses, with special provision made for prescriptive remediation;
3. increased opportunities for counseling in order to provide for a more meaningful and significant educational experience than they have yet experienced;
4. special types of motivating experiences for pupils who cannot or have not been able to function satisfactorily in the regular classroom program.

School nurses assigned by the Department of Health Services provide health services to the school under the direction of the school principal or his designee and with the professional assistance of staff members in the Department of Health Services.

In the spring of 1972 the ratios for various pupil services staff members in the schools, excluding those funded by special state or federal programs, were as follows:

POSITION	RATIOS
Junior high school counselors	1–385 pupils
Senior high school counselors	1–207 pupils
Social workers	1–1378 pupils
Psychologists	1–5600 pupils

Social workers and psychologists do have some noncertificated employees, in limited numbers, who assist them. In addition, eleven counselors are assigned among fifteen elementary schools.

The budget for the Denver Public Schools is different from the budget in a number of other school systems in terms of the items that are included in it; so, no effort is made here to relate the cost of each of the services to the total operating budget of the Denver Public School Systems.

Pupil Services staff members have worked with administrators and others in the interest of developing guidelines that could be used in constructing pupil services facilities in new buildings. A counselor on special assignment in the Office of Guidance Services coordinated the work of a committee, focusing specifically on facility needs in an elementary school.

The recommendations developed for the elementary school, with some minor modifications, are applicable also to junior and senior high schools.

General Description

A well-organized program of pupil services demands specially designed facilities in order to function most effectively. These facilities serve as a vehicle and environment for the pupil services programs and enable the staff to serve identified needs. Pupils and others will be served better if the environment of these facilities is planned to complement the pupil services staffs' professional preparation and background.

The rooms and offices in the pupil services complex should provide for maximum use of time and energy of the staff. The various components of the facility should form a highly coordinated unit with no isolated areas. Each room should be designed for specific functions but provide for sufficient flexibility and optimal utilization. All rooms should contribute to a unit which facilitates all functions of the pupil services activities.

Because the pupil services are so closely related, facilities should be planned to provide for convenient access from one service to another. Ease of mobility between offices, conference rooms, and all other areas within the facility will encourage frequent exchange of information and ideas between staff members.

Offices
1. Each service offered in the pupil services complex requires special

physical arrangements. For example, the facility, its furnishings, equipment, and decorations must reflect such basic conditions as auditory and visual privacy that are so essential.

2. Certainly the arrangement must convey to the client a sense of assurance that information will be kept confidential.

3. To convey the impression visually that the pupil services facility is one encouraging relaxation and comfort, it should be pleasing esthetically.

4. The offices should provide a setting in which the pupil services staff member may meet comfortably with individual pupils and with small groups of pupils.

Conference Rooms

1. Conference rooms should be provided away from the normal flow of traffic and noise but within the general complex of the pupil services facilities.

2. These rooms would also provide facilities in which to administer tests to individuals or to small groups.

Reception Area

The reception area should be incorporated to facilitate the coordination of pupil services activities. This reception area is the center of the traffic flow for those who desire assistance from pupil services —pupils, teachers, parents, administrators, and community visitors. Therefore, the facilities in this area must be designed to provide comfortable, attractive surroundings for the people who are waiting for services, reading material that will aid in orienting them to the activities of pupil services, and space for a receptionist-clerk, who will make appointments, answer questions about services and materials available. The traffic flow from the reception area to the various rooms and offices requires careful routing in that pupils, faculty members, and parents should be able to pass directly from the reception area to the various rooms without having to pass through other areas first.

Activity Room

- An activity room should be incorporated into the plans for the pupil services facility to provide for numerous unique and varied opportunities for pupils and staff to function and interact in a multi-purpose open and relatively free environment.

Storage

- The storage area(s) should be readily accessible to the people who must use it.

268

- Since various records are basic to pupil services work, they must be filed in convenient, handy, and secure locations.
- Security precautions should be considered in designing storage facilities in order to protect not only personal records but also tests, office supplies, and valuable equipment such as tape recorders, videotape equipment.

Observation Room
- A multi-purpose observation room should be provided to facilitate both visual and auditory observation of the activity room and one or more of the offices or conference rooms. This room should be equipped with "one-way glass," a communications system which would allow the activities and conversations in the adjoining rooms to be heard, and videotaping equipment.

Location
- The interchange of information and service between school programs is continuous; therefore, plans for the location and design of facilities for each program must include consideration of the relationships between activities.
- Pupil services facilities should be located near, but apart from, the administrative offices.
- The pupil services facilities should be reasonably close to the library.
- It would be preferable if these facilities are located near a main entrance.

Toilet Facilities
- Since the pupil services area is used by outside persons as well as by pupils, suitable toilet facilities should be included as a part of the unit.

Communications
- Each office as well as the reception area should be equipped with a telephone and an intercommunications system.
- In addition, an inter-room communications system for the entire school is desirable.

Glass
- If the physical design of the building will permit, the pupil services offices should have outside windows for better natural light as well for as a more pleasant atmosphere.
- Areas bordering on corridors or hallways should have a section of "hammered" glass or other translucent material as a part of the wall in order to provide for a more "naturally lighted" effect.
- The doors to the various offices, conference rooms, and the activity room should be solid wood doors with a small section of clear glass

269

inserted at eye level in order to provide for at least some outside vision into the room.

Figure 8.4 shows the pupil services facilities as part of the layout of the new Cheltenham Elementary School. These facilities conform to most of the recommendations listed above.

Figure 8.5 shows the pupil services facilities as part of the layout of Place Junior High School where, again, most of the recommendations listed previously concerning such facilities were followed.

No new senior high schools have been built recently. However, as some have been remodeled, the recommendations listed earlier generally have been observed.In addition, special consideration has been given at the senior high school level to the need for more space and equipment related to the many information-type activities conducted by guidance staffs in the senior high schools, for example, jobs, careers, college, and related activities.

Summary

Since the pupil services activities are adaptable to the local school situation, the facilities must be in harmony with both present and projected services. As the program, services, and activities change, the facilities will need to change. Therefore, the original structure should be planned for the utmost flexibility with possible future alterations in mind.

In the area of pupil services, the needs of the clients aid in determining the program functions. As a result, physical facilities of an adequate, private, well-ventilated and functional nature are essential.

Effective pupil services, as an integral and essential part of the total educational program, can best be carried out in facilities specifically constructed for this purpose. Greater dividends will accrue where tensions are eased, physical exhaustion is lessened, and confidence and interest are activated.

Unique Characteristics of the Denver Program

The Denver Public Schools is indeed fortunate to have a well-qualified professional staff in all the special disciplines within the Pupil Personnel Services. Consequently, a wide variety of programs are under way throughout the school system, including a number of activities which are considered to be pilot efforts for innovative practices. In addition to a full range of regular types of programs and

270

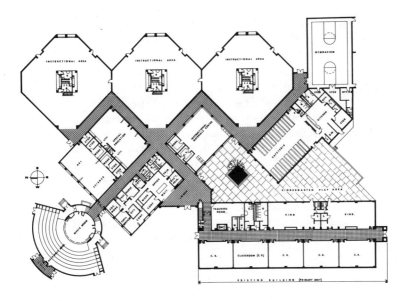

Fig. 8.4. Pupil services facilities in Cheltenham Elementary School shown at lower left.

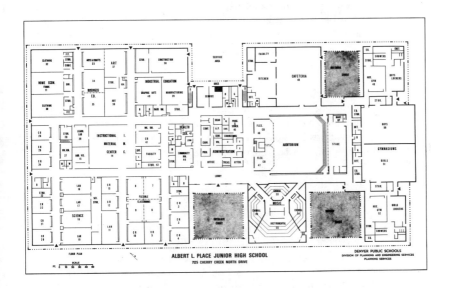

Fig. 8.5. Pupil services facilities at Place Junior School are shown at center left.

271

activities evident in the job descriptions cited earlier in this chapter, some of the more unusual activities within the Pupil Personnel programs are as follows:

Drug Education

- Drug Consultants are assigned to the Department of Pupil Services who have responsibility primarily for activities related to the identification and assistance of pupils involved in drug abuse, for liaison with individuals and agencies in the community that may be of assistance to pupils and families, and for planning and conducting continual staff development activities in relation to drugs.
- A peer counseling program is under way in which some junior and senior high school students work with some elementary pupils, essentially on value clarification activities which should have a positive impact on their attitudes toward drugs.
- Funds are available for planning and conducting activities to help develop key staff members to become resource people for their respective schools in the area of drug education.

Guidance Services

1. A corps of volunteer mothers work under the general supervision of counselors in hosting representatives from various colleges during their visits to high schools.
2. Staff members in guidance services have cooperated with staff members in other departments in the school system, with the Chamber of Commerce, with various businesses and industry in the community in producing twenty-four thirty-minute career guidance films which can be used with small groups or can be shown over television.
3. One junior high school has worked with a local university in helping to develop a career-oriented junior high school in which virtually all activities are governed by the extent to which they are seen as being helpful in the career development of a pupil.

Psychological Services

1. Psychologists are an integral part of an elementary school program aimed toward early identification of pupils with special learning problems and providing direct assistance to them as well as teachers and parents working with the pupils.
2. As part of a program for helping pupils with varying degrees of alienation at the elementary school level, a school psychologist has prime responsibility for planning activities related to improving teachers' competencies in working with these pupils and assisting administrators and other staff members in the early identification of alienated pupils and in helping such pupils.
3. School psychologists regularly schedule evening programs for teachers on a voluntary basis in order to help them develop skills

in areas of interest to them, notably, behavior modification, identification and assistance to pupils with learning disabilities, diagnostic testing and prescription procedures, and other related matters.
4. Psychologists provide special training programs for parents in the interest of helping them develop greater competency for having a positive impact on the behavior of their children and also to improve parent-school relationships.
5. Psychologists work with teachers of educationally handicapped and others in developing skills in the administration of various evaluative instruments that can be of assistance in diagnosing and prescribing learning experiences for pupils.

Pupil Attendance
1. A voluntary open enrollment program is administered by this office which enables pupils to transfer from one school to another when integration in the sending and the receiving school are improved by such transfer.

Social Work Services
1. Within the schools to which social workers are assigned, they provide special programs for the parents of preschool children, focusing primarily on parental techniques related to reinforcements of desired behavior of the children.
2. Social workers in an area in which schools have a high absentee rate have formed a network of communications and initiated activities to provide direct assistance to children with high absenteeism and to modify the environment in the schools and the community in the interest of helping these pupils.
3. Social workers serve as consultants to teachers in the development of their skills in the use of techniques such as the Magic Circle and other techniques aimed toward helping in the classroom management practices.
4. Special programs have been developed by social workers in cooperation with mental health programs on military bases in the interest of helping the children of military families who are in need of special assistance.

Special Education
5. A pilot effort is in its final stages in relation to the implementation of a planned program budgeting and evaluation system involving special education.
6. Insofar as practical, some speech correctionists are working intensively with language development problems as different from the usual speech handicaps in the interest of averting potential learning problems for pupils who use nonstandard English.
7. Each year, more teachers in the area of the educable mentally

273

handicapped and of the educationally handicapped are moving from the self-contained classroom setting into the resource teacher role in which they have pupils with them only a part of the day. These resource teachers then help other teachers who have the handicapped pupils for other parts of the regular school day.

8. A pilot effort of providing wholesome educational programs for autistic-like pupils is under way.

9. Increasing effort is being focused on preschool and early elementary school detection and remediation of learning handicaps.

10. A work-study program for hearing handicapped pupils is being implemented.

11. A series of extension centers which are located in nonschool settings is operative in the interest of providing educational experiences for disruptive pupils who have not been able to adjust to the regular junior high school program and environment.

12. A special education work experience and study program is operative in secondary schools which leads to a special education work-study diploma upon completion of the work and study requirements.

13. An extensive adaptive physical education program has been implemented primarily through the services of a resource teacher who assists other teachers in adapting physical education activities to meet the needs of pupils who may have physical or mental or emotional problems which limit their successful participation in the regular physical education classes.

14. Instructional resource centers are available to provide staff development activities related to exemplary teaching techniques as well as to keep them abreast of current research developments.

Testing and Pupil Records

15. Computer assisted test analysis programs are operative which identify various subskills within major skill development areas, such as reading and mathematics. Instructional supervisors cooperate in identifying prescriptive activities aimed toward helping teachers help pupils who have identified skill deficiencies.

This listing is little more than a sample of activities involving various pupil personnel staff members. The Department of Pupil Services, the Denver Public Schools, the community, the parents, and the pupils have a vested interest in having self-renewing professionals in these positions.

ISSUES AND ALTERNATIVES

There are a number of issues facing the pupil personnel program in Denver which may be different in kind and intensity than those

274

found in other school systems. Following are some current issues and comments about these issues which are in need of better answers than have been developed thus far:

Minority representation on pupil services staff. There is a great dearth of Black and Hispano counselors in all pupil services positions at all school levels. Participation in subsidized introductory guidance courses and in year-long EPDA institutes has enabled a few staff members from minority groups to be employed as school counselors. The lack of properly certified pupil services employees from minority groups, the lack of turn-over in these positions, and no increase in numbers of pupil services staff members work against any quick solutions to increasing the number of workers from minority groups.

Differentiated staffing. Certificated pupil services workers continue to perform duties that could be performed by staff members with far less training and at lower cost. Some progress has been made by the employment and effective job performance of assistants to school counselors, school psychologists, and school social workers. These assistants generally have had some formal education beyond high school and some are college graduates. It seems probable that persons with less training than this could assume a number of the less skilled tasks performed by pupil services specialists with no loss in efficiency and at lower cost. However, limited finances has delayed further exploration with differentiated staffing within the pupil services area.

Accountability. Pupil services activities, as well as instructional services activities and administrative services activities, have not been subject to rigorous evaluation of the product of these services. Preoccupation with what one is doing and the lack of skill necessary to implement accountability procedures contribute largely to lack of progress on this issue. Increased pressure, however, from legislators who have enacted state accountability laws, as well as from within the community, has resulted in an acceleration of planning and implementing of accountability activities. Some of the better examples of accountability are the result of the requirement of evaluations annually of all federally funded projects. Claims that much of what the pupil services worker hopes to accomplish is not susceptible to measurement are not acceptable.

*New pupil services roles.*Pupil services workers have maintained the integrity of their respective disciplines, despite the fact that there is considerable overlap in the training of staff members such as counselors, psychologists, and social workers. More recently, school nurses also have been getting additional training in relation to mental health problems and are making positive contributions in mental health activities. In a typical day, in some elementary schools, the

275

following pupil services and health services may be available to a school: one-half day social worker, one-half day counselor, one-half day nurse and, perhaps, a limited amount of a school psychologist's time. A pupil in need of assistance from the various services may meet with each one of these workers at one time or another. The parent and the principal, interested in knowing about such a pupil, also may have to meet individually with each worker to get such information. In such instances, school principals have raised some of the following questions:

1. Can our school counselor learn some of the skills of the social worker and be available for a full day rather than his being available one-half day and the social worker being available one-half day?
2. Can we forfeit the services of a counselor for one-half day and add this to the time of our one-half time social worker so that she would be available full-time and perform those duties we otherwise would expect of a social worker and a counselor?
3. Can we arrange for our social worker to develop evaluation skills that would enable her to conduct routine evaluations otherwise requiring the services of the school psychologist?

These questions deserve serious consideration and response. Strong interest on the part of various pupil services workers in maintaining the integrity of their disciplines and difficulty in arranging budget trade-offs involving budgets in various departments have delayed any movement toward the merging of pupil services roles.

Staff development. A knowledge explosion has been occurring in the various disciplines in pupil services and a real concern exists about the extent to which staff members keep renewing their skills and continue their search for more effective ways of helping children. Voluntary participation of various workers in staff development activities on their own time is limited. The most effective way to insure professional renewal seems to be to conduct such activities during the regular work day. A second preferred method for getting a positive response to staff development activities is to pay staff members for participating in such activities. Better answers are needed.

Local school autonomy. Vital decisions concerning the conduct of pupil services programs in schools are being made at the local school level. Such authority should enable the program to be responsive to the needs of the pupils and other needs at the local school level. The presence of local pupil services coordinating committees and the availability of consultant services should help maintain an effective program. However, some valid data are needed at the local school level and by decision-makers at the system-wide level in order to determine the effectiveness of programs and to provide assistance needed for

276

maintaining or improving the programs. Increased availability of computers for processing data should prove of immense value in this effort. At the present time, no hard data are available concerning the productivity of the pupil services programs, but then, neither are such data available concerning many programs in the instructional and administrative areas.

Program Evaluation

Ample data are available concerning what pupil services specialists do. Virtually no data are available concerning the impact of these services on pupils, other staff members, or programs. That there is some impact is obvious. That this impact is positive is probable. Information about the extent of the positive impact—which would be most helpful in determining priorities or budget outlays—generally is not available.

Information about what pupil services and health services staff members do, the percent of time spent in various activities, sources of referrals, and related data are useful benchmark data and do provide some bases for modifying these aspects of the pupil services and health services programs. However, when finances are limited, the inability to produce hard data about the impact of some staff members has eased the road for making reductions in these services.

The most comprehensive evaluative activities in the pupil services area have been those conducted in relation to the elementary school guidance program and, more specifically, the activities of elementary school counselors. Sound evaluative designs were developed and implemented and useful data gathered from records, pupils, parents, teachers, and administrators. This type of design and these data were required in relation to elementary school counselors funded by the Elementary and Secondary Education Act. However, such evaluation also took place in schools having counselors not supported by ESEA funding.

Repeatedly, the evaluative data substantiated the positive impact that counselors were having on pupils, teachers, parents, and administrators. Still, when federal funding of the elementary school counselor activities ceased, only the strong outcry from local school principals and members of the school communities were decisive in retaining counselors in those schools. The evaluative data were not sufficient. The primary reason that these data were not sufficient was that school principals in the affected schools were told that counseling time would have to be taken out of their allocated teacher time. To do so, of course, would result in increased class size for other staff members. Special pleas, however, by school principals and members of the community were instrumental in retaining counselors in schools under local funding who formerly were funded by a federal program.

Principals and staff in each elementary school continue to have the prerogative of trading off teacher time for counseling time, since funds for both of these kinds of staff members come out of the same budget. Faced with this choice, school principals and staffs in schools where elementary school counselors have not been employed, have opted for teacher time over counselor time.

It seems likely that only when a comprehensive accountability/evaluation program is implemented and hard data are available about the needs of pupils and the impact of the activities of teachers and pupil services specialists on pupils in relation to the goals of the school system will proper type of data be available for decision making. Just as searching questions are being asked about the value of pupil services workers, such questions also must be asked about the value of what our teachers are attempting to teach and the end product of teacher/pupil interaction. In all areas of educational activities, there must be a shift away from the concern about what people *do* and an increased concern about the *value of what they do*. The task of the pupil services staff members is clear in terms of the need to work toward the establishment of a comprehensive accounting/evaluative program for all educational activities with special attention to the contribution of the pupil services programs toward reaching our educational goals.

1. Denver Chamber of Commerce, "Goals for Greatness" (Denver, Colo., unpublished document, Aug. 1969).
2. Minutes of Denver Goals for Greatness Dept. Council, Denver Chamber of Commerce, Denver, Colo., Feb. 1971.

CHAPTER 9

Pupil Personnel Services in the
Independent School District: Osseo, Minnesota

JEROME KOENIG

THE COMMUNITY SETTING

FOR sixty-six square miles, Independent School District No. 279 spreads out embracing eight different communities. It is larger in land mass than its neighbor of less than ten miles, the city of Minneapolis. It was not always this way. In 1925 its students came from a six and one-half square mile area. But the 1950s and 1960s brought state pressure for school districts to consolidate. This resulted in the merging of fourteen rural North Hennepin County districts with Independent School District No. 279.

Population

With the enlarged land mass, the district inherited its population. This, together with the return of World War II veterans and the movement of young families to suburban communities, saw student population swell from 527 in 1950 to nearly 14,000 in 1971. Figure 9.1 shows this growth for five-year intervals beginning with 1950.

While the student population tripled during the decade following the 1960 census, the entire population nearly doubled. And there were some noticeable shifts in the age composition of the 50,984 people reported in 1970. For example, the under-five year age group claimed a smaller percentage of the total figure. In 1960 this group made up 22 percent of the total, whereas in 1970 it made up only 12 percent of the total. In another comparison, there was an increase in the percentage of the population claimed by the 5–19 year age

280

group. In 1960 they comprised 27 percent of the total 25,763 area population. In 1970, they claimed 35 percent of the total. Both census years estimate that the 20–35 year age groups made up 27 percent of the population, with the over 35-year-olds accounting for 24 and 26 percent, respectively, for 1960 and 1970. Table 3 depicts the population age distribution for the two recent census years.

Socio-economic and Ethnic Factors

The community is populated by what might be characterized as a predominately young white middle class citizenry. Preliminary census data indicates that over seventy percent are under age 35. Less than one percent are nonwhites.

Three occupational groupings account for about sixty percent of the workers. These are: clerical and kindred workers; professional, technical, and kindred workers; and craftsmen, foremen, and kindred workers. The latter two categories seem to contribute most to the total. Income level has increased considerably since the 1960 census, when fifty-two percent of the families had incomes between $5,000 and $8,000. Current data suggests that, for the 1970 census, the mean family income will be approximately $12,500. Employment for the recent census years was at about ninety-seven percent.

Educationally, some 73 percent of those 25 years of age and over have completed high school or more. Of this group, 22 percent have some college training. Ten years earlier, only 59 percent of this age distribution achieved high school graduation or more.

Residents inhabited 13,974 housing units in the district as of 1970. This reflects an increase of over 7,000 units in the ten-year period after the 1960 census. The total additions were split about equally between renter-occupied and owner-occupied type units, bringing the total rented units to 4,035 and total owner-occupied units to 9,300. Vacancies account for 639 dwellings. Of the owner-occupied units, 6,500 were valued at $20,000 or more. Ten years earlier only 411 units were valued at more than $19,999.

History and Nature of Educational Support

In the ten-year period between October 1958 and October 1968, voters approved nearly twenty-five million dollars for building construction through bond elections. These monies funded two additions to a senior high facility, *and* the erection of a district warehouse, and fourteen new instructional units. The latter included ten elementary schools, three junior high structures, and one senior high

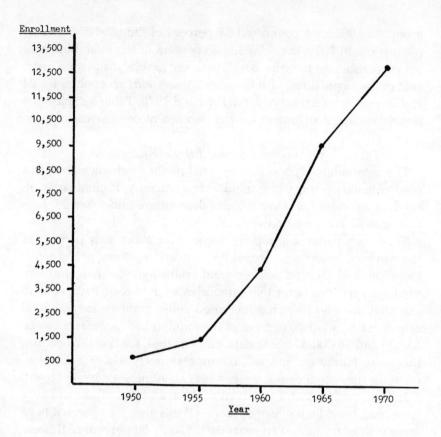

Fig. 9.1. Student population growth, 1950–70.

TABLE 3

*POPULATION DISTRIBUTION BY AGE GROUPS FOR 1960 AND 1970
CENSUS YEARS*

	1960 Census	% of Total	1970 Census	% of Total
Under 5 Years	5713	22.17	6142	12.05
5–9 Years	3775	14.65	7013	13.76
10–14 Years	2152	8.35	6786	13.31
15–19 Years	1081	4.20	4269	8.37
20–24 Years	1438	5.58	4822	9.45
25–34 Years	5591	21.70	8774	17.21
35–44 Years	3006	11.67	6611	12.97
45–54 Years	1365	5.30	3619	7.10
55–59 Years	448	1.74	941	1.84
60–64 Years	352	1.37	652	1.28
65 Years and Older	842	3.27	1355	2.66
Totals	25,763	100.00	50,984	100.00

282

plant. Table 4 lists pertinent data relative to the bond elections and building constructions for the ten-year period.

The extent of public acceptance of the building programs can be seen from the fact that seven of the nine bond issues succeeded the first time. On the two occasions when the bond elections failed, less than a year passed before subsequent ones were approved.

Between 1960 and 1970 the taxpayers felt successively bigger bites from their income to pay for increased educational services and inflation. The mill rate increased from 163 to 295.10 during that

TABLE 4

BOND ELECTIONS AND BUILDING CONSTRUCTION FOR THE PERIOD
1958–68

		VOTE		
Date	*$ Amount*	*Yes*	*No*	*Facility*
October 1958	1,300,000	1099	170	Garden City Elementary
				Park Brook Elementary
July 1959	3,400,000	675	113	Edgewood Elementary
				Crest View Elementary
				Osseo Senior High Addition
August 1961	3,000,000	662	135	Brooklyn Junior High
				Fair Oaks Elementary
April 1962	1,000,000	533	65	Osseo Senior High Addition
July 1963	4,000,000	498	846	Defeated
October 1963	4,000,000	2225	1433	Osseo Junior High
				Osseo Senior High Addition
				Palmer Lake Elementary
				Orchard Lane Elementary
December 1965	2,000,000	918	352	Birch Grove Elementary
				Zanewood Elementary
November 1967	5,000,000	1133	1973	Defeated
October 1968	10,250,000	7257	2992	Cedar Island Elementary
				North View Junior High
				Park Center Senior High
				Warehouse

283

period. Recent legislation to increase the state's contribution to education, and increases in assessed valuations have helped bring significant relief to homeowners, however. For example, the 1971–72 mill rate dropped to 166.09, approximately what it was eleven years earlier. For the school district, the per pupil unit cost of education continued to climb over the years. It ended the 1950s at $396.35 and began the 1970s at $904.50. The estimated figure for 1972–73 is $978.88.

Availability of Supportive Services

The community has a wealth of services within its boundaries or within easy driving distance. Churches, parochial schools, doctors' offices, homes for the aged, weekly newspapers, parks and playgrounds, post high school vocational training schools, and a junior college are among the in-district conveniences. The surrounding area offers more of the same, plus all the benefits of having access to facilities and services of the Greater Minneapolis and Hennepin County areas. These include several top-notch hospitals, four-year private and state colleges and the University of Minnesota, state employment offices, youth centers, radio and TV stations, daily newspapers, cultural centers, day-care centers and nursery schools, public welfare, civic and human relation organizations, and a vast array of social service and mental health facilities. Another type of service of fairly recent origin are those involving telephone counseling. At least eighteen agencies concerned with issues such as suicide prevention, runaways, drugs, and sexuality employ hot-lines. One group, a Minneapolis-based Community Information and Referral Service, provides information to callers who want to know where to get help for any need or concern.

In spite of the abundance of services available within close proximity to the district's citizens, many are reluctant to go beyond their immediate locale. Because of this, efforts have been sparked to decentralize some of the Greater Metropolitan area services and make them more convenient to local residents.

In general, it may be said that an abundance of services are available in the community and its nearby cities.

Major Community Needs

There is no clear evidence of any needs defined as such by the community as a whole. However, over the years, several issues related to the school have achieved action through involvement with

284

segments of the citizenry. The following serve as some examples of these.

1. 1965. An interested P.T.A. group sparked movement toward developing a K-12 family-life education curriculum.
2. 1968. Community civil rights groups joined with the school district in developing human relations proposals for the district covering staff in-service training, student education, and minority hiring.
3. 1968. Village park and recreation departments, in cooperation with the Board of Education, developed a "community school" concept. This opened school facilities during the community's leisure time for recreational and adult education opportunities.
4. 1970. A citizen's group was concerned about current enrollment projections which indicated that school facilities will be filled beyond capacity by 1976. They wanted to investigate using the schools on a year-round basis. The Board of Education, the school administration, and the PTA Council formed a research committee to study this possibility.
5. 1971. Efforts spearheaded by the District's Superintendent of Schools, combined with concerned citizen groups, resulted in the development of a K-12 drug education program.
6. 1972. A citizen's group concerned with alternative forms of education asked the Board of Education to establish a committee to investigate this matter. This was done, and funds were granted to cover the costs of administrative and clerical staff time and materials needed for the investigation.

In 1972 an effort was made by one of the elementary schools to determine to what extent parents felt that unit was fulfilling various goals and objectives of the district's educational program. From this, they hoped to infer needs. Only about twenty percent of the 500 questionnaires were returned.

If the district is to take into account community needs in developing its programs, appropriate vehicles and methods of assessment must be employed. Further, efficiency would suggest that the community at large and the schools must cooperatively decide who will provide what services.

Community Setting in Summary

What was once a district serving the children of potato farmers has now taken on the complexion of a middle-class white suburban community. Acres of farm land have given way to massive highway networks; vast housing developments, including private dwellings, townhouses, and huge apartment complexes; seventeen-district op-

285

erated school plants; parks and playgrounds; and an assortment of small business, large shopping centers, and various commercial and industrial plants. Services for virtually every need are available in the area or adjacent communities. However, the district's community proper may need to evaluate formally the need for specific types of services within the community itself, and under whose auspices they shall be conducted.

THE SCHOOLS

Organizational and Administrative Structure of the District

Valiant attempts were made over the years to accommodate the administrative structure to the staggering growth experienced in the district. School personnel increased as well as student population. The task in 1971 of administering educational programs for 14,000 students (up from 527 in 1950) became compounded with the need to employ, organize, coordinate, supervise, and pay 685 certified personnel (up from 20 in 1950) and 400 noncertified employees (clerks, cooks, custodians, etc.). The informal but real structure, which was characterized by a strong central office guiding the operation of each building unit, is gradually being modified. A "Central Office Management and Staffing" study, completed by a consulting firm in April 1970 provided recommendations and models for revising the organizational framework.[1] Considering the district's potential growth to some 70,000 enrollees within the next thirty years, consultants drafted proposals they believed would allow the district to achieve a level of effectiveness that would enable it to meet future demands. Essentially, the study influenced regrouping and definition of responsibilities, some decentralization, management by objectives, and accountability.

Key Systems of New Management Model

Four systems were conceived of as comprising the framework of the district: (1) planning and control, (2) personnel support, (3) management support, and (4) instructional.

The first system consists of the Board of Education, the Superintendent of Schools, an Administrative Assistant for Community Relations, and one for Information and Research. This group is responsible for the planning of educational services in the context of total community development. In addition, it is concerned with developing informational feedback systems and assessment procedures in

286

determining the effectiveness of institutional programs and pinpointing emerging problems. This system is depicted in Figure 9.2.

The personnel support system consists of the Director of Personnel, his assistant, and clerical staff. This office is expected to deal with recruitment, employment, fringe benefits, etc., of both certified and noncertified personnel. Figure 9.3 sketches this position.

Five functions are included in the management support system. They are: (1) the business office, (2) plant operation and maintenance, (3) transportation, (4) food services, and (5) negotiations. Supervisors of these areas report to the Director of Administration. See Figure 9.4 for an outline of this arrangement.

Finally, an instructional support system is delegated responsibility for the various educational programs of the district. Seven persons report to its director, the Assistant Superintendent for Instruction. Included in this category are two directors of instructional programs, K-12, an administrative assistant for program evaluation, and coordinators for special education, vocational education, instructional media, and community schools. All of these personnel are concerned with the coordination of district-wide programs. The Instructional System design is illustrated in Figure 9.5.

Levels: The Pyramid Model

While traditional elementary, junior high, and senior high levels can easily be identified, these units have administratively been regrouped into what now make up two subsystems, or pyramids. Each pyramid, under its Director of Instructional Programs, is responsible for developing and carrying out its own K-12 instructional programs independent of one another but consistent with district goals and objectives. The West pyramid consists of six of the districts twelve elementary schools, one of the three junior high schools, and one of the two senior high schools. The remaining six elementary, two junior high, and one senior high buildings form the East pyramid. In each pyramid its elementary schools are feeder schools for its junior high(s), and the latter feed its senior high. Enrollment data for each pyramid and building is given in Table 5.

Note that the largest difference between the two pyramids is at the secondary level. Uniquely, this type of model will allow the district to form additional administratively manageable building units or pyramids as student enrollment swells in various regions within district boundaries.

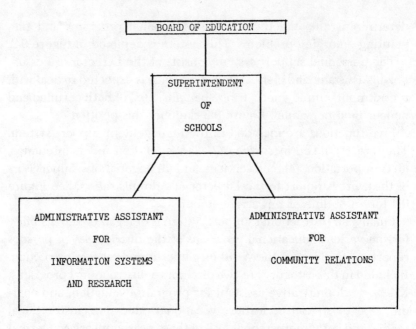

Fig. 9.2.   Planning and control system.

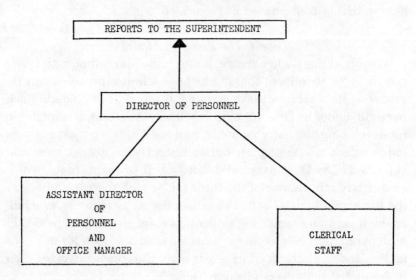

Fig. 9.3.   Personnel support system.

288

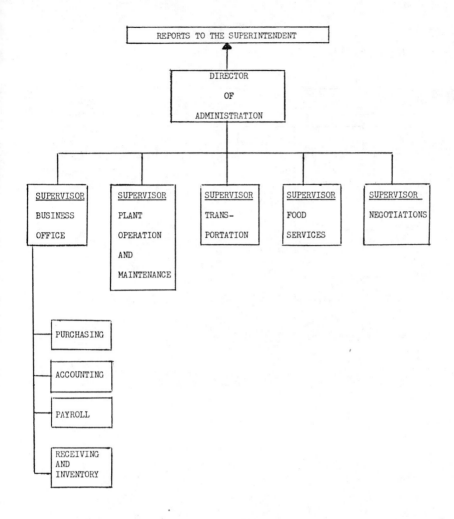

Fig. 9.4.   Management support system.

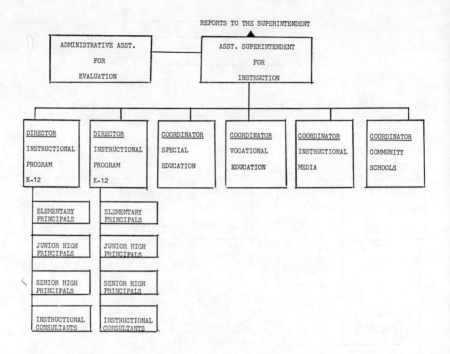

Fig. 9.5. Instructional system.

Typical Organizational Plan at Each Level

There is some variance between the management study recommendations for the administrative structure at each level and actual practice. There are also administrative differences between buildings at the same level. Such disparities can be accounted for in part by financial hardships, building leadership preferences, and reshaping of duty assignments.

At the senior high level, each building was to have one principal, one assistant principal, and two administrative assistants. In the fall of 1972, one of the schools completed this staffing, while the other had all but one of the administrative assistants. Among the primary duties of the principal are included: coordination of instructional

290

TABLE 5

PROJECTED ENROLLMENT DATA FOR INDEPENDENT SCHOOL DISTRICT NO. 279 BY PYRAMID AND INDIVIDUAL BUILDINGS, SEPTEMBER 1970

EAST PYRAMID	NO.	WEST PYRAMID	NO.	DISTRICT NO.
Elementary Buildings:		Elementary Buildings:		Level:
Birch Grove	601	Cedar Island	731	Elementary:
Fair Oaks	909	Crest View	644	
Garden City	590	Edgewood	840	
Orchard Lane	542	Osseo Elementary	515	
Palmer Lake	879	Park Brook	494	
Willow Lane	517	Zanewood	673	
Total Elementary	4038	Total Elementary	3897	7935
Secondary Buildings:		Secondary Buildings:		Secondary:
Brooklyn Junior High	1160	Osseo Junior High	995	
North View Junior High	1070	Osseo Senior High	1210	
Park Center Senior High	1556			
Total Secondary	3786	Total Secondary	2205	5991
Total East Pyramid:	7824	Total West Pyramid:	6102	Total District: 13,926

activities; allocation of staff, time, and space; development and control of the school budget; and development of written policies and procedures for building staff. His assistant generally supervises the discipline system and the extracurricular programs, directs the registration, programming, and scheduling of all students, and serves as acting principal when necessary. One administrative assistant is essentially a business manager, managing the school office and supervising noncertified personnel, processing and accounting for requisitions of materials and supplies, and other office management type duties. The second administrative assistant is concerned with such matters as attendance, study halls, and transportation. Since these latter two positions are new to the system, the administrative team is expected to readjust responsibilities and functions as need dictates.

Two of the three junior high schools have not yet implemented the administrative assistant positions, while the third junior high school has one such employee. In their absence, principals and assistant principals continue to carry out their traditional wide-range activities.

In addition to the above, both secondary levels are moving in the direction of developing strong department chairmen. These depart-

291

mental leaders, together with the building principal, form the core instructional leadership body of the building. Programs and budgets are hammered out in their Council Meetings.

The elementary schools all have principals. Some of them had instructional assistants, who acted much as an assistant principal. However, these positions were recently abolished by the school board. As of the fall of 1972, no elementary buildings have employed business managers to function similar to those at the secondary level.

The Schools in Summary

Organizationally, the district is in a period of transition. Having been forced by expediency alone to grapple with survival issues, it is now taking time to realign its organizational and operational structure to enhance the smooth and effective operation of its educational programs.

PUPIL PERSONNEL SERVICES

Employment of a full-time counselor in 1959, followed in 1961 by the entrance of a full-time school psychologist, formed the foundation for today's two broad pupil personnel programs: Guidance and Counseling, and Special Education. These areas grew up side by side, but have never been united under common coordination.

Two distinct efforts were made to bring about some joint planning of their services. In one instance, seven specialists met with the Assistant Superintendent in 1963 to work on revising the cumulative record system. At one of their meetings they unanimously affirmed the desirability and need to have one administrative head who would coordinate the work of all special services people, and who would serve as their administrator. A second effort was made in 1967. This time four district office administrators, three secondary and two elementary principals, the coordinator of special education, and the coordinator of guidance formed a District Committee on Guidance, Counseling, and Testing. They attempted to be a steering body, and managed to establish subcommittees to work on: (1) revising the cumulative record system, (2) developing a coordinated district testing program, and (3) research. While it was not an organization of strictly pupil personnel workers, it did show promise of giving some overall direction to these kinds of services. Nevertheless, neither the

1963 nor the 1967 efforts resulted in achieving a permanent common vehicle for the coordination of pupil personnel programs.

Current Organization and Structure

The district has consistently funded separate leadership for guidance and counseling, and for special education. Combined, these two areas today account for sixty-four full-time workers. A breakdown of the various personnel included in each of these broad categories can be seen in Table 6.

Organizationally, the Coordinator of Special Education holds responsibility for the areas of special education and school nursing services. Thus, technically, seventeen school nurses could be added to the forty-eight workers listed under the Special Education Heading in Table 6. Budgetarily, however, they are accounted for under Health and Physical Education.

A recommendation made by the 1970 district management study was that a Director of Guidance be employed for each pyramid. Nothing was said as to district-wide coordination of guidance and counseling services. As of September 1972, no separate directors had been assigned to the guidance function of either pyramid. However, in 1971 the existing position of Coordinator of Counseling was redefined as District Coordinator of Guidance and Counseling, K-12. This position more precisely stipulated district-wide K-12 coordina-

TABLE 6

PUPIL PERSONNEL SERVICE WORKERS IN IND. SCHOOL DISTRICT NO. 279 JUNE 1972

SPECIAL EDUCATION

1	Coordinator of Special Education (Coordinator of Student Support Services)	2	Teachers of Trainable Mentally Retarded
1	Coordinator of Special Learning and Behavior Problems	20	Teachers of Special Learning and Behavior Problems
		3	School Psychologists
1	Supervisor of Clinical Speech, K-12		
1	Vocational Adjustment Coordinator		*Guidance and Counseling*
8	Speech Therapists	1	Coordinator of Guidance and Counseling
11	Teachers of Educable Mentally Retarded	15	Full-time Counselors

293

tion responsibilities. Up to that point the Coordinator of Guidance had been functioning primarily at the secondary level. It is not clear how guidance services will be coordinated beyond the 1972–73 school year.

In addition to the overall coordination of the two major pupil personnel areas, there are some subcoordinators. For example, each secondary building has its own guidance department chairman. They function much the same as chairmen of other building departments: see to the smooth operation of the program, provide departmental leadership, and develop a budget. Guidance chairmen have counseling assignments, just as other building chairmen have teaching assignments.

Special education has two supervisors: one for special learning disabilities and one for speech therapy. These individuals work throughout the district with programs and personnel related to their speciality. The Speech Coordinator also devotes some time in one or more buildings to the active practice of his skill area.

Finally, all special personnel assigned to an elementary or secondary building unit are immediately responsible to its local principal. He controls all programs within his building, including guidance and counseling, and special education. His primary guidelines in developing building programs are state law, district and pyramid goals and objectives, building chairmen and staff recommendations, and district consultant advice.

Job Descriptions

Lengthy descriptions have been developed for the duties of eight pupil personnel workers. Summarized, they are as follows:

1. *District Coordinator of Guidance and Counseling, K-12.* This person is to plan, supervise and coordinate guidance and counseling services for students at all grade levels. A developmental guidance approach is to be the primary thrust of programs planned, but areas of special need, such as drug counseling, sexuality, and interpersonal relationships should also be provided for. In-service training of counselors and consultation with administrators are among assigned duties.
2. *School Counselor.* Five functions defined by one of our secondary buildings can describe the direction guidance and counseling is currently taking in this district. The functions include: (1) acting as a change agent for the entire school by analyzing and assessing its learning environment; (2) consulting with teachers on communication skills, small group processes, and behavior problems; (3) mak-

ing direct or indirect interventions to improve human effectiveness (individual counseling or changing the school environment); (4) acting as an advocate of a student's welfare through staff meetings and case conferences; (5) being a linkage person between and among teachers, parents, administrators, community agencies, and others.

3. *Guidance Technician.* Demonstrating developmental guidance materials for teachers, assisting in parent and teacher education classes, editing and preparing various guidance newsletters for publication, and assorted clerical activities are included in the duties of this position.

4. *District Coordinator of Student Support Services.* Some of the duties of this position are: developing special education classes and services for eligible district students; budgeting and managing allocated resources; seeing to the completion of required federal, state, and local reporting forms for special education programs; providing the means for staff development; evaluating programs for children; and informing the community about the needs of handicapped children.

5. *District Supervisor of Clinical Speech, K-12.* This individual is to supervise the work of the various speech clinicians; facilitate development and implementation of the speech therapy curriculum; and advise administrators about existing programs and future needs in the district's speech program.

6. *District Supervisor of Learning Disability Programs, K-12.* An effective program of screening, diagnosis, and remediation directed toward preventing and alleviating problems of the learning-disabled child is the primary concern of this position. Included among the duties are supervision of its instructional staff, and serving as a resource to district personnel regarding improving educational services for all students.

7. *School Psychologist.* Among the duties of these workers are: making school personnel aware of student needs, performing psychological evaluations and diagnostic studies of individual student; recommending appropriate programs for students; consulting with parents; helping administrators and staff evaluate and improve their programs; working with community groups to further the mental health and education of children; and carrying out the functions necessary to maintain a program of psychological services (record keeping, evaluation of services, professional growth, etc.).

8. *School Nurse.* Some responsibilities shared by all district nurses include: (1) providing for student health appraisal and record keeping; (2) providing for emergency cases of accidents or illness at school; (3) conducting a program of communicable disease control; (4) maintaining and supervising an office and rest facility for students; (5) planning special procedures for handicapped and ailing students in case of an emergency evacuation; and (6) providing

appropriate classroom instruction to students on various health matters (i.e., Red Cross first aid instruction at elementary level, personal health issues at the secondary level).

District Pupil Personnel Policies

Written policies are scarce for issues that are closely related to pupil personnel matters. Two exist that are frequently used. These involve the age of school entrance and attendance, and the current practice regarding pregnant students.

The Two Written Policies:

1. Essentially, the policy relative to the age of entrance and attendance stipulates that children who reach the age of five years after September 1 and prior to December 31 of the current year may be enrolled provided that such enrollment be recommended by a school psychologist.

2. The common practice regarding a pregnant student has been to provide her with home-bound instruction in accordance with state regulations regarding "handicapped" children. This makes a girl eligible to receive one hour of instruction for each day she is absent by a physician's recommendation.

During the 1971–72 school year, pregnant girls were given the option of attending special evening school classes at one of the district senior high buildings. Elective and required courses were offered, as well as individual instruction. They were also given the opportunity to take classes at a nearby vocational school. If the girls chose neither of these programs, individual instruction was provided at their residence.

Currently under consideration is a provision that would facilitate regular school class attendance for pregnant girls who would prefer it over the other options.

Committees Formulating Policy Proposals

At least two groups began meeting in 1971 to develop policy proposals. At issue were student records and a district testing program. Both of these areas had been addressed in the past and disposed of momentarily. However, issues of student or parent concerns over student rights, invasion of privacy, discrimination, libel, sparked the establishment of the two committees by the assistant superintendent for instruction. They were to grapple with the hard issues and to recommend procedures for implementing realistic and beneficial policies.

Some of the elements of record keeping which that committee is studying include the collection, storage, use, and release of student information. The testing committee is attempting to pinpoint the various purposes, methods, instrumentation, and uses of evaluation. Neither group completed its task during its first year, but targeted the 1972–73 school year for finality.

BUDGETS

Of the $14.8 million total district budget during the 1971–72 school year, 6.7 percent was spent on the combined pupil personnel services of guidance and counseling, and special education. Special education, with personnel and services at all grade levels, accounted for 5.2 percent. The remaining 1.5 percent was spent, for all practical purposes, on secondary school guidance and counseling. Of the one million dollars combined total of two services, 23 percent went to guidance programs, and 77 percent to special education. Table 7 details these data on dollar and percentage comparisons for the calendar year of 1971–72.

Salaries took the lion's share of each department's expenditures. Only two percent of the total guidance budget was used for nonsalary items of supplies or capital outlay. In special education, 17 percent of its funds were expended for such accounts as library, audiovisual, and general supplies; transportation; capital outlay; tuition; travel; and in-service training. For the combined budgets of the two major pupil personnel areas, 86 percent of the funds paid salaries of professional and clerical personnel. Proportions of pupil personnel budgets spent on salaries for the calendar year 1971–72 are shown in Table 8.

The district's secondary schools as a group provide extensive guidance services. Since each building principal is somewhat autonomous in developing his various programs, each building may differ in staffing its guidance department. This being the major expenditure, one can expect to see some variance in cost figures among the five secondary units. For the 1971–72 school year, they do in fact range from a per pupil cost of $32.06 to $47.34. In terms of the percent the guidance budget represents of a total building budget, the range is 4.5 to 6.2. There is less difference in these percentages when the buildings are combined according to the pyramid to which they are administratively and budgetarily assigned. The West pyramid schools together expended 5.8 percent of their total education funds

TABLE 7

DOLLAR AND PERCENTAGE COMPARISONS OF TWO PUPIL PERSONNEL
SERVICES BUDGETS AND THREE TOTAL DISTRICT BUDGETS FOR 1971–72

Department	Dollar Amount (Includes All Expenditures)	% of Pupil Personnel Budget	% of District Instructional Budget	% of Total District Budget
GUIDANCE AND COUNSELING	233,702	23	2	1.5
SPECIAL EDUCATION	770,758	77	8	5.2
1. TOTAL DIST. PUPIL PERSONNEL BUDGET (Guidance and Special Education)	1,004,460	100	10	6.7
2. TOTAL DIST. INSTRUCTION BUDGET	9,807,545			
3. TOTAL DIST. OPERATIONAL BUDGET*	14,787,471			

*Includes Instructional Budget, plus capital outlay, debt redemption, employee benefits, district operational expenses, interest, etc.

TABLE 8

PERCENTAGES OF PUPIL PERSONNEL BUDGETS SPENT ON SALARIES,
1971–72

Department	Dollar Amount Spent For Salaries	Percent Dollar Amount is of Total Department Budget*	Percent Dollar Amount is of Total District Pupil Personnel Budget*
GUIDANCE AND COUNSELING	228,992	98	22
SPECIAL EDUCATION	642,808	83	64
PUPIL PERSONNEL SERVICES (Guidance and Special Education)	871,800	86	86

*See Table 7 for total department and District dollar amounts for all expenses.

for guidance services, and the East pyramid schools shared 5.4 percent of their money for the same. The two pyramids comprise all the district schools, and thus 5.6 percent of all district secondary funds were spent on guidance services. Table 9 provides pertinent financial details for each secondary educational unit.

In historical perspective, the first school year guidance services were offered in 1959–60, the total budget was $7,649. The student counselor ratio was 1136–1. Twelve years later the budget increased

TABLE 9

EXPENDITURES FOR GUIDANCE SERVICES FOR EACH EDUCATIONAL UNIT, 1971–72

Educational Unit	Total Unit Budget in $	Total Guid. Budget of Unit in $	Percent of Total Unit Budget Used For Guidance	Per Pupil Costs For Guid. in $	Number of Students	Number of Certified Counselors
West Pyramid Secondary Schools						
Osseo Junior High	755,448	46,636	6.2	47.34	985	3
Osseo Senior High	955,745	51,816	5.4	46.72	1109	3.5
Total West Pyramid Secondary Schools	(a.) 1,711,193	(a.) 98,452	5.8	47.03	(a.) 2094	(a.) 6.5
East Pyramid Secondary Schools						
North View Junior High	730,272	33,255	4.5	32.06	1037	2
Brooklyn Junior High	705,243	42,484	6.0	41.52	1023	3.5
Park Center Senior High	1,030,429	59,511	5.7	45.31	1311	4
Total East Pyramid Secondary Schools	(b.) 2,465,944	(b.) 135,250	5.4	39.63	(b.) 3371	(b.) 9.5
District Secondary Total (a) + (b)	4,177,137	233,702	5.6	43.33	5465	16

299

more than thirty times its original figure, and today's ratio is less than one-third of what it was then.

Expenditures For Education and Counseling

Nine service areas are funded under special education. Over forty percent of the monies in 1971–72 were allocated to the learning disability section alone. Less than five percent per program went for the trainable mentally retarded, the hearing handicapped, or for vocational rehabilitation, with the visually handicapped receiving less than one percent of the department's $770,758 total budget. These figures reflect the difference in incidence of the various types of handicaps. Dollar expenditure for each special education service area and their relationships to the Special Education Department budget are shown in Table 10.

Earlier it was noted that seventeen percent of the total departmental budget was used for items other than salaries. Without detailing all the breakdowns of that amount, it may be of some interest to note that transportation and tuition costs together accounted for twelve percent of the nonsalary expenses. Transportation alone was an eight percent item of over $62,000.

Thus far, this department's budget has not been costed out on a per

TABLE 10

SPECIAL EDUCATION EXPENDITURES BY SERVICE AREAS, 1971–72

SERVICE AREAS	EXPENDITURES IN $	PERCENT OF TOTAL SPECIAL EDUCATION BUDGET
Educable Mentally Retarded	120,850	16
Trainable Mentally Retarded	31,000	4
Learning Disabilities	324,155	42
Speech Handicapped	81,229	11
Hearing Handicapped	18,530	2
Visually Handicapped	2,700	.3
Vocational Rehabilitation	18,741	2
Coordinator of Special Ed.	121,537	16
Psychological Services	52,016	6
Total:	770,758	99 +

300

pupil, building, or pyramid basis for any or all of its services. Since the programs are monitored as district-wide services, and since state special education reports necessitate district figures, accounts are kept accordingly.

But to provide some kind of picture of a per pupil cost an estimate was computed for one service for the 1971–72 school year. Approximately 425 students were enrolled in the learning disabilities program. With an expenditure of $324,000, this results in a per pupil cost of some $760 over and above the average maintenance cost of educating pupils in the district.

FACILITIES

Space is a premium commodity in the district. Some personnel and service areas shift location from one year to the next. But accommodations are always sought which will reasonably facilitate the kind of work to be performed and the various needs of the personnel involved.

Since the kinds of special services to be provided to students have grown with the years, none of the seventeen buildings has a formalized pupil personnel services suite. In the special education field, some of the building units house particular services centers to which students from throughout the district are bused. In other cases, the specialist goes to the students, occupying whatever facilities the principal can make available. Thus, the same quarters may be used for more than one service. A staggered day and time schedule assures room availability and privacy for each worker. There has been some minor remodeling of facilities to accommodate special programs for handicapped youngsters.

At the secondary level, counselors are housed in a common suite in each building. In all cases, they are adjacent to the administrative suite.

Guidance and Counseling Facilities

Four of the five secondary buildings have been constructed since 1961. Their guidance suites were planned to provide separate offices within that suite for each counselor. One senior high building, which has had four additions since 1957, has not always been able to do this. However, by sacrificing a conference room within the guidance center and some clerical-waiting room space, remodeling has now provided each counselor with his own office in the same complex.

The following generalities apply to all guidance areas. Each has: (1) sizable private offices for each counselor; (2) an adequate reception and clerical area; and (3) room for storage and use of cumulative records. Table 11 itemizes the space allocations for guidance suites in each building.

Conference rooms for special meetings and group counseling are available in all buildings. They are located in the guidance suite in all but one of the units. While counselors are heavy users of that room, it is considered, in all cases, not to be for their exclusive use. Thus, teachers, administrators, students, parents, or counselors must cooperate in the scheduling of that facility.

In instances where the guidance unit has more office cubicles than counselors, other personnel have been given residence. Such individuals usually include the part-time special education workers. The recent advent of business managers has found some of them being housed in this location.

Every guidance unit is centrally located and easily accessible to everyone. In two instances it is a center unit, flanked by the principal's and nurse's offices. In three buildings it is at one end of the principal-nurse-counselor section. Entrance is possible directly from the corridor, or through the hallway joining all three divisions. The

TABLE 11

NUMBER AND TYPES OF ROOMS IN EACH GUIDANCE SUITE

BUILDING	NUMBER OF COUNSELOR OFFICES	RECEPTION-CLERICAL AREA	RECORDS ROOM	CONFERENCE ROOM IN SUITE	ADDITIONAL ROOMS HOUSING OTHER RESOURCE PERSONS
Osseo Senior High	4	Yes	Yes	No	2
Park Center Senior High	4	Yes	Yes	Yes	2
Brooklyn Junior High	4	Yes	Yes	Yes	0
North View Junior High	3	Yes	Yes	Yes	2
Osseo Junior High	3	Yes	Yes	Yes	0

units are adequately furnished with office equipment and supplies and appropriate reading materials for the waiting area.

When classroom space became available in two buildings, the guidance staff secured them for guidance resource rooms. Their uses have been varied, including testing, meeting with post high school representatives, career information sessions, group counseling, guidance classes, and rap sessions. Educational-vocational literature files are located there. In schools without a guidance resource room, the literature files are found in the guidance reception area or the school library, or both. Counselors in the latter buildings are hoping to find empty areas to serve as resource rooms.

Where there are storage rooms or vaults, these are usually the property of the administrative wing, though they may house some guidance material.

A diagram of the facilities of one of the district's junior high guidance departments is represented in Figure 9.6. A senior high facility is shown in Figure 9.7

Perhaps a phenomenon of the times is the fact that, in the 1970s, the district counselors are not particularily covetous of facilities. They are moving more in the direction of providing services wherever the action is: classrooms, hallways, study or rap areas, faculty or administrative meetings, cafeteria. In this way, they use any existing facilities, as well as those that are centered in a particular corner of a building and labeled "Guidance Office."

Special Education Facilities

In this department, facilities may differ widely from building to building. Since some of the specialists service more than one school, they share available office space in each unit. Thus, speech therapists, school psychologists, and the vocational adjustment counselor often occupy the same corner of a guidance suite.

SPECIAL GUIDANCE PROGRAM FACILITIES

One unique area in an elementary building was especially developed for what has come to be called a Special Guidance Program. It houses intellectually able students who require special attention because of a combination of behavior problems and learning deficiencies.

Two regular size classrooms were combined to provide four distinct areas. A large study area is used for all academic activities and

303

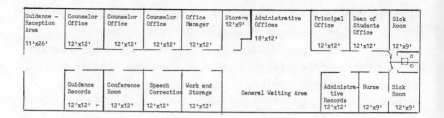

Guidance – Reception Area 11'x26'	Counselor Office 12'x12'	Counselor Office 12'x12'	Counselor Office 12'x12'	Office Manager 12'x12'	Storage 12'x9'	Administrative Offices 18'x12'	Principal Office 12'x12'	Dean of Students Office 12'x12'	Sick Room 12'x9'
	Guidance Records 12'x12'	Conference Room 12'x12'	Speech Correction 12'x12'	Work and Storage 12'x12'	General Waiting Area		Administrative Records 12'x12'	Nurse 12'x9'	Sick Room 12'x9'

Fig. 9.6. Adapted floor plan of North View Junior High School, Brooklyn Park, Minnesota.

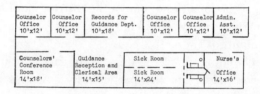

Counselor Office 10'x12'	Counselor Office 10'x12'	Records for Guidance Dept. 10'x18'	Counselor Office 10'x12'	Counselor Office 10'x12'	Admin. Asst. 10'x12'
Counselors' Conference Room 14'x18'	Guidance Reception and Clerical Area 14'x15'	Sick Room 14'x24' Sick Room			Nurse's Office 14'x16'

Fig. 9.7. Adapted floor plan of Park Center Senior High School, Brooklyn Park, Minnesota

is equipped accordingly. Children wishing some privacy may utilize the portable screens in the area.

Adjoining the study room is an activity area. The two are separated by a wall with a connecting door. Play, art, and craft materials are available here for informal "after study" enjoyment. In one corner of the room is a third area: a quiet room. It measures six feet long and

304

five feet wide. Only one student at a time may use this room when he feels the need to be alone.

A fourth area doubles as an observation room and a teacher aide's workroom. It is equipped with two one-way mirrors: one for the study area and one for the activity room. It has a desk so that the teacher's aide may complete her clerical tasks. The room is also used for storage of materials and supplies.

Special Resource Centers

Another distinct type of facility used by this department are special instructional centers for learning-handicapped children. These students may or may not have some form of moderate behavior problems. Each elementary and secondary school in the district has at least one such center, and there is much variation among them in their facilities. They may have as few as two or as many as seven school desks and chairs. In addition, there is at least one round table or 3x6 table with chairs. Among the items of equipment can be found: a phonograph, tape recorder, two or three cassette recorders, and a filmstrip projector. Some rooms also have an overhead projector and controlled readers. Instructional books and materials pertinent to developing basic skill competencies are in abundance.

School Psychologist Offices

A complex in a high school which once served as the district office suite now houses the three school psychologists and their secretary. Essentially, it consists of their respective desks in a common office area, and a separate conference room. There is a vault and ample storage area for testing equipment and other supplies. The area also has a number of cabinets for the filing of psychological reports. This office also acts as their home base when they are not working in one of the elementary or secondary buildings.

District Coordinator Offices

The District Coordinator of Guidance and Counseling, K-12, has always been housed in a senior high building. The exact location varies from year to year. Most recently he has been headquartered in a senior high administrative suite. The same area houses the building principals and business manager, three secretaries, and a conference room. The Coordinator of Student Support Services, who is responsible for special education, is located in the District Office wing of a high school complex. Her secretary has an office among a row of open clerical cubicles directly across the hallway. The coordinator's office proper is large enough to house a conference table and chairs for group meetings.

Pupil Personnel Organization in Summary

Sixty-four full-time professionals comprise the two major pupil personnel areas of guidance and counseling, and special education. They each have their separate coordinators. Special education spent the bulk of the district's $1 million used for pupil personnel services during 1971–72. Salaries are the major expenditure of both programs. All secondary buildings have functional and adequate guidance facilities. Space and equipment are provided in each elementary and secondary building for one or more special education programs. The nature of the rooms and furnishings depends upon what the building principals have available and the needs being serviced.

UNIQUE CHARACTERISTICS OF THE PUPIL PERSONNEL SERVICES

The guidance program has attempted to deliver services for the general student and staff populations. Special education has developed programs to relieve the limitations placed on student academic and social progress resulting from some handicap. A few of the noteworthy elements of these programs are discussed below.

Guidance and Counseling

Perhaps the most distinguishing feature of the district's guidance and counseling programs is the nature of its staff. They are an active and involved group who are neither satisfied with the status quo nor hesitant to explore new frontiers. A departmental summary report (Appendix B-1) exemplifies the diversity of involvements of the counselors at one building during the first semester of 1971.

Traditional services such as individual counseling, registration, providing educational-vocational information and testing are not sneered upon in the search for creative applications of counseling skills. But the "who" and the "how" of offering them are eyed carefully. Counselors are concerned about making optimum use of their skills and time. This helps account, in part, for five unique areas described below which aptly characterize district guidance departmental activities and involvements.

1. Implementing a Contemporary Role Model

By the end of the 1971–72 school year, each of the five secondary building units for the first time had developed a set of measurable goals and objectives for the following school year. The writing of goals and objectives was not in itself new. But doing it with enough precision that pupils, parents, teachers, administrators, and counselors alike could recognize and evaluate results was both a new and traumatic experience. The final document of each unit was interrelated with the goals and objectives established by its particular building, pyramid, and those established by the district.

The total process resulted in a more organized approach to a greatly expanded concept of counselor functioning which had been emerging haphazardly for some time. And therein was tremendous pay-off to the counselors. They were able to feel good about things they had been trying both in and beyond the confines of the guidance suite. They are finding new possibilities for their varied professional and preferential skills. They are seeing more purposefulness and opportunities to identify accomplishments in their work.

Fundamental framework for the implementation process was provided through a collaborative arrangement between the school district and the University of Minnesota. The University staff was looking for intern counselor training stations for those involved in their revised program. The district was looking for assistance in fashioning objectivity and accountability without losing humaneness in its guidance program. The district agreed to hire two interns on a half-time basis. The University agreed to provide on-site supervision and consultation one-half day a week by one of their doctoral faculty.

Primary action was centered in one junior high and one senior high building, where interns were assigned. A comprehensive process was initiated which included: examining of the needs of people in the building unit and its attendance areas; surveying resources available to fill those needs, and establishing priority goal assignments based upon pay-off potential and probability of success; designing and initiation of projects; and evaluating the project. This was a mammoth operation involving input from students, parents, and teachers, as well as administrators and counselors. It necessitated and had high counselor and administrator commitment. It required huge blocks of planning and organizational time, while still maintaining what appeared to be many fundamental traditional guidance and counseling activities.

Examples of a few projects conceived during the initial year of the intern program and scheduled for implementation during the 1972–73 school year by the Brooklyn Junior High Guidance Staff, are those shown in Appendix B-2. They are excerpted from among twenty nine listed in their department's immediate and long-range goals booklet.

For each of these projects thorough planning will be detailed, including assignment of responsibilities, time allocations, methodologies, and evaluation procedures. Further, the guidance and administrative staffs will hold regular review meetings to track the progress of all projects and make any pertinent modifications they deem necessary.

Counselors in buildings not having interns did not want to be left out. Abstracting some of the basic concepts and methodologies of the new contemporary schemes, the District Coordinator of Counseling began holding meetings with other guidance staffs. Ideas were presented on how to develop and write goals and objectives, how to decide on priorities and allocate time, and how to plan and dispose of projects. In addition, some sessions were held with the University consultant. Counselors in these buildings were encouraged to undertake the development of some minimum goals and objectives using the new design. The intention was not to foster rivalry or raise anxieties, but rather to encourage teamwork on planning and achieving common objectives. That this point was made seems to be suggested by the following quotation taken from the introduction to the Park Center High School Guidance Plan for 1972:

> Since our purpose is to function as a department unit with common objectives, the counseling staff, along with secretarial assistance intends to work as a team in completing the goals and objectives contained on the following pages. Finally, the staff agrees to the concept of (reviewing both philosophy and objectives) and making changes or additions when deemed appropriate.

The Board of Education renewed funding of the intern program for the 1972–73 school year. The job of implementing a contemporary role model for counselors has a long way to go. But, in one year it did make giant strides in taking the best from past practices, combining this with the skills and energy of the guidance staff and the organizational, analytical, and planning techniques of the University program.

2. Group Guidance and Counseling Practices

This district was one of the first in its state to employ group techniques on a massive scale. A modest beginning was made in 1962 involving seven underachieving-acting out boys,[2]. Improvement in grades and citizenship was demonstrated. By 1965, student response to groups was so favorable that counselors were unable to provide enough staff to man groups for more than 300 of the 600 interested students. At that time twenty-six groups were organized, involving such topics as: Family and Social Concerns, Getting Along with Others, Expressing Myself with Others, Understanding Myself, Personal Problems, Improving Myself in School, Vocational Planning, and College Planning. An in-district study that year demonstrated the effectiveness of using group procedures to modify specific coping behavior.[3] Findings such as this motivated the counselors to continue their group efforts, vary topics and methods, and carry on both formal and informal research.

One approach taken at Osseo Senior High School was for counselors to become coordinators for specific types of groups. This meant that one person was responsible for planning intervention strategies, gathering resource materials and personnel, providing in-service training for colleagues, developing a research design, and arranging the details of announcements, time and facilities—all for one specific kind of group. Thus, coordinators emerged for the following group areas: Human Relations, Communications, Sexuality, Occupational Development, College, Vocational-Technical Training, and Family Relationships.

Student types also became a concern. Most groups developed because of student self-selection. But certain student types were viewed as target possibilities. Among them were: potential dropouts, isolates, students with learning difficulties, absentees, behavior problems, and "problem" students entering from the junior high. The kinds of students and groups offered in any given year varied according to counselor interest and time availability, student interest, and administrator's wishes. Thus, there was variety from year-to-year and among buildings.

Counselors have made efforts to keep the public informed about group procedures. Through district and community publications

309

they have explained, described, and pictured groups at work. For some public meetings, they played segments of group sessions which had been approved by its members. In addition, parents of students who wanted to be involved in some Love and Human Sexuality groups received a letter from a counselor describing the nature of this type of group. Recently, in an unpublished project by four Osseo Senior High Counselors, parents were asked to participate in a study involving 105 students enrolled in self-awareness groups and 70 students assigned to control groups. Parents completed a pre- and post-counseling check lists indicating their perceptions of their children. Statistically significant differences were found in parent perceptions of increases in warmth, emotional stability, activity, and dependability, and decreases in depressiveness, tenseness, and reticence in their children.

Currently, counselors are looking carefully at two areas: (1) working more closely with teachers to accomplish some of the group counseling goals; (2) making groups more than "talk" sessions.

In the first case, English, Social Studies, Family Living, and Home Economics classes, work-experiences classes, psychology, and geometry are among the subject matter areas that have used counselors for extensive projects involving group dynamics. Teachers and counselors team up in both the planning and conduct of group experiences.

In the second case, two situations might be illustrative:

Situation 1. During the second semester of 1972, counselors at Osseo Senior High initiated a two-hour semester class called "Personal Growth Through Involvement." Enrolled students took a battery of tests, received test interpretations, participated in counseling group sessions, and spent approximately half their class time doing volunteer work at community agencies and making field trips to businesses and industry.

Situation 2. In a group counseling project at North View Junior High School, counselors visited students in their classes, took a field trip, and arranged for students to do volunteer work and tutoring.[4] These activities were in addition to weekly group counseling sessions.

It would appear that developing a contemporary role model for district counselors will necessitate adapting group skills to a variety of settings and not reserving them for formalized talk sessions in a conference room. To this end, a beginning has been made. For the district, group procedures have been a developmental growth-pro-

310

ducing process for counselors as well as students. It appears that this area will continue to be a vital concern of the counselors.

3. Counselors as Resource People and Project Leaders.

Counselors are working closely with faculties and parents, and as special resource leaders in two district-directed priority areas. Examples of a few of these involvements follow.

Working with Faculty Members. An extensive project has been undertaken by a teacher in which he is analyzing components of the kinds of behaviors he wishes to result from his classes. Together, he and a counselor have thus far constructed booklets of very specific and identifiable behaviors for areas involving the school and class proper, home and family, interpersonal relationships, and boy-girl relationships. The teacher wishes the counselor to work with him and his class as they deal with units such as career development, family systems, sex, and educational planning.

In another building two counselors have teamed up with two social studies teachers. The teachers have long been concerned about the difficulty seventh graders appeared to have in being integrated into the school. With the help of the counselors, they devised specific group procedures to help their students get acquainted with one another, become better listeners, describe their feelings, and learn how to work together in a group.

Much has been done in the line of observing classroom dynamics and reporting the data to the teacher. This is done by teacher invitation, and is usually preceded and followed by consultations dealing with the teacher's wishes as outcomes for the class. One series of such observations resulted in a teacher-initiated after-school voluntary study group concerning classroom management. Counselors were asked to be primary resource members for the group.

The principal of one building asked his counseling staff to conduct a teacher evaluation of the building's leadership and communication systems. An intern counselor carried out the project. Forty-seven teachers were individually interviewed on the broad areas of their input on the decision-making process, their view of the principal as a building leader, understanding of roles of the two building principals, and other comments the teachers generally wished to make.

Working with Parents. In the mid-sixties, counselors inaugurated and coordinated a series of Family Life Education classes for parents. Among the topics were: family communications, drug abuses, and how to give sex information to children. Outside speakers were

311

brought in for what were usually six-session commitments per series. To some of the sex education sessions parents were allowed to bring their children. The programs in the Family Life Series, supported by the P.T.A., always enjoyed large attendance. Beginning in 1970, counselors became involved in classes for parents during the daytime hours. Sometimes they team with a school psychologist or guidance technician. Ninety-nine percent of the participants have been mothers. Each series averages eight to twelve sessions dealing with family communications or child management practices. Modifications are constantly being made in content and process, and parent responsiveness increases with each new series. These school-day programs are usually offered through specific buildings for its attendance area, and are organized by the principal and his P.T.A. They, in turn, enlist a counselor or psychologist to provide the instruction. Classes are kept small—usually no more than twelve, with heavy emphasis on group participation. More therapeutically oriented are some evening parent group counseling efforts begun by a counselor and a school psychologist team. Specific sets of parents are invited to attend, and the group is usually limited to four couples. The basic purpose of these groups is to help the couples find mutually acceptable and useful ways of positively influencing their children's behavior.

For the 1972–73 school year some form of parent education or counseling has been established as a goal by counselors in each building unit.

Another way that counselors have been involved with parents is through committee work. For example, one counselor has been heavily involved with both parents and teachers in developing a family life education curriculum for the district. Another has been working with a similar group investigating the pros and cons of "open" education. In three of the buildings, counselors have stated intentions of working with parents to find adult "friends" for fatherless boys or motherless girls. One such committee found the summer of 1971 a good time to outline their plans for such a program. The committee, which included students, parents, teachers, an administrator, and a counselor, decided that counselors were to play a significant role in facilitating the project.

Working with District Priority Projects. When the Superintendent of Schools inaugurated a drug education program in the district, he asked one of the counselors to coordinate it. This further led to the establishment of a drug curriculum committee, chaired by the counselor. This group developed a complete K-12 curriculum, as well as audio-visual explanatory materials for use in the community and with the faculties of the district's seventeen schools.

A second major priority area of the district is that of career development. Among the range of traditional counselor involvements have been: organizing small groups to investigate careers and related topics; bringing in representatives from local businesses and industry, colleges, and military services; providing films on a variety of career opportunities; offering field trips to community businesses and industries; administering and interperting aptitude tests and interest inventories to students wishing them; and stocking a healthy supply of literature in career libraries.

One project initiated by a counselor in 1971 met with exceptional acceptance by students, community, and faculty. Entitled "Summer Scene," representatives from volunteer agencies and leisure-time activities, as well as those knowing of summer job opportunities were made available throughout the school day to offer students a wide range of summer opportunities. These included: political action opportunities, job data from the State Employment Office, leisure art classes, helping and relating to handicapped persons and inner city youth, leadership opportunities in camps and hospitals, park and recreation programs, as well as information on enriching and renewing experiences such as hosteling trips, scuba diving, sky diving, whitewater canoeing, camping, wilderness survival training, mountain climbing.

Another exciting development of the 1970s was the appointment of a district vocational director. His responsibility was to coordinate, expand, and modify the many career development and related activities. This has resulted in the establishment of a K-12 district-wide career development curriculum planning and writing committee on which counselors sit. And counselor involvement in the careers field is assuming more the role of assisting teachers to implement career development into their curriculum. Counselors in one building, for example, are establishing a career resource room for teachers. Here will be available materials and lessons for classroom use. The object is to build career relevancy into school subjects. Two other buildings have established career resource centers for students. Job-related aptitude and interest testing, literature, films, and group meetings are available there. In general, while teachers will be more responsible than ever before for helping student investigate career opportunities, counselors see themselves involved with students another way. They expect to be spending an increasing amount of time help-

313

ing students with value clarification, and then identify careers compatible with those values. In addition, they expect to devote more time helping students develop interpersonal communication skills contributing to career success.

4. Promoting Elementary Guidance and Counseling

Three interrelated factors have influenced movement in the elementary guidance field since 1971: (1) a committee was established to investigate guidance and counseling possibilities for the elementary schools; (2) a Title III proposal was funded, which made possible the development of an in-service course for teachers; it was aimed at helping teachers utilize counseling theory and techniques to facilitate the social-emotional growth of elementary pupils; (3) an elementary counselor intern program was begun in cooperation with the University of Minnesota.

The guidance committee served as stimulus for grass-roots endorsement of elementary guidance in some form. Its membership was represented by at least one teacher from each of the elementary buildings, as well as principals, a school psychologist, and the District Coordinator of Guidance. They studied the work of elementary counselors in other school systems, and supported the ideas of both the in-service training classes and the intern program.

Under the Title III project, a team of ten, including counselors, psychologists, and elementary teachers, developed the course described above during a five-week summer planning lab. They subsequently served as initial instructors for the course during the following school year. Eighty teachers in eight different schools took the course for credit during the 1971–72 school year. Other schools will be serviced as instructors can be provided.

The intern program was staffed by two half-time counselors. A doctoral faculty member from the University provided one half-day consultation and supervisory services each week. The program made direct guidance and counseling services available to the staff and students of one elementary building. Basic services included: providing individual and small group counseling; conducting developmental guidance activities within classrooms; consulting with teachers, parents, and administrators; producing a monthly elementary guidance newsletter for district-wide distribution; and conducting an evening course for parents dealing with communication systems in the family.

314

5. Professional Development

District counselors have a history of promoting their own in-service training opportunities. They have been fortunate in securing the best of state resource personnel to help them with their growth efforts. But besides speakers, they have employed audio recordings, personal video tapings, role playing, rap sessions, T-grouping, and both structured and informal gatherings. As a total group of district counselors, they meet at least three times each year for professional growth programs. Representatives from each building meet with the District Coordinator to design programs and see to their conduct and evaluation. Usually, district office and building level administrators are invited to all-counselors sessions. Periodically throughout the year, the junior high and senior high counselors may arrange special interest divisional meetings.

Continuation of formal education has played a significant role in counselor development. In some cases, special funds have helped the process. For example, four counselors were successful in obtaining federal funds to attend short training periods at the National Training Laboratories, and at the American Institute of Family Relations. Two were awarded workshops in sex and family life education. Another was the recipient of a drug education workshop, and still another of one in career development. And someone is usually enrolled in summer school or late afternoon credit courses through the University or one of the local colleges.

In June 1972 a committee of counselors developed and approved the outline for a proposed in-service training course for themselves and interested teachers. Entitled "Contemporary Guidance and Counseling Practices," the course is divided into three segments: Consultation Skills, Group Procedures, and Evaluating Outcomes of Human and Learning Goals and Objectives. The group is asking the District Professional Growth Committee to recognize the course for three Board Credits.

In a slightly different direction, counselors contribute to one another's growth through a sharing process. A district-wide guidance newsletter is published monthly. In this, counselors describe some of the guidance activities and developments in their respective buildings. This sometimes stimulates ideas others may wish to try or learn more about. The newsletter also serves as a vehicle for general announcements and other information the District Coordinator wishes to bring to everyone's attention. Administrators and some teachers receive copies of each edition.

315

SPECIAL EDUCATION

Independent School District No. 279 provides a broad spectrum of special education services for its students having exceptional needs. The general intent of the services is to help a child learn as best he can, given his type of disability, and, where possible, to modify the disability. It includes among its services a range of options from consultative help for regular classroom teachers to special stations for students with severe handicaps. Two of these programs are described below.

1. Program for the Educable Mentally Retarded

This program is for children who score at the lower end of the I.Q. range (approximately 50–80) and are experiencing difficulty in the academic areas of regular classrooms. Its goals are to improve the self-image, basic skill areas, and social behavior of its enrollees. Efforts are directed primarily through "resource teachers" in what are called "Supplemental Resource (SR) Rooms." Prior to 1970, Educable Mentally Retarded (EMR) children were educated in special classrooms. Today, they are assigned to grades and regular classrooms compatible with their age, size, and social maturity. Together with their classmates, they attend classes in art, music, physical education, social studies, and science, and have their lunch and library periods. Together, their regular classroom teachers, a psychologist, a resource teacher, and the building principal decide in what specific areas the children need supplemental help. For these select needs alone do they utilize the SR room. Here the resource teacher will give them assistance in the various academic areas, such as reading, math, and spelling.

Ordinarily, children in the elementary programs are promoted to seventh grade near age twelve.

A heavy vocational emphasis accents the secondary level EMR program. Resource teachers give considerable attention to such work-related matters as personal appearance, attendance and punctuality, responsibility, dependability, and relationships with supervisors and coworkers. Academic skill-building is directed toward making them functional for job requirements. Interested junior year students may attend a neighboring vocational school for job skill evaluation. This often leads to becoming involved in a work-study program, which offers them the opportunity to attend school part of the day and hold a paying job as well.

Students in the EMR program are given academic credit for course work and job experience (if a part of the work-study program). When they achieve the number of credits required by the district for graduation, they are granted a regular diploma.

2. Special Learning and Behavior Problems Programs

This program is for students who are not mentally retarded but who are experiencing learning problems and are not being serviced under other special help programs. One district report on special education suggests that such children may be hyperactive or hypoactive, distractable, lack understanding of time or space, have difficulty following directions, be unable to generalize or develop concepts, have poor coordination, be unable to memorize adequately, or have specific problems in learning basic skills. The program's aims are to prevent failure, to make academic functioning reflect general ability, and to promote self-confidence and self-worth. It uses resource teachers and tutors to accomplish these goals.

As with the EMR program, students go to resource centers for assistance. Usually, they are there for about one hour a day. The resource teacher, who may work with a maximum of fifteen students a day, focuses instruction on the basic skill areas of reading, arithmetic, handwriting, spelling, and spoken language. Beyond these sessions, the resource teacher confers with other classroom instructors of the children being seen. Together, they decide and plan the kinds of learning experiences expected to be most useful in the environs of the regular classroom.

If a learning disability is primarily emotional in origin or manifestation, children may be assigned to an SLBP Guidance class for a portion of each day. The amount of time spent in the Guidance class will be determined by the guidance teacher and the classroom teacher, the decision being based on the needs and characteristics of those being served. Generally the guidance teacher will work with no more than four children at a time, frequently less. A teacher's aide assists the teacher with the children and does clerical tasks, such as typing conference reports and keeping records.

The major goal of the guidance class is to improve social and emotional status of children so that they can function better in the regular classroom. As the students improve in functioning, time in the SLBP Guidance room will be diminished, and time in the regular classroom will be increased.

The curriculum in the guidance room is flexible with instruction based on individual needs. Programmed materials, tape recorders, and other audio-visual equipment are used extensively in the teaching of academic skill subjects. Arts and crafts provide outlets for creative impulses, as well as frustrations. Periods for talking through problems are held every day. Individual and group counseling and behavior modification techniques are used.

Since only a small number of children need the SLBP guidance services, classrooms are located in only two of the twelve elementary schools. Students from other schools are bused to this central location. Room dividers or screens allow students to be separated from the group when they feel too distracted or uncomfortable in group activity. The two teachers are fully certified elementary teachers with experience and master's degrees in the teaching of emotionally disturbed, socially maladjusted children.

Accountability Model. In the spring of 1971, the school district received funds to develop an accountability model. The funds were obtained through Title III of the Federal Elementary and Secondary Education Act of 1965. Special education was designated as one of two district areas in which to pilot the project. This launched a comprehensive six-phase process. Its components involve: specifying, evaluating, and revising student-centered objectives; and describing, evaluating, and revising instructional procedures.

Core areas initially under study by the Special Education Department include: word recognition in reading; articulation in speech; and addition, subtraction, multiplication, and division in math.

While the project will eventually expand to include other special education skill and curricular areas, there is concern for more than academic achievement. It is hypothesized that the process involved in this project can be applied to social-emotional growth, also. Demonstrating this is an anticipated, although not immediate, goal.

Unique Characteristics in Summary.

Counselors in this district are directing their efforts more concretely toward serving as learning consultants. The proportion of time spent working with adults and students is virtually being reversed. Group meetings of various types will probably be the preferred method for dealing with most student problems.

Special education personnel are available to help students who have difficulty functioning in the mainstream of the school. However, they are reversing a previous emphasis of providing a wholly separate learning station for the day-long attendance of such children. Resource centers are being staffed to assist youngsters with specific needs while allowing them to spend the majority of their time in the regular school environment.

ISSUES AND ALTERNATIVES
PROGRAM EVALUATION

Scrutiny of the preceding data will make obvious several general and specific items within the pupil personnel domain of this district with which one might take issue. Four elements which have broad implications are surveyed below. They are not to be considered as the only issues.

The reader is encouraged to compare comments made in this section with his view of each situation. He is invited to develop responses to or methods of answering the four basic questions posed, assuming that he were a member of the management team of this district. Finally, he should develop his own list of issues and recommendations based upon the preceding data.

1. Accountability

For Independent School District No. 279 there really is a "Million Dollar Question." It is: "Is the more than $1 million now expended annually by the two major pupil personnel service areas being spent productively?" Hope for answering this question in somewhat objective terms may be available through two vehicles previously mentioned. One is the generation of a contemporary role model for counselors, assisted by ideas from the counselor intern program. The other is the Title III Accountability Model. Both seek in one way or another to define needs; specify concrete, demonstrable goals and objectives; plan and implement strategies related to them; and produce evidence of results.

Critics might object that the really important human needs cannot be quantified. But advocates of accountability suggest that tangible productions are the ally of such needs, not their foe.

Accountability is not a new concept to district pupil personnel workers. The workers have a long history of attempting to sample the success of their efforts, at least in terms of satisfaction of clients. Almost annually they have used survey forms to ask students, parents, or teachers to evaluate their programs and services. Results have been used as a guide to continue or modify approaches and services for subsequent years.

Thus, surveying clients has been the primary method used to confront the issue of value of pupil personnel services. Other data gathering, summarizing, and inference making reports have been completed in the areas of group counseling, testing programs, follow-up studies, and the post high school plans of seniors. Pupil personnel workers are not willing to dismiss these kinds of studies as valueless. But they are looking forward to the challenge of designing methods for revealing to what extent they can objectively demonstrate that a preplanned goal was attained.

2. Changing Role of the Counselor

In relation to the general issue of accountability there is another significant question to be faced: to what extent should counselors modify their role? Essentially, the role change will greatly diminish the amount of time spent in individual conferences. Elevated will be the time spent in classrooms, with teachers, designing problem-solving strategies throughout the school environment, and doing more overall consulting work on school affairs. These functions will replace dealing directly with students for large blocks of time. Obtaining evidence on the extent of value of these activities in relation to the more traditional services would seem to be useful.

Human consideration will also need to be taken into account on such a role change. At the least, these will include the skill and emotional readiness of counselors, acceptance by teachers, and adjustment of students.

3. Unification of Pupil Personnel Efforts

Would a unified organizational structure for pupil personnel services be advantageous to the district? The present one has seen both the guidance program and special education develop and flourish side-by-side under distinct leadership. They determine their own goals and objectives and programs. But there are some issues which the coordinators find they have in common. These include: (1) promoting a team effort approach among pupil personnel workers themselves and they with other school staff; (2) assessing the developmental and exceptional needs of all students, assigning priorities from among them, and developing appropriate delivery vehicles; (3) developing policies; and (4) effectively using resource personnel and services outside the school itself. Some additional issues that fall in the pupil personnel domain and prompt attention are: (1) establishing a functional testing program that meets student as well as district

320

needs, (2) implementing a modern student record keeping system, and (3) investigating the application of modern technology, such as computerized counseling systems.

That there is both commonality and uniqueness of purposes and problems among the various pupil personnel services is not new. This district must decide whether the present structure facilitates adequate and effective attention to these similarities and differences.

4. Elementary Guidance and Counseling

What provision should the district make for such services? The intern counselor program has demonstrated that both teachers and students will make use of staff counselors, and they express satisfaction with results. Principals have requested full-time counselors for their buildings. Elementary teachers have responded to guidance and human relations classes for them offered through district in-service training programs. Developmental guidance and affective education materials have been purchased and used in several classrooms. The concern, interest, and efforts are evident. But finances are a factor. Staffing each of the elementary buildings with but one counselor would cost in the neighborhood of $150,000. This realistic fact cannot be ignored.

Among some apparent options for servicing elementary guidance needs are the following: (1). expand in-service training opportunities for teachers in the types and uses of developmental guidance and affective education materials; rely upon the teachers to handle all guidance and counseling needs; (2) employ a counselor for each pyramid; this person would serve as a guidance resource person for all the buildings of the pyramid; he/she would coordinate the testing programs, offer parent education classes, consult with teachers, work with some students in groups or individually, and offer some guidance classes for teachers; (3) allow any principal who wishes and can manage the funding to hire a counselor.

And there are other possibilities. Whatever the decisions, they must be made thoughtfully and deliberately. They must be based upon a consideration of the needs of children, and the means most likely to deliver results for the finances available.

Issues in Summary

A million dollar investment of public funds for pupil personnel services demands responsible use. The issues referred to in this section suggest that monitoring and modifying programs are ways to safeguard that investment. The reader was urged to appraise the data in this chapter and compare the specific issues raised with his own list. He was also advised to speculate on possible solutions.

1. Educational Management Services, Inc., *Central Office Management and Staffing*, report prepared for the Board of Education of Independent School District No. 279, Osseo, Minn. (April 1970), pp. 2–12.
2. Harold Schindele, "Group Counseling Work with Seven Selected Boys," *Minnesota Counselor* (Feb. 1963), pp. 8–13.
3. Ronald L. Benson and Don H. Blocher, "Evaluation of Developmental Counseling with Groups of Low Achievers in a High School Setting," *The School Counselor* (March 1967), pp. 215–20.
4. Jerome Koenig and Bess Marmas, "Three-Pronged Strategy Perks Up Boys," *The School Counselor* (Jan. 1973), pp. 211–15.

CHAPTER 10

Pupil Personnel Services
in Community School District 7: The Bronx

NATHAN YOUNG

THE COMMUNITY SETTING

Population. New York City contains approximately eight million people, almost half the population of the state of New York. For educational purposes, the city is divided into thirty-one community school districts, so that several of these districts fall into each of the five boroughs[1] into which New York City is divided. Community School District 7 lies in the extreme southern part of the borough of the Bronx. Approximately one quarter of a million people[2] inhabit the geographical area in which Community School District 7 is located. This does not include the many business people, school personnel and other professionals who work in the area but reside in other communities.

Socio-Economic and Ethnic Factors: District 7 is one of the most disadvantaged areas in New York City, even though it has not quite achieved the notoriety of the Harlem and Bedford-Stuyvesant areas.[3] The extent of unemployment, death from disease, narcotics addiction, crime rate, insufficient and substandard housing, and dearth of medical facilities match those of any other blighted area of the city. Coupled with these misfortunes is the very high mobility rate of the population. Gone are the substantial Irish, German, and Jewish populations of a generation and more ago. Today at least two-thirds of the population is Puerto Rican in origin, with the balance black American. It is these groups that must struggle to raise their children under the highly unfavorable conditions described above—conditions

324

which are at least partly responsible for the mobility of the population, and the growing lack of faith in, and bitterness toward the established order.

History and Nature of Educational Support: Although education is considered to be constitutionally a state function, the source of funds for each school district in New York City is the city itself, which in turn gets a substantial amount of financial help from New York State. Since the steadily rising property tax is the major source of income for New York City (with the relatively new and unpopular city income tax threatening to rival it as a necessary source of revenue some day), there is growing pressure to have New York State assume the entire cost of public education in New York City. For the school districts within the city there is no specific education tax as such. Consequently, there is total financial reliance upon the political governmental structure.

Prior to the development of the national antipoverty program, the financial role of the federal government was limited to the rather meager contributions that came to New York State through the various vocational education acts. However, in recent years there has been an increasing input by the federal government through the Elementary and Secondary Education Acts, the various Title Programs included in the antipoverty operations (especially the Title I Programs, which emphasize educational programs in disadvantaged areas), and the Model Cities Program. District 7 has benefited substantially from the new role of the federal government because it is a prime target area for antipoverty programs. Coupled with the growing control over educational activities being given to local school districts in New York City under the 1970 decentralization law, the emerging role of the federal government has helped to make the total educational funding picture more involved than in the past. The prime source of funds for Community School District 7 is still New York City, whose total educational budget is still determined by how much it gets from New York State to augment its own limited resources. However, decentralized districts such as ours, which are target areas for educational programs for the disadvantaged, are also moving increasingly in the direction of getting help for special funded programs directly from federal government agencies and the New York State Education Department, with the New York City Central Board of Education playing only a nominal role in the process. A brand-new development in this direction is Project Redesign.[4] Under this program the New York State Education Department has selected four school districts in the state for special help in redesigning their total educational programs. All the financial specifics have not yet been spelled out. However, one of the special possible consequences of this arrangement is a hoped-for financial benevolence on the part of New York State as far as District 7 is concerned.

Availability of Supportive Services: There is a serious lack of the various supportive services that help to make an educational system viable. Both public and private hospitals have constantly reduced their services to the point where there is only one hospital in operation, with very limited help available.[5] Medical help frequently requires a long waiting period; and mental health facilities are limited to very pressing cases. The situation has also been aggravated by the departure of private agencies from the South Bronx. The reasons given usually involve lack of funds. However, problems of identifying with the needs and coping with the problems of the newer population groups appear to have played a significant role in the departure of these traditional private agencies. To a very limited extent the vacuum is being filled by indigenous groups, which are organizing facilities through antipoverty funds. One of the most significant of these groups is the Hunts Point Multi-Service Center, located in the northern part of Community School District 7. Through an influx of federal funds this organization is making considerable strides in providing out-patient services in health and mental health, as well as socio-economic services in the areas of employment training, family problems, housing needs, and community needs. A major problem for these new groups is obtaining professional personnel; particularly since every effort is made to choose personnel who identify with the needs and aspirations of the community.

Major Community Needs: There are serious physical plant needs throughout the District 7 area of the South Bronx. There is, for example, a tremendous need for new housing, not only to provide adequate homes for the total population, but also to replace the many slum dwellings that still remain, and which help provide breeding places for disease and crime in general, and for the very serious narcotics problem in particular. The Model Cities housing program is moving very slowly in the direction of providing the new buildings. However, the new housing must be matched by a school building program to relieve the severe overcrowding in the schools. This, too, is proceeding rather slowly. It is also essential that the school building program include provisions for community recreation centers that

326

will not limit the facilities available to the school gymnasiums and playgrounds when school is not in session. All this must, in turn, be matched by a considerable medical building program to help lift the health level of the community to one of minimum acceptability.

The unemployment problem is an extremely serious one. Current welfare programs are not the answer to demoralized people who want to lift themselves out of the cycle of poverty and degradation. A planned, organized effort to provide meaningful training and employment opportunities for the people of the South Bronx is still lacking. Current efforts have only scratched the surface. The unemployment level is the worst in the city. Perhaps the combined efforts of private enterprise, government, and the educational system should replace the scattered efforts of antipoverty training programs, employment agencies, and individual companies in this area.

The narcotics problem is one of the worst in the nation. It is generally conceded that New York City has over sixty percent of the over half million narcotics addicts in the United States. The South Bronx is one of the most addicted areas of the city. The limited prevention and rehabilitation programs that have been undertaken have had very little impact, and have given the people of the community little reason to believe that the problem is being alleviated in any way. However, any massive approach to this problem must be accompanied by corresponding massive approaches to the housing, health, schooling, and unemployment problems in order to have any chance of meaningful results.

Underlying all the serious economic and social needs referred to in the preceding paragraphs is the political need to develop a unity of purpose and spirit of cooperation among the people of the community. There is considerable movement for increased community control over the various phases of community life. The current problems are heavily identified with the established institutions and forces of government. Wrapped in the struggle for community control is the belief that taking control away from the established leadership, which has failed to meet the needs of the current population, is an important step in the direction of meaningful solutions. Community control has already made some beginnings in the area of education.[6] There are many who believe that this control over education should be increased and extended to sanitation, fire, police, hospitals, and other city government functions. However, this movement for community control is not presently accompanied by a unity of democratic spirit. There are serious clashes among the various segments of the current indigenous population with respect to decision making and budgetary development, which significantly delay and hamper meaningful community effort.

THE SCHOOLS

Organizational and Administrative Structure of the District: Under the 1970 New York City Education Decentralization Law, Community School District 7 is headed by a nine-member community school board elected by the local population for a three-year period. The term of office of the current board expires July 1, 1973. The board chooses its president and other officers from its own membership. The board receives budgetary allotments from the Central New York City Board of Education, and, within specified limitations, may decide how the monies are to be spent, and which types of educational programs and pursuits are to be followed. The limitations include the by-laws of the New York City Central Board of Education, the contracts of the Central Board with the United Federation of Teachers and the Council of Supervisors and Administrators, and the limitation of community school board jurisdiction to the elementary and junior-high-intermediate schools. All high schools and special schools are still under the direct control of the New York City Central Board of Education.

The Community School Board may also hire and dismiss personnel within limitations. They may choose the new personnel they wish, provided they meet minimum qualifications; and they may dismiss personnel, provided all the legal steps are accomplished.[7] The administrative structure of the school district is headed by a community superintendent, chosen by and directly responsible to the community school board. He is assisted by a deputy superintendent to help reduce the routine responsibilities of the superintendent. The principals of the elementary and junior high-intermediate schools are directly responsible to the community superintendent. Also directly responsible to the superintendent are his executive assistants, the district business manager, the administrative director of pupil personnel services, the director of curriculum, and the directors of the federal and state funded programs. The number of people directly responsible to the immediate members of the superintendent's staff is constantly growing as more and more functions and responsibilities are transferred from the New York City Central Board of Education to the community school boards. A fundamental aim of the decen-

328

tralization law is to gradually curtail the personnel and responsibilities of the Central Board of Education, and limit its functions to setting fundamental policies and minimum standards, and serving as an overall resource agency for the community school districts. Figure 10.1 shows a more streamlined presentation of the community superintendent's staff:

It should be remembered that the above organization may be subject to change at any time. This may happen in the not too distant future, since the district is currently in the process of selecting a new community superintendent (the last superintendent retired in the spring of 1972).

Elementary Schools: At the present time there are nineteen elementary schools in the district, with classes ranging from kindergarten through fifth grade. In registration, the schools range from eight hundred to eighteen hundred. The total elementary school enrollment for the district is approximately twenty-two thousand pupils, with average class size in the low thirties. One of the schools is a bilingual school. There children may receive their instruction in

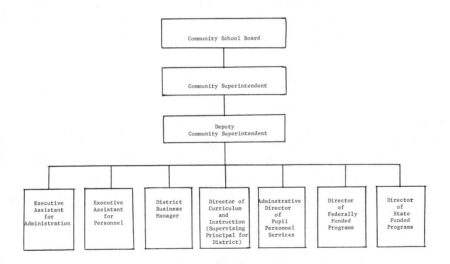

Fig. 10.1. Organization of Community Superintendent's staff.

English or in Spanish, with parallel classes on each grade. This makes it possible for children coming from Puerto Rico and other Spanish-speaking areas to receive instruction in all subjects in their native tongue until they show a sufficient mastery of English. Thus, a possible academic retardation attributable to language handicaps is avoided.

Junior High-Intermediate Schools. There is now one junior high school in the district (grades 7–9) and four intermediate schools (grades 6–8). In enrollment, they range from fourteen hundred to eighteen hundred. The total junior high-intermediate school enrollment for the district is approximately eight thousand pupils, with class size again in the low thirties. The trend is toward the elimination of junior high schools in favor of intermediate schools. The process has been slowed down by the overcrowded conditions of the high schools. It is expected that a bilingual intermediate school will be opened this year, with provision for learning in both English and Spanish.

High Schools. Under the 1970 New York City decentralization law, high schools throughout the city are under the jurisdiction of the Central Board of Education. All the regular academic high schools have zones or district lines, which in many cases overlap the community school districts; therefore, particular high schools may draw their student population from the junior high-intermediate schools of more than one community school district. The zoning regulations cover the regular academic high schools. Students are automatically entitled to go to the high schools in their home zone, the zone in which they live. However, students may also attend one of the special high schools for the gifted if they pass the competitive entrance examination with a sufficiently high rank to be included in the incoming classes. To some extent, extra consideration is given to potential when the students come from disadvantaged areas such as District 7. Students may also choose to attend one of the many vocational high schools in the city without regard for zoning regulations. Whenever applications at a particular vocational high school are oversubscribed, quotas and priorities are established. Enrollment in the high schools varies from about fifteen hundred in some of the vocational high schools to over five thousand students in the overcrowded academic high schools. The graduates of Community School District 7 junior high-intermediate schools also have automatic access to one all-boy high school and one all-girl high school.

Special Schools. When one speaks of special schools in New York City today one does not usually mean the special high schools for the gifted, such as the High School of Science or the High School of Music and Art. The term "special school" technically designates the school for the youngster who is having adjustment problems in the regular school setting. If a student is eleven years of age, and it has been demonstrated that behavioral adjustment is not possible in the regular school setting, he or she may be transferred to a special school in which class size is fifteen or fewer; the total school registration may be two hundred to three hundred students, or even less. These schools are all under the jurisdiction of the New York City Central Board of Education. The transfer involves an application process. Return to the regular school setting may be accomplished when the child is considered ready for it. For children under eleven years, junior guidance or special classes may be set up within the regular school for those who cannot adjust to the regular school setting. These classes are small (from six to fifteen in size), and usually receive extra guidance and psychological services. Also under the jurisdiction of the Central Board of Education are schools for the deaf, the blind, and those with multiple handicaps. Classes for the mentally retarded are under Central Board of Education jurisdiction, but they are housed in the regular community district schools as well as in the high schools.

Typical Organizational Plan: An Elementary School. The following describes an elementary school in Community School District 7 that has about fourteen hundred pupils: The school has classes ranging from the kindergarten through the fifth grade:

one principal
one assistant principal for upper grades
one assistant principal for lower grades
one assistant principal for pupil personnel services
one guidance counselor
one part-time psychologist
one bilingual teacher
three resource specialists (speech, early childhood, the retarded)
seventy teachers (fifteen of them specialists, serving several classes)
forty educational assistants (classroom paraprofessionals)
one guidance assistant
one attendance aide
ten general school aides

Although one speaks of average class size in the low thirties, special classes and classes for the mentally retarded range closer to twenty.

The principal of the school and the assistant principals are full-time administrators and supervisors. They do not teach any classes, nor do they usually give demonstration lessons. This is generally the role of the specialist and the teacher who serves as the grade leader for the teachers on a particular grade level.

The above organization does not include the periodic services of the district specialists in the curriculum areas, who visit the school at least once a month.

An Intermediate School. The following describes an intermediate school in the district that has a school population of about sixteen hundred pupils: The school has classes ranging from the sixth through the eighth grade:

> One principal, three assistant principals in charge of the grades. Each of the three assistant principals also has subject area responsibilities.
> one assistant principal in charge of programming and scheduling
> one assistant principal in charge of pupil personnel services
> one assistant principal serving as administrative assistant.
> three guidance counselors: One for each grade
> three teachers serving as part-time grade advisors, thereby relieving the deans and guidance counselors of many minor items.
> one dean of boys and one dean of girls
> three specialists for library and corrective reading
> six part-time teachers who serve as subject area chairmen for areas not covered by assistant principals.
> fifteen teachers who perform special services instead of having a homeroom class.
> one part-time social worker
> one full-time attendance teacher
> one laboratory specialist
> six teachers of industrial arts subjects
> six teachers of home economics
> fifty-five teachers of regular academic subjects who are also in charge of homeroom classes.
> two guidance assistants
> one bilingual teacher

The principal and all assistant principals are full-time supervisors and administrators.

The above organization does not include the periodic services of the district specialists in the curriculum areas, who visit the school at least once a month.

332

High School. The following describes one of the Vocational High Schools that is geographically located within the area of Community School District 7. It has a student population of fourteen hundred, and is an all-boy school.

> one principal
> one assistant principal for administration
> one assistant principal for pupil personnel and related services
> ten department chairmen who supervise and teach part-time. This
>   includes all the shop areas and the academic areas.
> one full-time chairman of guidance, assisted by two full time guidance
>   counselors and eight teachers serving as part-time grade advisors
> one full-time dean of boys
> one full-time attendance coordinator (teacher-assigned)

Although there are ninety-five people on the total staff of the school, this does not prevent many academic classes from reaching into the thirties. The shop classes must be kept small.

The Academic High School nearest to the geographic area of District 7 has a principal; an assistant principal for administration; an assistant principal for pupil personnel services; teaching chairmen of departments for each of the academic, commercial, and industrial arts areas; deans and assistant deans for boys and girls; an attendance coordinator; a college advisor; a guidance counselor for each of the grades, assisted by part-time grade advisors; special psychological and social worker services from the Bureau of Child Guidance; and a number of special services obtained through funded programs. The school has over four thousand students with overlapping sessions, and has been operating at about one hundred and forty percent of capacity.

Special School. The special school for elementary boys eleven years and older, which is geographically located in District 7 has a principal and assistant principal, and a staff of twenty-five, including pupil personnel and curriculum specialists for a student body that varies between one hundred and fifty to two hundred students.

PUPIL PERSONNEL SERVICES

Organization and Structure. The structure of pupil personnel services in Community School District 7 is a little more complicated than in districts outside of New York City, owing to the changes set in motion by the decentralization law. In overall charge is the administrative director of pupil personnel services, directly responsible to the community superintendent. Within the basic pupil personnel services are included the guidance services, the attendance services, the psychological and social work services, and the psychiatric services. The guidance counselor services are the most extensive, and are in a supervisory as well as administrative relationship to the director of pupil personnel services. In connection with the supervisory aspects of his role in this area, the director is assisted by the head of guidance services for the elementary and junior high-intermediate schools. However, the director is responsible for such items as appointments, transfers, administrative reports, and the nature of the overall program; and he shares with the principal of each school the rating of guidance counselors. Each of the junior high-intermediate schools has three guidance counselors, one for each grade. The elementary schools have one counselor each, with the exception of the larger elementary schools (sixteen hundred or above in registration), which have two counselors. Actually, the number of schools having more than one counselor varies from year to year, depending upon the budget. Within each school building, the counselors maintain a direct administrative relationship to the school through both the principal and a designated assistant principal. In the years prior to 1970 the New York City Central Board of Education, through the Bureau of Educational and Vocational Guidance, was responsible for the appointment and training of counselors, and the development of all guidance programs. Under decentralization, the Bureau has been moved more and more into the status of a supportive, advisory, resource agency.[8] Through federal and state funding, each school guidance office now has a minimum of one guidance assistant. Each person who serves as a guidance assistant is an indigenous paraprofessional, who helps the guidance counselor increase his services to the children, the parents, and the school.

The attendance services of the district are under the supervision of a supervisor of attendance who relates administratively to the director of pupil personnel services. He is responsible for the supervision of the attendance teachers, as they are known in New York City.[9] The policy-making relationship of the Central Board Bureau of Attendance to the districts remains stronger than that of the Bureau of Educational and Vocational Guidance because of the legal mandates of the state with respect to school attendance. Each of the junior high-intermediate schools in the district is assigned one full-time attendance teacher. However, in the elementary schools, there is an attendance teacher for every two schools, except for the two largest schools, each of which has an attendance teacher.

The services of the social workers, psychologists, and psychiatrists are allocated to the district by the Bureau of Child Guidance, an agency of the Central Board of Education. Decentralization has not had the same effect upon this central bureau as it has had upon most central bureaus because most of its funding comes from New York State and New York City agencies that lie outside of the province of the New York City Board of Education. The district relationship, therefore, is as follows: a liaison supervisor from the Bureau of Child Guidance is responsible for the overall supervision of social work, psychological and psychiatric services in the district. However, that supervisor relates administratively to the director of pupil personnel services with respect to the distribution of personnel, the planning of assignments, and the directions and emphases of the overall mental health program. Under the Bureau of Child Guidance allocation formula, there are two psychiatrists for the entire district, and only five psychologists and seven social workers. Most of the schools are serviced by having a social worker or psychologist serve two schools, with reciprocal arrangements for back-up social work or psychological services. However, owing to lack of sufficient personnel, a few of the schools are served by a single psychologist who receives supportive help from his colleagues on an "as needed" basis. The limited mental health services available through the Bureau of Child Guidance makes it necessary to rely upon referrals to outside agencies, hospitals, and clinics for the bulk of in-depth mental health services.

The basic health services in terms of nurse and doctor services are not really provided by the Board of Education.[10] These are provided to the schools through the New York City Department of Health. This means the Mott Haven District Health Center, as far as District 7 is concerned. The chief health officer of the Mott Haven Center is the district health officer. His staff includes the district supervisor of nurses. Both relate to Community School District 7, and to the director of pupil personnel services in particular. A member of the staff of the director of pupil personnel services, the coordinator of health and related services, serves as a direct liaison between the PPS director and the district health officer and district supervisor of nurses. Unfortunately, there is a severe shortage of nursing services. The number of nurses and public health assistants available for service in the schools is in constant fluctuation. As a result, the nursing service

335

provided for some schools in the district is only occasional and very sporadic. Plans are under way to try to relieve the situation through such federally funded operations as the Hunts Point Multi-Service Center.

The district personnel who are administratively or supervisorily responsible to the director of pupil personnel services are shown in Figure 10.2.

The aforementioned services constitute the basic pupil personnel services for Community School District 7. However, there are cooperative supporting services within the district that work closely with the basic pupil personnel services. Foremost among these are the bilingual teachers in school and community relations. These are Spanish-speaking teachers (largely of Puerto Rican extraction) who help both parents and children to relate more effectively to the school and the community. This is especially helpful in view of the fact that over two-thirds of the school population are Spanish-speaking Puerto Ricans, with only a small percentage of the parents having been born in continental United States. Each elementary school has such a teacher, and provisions are being made to have one of these in each of the junior high-intermediate schools.

Through one of the major, federally funded, Title I programs, each school has a family assistant who works very closely with the parents to help them become more involved with the school's activities, and hence more effective in helping their children to experience a suc-

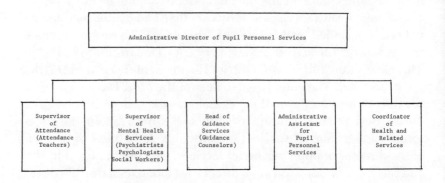

Fig. 10.2. Organization of office of Administrative Director of Pupil Personnel Services.

cessful school relationship. This person is also an indigenous para-professional.

It can readily be seen that both cooperation and clarification of roles are essential if the guidance office, the bilingual teacher in school and community relations, and the family assistant are to function harmoniously and productively. District guidelines are provided, but each school is given leeway for innovation and modification.

A relative newcomer among the specially funded programs in the district is the drug abuse or narcotics program. The program is headed by a director and five teacher coordinators, each serving one junior high-intermediate school and its feeding elementary schools. Within each school there is one drug abuse instructor and one neighborhood worker carrying on preventive work, and helping to make appropriate referrals for rehabilitative work.[11] Both the instructors and neighborhood workers are paraprofessionals, who in most cases have gone through narcotics experiences.

The District Pupil Personnel Council. It will be seen that the administrative director of pupil personnel services relates to a number of services in a variety of ways. With respect to the guidance services, he has both supervisory and administrative responsibilities. With respect to mental health services (social workers, psychologists, and psychiatrists) and attendance services, he has administrative responsibilities. With the drug abuse personnel, bilingual teachers in school and community relations (this title distinguishes them from bilingual teachers in the classroom), and family assistants, there is recognized administrative cooperation. With the health services, there is more limited administrative involvement. To some extent, all these relationships are formalized. This is done through the District Pupil Personnel Council, of which the administrative director of pupil personnel services is the chairman. The following people are members of this council:

Administrative Director of Pupil Personnel Services: Chairman
Supervisor of Attendance
Supervisor of Mental Health Services
Administrative Assistant for Pupil Personnel Services
The Head of Guidance Services
Coordinator of Health and Related Services
Supervisor of Bilingual Teachers
Coordinator of Family Assistants
Director of the Drug Abuse Program

Four elementary school assistant principals
One junior high-intermediate assistant principal
Representative of the District Parents Council.

A major function of the District Pupil Personnel Council, which meets at least once a month, is to provide leadership and supervision in getting all the pupil personnel services and cooperating supporting services to work together effectively within each school. Activities of this group have included: district-wide joint institutes of all the services represented on the Council; recommendations and direct involvement in the organization and operation of pupil personnel teams and committees in the schools; recommendations to the community superintendent and the community school board regarding special facilities and programs for pupils with adjustment problems; recommendations and proposals to the district for helping to establish alternative educational programs to meet the needs of all students; and proposals for expanding the pupil personnel services. Despite budgetary limitations, there has been some measure of accomplishment, as indicated in the next section on District Policies for Pupil Personnel Services.

District Policies For Pupil Personnel Services

Community School District 7 is dedicated to the belief that pupil personnel services are intended to: help children to adjust successfully to the school setting; develop in them a feeling of success and self-worth as they proceed through their educational experiences; and help them prepare meaningfully for the educational and career choices that lie ahead of them.

In line with the above belief it is the accepted practice that pupil personnel services are for all children, not just for those who manifest problems. It is expected that all children should be given the opportunity to function successfully, and realize their potential more fully as a result of the benefits of pupil personnel services.

It is also the accepted belief that each service can make its contribution most effectively if it operates cooperatively with the other services as part of a team approach. Thus, there is increasing emphasis on the pupil personnel team approach in the schools of the district. The team concerns itself not only with finding immediate solutions to hard-core problems (whether they be pupils or situations), but also with recommendations to the principal of policies and practices that will be preventive in nature, and will help the school to function

338

more effectively. Such recommendations may be instructional or administrative.

The district is currently placing great stress upon the role of the paraprofessional in the pupil personnel services. The concept of the paraprofessional educational assistant in the classroom has now been extended to the supportive services. Thus, one finds guidance assistants, family assistants, paraprofessional drug abuse personnel, attendance aides, and paraprofessional mental health workers working side by side with the professionals in the attempt to strengthen and enrich the supporting services to the school, the children and the parents. Not only does this trend help to enrich and strengthen the services, it also helps bring the services closer to the community and provides a career ladder for indigenous adults to move up through paraprofessional to professional ranks.

The growing emphasis upon the development of paraprofessional components in each of the pupil personnel services does not mean a lowering of standards. The district is anxious to have the best possible services for its children, and seeks only qualified people. Only fully licensed personnel, or personnel who possess all the requirements for the position, are placed in full-time pupil personnel positions.

There is considerable emphasis upon the role of the pupil personnel services in helping the schools to develop alternative educational approaches for the children. Consequently, in the training programs there is growing emphasis upon career education approaches, humanistic educational techniques, reality therapy techniques, learning disability programs, and increased community involvement.

Increasing emphasis is being placed upon helping to plan for and provide alternative educational settings and approaches within the regular school for the child with adjustment difficulties. The pupil personnel workers play a very active role in this area, and often seek to combine a more effective program for the individual child with supportive help or therapy from outside agencies. Transfer to a special educational setting outside the school or the district is a last resort. The dearth of adequate outside facilities and the great local fear of stigma help to reenforce this policy. However, the district has recognized the need for special class settings that may help particular children to prepare more effectively for adjustment to school, and to enable them to return to the regular setting later on. Within budgetary limitations, such classes are encouraged within each school.

There is growing emphasis upon group approaches. Working with the individual child is still considered an integral part of the total program. However, the effects of group interaction, the possibilities involved with many groups of children, as opposed to working with individuals, and the many other merits of small and large group work have resulted in a reduced emphasis on working solely with the individual child, and greater involvement with group techniques, approaches, and programs.[12]

The district does place a high priority on the need to expand its pupil personnel services, but budgetary limitations and union staff contracts create operational limitations. There is a tremendous need to raise the reading and mathematics levels of the children of the district. They are among the lowest in New York City. Under the circumstances, it is difficult to obtain the expansion of pupil personnel services at the expense of greater direct emphasis upon the instructional services, much as one may try to argue both the immediate and long-term merits of such approaches. The growing demand for instructional components in any specially funded program that provides for pupil personnel services does not help the situation.

Although decentralization is placing increased control over budgetary, personnel, and program matters in the hands of the Community School Board, Community School District 7 places great value upon the help, support, and advice it receives from the pupil personnel services agencies of both the New York City Board of Education and the New York State Education Department.[13] The administrative director of pupil personnel services and the supervisors who work closely with him maintain a close ongoing relationship with these agencies.

JOB DESCRIPTIONS

The Attendance Teacher. The basic responsibility of the attendance teacher is to help all pupils attend school regularly, and to provide such help as may be necessary to the pupils, parents, and school personnel to make that regular attendance possible. Thus, it becomes the province of the attendance teacher to make certain that the child is attending the right school in terms of his residence and educational level, and that he is placed, registered, and attending the proper classes in the school. It means that the attendance teacher must investigate causes for absence in order to help overcome and prevent truancy, and to render such assistance as may be necessary to help overcome obstacles that are interfering with proper school attendance. That assistance may take the form of explaining the educational attendance laws and procedures to parents and children; directing the family toward proper agencies for help if housing, economic, or family problems are impeding school attendance; making school personnel aware of school situations that may be contributing to nonattendance; hastening actions for medical attention and medical certificates; cooperating with the guidance services and other staff members of the school to help promote the best possible educational-learning setting for the child; and taking such legal action as may be necessary with respect to the parents, the child, or both in order to obtain the best possible educational circumstances for the child. As a member of the school pupil personnel team, he helps achieve group solutions and recommendations with respect to children and situations. He also serves as a direct consultant to the principal of the school.

The Attendance Aide. In order to provide paraprofessional assistance for the tremendous amount of routine chores connected with attendance procedures, each school is permitted an attendance aide to assure parental notification of all absences, and to expedite the delivery of suspected truancy forms to the attendance teacher in all cases of unverified lengthy absences, and all absences where there is a history of truancy. The aide may also assist with communications with parents and children in connection with attendance procedures and past absences, and help with the maintenance of appropriate attendance records.

The Guidance Counselor. It is possible to fill many pages discussing the variety of activities in which the guidance counselors may participate. This presentation will be limited to those services that are given a high priority in Community School District 7. Although there may be some repetition involved, it may be better to separate the elementary from the junior high-intermediate school counselors.

Elementary. Great emphasis is placed upon the early identification of talents and weaknesses in order to overcome handicaps and nurture the children's strengths at the earliest possible time; the development of an awareness of the world of occupations and their relevance to educational activities through actual community involvement beyond the school building; the provision of opportunities for decision making and choice making, so that children are better prepared to make meaningful educational and tentative career choices at appropriate junctions in their lives; arrangements for working especially closely with teachers and parents to help them serve the children more effectively, rather than emphasizing direct counseling activity with children; arrangement for direct activity with children in small groups or individual sessions whenever this is a demonstrated need of the child rather than the situation;[14] provision for maximum of teacher training activity and minimum of involvement in crisis situations; the development of a referral procedure to outside agencies and providing follow-up services; service as a key member of the school pupil personnel team, and involving the latter in all hard-core situations rather than trying to "go it alone"; and service to the principal of the school as a consultant.

Junior High-Intermediate. Great emphasis is placed upon having the counselors specialize at different grade levels. The counselor of the incoming grade will usually specialize in articulation activities connected with the coming of entering pupils from the feeding elementary schools, and orientation activities for these pupils and their parents. The middle grade counselor usually emphasizes occupational awareness activities in which there is considerable involvement with private business organizations in "Business-School Partnerships" and "Living Witness" programs.[15] The senior class counselor is heavily involved with orientation for high school and the preparation of high school applications. At all grade levels there is a constant emphasis upon developing better occupational awareness, and its tie-up with educational activity and educational choice making; a special emphasis upon developing parental involvement, which is less characteristic at this level than at the elementary level; a widespread attempt to reach more children through a variety of small counseling groups, half-class developmental counseling groups and large discussion-information-giving groups. At this age level it is essential that the counselor relate directly to the children rather than through other adults, since the student is now becoming involved in more immediate educational decision-making questions than was true at the elementary level. Too frequently, this activity has been entrusted to noncounselors, to the detriment of the children's best interests, and to the detriment of the guidance movement in general.

The Guidance Assistant. The guidance assistant has become a sort of junior partner to the guidance counselor in helping to provide counseling and guidance services to the students, the parents, and the school. A concerted effort is made not to turn the guidance assistant into an ordinary clerical helper, messenger, or receptionist. Through district and on-the-job training, the guidance assistant is prepared for direct involvement with the pupils and parents, both individually and in groups. Sometimes information-giving or referral service is involved. At other times, it may be a combination of tutoring and uninvolved help with decision making or problem solving. At other times, it may simply be the opportunity to talk with the guidance assistant that will provide the service. All guidance assistant activity must be under the supervision of and in consultation with the guidance counselor. Guidance assistants are encouraged to continue their education (most are only high school graduates) so that they may enter the professional ranks of guidance counselors and teachers.

The Social Worker. The seven social workers assigned to the district spend two days in each of the two schools to which they are assigned. The fifth day is spent at their district and borough headquarters for completion of paperwork, consultations and training sessions, and follow-up activities. Referrals to the social worker usually come from the guidance counselor, but may also result from a decision of the pupil personnel team in the school, or a request for back-up services from another school in the district that does not have a social worker assigned to it. When a case involves severe family problems beyond the scope of the school counselor, the counselor and the social worker make a joint decision as to whether the case can be taken on by the social worker (in terms of current case load and special characteristics of the case), or whether it should be referred to an outside agency. In addition to serving as a member of the school pupil personnel team, the social worker may sponsor or cosponsor training workshops for teachers and other staff members of the school.

The Psychologist. The five psychologists assigned to the district also spend two days each week in each of the two schools to which they are assigned. Here again, the fifth day is spent at their district or borough headquarters for the completion of paperwork, consultations and training sessions, and follow-up activities. Referrals usually come from the guidance counselor, but may also result from a decision of the pupil personnel team in the school, or a request for back-up services from another school in the district which does not have a psychologist assigned to it. When a case involves behavioral manifestations that are beyond the scope of the school counselor, or that may require special educational placement, the school counselor and the psychologist make a joint decision as to whether the case can be taken on by the psychologist (in terms of current case load and special characteristics of the case), or whether it should be referred to an outside agency. There is tremendous pressure to provide definitive action immediately, especially testing for mental retardation. Every effort is being made to resist this demand, and to have the psychologist decide what initial exploratory steps should be taken, which often will not involve testing. In addition to serving as a member of the pupil personnel team, the psychologist may sponsor or cosponsor training workshops for teachers and other staff members of the school.

The Psychiatrist. Fifteen hours of service is the full-time weekly load of each of the two psychiatrists assigned to the district. One of the psychiatrists has concentrated on individual referrals from the other mental health services. Usually, referral from a school will result from joint consultation of the psychologist and guidance counselor, or the social worker and guidance counselor, with the former in each case making the referral. However, in special situations, district headquarters and school principals communicate directly with the psychiatrist. The other psychiatrist concentrates on training sessions for groups of pupil personnel workers, and serves as a consultant for various special classes in the district and in the schools.

The Mental Health Trainees. This is a group of five paraprofessionals who have received training that enables them to assist social workers and psychologists. Each one is assigned as an assistant to a particular social worker or psychologist. They are encouraged to continue their training beyond their present high school graduation status so that they may eventually enter the professional ranks.

The Nurse. As previously noted, nurses and public health assistants are provided not by the Board of Education but by the Department of Health. The Mott Haven Health District must use these same people to work in their clinics part of the time, and also to make home visits. Therefore, they serve the schools rather sporadically, with the smaller schools receiving only occasional service. Frequently, therefore, emergency first aid may be provided by the principal, an assistant principal, a teacher, or a school secretary. No staff personnel may administer medication of any kind. The services of the school nurse are usually limited to bringing the health records up to date, and preparing the necessary cards for the periodic visits of the department of health doctor for inoculations and routine examinations. She has little time for referrals, and no time for involvement in preventive health activities. Wherever possible, she is welcomed into the pupil personnel team.

344

The Bilingual Teacher. The bilingual teacher in school and community relations is a regularly licensed teacher. In some districts, her language specialty may be Chinese or another language. In Community School District 7 it is Spanish. She (most are female) operates outside the classroom, and is involved directly with parents, pupils, and community agencies. Since she inevitably finds herself involved in personal, family, and educational problems in trying to be a source of all-round help, it is essential that she work very closely with other members of the school pupil personnel team. There are many areas in which there is interrelationship with the guidance counselor's activities. The two work very closely together.

The Family Assistant. This is a specially funded paraprofessional position. A major focus here is the establishment of a family room in the school, with a variety of meaningful activities and workshops to draw the family (especially parents) to the school. The work of the family assistant is frequently a means of bringing all the pupil personnel services closer to the parents. She is expected to limit the time spent on home visits, and to concentrate on conducting a meaningful daily program in the family room.

The Narcotics or Drug Abuse Personnel. These are also specially funded people. While the director and the five teacher coordinators are professional staff, the instructors and neighborhood workers in each of the elementary and junior high-intermediate schools are paraprofessionals. From prepared materials, they provide preventive instruction in the classrooms; conduct small group sessions with selected groups of students; work closely with the guidance counselors and deans in connection with specific cases; and are directly involved in referrals for rehabilitation, especially at the junior high-intermediate school level. The insight made possible by their unique personal experiences are frequently helpful at meetings of the school pupil personnel teams.

COSTS OF PUPIL PERSONNEL SERVICES

When one considers costs and the proportion of expenditures for pupil personnel services, as related to the total operating district budget, one must confine himself to those services which are technically considered to be pupil personnel services from a budgetary viewpoint. These include the attendance and guidance services. The health services are provided by the Department of Health and, therefore, do not fall within the district budget. The mental health

345

services (social workers, psychologists, psychiatrists) are limited to those provided by the Central Board of Education. No district funds are currently allocated to this area. The bilingual teacher, the family assistant, and drug abuse personnel, while they mesh with the pupil personnel services in actual operation, are technically not budgeted under that heading. The total annual operating budget of the district, and the amounts actually spent by the district for pupil personnel services for attendance and guidance services, are the specific figures used to determine the expenditure ratios.

Comparing the total operating budget of the district with the expenditures of out-of-district funds for pupil personnel services, one finds that, out of the funds allotted to it, Community School District 7 spent a little under three and one-half percent on pupil personnel services.

Is this a favorable operating ratio? It is favorable in comparison with what has happened to a number of other districts under decentralization, where the budget squeeze has been less kind to pupil personnel services. On the other hand, none of the district's own funds have yet gone into the strengthening of nursing and mental health services in the district's schools.

How can the operating ratio be changed? The following possibilities exist, but in the present severe budget squeeze these developments are very unlikely: (1) the district could put more of its state and federal program funds into pupil personnel services; this would have to be at the expense of other programs; (2) the city could give more money to the district with the stipulation that it be used for pupil personnel services; (3) community and parental pressure could change priorities in favor of more supportive services.

TABLE 12

1971–72 Operating Budget For Community School District 7

Regular tax levy funds received through the New York City Board of Education:	$23,006,707.00
Appropriations through federal & state funded programs	6,977,023.00
Total operating budget	29,983,730.00
Total budgeted for attendance services	293,930.00
Total budgeted for guidance services	742,018.00
Total district expenditures for Pupil Personnel Services	1,035,948.00

FACILITIES

Space. The space made available to the Community School District 7 Pupil Personnel Services falls into two categories: space made available for district headquarters, and the space provided in each school building. The headquarters offices for the basic pupil personnel services (attendance, guidance, and mental health) are all located on the fourth floor of a private office building about one block from the main district headquarters of the Community School Board, the Community Superintendent, and most of the district staff. The offices vary in size from two meeting and resource rooms that can comfortably accommodate about twenty people each, to very small offices capable of accommodating only one person. The fourteen offices involved cover a total space of about four thousand square feet. A diagram of the area would not adequately reflect the limitations of the space provided because it would not show the handicaps of construction that reduce the actual amount of space available for furniture and other facilities. At this point, the space is just about adequate to serve the official needs of the approximately twenty-five people who use these offices on a full-time or part-time basis. In each school building, the situation varies. All guidance counselors, since they are in their schools full-time, have offices. Most have private offices of their own; although a few are barely large enough to move around in. Where two counselors share an office, the offices are fairly spacious. However, attendance and mental health personnel, who are in each school on a part-time basis, simply have a desk in someone else's office, and do most of their interviewing on a "where space is available" basis. No, diagram could represent the typical facilities for the schools in the district.

Furniture. Generally speaking, there is an adequate supply of desks, chairs, tables, bookcases, file cabinets, typewriters, and general office supplies in all offices. However, audio-visual equipment is generally limited in amount, and, where it is available, security is a serious problem. The theft and vandalism rates are quite high. Attendance personnel and mental health personnel usually save most of their clerical chores for the time they spend in their district offices.

Telephones. All offices at district headquarters and all guidance offices in the schools have telephones with private lines, with one or two technical problem exceptions where they are hooked into the school switchboard. Unfortunately, attendance and mental health personnel in the schools must use any available telephone during the

347

course of their work. Usually it is the guidance office phone or the medical office phone. Every school has a medical office, which is, in turn, equipped with a telephone, even though the office itself may not be regularly used by medical personnel.

Secretarial Service. All pupil personnel services staff based in the schools must rely upon general office service for secretarial work or do it themselves (mostly the latter). Headquarters' supervisory staff have a limited amount of secretarial service directly available to them.

UNIQUE CHARACTERISTICS OF THE PUPIL PERSONNEL SERVICES

The following characteristics may not be unique to the pupil personnel services of District 7. Certainly many of them are evident in scores of other districts. However, they are worthy of note.

The services are for all children. Pupil personnel services, especially at the elementary school level, are usually regarded as being involved with the difficult child or the child who cannot adjust to the regular school setting. This has served to give the services a negative image in the eyes of the public, and a low rating in the popularity scale with budget makers. In District 7, a concerted effort is being made to associate each of the services with the needs of all children in a number of ways: through their involvement in the school pupil personnel team planning sessions; through active participation in training workshops; and through efforts to make themselves available to a variety of school and community groups. Even the attendance workers and mental health workers are moving steadily in wider directions. As noted in other sections of this chapter, the guidance personnel have become involved in numerous activities that bear directly on the needs of all children.

There is a special unity of effort, as shown by the District Pupil Personnel Council, the school pupil personnel teams, and the task force approach. The unity of effort among the pupil personnel services of District 7 is not limited to simply clarifying the role of each service and keeping one another informed of the activities in each service. There is joint activity in both planning and performance, and a frequent intermeshing of roles, depending on the strengths of the particular people and the needs of the particular situation. While basic recommendations may come from the District Pupil Personnel Council acting as a group, each school administration and each school pupil personnel team may originate and implement plans and proce-

348

dures that may have a particular type of task (perhaps in relation to certain family problems) performed by the guidance counselor in one school, the attendance teacher in another school, and the social worker in still another school.

This unity has reached its peak of operations in task forces of the pupil personnel services that have been organized for particular purposes. Worthy of special note here are the task force dealing with children having severe problems and the task force to determine community and school staff attitudes toward the pupil personnel services. The tasks undertaken by each committee member bore a greater relationship to the needs of the situation and the committee member's personal strengths and interests, than to the particular discipline from which he came.

There are many special programs and activities. There is a strong feeling that the pupil personnel services of the district have pioneered in a variety of directions. There is a Career Resource Center that makes its facilities available to pupils, staff and community groups, and which has been very instrumental in establishing close working relationships between the district schools and a variety of business organizations.

Through the pupil personnel services a variety of educational approaches have been pioneered, including: the Glasser Class Meetings Program,[16] a learning disabilities program, humanistic approaches in the classroom, and the establishment of special classes within the schools and at the district level for children who cannot adjust to the regular school setting.

There is a variety of undertakings on the part of coordinators on the staff of the director. At both the elementary and junior high-intermediate levels, the head of guidance services has made significant strides in moving occupational awareness activities into both the school guidance programs and a number of regular classroom programs. She and others have also been very much involved in the basic training of paraprofessionals to serve in the guidance offices, one of the proudest achievements in the district. The coordinator of health and related services has made substantial progress in bringing camp programs into the regular school year; thus, many children have experienced camping as part of their regular educational program rather than only during the summer. The administrative assistant to the director has been very instrumental in helping schools to reduce substantially the number of pupil suspensions, and to find educationally meaningful alternatives.

349

There is a special effort to promote the involvement of outside services to supplement our limited health and mental health services. The five psychologists and seven social workers provided through the Central Board of Education cannot begin to meet the needs of the thirty thousand pupils attending the elementary and junior high-intermediate schools of this heavily disadvantaged district. As previously noted, private and public agency resources are extremely limited. Therefore, maximum cooperation is extended in the direction of the relatively new federally funded agencies, which help make their personnel and facilities available. These include the mental health facilities of both the Hunts Point Multi-Service Center and the Mott Haven Mental Health Center. Arrangements have been made for some of their personnel to provide mental health services within the school buildings. However, these arrangements are voluntary, unofficial, and vary considerably from time to time. In the area of physical health, the district is now trying to work out a cooperative arrangement between the Hunts Point Multi-Service Center and the Department of Health Mott Haven Health Center to augment the limited nursing services provided in our schools by the latter agency.

The role of the paraprofessional has become an integral part of the total pupil personnel services program. The guidance assistant, the attendance aide, and the mental health trainees are here to stay. They are making significant contributions to the pupil personnel services, and are helping to bring the services closer to the community. Coupled with the special college opportunities that accompany the whole paraprofessional program, the positions provide excellent career-ladder approaches for indigenous adults.

The total pupil personnel services program is very much concerned with curriculum and the role of the teacher. There is a constant striving not to be a "crisis" or "finger-in-the-dike" operation. While we do not sidestep immediate problems, every effort is made to give an increasing proportion of our time to helping teachers relate more effectively to pupils through training programs, and through direct involvement with teachers in classroom activity. We are also very much involved in the search for alternative educational approaches, so that the emphasis may move away from adjusting the child to the educational setting toward providing the most viable and most productive educational setting for the child.

Despite resistance, there is steady chipping away of the crisis approach. Administrators and staffs are becoming more receptive to the idea of turning inward and developing alternative educational

350

approaches and new behavioral attitudes toward children, rather than being constantly ready to brand particular children as "impossible" and literally throwing them at the guidance staff and other pupil personnel workers.

There is a growing emphasis on the balanced use of time by pupil personnel workers. Each professional in the different services is given some discretion in the organization of his duties and in the particular activities he wishes to emphasize, although the district is constantly pressing for more group work rather than individual case-work, and more prevention activity rather than crisis work. However, each worker is required to keep a log of his activities, and to develop a daily program, in addition to his case records. This makes it possible for the individual worker to assess what he is doing, and provides a means through which the supervisor or coordinator can review with the worker the nature of his output in terms of balance and productivity.

Increased community involvement has become an integral part of the total approach to pupil personnel services. The staff of the pupil personnel services makes pronounced efforts to do the following: to be present at Community School Board meetings whenever possible, and to invite Community School Board members to join and observe their activities; to become actively involved in, or to be in, ongoing communication with at least one community agency; and to invite parents and other community groups to be actively involved in planning and carrying out pupil personnel services activities. At the May 1972 annual Community School District 7 meeting of all pupil personnel services, nearly five hundred people were present. More than half of those present were from the community, and had no connection with the pupil personnel services in the schools.

Each school is encouraged to develop its own special approaches to the rendering of pupil personnel services. Under decentralization in New York City, each community is developing its own educational personality. Within District 7, each school is encouraged to be innovative and unique. We follow this philosophy in the pupil personnel services. Desired directions are stressed; but within the framework of legal requirements and by-laws, each school, through its administration, pupil personnel team, and the individual services, is encouraged to be innovative in the directions that suit it best. Thus, not only will the programs vary, but the functions performed by guidance counselors, attendance teachers, psychologists, and social workers will vary somewhat from school to school.

351

ISSUES AND ALTERNATIVES

At one time or another the following questions come to the surface among pupil personnel workers, among professional school staff in general, and even in community groups. The following statements reflect some of the thinking in Community School District 7.

How should the qualifications of personnel be determined? Under decentralization there has been considerable impetus to have personnel in the schools who ethnically reflect the population of the areas in which the schools are located; the argument is that personnel who identify with the pupils and parents can relate more effectively to them, and at the same time can help the aspirational levels of the pupils themselves. Under the traditional New York City system, personnel up to the superintendency levels have obtained their positions through civil service examinations. Under these procedures, the number of blacks and Puerto Ricans who have come into the system to date represent a small proportion of the professional staff, and a very small proportion of the supervisory staff. There is some dissatisfaction with the rate of increase of these minority groups within the total staff membership. The following alternative schools of thought appear to have developed: some wish to maintain very high examination standards and academic qualification requirements, and frown upon the ethnic arguments; others wish to modify the requirements to help speed up the entry of blacks and Puerto Ricans into professional staff and supervisory ranks; and still others consider the academic and examination requirements outmoded, and wish to base elegibility upon ability to identify with the indigenous population and ability to perform on the job.

Should more budget be put into the classroom rather than into pupil personnel services? In the atmosphere of budget-cutting which pervades the educational scene today, pupil personnel services are frequently regarded as fringe benefits, and are among the first to be reduced; and when restorations are made, there are many who argue that the additional funds should be put into more teaching staff so that class size may be reduced. The argument used here is that more effective teaching and a good deal of pupil personnel work on the part of the teacher can go on if the teacher has a smaller class to work with. On the other hand, there is the general recognition in many quarters that guidance, attendance, and mental health services are specialized services; and that one is really shortchanging the children if one asks staff members who are not professionally trained and

352

experienced in those areas to perform the required services. Despite the atmosphere of general budget-cutting, District 7 staff members are constantly pressing for such items as a better allocation ratio of counselors to pupils. The present ratios of fourteen counselors for eight thousand junior high-intermediate school students, and twenty-five counselors for twenty-two thousand elementary school students are considered far from adequate; and five psychologists for the entire district is woefully inadequate.

Should group approaches replace individual counseling? There are those who argue that the basic process in guidance and pupil personnel services revolves around the one-to-one relationship, and to do otherwise is to destroy the service. On the other hand, one faces the operational reality that to limit all activities to a one-to-one relationship in terms of currently available personnel would mean no services for the vast majority of the students. One also faces the practical reality that group processes can often succeed where the one-to-one relationship seems to be making no progress. It is not proposed here to argue in depth the merits of one-to-one sessions versus group approaches. However, in District 7, staff members have frequently found that the effects of peer reaction and interaction, whether at the pupil level or the adult level, frequently bring more progress and change than the one-to-one operation. The latter certainly has its place. For a variety of situations it must be preserved. Nevertheless, in this district, at this moment, there is continued movement in the direction of giving a greater proportion of time to group rather than one-to-one approaches.

Should the immediate demands for crisis counseling and testing have priority over long-range training and planning? Unfortunately, this is a crisis-ridden society; and since this is also an action-oriented society, there is a compulsion to respond spontaneously to every crisis. In the pupil personnel services, and particularly in guidance counseling, one is constantly faced with the question of how one is going to eliminate or substantially reduce the number of crisis cases if one spends most of his time responding to the crises and very little time planning and preparing for their elimination. In this district it is felt very strongly, although some teachers and administrators do not agree, that most crises stem from pupil-teacher and pupil-pupil relationships, situational elements, and instructional approaches. Except where the evidence clearly demonstrates the need for working with the child, a great deal of emphasis is placed, therefore, on working with teachers and parents rather than on working with

353

individual children. This is especially true at the elementary school level.

Is there a need for more special classes and special placement facilities? "Please test this child. He obviously belongs in a class for the mentally retarded." "This child is intolerable. He cannot get along with others. Please place him in a special school."

The above are not unusual requests received by guidance counselors and psychologists. The space shortage in the schools could be eliminated immediately if one could and did honor all requests of this nature. Many of the requests are genuine in terms of the current status of the educational programs. However, many in the pupil personnel services feel that there is a need for the schools to turn inward as far as the needs of these pupils are concerned, instead of always trying to thrust the pupils outward.

In addition to teacher training, there is a great need to explore alternative educational approaches, and to help move each student into the educational approach that appears to offer the greatest possibility of success for him (with flexibility for change). In District 7, schools are gradually beginning to move in this direction with approaches that include the mini school, the open classroom, the open corridor, schools without walls for part of the day,[17] and a variety of classroom approaches which come under such headings as "Learning Disabilities," "Class Meetings," and "Humanistic Education." Some still argue for good old-fashioned testing and placement, which has really not yet gone out of style.

PROGRAM EVALUATION

Evaluation is an ongoing process in Community School District 7. There is constant concern about program content, personnel, performance, facilities, and support.

Program Content. Most new types of programs are installed through funding arrangements. Therefore, there is ongoing evaluation as well as annual evaluation. The ongoing evaluation for the program of guidance assistants, for example, consists of such items as: the evaluations at the weekly district training sessions, the evaluations at conferences of principals or parents, the observations of supervisors, and suggestions for change that are constantly solicited. The annual evaluation is usually done by an outside agency, through questionnaires, interviews, observations, and recommendations. For all programs supported by tax levy funds, supervisory observations, periodic revision committees, requests from personnel in the services, requests from parents, and pupil responses to questionnaires provide the evaluation content.

Personnel. Evaluation of staff is accomplished through: logs kept by the staff, reports submitted by them, ongoing evaluation in the school pupil personnel teams, supervisory observations, and reports and discussions by school administrators and district supervisors. Schools encourage evaluation in terms of the annual goals that are set up by consensus at the close of the previous school year. There is constant pressure to evaluate staff in terms of their possible contribution to academic improvement on the part of the pupils, a pressure that is constantly resisted by the services. All staff receive an annual rating of satisfactory or unsatisfactory. Unsatisfactory ratings for substitutes may result in immediate dismissal. Probationary staff may be given further opportunity after an unsatisfactory rating. In the case of staff members with tenure, dismissal becomes a difficult process, involving intensive documentation and hearings at a number of levels.

Performance. The reference here is to immediate program performance or effectiveness. Particularly in the case of funded programs, each program is in competition with other proposed programs for the limited funds available. The Community School Board and the district funding committees compare the accomplishments of particular programs with the potential contributions of other suggested programs. Programs are often dropped completely on that basis. In the requests for additional guidance counselors or psychologists, it is not easy to use short-term statistics in a competitive situation with reading and mathematics programs.

Facilities. Here the difficulty does not lie with evaluative procedures, but with shortages of space and, to some extent, money. There is little difficulty in demonstrating and convincing with respect to space shortages for some of the counselors and for the vast majority of attendance and mental health workers. The same applies to availability of telephone facilities. The answers must come through more building space in mini schools, housing projects, or the more traditional structures, if the pupil personnel services are to operate successfully as part of the regular school setting. In a crowded, deprived area such as the South Bronx, this is not a goal that is easily obtainable in the near future.

Support. One appreciates the support for pupil personnel services that has come from the Community School Board, the district and school administrations, and parents and school staff. In this era of severe budget cuts, one judges that support in terms of the comparatively conservative cuts to which our overall services have been subjected. It is hoped this bodes well for the future.

1. Politically, New York City is divided into five boroughs: Bronx, Brooklyn, Manhattan, Queens, and Richmond. Six of the community school districts are located in the Bronx. Community School District 7 is the southernmost and the most deprived of these districts.

2. The number of people who actually reside in the geographic area in which District 7 is located may very well exceed a quarter of a million. Some authorities feel that, as a result of population mobility and the very poor housing situation, a substantial number of people escape the census takers.

3. The South Bronx, Harlem in the Borough of Manhattan, the Bedford-Stuyvesant area in Brooklyn, and the Jamaica area in Queens are disadvantaged target areas which are the principal focus of antipoverty programs in New York City.

4. The four New York State school districts selected by the New York State Department of Education for Project Redesign are from various parts of New York State. Community School District 7 is the only New York City school district involved. It is also the only one of the four which is a large urban district.

5. The only hospital currently operational in the geographic area of Community School District 7 is Lincoln Hospital, which is currently operating with very limited staff and budget. However, construction has begun on the new Lincoln Medical and Mental Health Center. It is expected that this new facility will become operational by 1975. A small comprehensive family health care center may also become operational within the area within the next year.

6. Under the New York City education decentralization law, locally elected school boards of nine members: choose the superintendent and members of his district staff; are the source through which school staff are hired and dismissed (within the framework of state and city regulations); decide upon the specific educational programs of the district; and, within legal limitations, decide on how the centrally allocated funds are to be spent.

7. Staff members who have achieved tenure cannot be dismissed without intensive documentation and hearings, which have appeal steps all the way up to the Chancellor, the educational chief of the New York City Board of Education.

8. One of the major components of the Central Board of Education in New York City is the Division of Pupil Personnel Services and Special Education, currently headed by an acting assistant superintendent. Included in this division are: the Bureau of Attendance, The Bureau of Child Guidance, and the Bureau of Educational and Vocational Guidance. Prior to decentralization guidance counselors were appointed to the schools through the Bureau of Educational and Vocational Guidance. Now they are appointed to each district by the Central Board Office of Personnel after the district has officially requested the appointments.

9. Originally known as truant officers, and then as attendance officers, they now enjoy the status of teachers (including salary level), and are known as attendance teachers. Qualifications for the position have been raised accordingly. Under the decentralized budgetary arrangements, each district now decides how many attendance teachers it wishes to have out of its budget.

10. The Central Board of Education has a medical division through which periodic doctors' examinations are authorized. However, actual school health services are provided through the New York City Department of Health.

11. When children in a school are identified as drug users, referrals for rehabilitation

are made to agencies outside of the school, but this must be done with knowledge and consent of the parents. A very delicate problem is the requirement that police authorities be notified by the school when it is found that a child is involved in the use or traffic of drugs.

12. There is considerable flexibility from school to school. However, guidance personnel are asked specifically to schedule individual appointments, slot them to certain time periods only, and keep ongoing records to justify the sessions scheduled. There is increasing emphasis on helping teachers to work with the children, and, where direct involvement of the child with the counselor is called for, to stress group approaches rather than individual sessions.

13. Under decentralization, the bureaus of the Central New York City Board of Education are increasingly becoming resource agencies, while direct district relationships with the New York State Education Department are growing. The special antipoverty funded programs are strengthening the latter relationship.

14. Where direct observation and all the available evidence indicate the need for direct professional guidance and mental health service for the child, the decision of the guidance counselor is the initial step in deciding whether the child will be put into a group, given individual counseling, referred to the school psychologist or social worker, or referred to an outside agency. The psychologist or social worker will help make the decision when the third and fourth choices are involved. Only very difficult cases are brought before the pupil personnel team in the school.

15. A number of schools in the district have developed special relationships with particular organizations, such as Equitable Life Assurance Society, Chemical Bank of New York, and Prospect Hospital. Groups of students from the schools are involved in periodic all-day schedules at the business locality, and have developed "Big Brother" and "Big Sister" relationships with particular employees. In addition, groups of employees come to the schools on a regular basis, and go into the classrooms as part of a "Living Witness" program, to help develop more meaningful occupational awareness on the part of the pupils.

16. One of the psychologists in District 7 has been specially trained by Dr. William Glasser, as his representative in this part of the country. Dr. Glasser has great faith in the class meetings as part of his "Schools Without Failure" approach. The psychologist in question is serving as the principal trainer for counselors and teachers in this program.

17. Two of the intermediate schools in District 7 have developed programs which encourage particular groups of students to get a considerable part of their education at a variety of localities and agencies within New York City. However, owing to the traditional basic structure of our overall school organization, there are currently severe administrative limitations on the expansion of such programs.

CHAPTER 11

Pupil Personnel Services in Central Bucks County

HARRY J. KLEIN

THE COMMUNITY SETTING

THE name "Central Bucks" is really quite descriptive, but only if you are familiar with Bucks County, Pennsylvania. The county currently contains thirteen school district, with Central Bucks monopolizing just about the whole center section of the county. A quick listing of some pertinent statistics should begin to give you parameters for visualizing the district:

Location:	27 miles due north of Center City, Philadelphia; 90 miles south by southwest of New York City.
Governmental Structure:	Within its boundaries lie nine municipalities, three boroughs, and six townships.
Area:	125 square miles, in a relatively square configuration.
Population:	45,000 residents and a school population of about 12,000.

Like a bikini, what these statistics reveal is interesting, but what they conceal is vital.

Population and Geography

Location, geography, climate, and sense of history make Bucks County a very attractive place in which to live. The county's southern border abuts the city and county of Philadelphia. Its eastern boundary is the Delaware River, which separates Pennsylvania from

New Jersey. The northern line separates it from Lehigh County, and the western boundary line (appropriately called County Line Road) separates it from Montgomery County, Pennsylvania.

At almost the geographic center of Central Bucks and Bucks County stands Doylestown, the county seat of government, with a population of about 8,000. Here, as part of the county government, is housed the county school office called the Intermediate Unit (I.U.). Doylestown is also the site of the Central Bucks Administration Center, which is the administrative offices for the school district.

Within Central Bucks School District, approximately eighty percent of its land is open and still awaiting building. Density varies from the southern end which is very suburban in nature, to the central portion which contains several small towns and villages dating back to Revolutionary War days, to the northern end which still has a heavily rural flavor. Very rapidly, however, the district is becoming more suburban as the rapid growth continues.

According to a recent survey, about forty-seven percent of the wage earners in the district are professionals, owners, or managers; except for housewives who comprised fourteen percent of the population, no other area of work or retirement exceeded five percent. It is probably safe to characterize the district as upper middle class. Though this is the dominant characteristic, there is still considerable heterogeneity within the district. To make the meld more interesting, Central Bucks has no "poverty pocket" as such. There is no single "patch" or "other side of the tracks" in the district. No one school or area in the district contains a preponderance of disadvantaged children.

Another important characteristic of Central Bucks is its "bedroom community" aspect. Except for county and local government jobs, several small industries, and local stores and service shops, people who live in Central Bucks work elsewhere. Housing is expensive, with very little low-cost housing. Ninety-nine percent of the population is white. Educational background of the average wage earner is relatively high.

Support

Both a boon and a bane to the school district is its growth rate. The population of the school district in 1961 was about 29,500. By 1971 the population had risen to 44,000 people. This influx has created a continuing need for schools. From 1969 through 1971, the school district averaged a new classroom about every eight days. The tax

360

rate over the same period of time rose about twenty-eight mills to bear this added cost. Prior to 1972, the district experienced little or no difficulty in obtaining the support necessary to maintain a good level of education. This support was not there in 1972. A number of factors seem to have had bearing on this change of attitude. Middle management, of which Central Bucks is largely comprised, was one of the first to feel the economic axe. Meanwhile, a new Pennsylvania State Income Tax came due for the first time in May 1972. Federal taxes were payable as usual in April. The "topper" was the announcement by the Bucks County Commissioners that a long-delayed real estate reassessment program would be applied in the summer of 1972. Against this backdrop, the Central Bucks School District presented its 1972–73 budget in April calling for an increase in school taxes. The original budget, as presented, was severely cut. Accountability and economy are now very real words in Central Bucks, as they are in many districts around the country.

Table 13 provides some idea of the present operating budget and the nature of support from the varying sources over the past few years. It indicates that 70.14% of current budget must come from local sources to make up the $16,749,000 budget for the current year.

Supportive Services

As part of the backdrop for the district's pupil personnel services, it is important for you to understand the supportive services sector. To the extent that such services are available, they both enhance and compliment district services and have implications for program development and budget formulation. This is one of the variables

TABLE 13

CENTRAL BUCKS SCHOOL DISTRICT SUMMARY OF REVENUE, 1973–74 BUDGET

Source	1971–72 Actual	1972–73 Budget	1973–74 Budget	%
Beginning cash balance	(149,185)	160,000	———	0
Local sources	9,530,197	10,317,012	11,748,576	70.14
State sources	4,369,027	4,644,714	4,894,924	29.23
Federal sources	259,726	135,000	62,500	.30
Contra to expenses	91,593	430,334	43,000	.23
Grand Total	$14,101,358	$15,687,060	$16,749,000	100

which make comparison of per pupil costs for pupil personnel services difficult from district to district.

Many of the direct services to pupil personnel services come from the intermediate unit. The underlying philosophy of services provided from this unit is based on the premise that I.U. services are provided in those cases when it is not feasible for a district to supply the same services from either an economic or program standpoint. As a result, classes for the hearing impaired, profoundly retarded, learning disabled, emotionally disturbed, and orthopedically handicapped are conducted by the I.U. on referral from the individual districts. However, when a district has sufficient numbers of these children in any of the special education categories, it is expected to inaugurate its own program.

In addition to the operation of special classes, the I.U. also provides itinerant services to districts for speech and hearing, visually impaired pupils, including sight-saving materials, learning disabled, and psychiatric consultation. All itinerant specialists are on a schedule of apportioned days, based on actual students to be served, except for the services of the psychiatrist, who is assigned time on the basis of district population. In the case of Central Bucks, the I.U. provides about twenty-eight days of psychiatric time over the course of a school year.

The offices of the Department of Child Welfare and the Department of Public Welfare are both located within the school district, and liaison with these department is affected through the school social workers.

The Juvenile Probation Office for the county is also physically located in Doylestown for the increasingly necessary contacts and coordination.

A county psychiatric services unit is housed within the confines of the school district. A good relationship exists with this unit, and it is of tremendous help in both referral, consultation, and follow-up work with students.

Since the county seat is within the district, a further advantage is experienced with the location of a number of private agencies here. Family and Children's Service of Bucks County, Big Brothers of Bucks County, Bucks County Association for Retarded Children, and Bucks County Legal Aid Society are just a few of the private agencies located in close proximity for our pupil personnel staff. A drug treatment center, TODAY, Inc., is housed close to Doylestown and contains both an in-patient and out-patient program of services.

In general, then, the Central Bucks School District is well situated to take advantage of a variety of governmental and private agencies which assist and complement the work of the district's pupil personnel services staff.

Having no classes in the district for learning disabilities or socially and emotionally disturbed children (and limited number available from the I.U.) presents a real disadvantage. Under Pennsylvania Law, a handicapped student, properly diagnosed, may attend an approved private school with both district and state financial assistance up to seventy percent of cost for day programs and forty percent for residential programs. Transportation is also provided by the district to these approved private schools for day programs. A number of approved private schools are within thirty-five minutes transportation time of the district, and, currently, a number of Central Bucks students are being provided for in such approved private schools, where programs are not available in the district or from the I.U.

Community Needs

As a community, the Central Bucks area has growing pains. It is growing out of its "britches" faster than they can be altered. This is the most pressing need.

A lingering holdover from the past is the "green belt" zoning philosophy. Most of the area is zoned in such a way that heavy commerical and industrial uses, along with low-cost housing, are discouraged. At some point, those who expound this philosophy must come to grips with its natural consequence—an expensive bill for services and education to those who live here.

The most scarce labor in the Central Bucks District is unskilled and semiskilled workers. The lack of low-cost housing forces employers daily to import or transport its unskilled and semiskilled workers from other areas. At some point, recognition of the necessity for planned community zoning must be faced.

Growth of new housing developments without concurrent plans for water and sewers has resulted in septic tanks and drilled wells for two-thirds of the residents. A high water table and poor percolation will begin to create unsanitary situations as density increases; then taxpayers will be faced with increasing taxes for sewers and water.

Other municipal services are being outstripped by the growth, also. Fire protection in the area is all volunteer. Police coverage is spread too thin. More people and houses will increase the probability of fire and crime. This, in turn, will call for a more sophisticated delivery of services not currently receiving sufficient planning.

The increasing population has created and will continue to create heavier demands on county services for people. Mental Health, Child Welfare, Juvenile Probation—all are understaffed and insufficiently organized.

Within the province of education, the major need is for more and varied methods of community involvement and decisions in the schools and their problems. Only in this way can education be understood and supported by the community at large.

THE SCHOOLS

Organizational and Administrative Structure of the District

Central Bucks School District citizens are represented on the Board of Education by nine members. Each member represents a geographic area and is elected by the voters from that area. Terms extend for six years, with overlapping terms so that three members are elected every two years on a partisan ticket. School board powers are similar to those elsewhere in the country but, unlike some, have the power to assess certain taxes.

The school district is administered by a central office staff, (Superintendent's Cabinet) and a Principals' Advisory Council. The composition of the cabinet can best be seen rather than explained (see Figure 11.1).

The Principals' Advisory Council is composed of the eighteen principals and eight assistant principals in the district, plus the superintendent, three assistant superintendents and, often, various of the directors.

The cabinet meets weekly, and the Principals' Council meet every

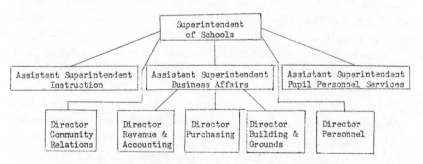

Fig. 11.1. Organizational chart, Central Bucks School District.

other week. Secondary principals and elementary principals meet separately and on alternate weeks. Periodic meetings of the combined principals convene on a need basis.

Curriculum recommendations are generated at monthly department meetings and passed on to the appropriate principals' council for decision. Each department of three or more people in each secondary building is headed by a coordinator who receives added pay and released time. Time and pay are apportioned according to department size. These six department coordinators meet monthly with a secondary administrator, who is assigned to that department. It is the administrator's responsibility to convey department plans, progress, and recommendations to the Principals' Council and relay decisions or requests for studies from the council back to the coordinators' group for that department.

Departments of less than three people have no coordinator. They meet monthly as a total district department with a designated administrator. One department member from the district is assigned as department representative to coordinate the departmental minutes and budget. This post carries with it a pay differential for the added responsibilities, but no released time.

At the elementary level, subject area curricular committees headed by an elementary principal meet regularly to evolve curriculum changes, courses of study, and evaluation procedures. Here, again, the administrator acts as the intermediary between the needs and plans of the committees of teachers and the decision-making body, which is the Elementary Principals' Council.

No full-time department heads or curriculum director function in the district.

K through 12 coordination is accomplished through joint elementary and secondary meetings for the avowed purpose of continuity and the same objectives. Other needs are met through summer curriculum workshops.

Levels

An unwritten, but adhered-to district philosophy dictates a structure of elementary schools organized K through sixth grade; junior high schools contain seventh through ninth grades; and senior high schools composed of tenth through twelfth grade students. Further, the philosophy sets the numerical limit for schools at each level. No elementary school should exceed 750 students; no junior high school should exceed 900 students; and no senior high school should enroll more than 1,600 students. Buildings are planned and built on this premise. The current lineup of schools in Central Bucks for the 1972–73 school year is:

1. Elementary Buildings: Twelve in number; total enrollment, 6,192

Enrollment	No. of Buildings
Over 700	2
600 to 700	2
500 to 600	3
400 to 499	2
Under 400	3
	12

It is important to know that the elementary schools were joined into the district from four separate elementary entities in 1966. Some geographic and philosophic differences existed prior to that time and governed the size and expandability of the schools built prior to 1966.

A three-school complex in the southwestern part of the district is now receiving rather intense attention. Several sets of preliminary plans were submitted; educational specifications for the buildings have been written, and all departments have had their input at each stage. If all goes well, the elementary school should begin next year.

2. Junior High School Buildings: Four in number; total enrollment, 2,936. All four junior high schools house between 685 and 785 students.

The oldest junior high school is just fifteen years old; the newest entered its second year of operation in September 1972.

3. Senior High Schools

Two senior high schools currently house 2,750 Central Bucks Students in grades 10 through 12. Location is the name differential. There is Central Bucks, EAST, and Central Bucks, WEST.

Central Bucks, EAST, is the newer of the schools. It was opened in 1969 and currently enrolls 1,175 students. In 1973, a twelve-room addition raised its rated capacity to 1,600 students. The addition consists, basically, of classrooms since the multi-use areas in the original building were designed with the addition and total capacity in mind.

Central Bucks, WEST, was built in 1952. Phase one of a two-phase renovation project was completed during the summer of 1972.

WEST currently contains 1,575 students. The addition to EAST, with its subsequent attendance area change should keep WEST relatively static at 1,600 for several years, as attendance area changes will channel the growth to Central Bucks, EAST.

A discussion of the two senior high schools would not be complete without including the Middle Bucks Vocational Technical School. Middle Bucks Vo Tech is operated by a joint board of education composed of four Bucks County School Districts, including, of course, Central Bucks. Roughly, about eighteen percent of C.B. senior high students avail themselves of the twenty-four vocational and three technical courses at Middle Bucks Vo Tech. The percentage is about the same for both EAST and WEST. These students attend Middle Bucks for one-half day and their home school one-half day.

4. Special Schools

A six-room elementary school was abandoned as a regular institutional site last year when it was replaced by a newer and larger open space elementary school. One Central Bucks retarded, trainable class is now housed there, and four classrooms are rented to the Intermediate Unit for their classes of retarded, pre-trainable children.

Within the boundaries of the district are three parochial and two private grade schools, which contain grades one through eight. Two of the three parochial schools draw only from Central Bucks residents. The third draws from several districts in two counties. Total private and parochial school enrollment is about 2,100 students. Medical, nursing, guidance, and psychological services are provided to these schools, so that they swell the population served by pupil personnel services to 13,978 students, even though the public schools enroll only 11,878.

PUPIL PERSONNEL FACILITIES

Facilities vary from school to school and, as in most districts, staff members who are not consistently located within a building must share space with others who are itinerant. Several examples of how this is accomplished can be noted in Figures 11.2, 11.3, 11.4, and 11.5.

PUPIL PERSONNEL SERVICES IN THE CENTRAL BUCKS SCHOOLS

Organization and Structure

Probably the best manner of presenting the organizational structure of the school district is through a schematic. Figure 11.6 some-

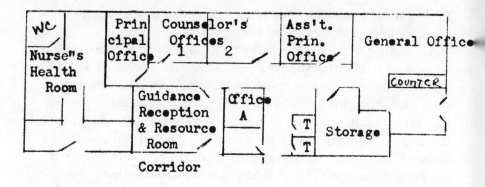

Fig. 11.2. Junior high school. (a) Two counselors use offices 1 and 2, as indicated. (b) Reception and resource room houses guidance clerk and guidance research and resource materials. (c) Psychological and social work personnel use Office A when serving this building. (d) Nurse's Health Room has reception area, rest areas, washroom, and office/examining room. (e) One special education (EMR) class in another wing is not shown.

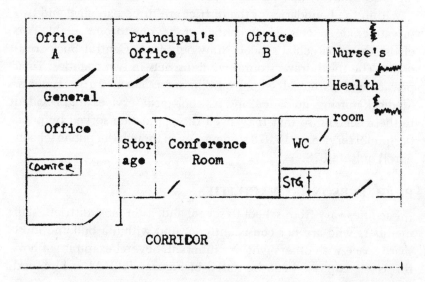

Fig. 11.3. Elementary building. (a) Psychologist and social worker use Office B when in the building. (b) Elementary counselor has an office apart from the general office complex in a conference room of a classroom wing. (c) Health room with large examining room, office, and dividable rest area is show just inside front door. (d) Two special education rooms (EMR) are not shown. One is in the primary wing, and the other is in the intermediate wing.

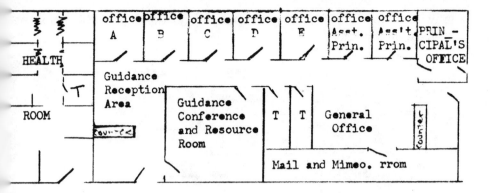

Fig. 11.4. Senior high school facilities. (a) Four counselors use offices A, B, C, and D. (b) Office E is used by a psychologist and social worker when in the building. (c) Health room, with its washroom, examining area/office, and rest areas, is shown. (d) No special education classes exist at this school.

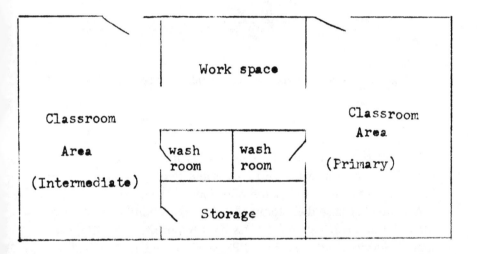

Fig. 11.5. Elementary special education facility. Note: The two-class complex depicted above is the model that will likely be used for special education facilities for EMR and TMR classes in the district. The two large classroom areas are carpeted and can be subdivided into learning centers or work areas with movable furniture. The work area in the center is tiled and contains an oven/range and refrigerator.

what graphically depicts personnel and relationships within pupil
personnel services.

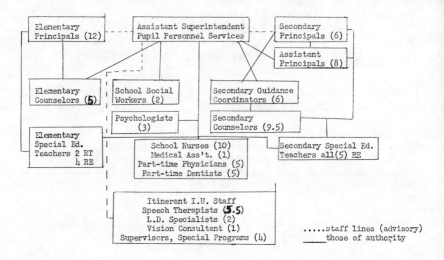

Fig. 11.6. Personnel and relationships within Pupil Personnel Services.

Examination of Figure 11.6 should clarify many things for the
reader, but will probably also raise some questions. The following
facts may serve to clarify some questions of structure.

A somewhat false dichotomy of line responsibility exists between
the building principal and the Assistant Superintendent, Pupil Personnel Services, in regard to PPS staff housed in the buildings.
Theoretically, the staff is responsible to the building principal for
administrative matters, such as length of day, starting time, office
supplies, building meetings, etc. The same staff is responsible to the
Assistant Superintendent, PPS, for professional matters, such as the
setting of priorities in areas where time is spent, techniques used,
professional materials ordered, etc. Figure 11.6 depicts the theoretical model, but, in reality, the principal has the line relationship with
secondary counselors. The other PPS staff are on line relationship
with the Assistant Superintendent, PPS, and a staff relationship with
principals for all practical purposes.

370

Elementary counselors are scheduled by the Assistant Superintendent for PPS, who is also accountable for their overall administrative function. These counselors have their home base in an elementary building for mail and phone purposes. Time of reporting and activities planned within a building is a matter that each counselor works out with the building principal.

In order to assure district continuity and some uniformity in program and to coordinate such things as testing and, record keeping, the elementary counselors meet monthly with the Assistant Superintendent, PPS, and a committee of elementary principals.

The two school social workers also work under the direction of the Assistant Superintendent, PPS. One is housed in the district administration building, and the other is housed just across the street from the administration building in Central Bucks, WEST. Since social workers serve across the district in all nineteen buildings, referrals are the basis for their operation. Time is apportioned on the basis of need, but the larger buildings, of necessity, see more of the social worker than do the smaller buildings. Because Child Study Team Meetings are an essential part of PPS operation, the social workers are scheduled on a set basis for such meetings in each building at least once a month. The Child Study Team concept will be dealt with separately a little later in the chapter.

The district's three psychologists operate under the direct administration of the Assistant Superintendent, PPS. Two psychologists are housed in the district administration center and the other just across the street from his colleagues at Central Bucks, WEST High School. The nineteen district buildings are divided three ways among the three psychologists. Each one carries a roughly equivalent load of schools and students, which, when broken down, means an assignment of six buildings which have a total student population of about 3,900. A factor in assignments is the number of special classes in the building to be served, since special classes demand more consultation and periodic evaluations.

All psychological and social work reports are funneled through the PPS secretary in the central office. Depending upon the style of the psychologist, this is accomplished by either hand-written reports or dictating equipment.

Coordination of the efforts of the psychologists and social workers is obtained in weekly staff meetings with the Assistant Superintendent, PPS. The purpose of these staff get-togethers is to share information all need to know, to plan for activities in which several share,

371

and to review cases or situations where the group can offer suggestions or help.

Secondary counselors are assigned to buildings, and are hired for a particular building by both the principals and Assistant Superintendent, PPS, with the guidance coordinator from that building. Counselor load is apportioned on an alphabetical arrangement across grade levels. Often, various coordinating aspects of guidance and counseling will be assumed as a responsibility by a counselor within a building. For example, one counselor within a building may keep track of, and make arrangements for, testing within that building. Another may take special education classes as his or her province for special attention within a building.

School nurses are assigned to buildings for time in proportion to the number of students in that school. Pennsylvania now mandates a school nurse for each 1,500 students, at least, in order to qualify for reimbursement for a school health program. In Central Bucks, the average weekly load for each nurse is about 1,350 students. As a result, a school is assigned one day of nursing service for each 270 students in enrollment. Most nurses serve two schools, a few serve three, and only one nurse has a sufficient load to serve only one school. The coordination and program idea sharing for health services is accomplished through monthly meetings of all nurses with the Assistant Superintendent, PPS, and a small principals' committee.

The itinerant staff members assigned by the Intermediate Unit are responsible to the Assistant Superintendent, PPS, in Central Bucks for the general assignment to buildings and the flow of communication. Other administrative and supervisory functions with these specialists are the responsibility of the Intermediate Unit's Assistant Director of Special Pupil Services.

Another item which may be of interest under this general heading would be length of contract for various staff members. School nurses work a school year of 191 days, as do teachers. Counselors' contract is for 201 days, as are those of the social workers and two psychologists. All guidance coordinators, one elementary counselor, and one psychologist are on twelve-month contracts.

Structurally, special education follows the same pattern as other classes. Teachers are scheduled by, and administratively responsible to, the building principal. Program guidelines, placement, continuity, and coordination are the province of the Assistant Superintendent, PPS. This is affected through a committee of special education teachers, a psychologist, social workers, several principals, and several counselors. The committee is chaired jointly by a department representative and the Assistant Superintendent, PPS. This committee meets monthly.

Pupil Personnel Job Descriptions

Currently, all job descriptions within the school district are under revision as an adjunct to evaluation by a compensation committee appointed by the Board of School Directors. Though written job descriptions are not currently appropriate for inclusion in this chapter, a discussion of role and function seems a necessary aspect if you are to understand the services offered. These will be followed by a discussion of how the service operates in the Central Bucks School District.

Pupil Personnel Service Functions

1. Administration. In Central Bucks, the administration of pupil personnel services is the responsibility of the Assistant Superintendent, Pupil Personnel Services. Since the author of this chapter fills this function, be warned, now, of the bias and somewhat colored objectivity.

Philosophically, the function of this pupil personnel administrator follows that set down by the *Postion Paper on Pupil Personnel Services* published by the National Association of Pupil Personnel Administrators.[1] As a charter member of the association since its inception in 1966, the author concedes its very great influence on his function as a PPS administrator.

The operation of the Central Bucks PPS Administrator hinges on four basic tenets. The PPS Administrator shall be: (1) an administrator, not a functionary within a discipline; (2) a facilitator to obtain agreement from each PPS discipline on their separate as well as concerted services; (3) a facilitator for the mobilizing of money, materials, and facilities to assure the smooth, efficient delivery of the services agreed upon; (4) an advocate and change agent for affective sensitivity in all phases of district operation.

These principles may sound very theoretical. In reality, they dictate a mental set and method of operation that is reasonably narrow in scope. Some brief elaboration may clarify this.

The administrator, regardless of his background does not counsel students, administer T.A.T.'s, visit homes, calibrate hearing, or teach children. He does meet with his staff separately as discipline and together as a department. The purpose of these meetings is to explore with them the priorities for the best use of their time in order to help students. The PPS administrator is then obliged to convince other administrators and the board of education to provide the freedom, funds, or facilities to meet the goals set by the PPS staff. As a district administrator, he uses his position to influence programs, policies, and decisions so that they take into account affective learning and what seems best for students at the developmental level under consideration.

Another very necessary aspect of the PPS administrator's role centers around evaluation. The administrator must keep attuned to how PPS services are used, perceived and supported by students, staff and administration and, to some extent, the community.

The National Association of Pupil Personnel Administrators has just published the first in a series of monographs which treats the training, certification, and accreditation of pupil personnel administrators and programs. It is officially entitled, *Pupil Personnel Services Guidelines for Training, Certification, Accreditation.*[2] Along with *Pupil Personnel Services: A Position Statement,* also published by the same association, a student of PPS services in schools should find these an excellent source for establishing a good fundamental knowledge of the field as perceived and supported by a number of well-qualified practitioners in PPS.

2. School Psychologists. The three school psychologists in Central Bucks possess Pennsylvania certification to function in this capacity. They have graduated from a state-approved school psychologists' graduate program with a master's degree, at least.

The case load for each psychologist is six schools and about 4,000 students.

Psychologists use consultation and evaluation skills in order to help diagnose the learning difficulties of students, as well as to help in understanding the dynamics at work in a student, class, or school. To this end, Central Bucks psychologists perform the following services:

1. Serves as a prime consultant when questions concerning the dynamics of learning are raised.
2. Consults with school staff in the development of curriculum adaptations and classroom practices for the specific needs of all pupils or a given student.
3. Conducts detailed individual analyses for particular children in order to furnish deeper insights into their educational and behavioral problems.
4. Provides leadership in conducting staff development activities and

374

in planning programs which will promote the use of sound mental health procedures in the school and home.

5. Interprets diagnostic findings to the individual, appropriate school and agency personnel, and parents.
6. Initiates and follows up on referrals requiring specialized diagnosis or remediation not available through school.
7. Functions as an integral part of the Child Study Team in a building, using his skills and background to accomplish the team objective.
8. Sees students for short-term counseling when necessary and upon agreement of the Child Study Team.

In Central Bucks, typical referrals come to the psychologist through the counselor in that building. Generally, the principal, psychologist and counselor go over referrals and decide priority needs for the psychologist's attention. In this process, a decision is made on two basic questions: (1) Can the psychologist really add to what is known about this student? (2) What service seems needed as a starting point in this case: classroom observation, specific evaluation, consultation, or counseling? On the basis of these decisions, the psychologist pursues each referral.

Periodically the same people review the referrals pursued to answer three more questions: (1) What has been learned about the referral? (2) What are the next steps needed in this situation, i.e., outside referral, Child Study Team referral, added data from another source? (3) Who will take responsibility for the next action agreed upon?

Each week the psychologists and social workers meet with the Assistant Superintendent for PPS to review the past week and look ahead to the coming week. This staff meeting also serves as a clearing house for sharing information and evaluation effectiveness.

Psychological reports are prepared in the central office. Three copies of each report are prepared. One is slated for the building file, another stays in the psychologist's file, and the third goes into the central file which is a composite, by family, of psychologicals, case-work records, and psychiatric reports. In the central file, too, are outside school reports of medical, education, and agency information released by the parents to Central Bucks.

3. *School Social Workers.* Central Bucks currently employs two school social workers. Each has a load of about 6,000 students. In order to understand the function and certification of these individuals, a brief history is in order.

Once upon a time schools employed truant officers to enforce compulsory school attendance regulations by use of the "search and collar" authoritarian method. In the evaluation of education and compulsory school, this was a necessary beginning, probably. Over a period of time, school attendance became better accepted, and realization grew that poor attendance was only a symptom of some problem the student had. Various titles across the country then were assigned to this role: attendance officer, attendance teacher, home and school visitor, pupil personnel worker, and so forth. In the evolutionary process, the role expectation began, more and more, to resemble (and need) social work practices. At the present time, the transition from pure attendance to social work concepts is still in process. Training and certification to fill the position hover in a Limbo. Many schools of social work still train only classic, clinical social workers. Within Pennsylvania, at least, this is the case.

Today the role of the school social worker in the Central Bucks Schools is currently one which stresses specialized casework service, which is based on an understanding of social dynamics, skill in human relations, and the ability to combine these skills and understandings in working with the family, the school, and the resource agencies of the community. The Central Bucks school social workers' contribution is summarized in the following statements:

1. They help interpret to the school, the family, and the community the cultural forces which impede or enhance adjustment to the learning process.
2. They provide casework services with parents—to increase their understanding of their child, to encourage their constructive participation in the educational process, and to assist them in the use of school and community resources.
3. They consult and collaborate with other school personnel—to gather and give information on a case, and to establish and plan for respective roles in the modification of pupil's behavior.
4. They identify appropriate referral sources for a child or family; prepare the child or family to accept referral; contact the proper referral agency for efficient intake, and follow up the referral.

In spite of this broad role set forth, the role of the school social worker still involves considerable work with attendance. Some of this is a holdover from the past, but much of it is realistic in schools. Often, the first symptom of student problems manifests itself in erratic attendance. Erratic attendance results from one of three reasons: (1) a psychological problem on the part of student or parent(s);

(2) poor health, to the point of incapacity of either the student or parent; (3) negligence by the parent(s).

Central Bucks principals or assistant principals carry first-line responsibility for checking attendance and keeping a wary eye on patterns and frequency of absences. When an administrator spots a problem in the attendance area which seems to fall into one of the reasons just cited, a referral to the school social worker is in order. Such cases run the gambit of perfunctory to very complex.

Regardless of the degree of complexity, benefit is derived from the referral since one of the first laws of learning is to have the learner where he can be presented the material to be learned as continuously and consistently as possible.

Central Bucks social workers also maintain contact with community agencies to feed out and back the kinds of information needed so that all those who work with a student or his family are presenting consistent support.

Parent groups are another aspect taken on by Central Bucks social workers. The parent groups are short-term (6 to 8 sessions) developmental groups, usually aimed at a given grade level, where the objective is to give parents a forum to learn from each other what the normal developmental milestones are for their children. Often these are conducted jointly by a counselor and social worker. The format is somewhat structured and centers around *Parent Effectiveness Training*[4] principles. Transactional analysis from *I'm OK, You're OK*[5] is also woven into the sessions.

Social workers in Central Bucks also do small group work with students. The students are generally ones with whom they have had contact in the past. The groups are assembled from students who face similar kinds of social or family problems but cope with them in different ways. A counselor will often act as coleader with the social worker.

With responsibilities that grow out of Child Study Team meetings, contact with the community agencies and the referrals from administrators and counselors, the Central Bucks social workers are active, involved and overworked people.

4. School Health Services. Central Bucks conforms to state guidelines in the employment and use of school nurses. The ten nurses and one medical assistant serve the public, parochial, and private schools in Central Bucks. This is mandated by the Department of Public Health in conjunction with the Department of Education.

Both departments have a set of guidelines which govern school nursing.

The Department of Education sets certification, and general role and function. The Department of Health mandates specific screening examinations, record maintenance, and school entry requirements. School Health reimbursement comes from the Department of Health, through a formula agreed upon with the Department of Education and by means of an annual report which reflects the accumulation of the data to meet the state mandates.

School nurses all possess R.N.'s as well as at least a bachelor's degree. They essentially meet the same certification requirement which teachers must have. As a result, they are on the teachers' salary schedule.

The purposes of the school health services program in Central Bucks are these: to bring each child, through health services and counseling, into an optimum condition of mental and physical health so that he may profit from the educational program; to create in each child a sense of responsibility for his own health, as well as the health of others; and to develop an understanding of the principles and practices upon which good health is based.

In order to comply with state mandates, much of the nurse's time is spent in scheduling, conducting, recording, and following up the various screening examinations and assuring that proper entries are made for all mandated information.

Central Bucks nurses spend much time in health counseling and guidance with students appropriate to the level. To this end they may talk with first graders about dental care, with ninth graders about skin and body care, or with eleventh graders about nutrition.

Inevitably, their presence in schools means referrals for first aid. Though time consuming, it is a valuable service. A Central Bucks nurse may often be the first to identify a student with a problem when the student consistently shows up in her office with a psychosomatic stomachache the same period several days a week.

The school nurse, then, is a valuable asset to both the pupil personnel team and the child study team because her information helps interpret the physical uniqueness of each child and its bearing on that child's learning. Further, school nurses are as interested in mental health as in physical health. As such, they are attuned to the factors which interrelate the two in the school setting.

Central Bucks employs one school physician, part-time, who writes the standing orders which govern first aid treatment and supplies ordered for such treatment. He is the consultant to nurses and administrators on a variety of questions which affect health practices for both students and staff. Six part-time medical examiners also serve Central Bucks schools to conduct required physicals not accomplished by family physicians. The medical examiners also do all sport physicals by season and attend home football games. Assisting, recording and follow-up for all of these examinations is the job of the school nurse.

Dental examinations are mandated periodically by the state. Many parents meet this requirement through their family dentist. Six school dentists serve the school district part-time for student examinations not done by family dentists. Again, arrangements, recording, and follow-up is the nurse's task in the school.

Counseling and Guidance Services

In discussing guidance services in Central Bucks, it may be best to deal with the three levels separately since they are entities that are different. After a brief discussion of the three levels, a summation of the coordination and continuity efforts may then help tie them together into a comprehensible package.

Elementary Guidance and Counseling. Central Bucks employs four elementary counselors to serve its twelve buildings. The average load per counselor, then, is three buildings and about 1,500 students. The load is twice what can be realistically handled, although the program in operation is enthusiastically received and seems to be working well.

Each counselor works just a little differently from each other counselor. Broad guidelines are agreed to and set down in "Blueprint for Elementary Guidance in Central Bucks." This guideline was organized and implemented by an elementary guidance committee, consisting of three elementary principals, two counselors and the Assistant Superintendent for Pupil Personnel Services. It was presented to and adopted by the Elementary Principals' Council and still remains the "official" stand, even though it is due for revision.

Elementary counselors have clerical aide time in each building to accomplish tasks such as record keeping, test sorting, distribution, reproduction of materials. As a result, elementary counselors are free to function professionally the greatest portion of their time.

In general, elementary counselors divide their time between developmental, referral, and guidance service activities.

379

Developmental activities include:

1. Parent groups (with social worker), which are short term, information and awareness oriented, usually with a group of six to ten parents of children at a particular grade level.
2. Teacher groups—for the purpose of alerting teachers to materials available for use in the classroom to enhance the effective interrelationships there. This entails regular meetings of volunteer teachers, usually at several consecutive grade levels within a building, who use the counselor to improve their techniques in incorporating affective dimensions into the learning process.
3. Pupil groups, usually a whole classroom, are also worked with on affective materials as demonstration lessons for teachers who are beginning to get involved in the teacher groups. As teachers feel more comfortable and confident with the process, the counselor phases out and the teacher phases in.
4. Another area of developmental concentration is kindergarten, pre-first grade, and first grade. Observations, screening, and prognostication are crucial at these levels to assure that children are placed, their learning modes identified, and as many factors as possible taken into account so that learning is maximized as much as possible for each child.

Referral activities result from:

1. Teachers, principals, or parents who have concerns about a student or group of students. From such referrals come a multiplicity of activities centered around being helpful to the person referring. Such help may take the direction of small group work, individual work with children, involvement of other pupil personnel services staff, a child study team meeting, or any combination of these. Key to a counselor's referral activities is follow-up and feedback. Unless teachers can feel that they are listened to and that some action results with dialogue and feedback, they are likely to stop referring. Without this staff involvement, satisfaction, and communication, an elementary counselor's job would soon become sterile.

Guidance service activities of elementary counselors are few but important. In this category fall such activities as coordinating the testing program in each building, arranging the orientation program for sixth graders with junior high school counselors, and coordinating the materials and recommendation for vocational awareness.

Junior High School Guidance and Counseling. At the junior high school level two full time-counselors serve each building. A clerical aide assists counselors with the paperwork involved.

Junior high school guidance really begins at the end of sixth grade. On several occasions counselors visit the elementary schools from which they receive seventh graders. A group session is conducted to answer questions and deal with general concerns students have about the transition to junior high. On another occasion, counselors spend time with sixth grade teachers and an elementary counselor, making notes on suggested academic placements for students in the varying subject areas in which students may have difficulty adjusting and determining which students have been getting special help and need to continue.

After these visits, the sixth graders visit the junior high they will attend. In the fall, only seventh and tenth graders report the first day of school. The objective is to make the new student feel welcome, less anxious, and well informed about his or her role in junior high. Through seventh grade, the guidance and counseling emphasis is on personal and academic adjustment to junior high. When appropriate and necessary, schedule changes are made, after parent and student conferences, when the change is in the best interests of a student and agreed to by both parent and student. Counseling over academic difficulties and personal adjustment difficulties, either in a small group or individually, takes place during the year.

Guidance and counseling emphasis in eighth grade takes two major directions: attention to students who continue to need support in order to cope with junior high and information and counseling around choices and implications available in ninth grade.

Guidance and counseling efforts in ninth grade have primary emphasis on career planning. A unit in which ninth grade social studies teachers and counselors cooperate explores the world of work. The concepts of what questions to ask and where to find answers about occupations is the focus of this unit. Considerable time is spent with each student in laying out a tentative senior high school selection of direction and courses so that students are forced to think in terms of intermediate and long-range plans. From this, each student selects, specifically, a program of study for the tenth grade year.

Junior high school guidance and counseling moves from protective attention for adjustment to transition, through exploration and information, to responsibility, with help from counselors, teachers, and parents, for tentative choices and decisions concerning the students' immediate, as well as their long-range, future. Developmentally, this is suited to what preadolescent students need and are capable of doing.

Senior High School Guidance and Counseling. Central Bucks has two senior high schools. One senior high operates with four full-time counselors for 1,600 students. The other high school has 3.5 counselors available for 1,200 students.

Senior high school guidance and counseling begins with the incoming ninth grader. Counselors and teachers combine to provide the student with the information needed to see the alternatives available and then to provide help in sorting out the alternatives. Choices and decisions, however, then become the students.

Recognizing that all transition entails some anxiety, tenth graders spend the first day of school by themselves in the building with the entire staff. This is their day. They follow their schedule for that day in abbreviated fashion; meet their teachers, ask questions; explore the building, and begin to feel comfortable with the role expected of them without the press of upperclassmen.

In senior high school, guidance services take the form of information giving. Some of these are: (1) career days and/or nights to provide information about occupations; (2) sessions with representatives of various institutions who offer education beyond high school; (3) group sessions to provide program planning information for their upcoming year; (4) opportunities to gather information in the guidance resource room through use of occupational files, filmstrips, tapes, higher education catalogs, resource books, View Deck selector, etc.

Counseling services in senior high defy categorization. They are as diverse as people are. Much counseling centers around academic needs of the now and of the future. Some counseling centers around behavior, its causes and consequences. Other counseling attempts to sort out alternatives available to a student whenever he is faced with a choice or decision in his life.

Paperwork of all kinds is the bane of counselors everywhere. As a result, an integral part of each senior high school guidance department is a full-time, twelve-month secretary.

Students in both junior and senior high school are assigned a counselor on an alphabetical basis. This provides continuity for three years, and also permits a counselor to become familiar with siblings. Students may, however, go to any counselor they choose.

Each secondary building in Central Bucks has one counselor designated as a guidance coordinator. He is employed twelve months and carries coordination and some supervisory responsibilities for that building's guidance and counseling program and staff. Coordinators' regular meetings provide the vehicle for communication and coordination at a district level. All other counselors are employed for the 191-day school year, plus an additional ten days for which they are paid on a pro-rata basis.

Summarizing the Central Bucks guidance and counseling program in oversimplified terms, it might go like this: Counselors in Central Bucks spend great emphasis and time at entry levels; kindergarten, seventh grade, and tenth grade. The rationale for this assumes that careful attention to both readiness and adjustment at these levels prevents remediation later. Both the guidance services and counseling offered is aimed at being both age-appropriate and need-oriented. In this way, the development of all children is assisted. Within its continuity, the Central Bucks program attempts to move youngsters from dependent deciders to independent deciders through a process of exposure to decision-making skills and the opportunity to use them.

Attendance Services

Attendance services centered in PPS are those which have people-contact implications. When attendance decisions involve affective as well as cognitive processes, PPS is involved in the decision. An attendance aspect where PPS could be involved is variances in attendance area for a building in order to assess whether it is in the best interests of the child. Another is absences of an unusual nature in order to assess what services might be brought to bear to help the student (i.e., home-bound instruction, medical assistance, or outside agency involvement). PPS might also investigate factors surrounding the residence of a student in the district with other than his parents or legal guardians.

Policies regarding illegal absences of students, absences for urgent reasons, and deviation from accepted attendance procedures are generated by and cleared through the PPS department.

All these factors have implications on the continuity and stability of a child's educational progress. Many of these fall into the province of the social worker or nurse.

Pupil accounting and census is the responsibility of the district business office.

Special Education

The Special Education Department in Central Bucks currently consists only of classes for the retarded.

As explained previously, the Intermediate Unit (County Office) provides classes for Central Bucks' children who are physically handicapped, hearing impaired, emotionally disturbed, or learning disabled. In addition, the Intermediate Unit conducts a class and work-

383

shop for older (over sixteen) trainable retarded students. Various itinerant services, such as speech and hearing therapists, vision consultants, and learning disability specialists, are also provided to county districts by the Intermediate Unit. As a result, some eleven of these itinerant staff serve Central Bucks on a full- or part-time basis. Liaison and coordination for these people falls to the Assistant Superintendent for Pupil Personnel Services, but the general administration and supervision rests with the Intermediate Unit.

An Intermediate Unit class for the learning disabled is located in a Central Bucks elementary school and contains only Central Bucks children.

The Central Bucks Special Education Department consists of eleven teachers who serve children from K through 12 in a special program.

A. Trainable Retarded Program
  1. Two classes each with a teacher and an aide.
  2. One class is for younger children (5 to 10 years of age), which is housed in the primary wing of an elementary school. It contains eleven children.
  3. The other class serves older children (11 to 16 years of age) and is located in a small district building where the remaining rooms are rented to the Intermediate Unit. This older class currently houses eight students.
  4. Students beyond sixteen attend the Intermediate Unit class and workshop until age twenty-one.
B. Educable Retarded Program
  1. Elementary Program
    There are four classes—two classes in each of two buildings. Each of the two buildings has a primary class and an intermediate class, limited to eighteen or less students. The children in these classes may move out into a regular grade or room for aspects of the program with which they can cope. Art, music, and physical education teachers work with the children several times a week also. Each class is taught by a teacher specially certified to teach retarded children. As you would expect, emphases in the classes are on basic skills taught through concrete activities. For example, a class may plan, cook, and serve apple strudel. In the process, they must read a recipe, measure, count, follow direction, keep track of time. Since the program is a continuous progress one, various groupings and interest centers are also arranged to assume progression through the program. As a continuous progress program, grade level designations are not emphasized. Most children who move through the elementary program are ready for

junior high school special class at age twelve or thirteen. Social, as well as academic, readiness is considered.

2. Junior High School Program

Although Central Bucks has four junior high schools, numbers warrant only three junior high educable retarded classes. At the moment, each of these is housed in a different junior high school. The special education plan calls for two classes in each of two buildings as soon as numbers permit. Each of the junior high classes now contain about eighteen children. Each class is generally self contained for major subject areas. Girls and boys do move out into regular physical education, art, and music classes. When possible, students do go to regular classes in subject areas where they can cope with regular class materials. In this way, a youngster may be in special class for English, social studies, and science but be in regular class for math, art, music, and physical education. The key to placement is the ability of the youngster to function in a regular class. Students in special classes receive the same report card as the rest of the school. Grades are awarded on the basis of work completed at whatever level they are working. In regular classes, of course, this criteria is also applicable. At this level, students are more conscious of grade level designations. By age fifteen or sixteen they have achieved a ninth grade status and move on to the senior high special program.

3. Senior High School Program

For teaming purposes and flexibility, the two senior high school educable classes are in one school rather than having one smaller class in each of the two senior highs. Here, again, students are scheduled for regular or special class in all subject areas. The differentiating criteria is the student's ability to succeed. A student moves out into a regular program or back to the special one according to his or her degree of comfort with, and success in, the program. Approximately half of the forty students in the senior high program attend the Vocational Technical School. About twelve of the twenty-six courses at the Vo Tech School are available to special education students. Experience to this point has been good, and most students placed do complete the program. A Vo Tech special student spends half day at the home school. Here he takes the basic courses in either special or regular program. The other half day is spent at the Vo Tech School in the program chosen. Senior high school students in special class who are not at the Vo Tech spend tenth grade in scheduled courses including some electives. Eleventh grade includes course work and a work-study program. Senior year includes some course work and a slightly expanded work-study program. All students who continue through the program graduate with their class and receive a regular high school diploma.

Several characteristics of the Central Bucks Special Education program are worthy of note: (1) at all levels, emphasis is on integration whenever possible; (2) by the nature of the community, many special education students test at the borderline level and, as a result, are capable of moving out of special education at any given time, either partially or completely; (3) a motor coordination program, with swimming and aquatic activity, is a continuous part of the program; (4) all students are formally re-evaluated biennially for continuation in the program; informal evaluation occurs each marking period; (5) activity learning and field trips are integral to the program.

All teachers in the department meet monthly with the Assistant Superintendent for Pupil Personnel Services, psychologists, and an appointed department representative, who is one of the teachers. The department representative functions as a coordinating agent for agenda items, budget requests, field trip and aquatics schedules, and as a leader in curriculum revision. The monthly meetings of the department serve as the vehicle for communication and provide the impetus for program revision.

Special education, technically, is an instructional program and, as such, probably does not belong in pupil personnel services. Unfortunately, this department in most districts is not large enough for a full-scale organizational chart. As a result, they have not really "belonged" to any aspect of organization. Because of the close working relationship necessary with many of the pupil personnel services, they seem to fit best and get more attention in the pupil personnel services program. Lumped also as part of "special education" are the placements in Intermediate Unit classes, placements in private schools (about forty-nine children currently), and home-bound instruction. These fall solely to the pupil personnel services department, and, in a district the size of Central Bucks, are probably best handled in this manner.

BUDGET

The following tables tell their own story. For those interested in the finance aspects of schools and pupil personnel services, the figures provide a means of making a number of comparisons and analyses. However, few basic ground rules for interpreting the figures may be helpful.

No attempt was made to break out the cost of special education in the following figures. The bulk of expenditures for special education is in 0200, Instruction. Some pro-rata costs for special education are in 0100, Administration; 0500, Transportation; 0600, Operation and Maintenance of Plant, and in 1200, Capital Outlay. Since they do not interrelate with costs of pupil personnel services, they were not listed in a table. It may be helpful to know that the per pupil cost of special education for 1972–73 was $1,496 per elementary pupil and $1,771 per secondary pupil. The cost per regular student for the same year was $1,320.

Table 14 lists all budget categories and three-year allocations for each.

Tables 15 and 16 provide a breakdown of the two budget categories applicable to pupil personnel services.

TABLE 14

CENTRAL BUCKS SCHOOL DISTRICT, DOYLESTOWN, PA.

SUMMARY OF EXPENDITURES
1973–1974 Budget

Code Number	Classification	1971–1972 Actual	1972–1973 Budget	1973–1974 Budget
0100	Administration	430,714	458,450	472,350
0200	Instruction	8,089,659	8,714,158	9,252,231
0300	Pupil Personnel Services	397,983	464,251	445,052
0400	Health Services	134,586	152,271	126,773
0500	Pupil Transportation	440,814	473,622	498,956
0600	Operation and Maintenance of Plant	1,151,511	1,266,269	1,433,417
0800	Fixed Charges	768,493	868,465	952,730
0900	Food Services	15,005	3,475	———
1000	Student Activities	134,551	174,882	175,161
1100	Community Services	12,518	4,000	5,000
1200	Capital Outlay	147,583	202,925	154,029
1300	Debt Service	2,179,644	2,289,246	2,409,145
1400	Outgoing Transfers	527,938	610,246	647,361
1500	Budget Reserve	———	4,800	5,000
3232	Improvement and Equipment Notes Payable	———	———	171,795
	Total Expenditures	$14,430,999	$15,687,060	$16,749,000

Total Number of Students, 1973–74   12,120
Total Cost per student, 1973–74 $1,380   (all budget categories)

TABLE 15
CENTRAL BUCKS SCHOOL DISTRICT
1972–1973 Budget Summary Sheet

0300—PUPIL PERSONNEL SERVICES

Account Number	Classification	1971–1972 Actual	1972–1973 Budget	1973–1974 Projection
0311	Salaries, Directors*	14,750	15,950	16,350
0312	Salaries, Attendance Personnel	26,894	30,797	31,273
0313	Salaries, Guidance and Psychological Personnel	336,865	396,000	375,425
0319	Salaries, Clerical†	11,265	13,371	13,871
0320	Materials and Supplies, Pupil Personnel Services	3,934	4,433	4,628
0330	Expenses, Pupil Personnel Services	2,035	1,500	1,825
0350	Contracted Services, Pupil Personnel Services	2,240	2,200	1,680
	Total 0300 Series	$397,983	$464,251	$445,052

*Remainder of salary is in 0100 portion of the budget (see Table 13).
†Some aide salaries are contained in the 0200 portion of the budget (see Table 13.)

TABLE 16

CENTRAL BUCKS SCHOOL DISTRICT
1973–1974 Budget Summary

0400—HEALTH SERVICES

Account Number	Classification	1971–1972 Actual	1972–1973 Budget	1973–1974 Projection
0412	Salaries, Physicians and Psychiatrists	9,355	5,000	8,000
0413	Salaries, Nurses	108,673	91,253	81,860
0414	Salaries, Dentists and Hygienists	718	1,850	1,500
0416	Salaries, Nonpublic School Health	8,411	33,165	18,463
0418	Salaries, Clerical and Non-Professional Dental Services	———	500	500

388

0419	Salaries, Clerical and Non-Professional Medical and Other Services	——	6,500	3,000
0421	Materials and Supplies, Dental	10	200	100
0422	Materials and Supplies, Medical and Other	3,735	5,100	5,100
0432	Expenses, Medical & Other	440	600	600
0433	Expenses, Nonpublic School Health	——	100	100
0445	Equipment (Replacement) for Health Services	604	703	850
0451	Contracted Dental Services	2,523	1,800	3,000
0452	Contracted Medical and Other Services	117	4,500	3,200
0453	Contracted Services, Nonpublic School Health	——	1,000	500
	Total 0400 Series	$134,586	$152,271	$126,773

Having perused both the budget in general and pupil personnel services in specific, Table 17 is designed to accumulate a number of meaningful statistics and put them together in one table for analysis, using 1972–73 data.

Gaskin's Study,[6] published in 1968, presents a mean expenditure of $31.47 per pupil for pupil personnel services in the North Atlantic States. The data was based on the 1966–67 school year, or 1966 calendar year; however, the Central Bucks figure of $78.07, as a mean expenditure, may be close to the mean expenditure for this region, since Central Bucks was very near Gaskin's mean in 1966.

Since the 1972–73 per pupil expenditure on total budget is $1,320, the per pupil expenditure for pupil personnel services of $78.07 represents .059 percent of that amount.

Table 16 reflects actual amounts as opposed to the figures in Tables 14 and 15. As a result, the total cost amount in Table 17 does not quite equal the addition of totals from Tables 14 and 15.

UNIQUE CHARACTERISTICS OF PPS IN CENTRAL BUCKS

A list of things unique to PPS in Central Bucks is neither extensive nor difficult. Such a list would include such things as:

TABLE 17

PUPIL PERSONNEL SERVICES

Ratios, Total Cost per Service

	Service	No.	Student Ratio	Cost Total	Cost per Pupil
1.	Psychologists	3	1–3726	$47,440	$3.99
2.	Social Workers	2	1–5939	30,707	2.59
3.	Nurses	10.5	1–1322†	130,418	9.10
4.	Physician & Dentists	(10)	1–1385†	14,150	1.19
5.	Guidance				
	Elementary	4	1–1548	57,044	9.21
	Secondary	15.5	1– 367	259,744	45.68
6.	Administration	1	NA	15,950*	1.34
7.	Material Supplies &				
	Other Expenses	NA	NA	14,836	1.25
8.	Clerical & Aides	9.5	NA	44,171	3.72
		55.5		$614,550	$78.07

†Includes parochial enrollment in ratio.
*Proportion of salary, remainder in 0100 category.
() Designates part time personnel.

NOTE: Cost total, except in number 7 of the table, reflects only salaries. All professional materials and supplies are contained in number 7. General supplies and materials are contained in the 0200 section of the budget. (see Table 13).

1. provision for coordination of pupil personnel services;
2. provision of staff to man services in a workable if not optimum manner;
3. provision for inclusion of instructional staff in Child Study Team sessions, which are well received;
4. provisions for communication including a spelled-out policy on maintenance, use and release of records;
5. provision for administrative-PPS representation in planning and decision making;
6. provision for new staff orientation to PPS attitudes;
7. provision for much community involvement in district programs;
8. provision for many kinds of parent-staff-student group sessions.

The uniqueness of the above list is doubtful. Most PPS organizations in a school district could probably boast the same list. What seems to make Central Bucks unique are the attitudes that have been established in the district both within and without PPS.

A number of factors outside of PPS contribute to this overall effect. Key factors are: good curricula; a sense of progress and momentum in instructional innovation; a feeling of general harmony in the district; decent rapport between Teacher Association, Board of School

Directors, and administration, and a community which is fairly interested in a well-rounded education for their children. Within such a climate, PPS can flourish. In fact, good PPS departments cannot exist in districts without good instructional programs and adequate community support. One cannot adjust, adapt, or even interest a student in a stultified educational system that is not itself willing to adjust and adapt for the students. By the same token, most communities get what they want from their educational system. A community which is not willing to insist on a good instructional program for its children will neither seek nor want a good PPS program.

Given, then, a nurturing and receptive climate, Central Bucks PPS has been able to develop several significant attitudes among staff and community which are desirable. Over the years, the PPS staff have had their impact in creating one of these attitudes best summed up in this statement: "Let's all look at kids and use each other to decide what is best for them." As a result of this attitude, there seems to be trust and use of the PPS staff. Such an attitude not only opens many doors but it puts a stamp on the services that sets a tone. The staff works to perpetuate this helping tone.

Another attitude is the willingness to share and be comfortable with overlap. No one discipline seems threatened by another. There is a real openness here that can only be appreciated if one has worked in a setting where it is not so. This aspect is one we often assume will be present, but too often is not. It is crucial, however, if we are truly to be of service efficiently. A counselor cannot pout if a psychologist sees one of his students for short-term counseling. A psychologist cannot get peeved if a counselor gives an ITPA or a Slosson. A social worker must accept that a nurse will sometimes make home visits. In short, there are areas of overlap where expediency and common sense seem to dictate a course of action. The key, however, is communication. In Central Bucks, this comfort and communication seems to work well.

A significant attitude that is unique but crucial is an administrative attitude that perceives PPS as an integral part of education to fully achieve growth and development in students. Since administrators set a tone for buildings and districts, receptivity to PPS, as a tone, goes a long way to gaining receptivity from staff for PPS concepts. In this, Central Bucks is fortunate. Administrative staff are receptive and supportive to the efforts of PPS staff.

Another "given" in any good PPS program are the qualifications of staff. In Central Bucks, PPS staff are all well-qualified for their

391

function. As a result, they gain the respect of those with whom they deal and are able to carry out their role in a confident manner.

From the previous, somewhat glowing, testimonials stems the last unique attitude. There exists among the PPS staff a harmony and an enthusiasm that promotes cooperation and a willingness to work out obstacles. As interpersonal problems arise, they are dealt with in a positive, open manner. This harmonious working relationship within the department has much impact. It promotes trust from others and is a necessary ingredient in having PPS truly perceived as a team.

Central Bucks uniqueness, then, is an intangible. Putting all the unique factors together is not enough. A gestalt relationship exists where the whole is really greater than the sum of the parts, since the intricate interwoven network of relationships create a pattern not quickly or easily appreciated.

ISSUES AND ALTERNATIVES

PPS faces many issues and alternative directions in its present operation and immediate future.

In the section, ready answers are not available or no issue would exist. As a result, an issue will be stated and certain questions posed. Solutions are to be sought by student and practitioner, alike.

Issue 1: PPS must consider various forms of differential staffing.

QUESTION 1:   To what extent can paraprofessionals be used effectively by the various PPS disciplines?

QUESTION 2:   Should discipline lines be eradicated to provide a generalist PPS worker? What are ratio implications?

QUESTION 3:   Should the various disciplines further subdivide to provide a hierarchy of differentiated work with certificate and salary implications? (That is, instead of school psychologist have psychometrist-consulting psychologist-counseling psychologist.)

Issue 2: A number of alternative educational settings are springing up.

More are necessary for the future (i.e., year-round schools, extended day, other organizational models).

QUESTION 1:   What role should PPS play in such alternative educational plans?

QUESTION 2:   What implications do these alternative plans have for the operation of PPS?

QUESTION 3:   Are there aspects of alternative educational arrangements which are antithetical to the philosophy of PPS?

Issue 3: *Community agencies are increasingly being seen as a substitute for many of the pupil personnel services.*

QUESTION 1: Can social work services, psychological services, school health services, and psychiatric consultation be provided to schools from community agencies?

QUESTION 2: Would a broad-based community agency program for services be cheaper and more efficient than a school-based PPS?

Issue 4: *Special education philosophy is in a transitional state.*

QUESTION 1: Exclusion of any school-age child, regardless of handicap, is fast becoming illegal. What implications has this for education in general and PPS in particular?

QUESTION 2: Where should PPS stand on the question of containment in regular class versus special placement for varying types of handicaps?

QUESTION 3: Can PPS accurately pinpoint the primary handicapping condition in a multiple-handicapped child?

Issue 5: *The use and reliability of all kinds of testing is currently under considerable fire.*

QUESTION 1: For what children, and to what extent, do tests provide significant differential data?

QUESTION 2: Are group tests worth the time and money spent in light of increasing differences in curricula and current use?

QUESTION 3: If various individual assessments in a psychologist's bag of tricks are regarded dubiously, what does this mean for the future of school psychological services?

Issue 6: *In light of all the current unresolved issues in PPS, community support is difficult to muster.*

QUESTION 1: Can PPS sell itself to the community as an integral, necessary part of education?

QUESTION 2: What modifications must PPS make to be more useful and accountable in education?

QUESTION 3: Does collective bargaining by professional groups in education hinder or help PPS?

Issue 7: *Student rights and responsibilities are not clearly defined nor understood in the school setting.*

QUESTION 1: Should pupil personnel staff be student advocates in relation to their rights and responsibilities?

QUESTION 2: Are compulsory school attendance laws realistic and are they legal?

QUESTION 3: To what "due process" are students entitled to before suspension, expulsion, or other punitive action can be applied?

QUESTION 4: What records can (and ought) to be kept in schools; by whom should they be kept, and who has access to various records?

1. *Pupil Personnel Services: A Position Statement,* National Association of Pupil Personnel Administrators, April 1969.
2. *Pupil Personnel Services Guidelines for Training, Certification, and Accreditation,* National Association of Pupil Personnel Administrators, June 1972.
3. *Pupil Personnel Services in Pennsylvania: A Position Statement,* Pennsylvania Dept. of Education, Bureau of Pupil Personnel Services (Harrisburg: Pennsylvania Dept. of Education, 1971).
4. Dr. Thomas Gordon, *Parent Effectiveness Training* (New York City: Peter H. Wyden, Inc., 1970).
5. Dr. Thomas A. Harris, *I'm O.K.—You're O.K.* (New York City: Harper & Row, 1967).
6. John R. Gaskins, *Expenditures for Pupil Personnel Services* (Interprofessional Research Commission on Pupil Personnel Services, 1968).

CHAPTER 12

The Pupil Personnel Program in Perspective

RAYMOND N. HATCH

THE preceding chapters have been devoted to some of the more pressing issues and promising practices in pupil personnel work. It is to be hoped that they will provide the reader with an increased understanding of the problems faced by the administrator of a pupil personnel program and suggest ways by which such problems can be solved. A review of the material will reveal the fact that there are many unresolved issues, as well as many alternate ways of approaching an administrative issue. This is certainly the wish of the authors, for it has not been their intent to suggest solutions to all problems in this field or to draft a precise model to be transferred to all school settings. There are certain guidelines, however, which the pupil personnel administrator may follow with a reasonable degree of confidence, and some of these are restated here for emphasis.

The pupil personnel program of the future should profit from the growing stability of the professional field. This, however, will not be enough to perpetuate the continued acceptance and growth of the various services of the program. The flexibility that has characterized the program during the past decade must be retained if the personal needs of the pupil are to be met as dictated by the changes in his environment. To maintain the necessary adaptability, the staff must be especially aware of certain aspects of the material discussed in previous chapters which tend to guarantee this flexibility in program development. It seems desirable, therefore, to offer a brief review of some of these in this closing segment of the presentation.

PROGRAM PLANNING AT THE UNIT LEVEL

Suggestions for the identification of objectives and the proper evaluation of those objectives were reviewed in considerable detail in the previous chapters. The ideas presented were, in general, directed at the program of the total school district. This is essential to the effective programming of pupil personnel services but may fall short of the accepted goals unless there is planning and evaluation at the small unit or building level. Specific goals and plans for evaluation have unique characteristics at the smaller unit level, but the fact that individual staff members participate in the drafting of the plans should insure a more effective performance at all levels.

The district-wide goals represent the foundation upon which the smaller unit staff should define its needs and state its objectives. Failure to extend planning to this level may result in an ineffective program. The major elements of planning at the smallest unit level can be reduced to four simple steps for implementation. If the four steps suggested below are cast within the context of the objectives and plans of the school district, the total program should provide a more viable service.

STEP ONE—The goals, objectives, and plans of the school district should be analyzed by the members of the smaller unit, and the unique needs of the unit identified for additional strategies.

STEP TWO—The precise activities expected of the individual staff members in the attainment of a specified set of objectives (district and unit) should be determined in consultation with the local administrator. If at all possible, this should occur before the staff members enter upon their first official day of service in the school year. If this is not possible, it should be a matter of top priority in the early weeks of service.

STEP THREE—The agreed-upon role and the objectives to be reached should be explained to all individuals for whom the staff members' services are designed. The responsibility for seeing that this is done rests with the individual assigned to the administrative component of the local unit and the individual with whom the pupil personnel staff member has consulted in the definition of role. For most local units and pupil personnel staff members, this step suggests that pupils, teachers, and parents be given a clear explanation of what to expect from the pupil personnel worker. This step, also, should occur very early in the school year in order to insure effective use of the staff members' services at the earliest possible date.

STEP FOUR—An evaluation of the services provided by the staff member can then be made in terms of the role definition and the local objectives and should include all facets of the school family for whom services had been promised. The appraisal should also include considerable input by

397

the pupil personnel staff member to see if the role had been unrealistic or if inhibitors to the attainment of the objectives had been introduced over which the staff member had no control.

At first glance, these steps may strike the reader as an oversimplified resolution in the development of a more effective pupil personnel program at the building level. The fact remains, however, that most school counselors, school social workers, and others enter upon their jobs with former role perceptions of the duties to be performed and with very limited job descriptions available. To make matters worse, the administrators may have quite a different perception of their role, and all the individuals they are to assist may have limited or no knowledge at all as to how to use their services. This leads to confusion and ineffective service, and hinders objective evaluation. A major cause for the criticism that is frequently leveled at the pupil personnel worker is the ignorance of those being served regarding the proper role of the worker. The alert administrator will try to alleviate the problem by requiring that the steps noted here become minimum aspects of program planning and implementation.

THE DILEMMA OF ETHICAL PRACTICE AND LEGAL LIMITS

The problems faced by the pupil personnel worker in adhering to sound ethical practice and staying within the confines of the rather nebulous legal directives have been reviewed in detail in Chapter 3. Little can be added to that presentation, but there seems to be merit in noting a few additional factors, since this appears to be a very sensitive issue for pupil personnel workers in the foreseeable future.

The major problems to be faced, relative to this issue, stem from legal restrictions imposed by law and interpretations by the judiciary of the nation. This assumes, of course, that the professional ethics of the profession will be followed by practitioners in all the educational services. If these assumptions are correct, it may be further assumed that the changes that have been taking place in the social order will result in a far greater amount of change in legal interpretations in the future. This can be credited to such social changes as the deep concern many citizens have for "invasion of privacy" and the limits imposed by "privileged communication." The direction and the speed with which change takes place is impossible to predict, but it does suggest that a major concern of the pupil personnel administrator must be the development of a vigilant program of research and planning that will keep him abreast of the current legal limits within which the services are performed.

If there is to be a viable program to keep the pupil personnel staff appraised of the significant changes in the legal aspects of their services, a number of activities should be planned. Such activities must be selected in such a way as to insure a continuing improvement in the definition of acceptable roles for all staff members and at the same time provide for constant attention to those services which pose the greatest threat to questions of a legal nature. A few of the suggested activities which seem to fit this description are reviewed here.

Privileged Communication

The meaning and scope of the term, *privileged communication*, has been reviewed in Chapter 3. The significance of this factor in regard to the work of the pupil personnel worker has also been stressed. To recognize its importance and to accept its current application, however, is an inadequate approach to the problems inherent in a matter of such importance. The pupil personnel administrator and his staff should feel obligated to work through all available legislative channels to try and obtain a statute in their state which clearly defines the scope of privileged communication to which the various pupil personnel workers are entitled. A growing number of states have such a provision, but it will take vigorous and continued effort to increase the number and clarify the meaning of those statutes which have been enacted.

Student Records

During the past fifty years, our nation's schools have developed rather extensive student record files with little concern—and no need for concern—regarding the "right to privacy" of the individual student. Such records were kept in order to provide the best education possible for each student. The compiled information provided an invaluable profile from which the professional staff member could make an evaluation or assessment of each individual. The temper of contemporary society, however, suggests that this rather blasé attitude of collecting pupil information is due for a rude awakening. The change in the public's attitude, in regard to pupil records, is being quickened by the rapid increase in the use of data processing equipment (Chapter 4), which poses a far greater threat to the "right to privacy" of an individual than that contained in the older and more conventional cumulative record.

An issue of this significance will probably play a major role in the concerns of pupil personnel workers for the years immediately ahead. It may be necessary to re-evaluate the entire record-keeping system to see if the information collected, the way it is used, and how it is retained can be justified in terms of professional ethics and legal limitations. The staff, interested in updating the record system in order to bring it in line with current ethical and legal demands, should find considerable help in the references noted in Chapter 3 and in the many new publications now appearing in the professional field. Such reviews as the one prepared by Butler et al.,[1] for example, is an excellent report of the history of student record keeping and the legal limitations currently in force in the various states. With the present emphasis on the concern for individual rights, undoubtedly many more such publications will soon be made available to the staff of the pupil personnel program.

These two areas of concern in the ethical-legal aspect of pupil personnel work are by no means the only categories to which the staff must devote its attention. A few of the other areas will be touched upon under subsequent topics, since all pupil personnel work is subject to ethical criteria but may not be as closely related to legal limitations as the ones noted above.

THE FUTURE OF TECHNOLOGY IN PUPIL PERSONNEL WORK

The current status of technology as it is utilized in pupil personnel work is reviewed in Chapter 4. The possible growth of its various components are also noted in the chapter with little to be added except the possible speculation of another writer. It is within this vein that the following comments are offered.

The various conditions which have inhibited a more rapid acceptance of technology in education have been noted: human reluctance to accept the machine as a partial replacement, the lack of sophistication and knowledge of equipment, and added costs. Historically, educational innovations have faced the same conditions, and usually have been overcome if the idea proved to be more than an educational fad. Cost, traditionally, has remained a major stumbling block to project implementation on a large scale. This may well be the case in the increased use of technology in education unless a way can be found to provide for the various innovations in more effective ways than that proposed for schools in accordance with their present organization.

The areas of technology which seem to pose the most difficult financial problems for the administrator appear to be data processing equipment, television, and the reproduction and delivery plans of career information. In all of these, the unit cost has been reported to be prohibitive in terms of the benefits gained from its use. Granting that the amount of gain claimed is usually in relationship to the personal bias of the individual making the evaluation, and granting that there is limited hard evidence to support a position, the present author would like to suggest that the primary problem rests with current school organization and current methods of taxation for school purposes.

The schools of the United States have been developed in an atmosphere of local control and local support through the primary method of real estate tax. This has placed the responsibility for the operation of a school district with the local school board, with little or no control imposed on their jurisdiction from any level beyond its boundaries. Consolidation and urbanization have tended to decrease the number of separate districts and increase the number of pupils in a given district, but this has come about very slowly as the local groups tend to cling jealously to their control over the local autonomous unit. Many attempts have been made to broaden the control by the development of a larger administrative unit, such as the intermediate school district, but there have been only slight changes in the exercise of authority of the local board.

The second factor, characterizing the educational setting of the nation, that of the property tax for school operation constitutes a major block to innovations that represent added or unique costs. When the local school board must depend on this outmoded method of taxation for a major portion of its operational costs, there is little likelihood that it will support major innovative costs, since these must be explained and "sold" to a voting public which will cast a vote every one or two years. Add to this the hazard of asking a voter to increase his taxes when this may offer the only opportunity he has to rebel against tax increases, and the position of the typical board can be understood even though it may not be accepted.

The future growth of technology, therefore, may rest more on the degree of change in the administrative organization for education and the method of taxation for school operation than all the other

401

factors combined. There now appears to be a growing segment of the population interested in changing the method of taxation, but how far this will develop will depend on the alternate possibilities offered to the tax-paying public. School organization, on the other hand, may offer little in the way of change in terms of local authority. It may be that the most promising action in the administration of pupil personnel program for innovations of technology will be the cooperative efforts of several districts in mutually supported activities. If the administrators of such programs can develop an attractive project package which includes the more effective use of the computer, television, or similar technique and show the increased benefits at a minimal per pupil cost, this problem may be overcome. In any event, the role of the pupil personnel staff in expanding the use of the more expensive aspects of technology may involve collecting a body of evidence to support the increased use of one or more of the innovations and then cooperating with professional colleagues of surrounding districts in proposals which are financially feasible for all concerned.

STAFF ROLES AND CRISIS ISSUES

One of the major demands on the time of the school counselor during the past few years has been that of assisting the school staff to cope with crisis issues. These issues have evolved from the social revolution which has had an impact on the schools as a major social agency. Problems of drug use, racial conflict, sexual freedom, and related problems of venereal disease and threats of suicide have been the most common. Other members of the pupil personnel staff have also been called upon for assistance in some instances, but it has been the school counselor who has been placed in the forefront to alleviate the problems, which at times have reached crisis proportions.

The social problems noted here have always been a part of the normal counseling problems to be dealt with by the typical school counselor. The rapid increase in the frequency of the problems, with the implicit threat of violent action of some nature, has created a dimension of concern for the current work of the counselor and for his role in the future. The question that many counselors face today is one of either withdrawing from a leadership role, which attempts to reduce the problems, or overtly seeking the reduction of such problems as the responsibility of the counselor. If the latter course is the choice, then many other duties usually described as pertinent to the work of the counselor will suffer. There is, of course, the prospect of adding staff to insure adequate coverage of duties, but this may be wishful thinking unless a new source of funds can be uncovered. Thus, the future role of the school counselor in crisis situations becomes a serious administrative issue.

Criticism of Roles

Counselors have reacted to the demands of the social revoluation in different ways. Some have moved into the new role with vigor and determination in an effort to find answers and provide settings which will reduce the tensions. Others have withdrawn from the fray and redoubled their efforts to maintain their roles as prescribed by various professional agencies and training programs. This situation has resulted in open public criticism of the counselor and may even threaten his continuation in any role unless an appropriate role definition can be accepted by all concerned. An excellent example of the criticism that stems from this situation has been presented by Gribben, writing in the January 20, 1973, issue of *The National Observer*.[1] The author is extremely critical of the roles played by many school counselors when he asserts, "In many schools guidance counselors turn away recognizably suicide-prone youngsters, refusing 'to intervene.' They deny help and information to students who come to them with problems about drugs and sex." There are cases in the same article, however, in which the author commends the work of counselors, but the tone of the entire presentation is one of wondering why the counselor is not a more active participant in crisis situations.

One of the confounding aspects of the recurring negative comments made by both lay and professional people concerning the work of the counselor is that many studies indicate that counselors are involved in professional activities which are beneath the competency level of the well-qualified counselor. To add to this, there is some evidence to indicate that some counselors find satisfaction in routine activity. One may speculate as to the meaning of this condition, but the fact remains that there appears to be an increasing demand that counselors devote a major portion of their time to counseling, while some counselors express preferences for other activities. Dietz found, for example, that a sample of 246 certified counselors in Tennessee indicated greater job satisfaction in placement and public relations than in counseling.[2] In fact, counseling was rated seventh in a list of ten typical counselor activities. This is a small sample, to be sure, but a review of the recent literature indicates considerable counselor support for many activities which could be performed by paraprofessionals, thereby releasing counselors to fill the voids indicated by the spreading criticism of counselor activities.

The professional associations have become increasingly concerned about the apparent failure of certified counselors to become aware of the newer demands of the social revolution. For example, the American Personnel and Guidance Association has made a concerted effort to bring the problem into proper focus. One issue of its publication, *The Personnel and Guidance Journal,* was devoted entirely to the role of counselors in the social revolution.[3] Numerous other articles in subsequent issues and in other professional publications have also pointed out the need for a reorientation of counselors to meet the new demands. The impact that this may have on the counseling profession is most difficult to predict, since criticism of various phases of education is not a new phenomenon. Counselors may continue as they have in the past in the hope that the threat will go away. Ignoring such an obvious demand, however, will not resolve the problem. The current situation would seem to dictate that those responsible for prescribing counselor roles would demand a reappraisal of those roles and bring them more in line with the demands of a society to be served.

A Positive Look

The brief discussion of the counselor's role in the present social setting should serve to alert the reader to this issue in pupil personnel work. No doubt criticism will continue as counselors, counselor trainers, and administrators struggle to adapt to these new demands in relationship to the competencies now possessed by the counseling staff. An adjustment of this kind cannot be made overnight, for it calls for changes in value systems, a willingness to relinquish routine duties representing minimal involvement with the pressing problems of others, and a desire to gain competencies demanded by a changing role. In addition, it will require a change in the administrator's perception of the proper role for a counselor in order for the counselor's training to be properly used in a manner consistent to the changes which place new demands on his activities. This is a sizable adjustment to expect but a necessary one if counseling services are to fulfill their professional obligations.

Counselors and their administrators should find considerable help in adjusting to these new demands in the emerging literature devoted to the topic. The recent writing suggests ways by which the counselor can cope with immediate and emergency needs without being absorbed by them. Writings of this character tend to retain the basic elements of what has been considered the proper role for the counselor in the past, yet requires him to reappraise his values and to become more aware of the social setting in which he functions. A new publication by Wrenn is especially helpful in a reorientation of a new role for counselors.[4] Another recent publication edited by Kagan and Coles contains a series of articles dealing with the particular problems of the youth in their early adolescent years.[5] The chapters entitled, *A World They Never Knew: The Family and Social Change* and *The Creation of the Sexual in Early Adolescence* are but two of many fine chapters which should prove very revealing to the counselor and administrator concerned with a new role for counselors. A recent book by Shaw, although designed more for use as a general introductory guidance text, offers points of view in understanding a new frame of reference for the school counselor.[6] These represent the beginning of what will probably be a massive professional effort to help the pupil personnel staff cope with this new dimension in their field.

In summary, the primary elements of what has been projected for the work of the school counselor will probably remain intact, but there will be urgent need to readjust to the new demands. Counselors who have gained their titles by administrative edict, a "grandfather clause," or by some other avenue than a solid training program in areas of counselor competence, should not be expected to perform well in this new role. Administrators who have routine clerical tasks performed by a staff member should feel an obligation to name such staff by some title other than counselor, and counselors who enjoy such a role would be rendering a professional service by asking that their titles be changed. School counselors could then be expected to adjust their values, alter their activities to meet the new demands, and perform a satisfactory service in accordance with guidelines of good counseling practice.

STAFF ROLES AND CAREER EDUCATION

By the end of the 1960s, educators in all phases of professional education became acutely aware of two new terms which dominated much of the professional literature, constituted major portions of the agenda of professional meetings, and appeared to enjoy the accep-

405

tance of the general public. The two terms were *accountability* and *career education,* and both seemed to capture the temper of the times by appealing to the tax-paying public in holding public education more accountable for the attainment of accepted educational objectives. It was only a short time after their introduction, that legislative bodies began to endorse the concepts, and appropriations were made to expedite the implementation of programs in accordance with promises set forth by proponents of the guidelines suggested by the descriptions of the two terms. The principle of *accountability* has been discussed in earlier chapters. The model suggested is that of the definition of goals, the identification of objectives, the strategy for attainment and the techniques of evaluation. The problems inherent in applying the model to pupil personnel services were also noted, as well as the interrelationships that exist between the various components of the educational enterprise. The application of accountability was reviewed in the issues presented by the various school districts. There seems to be little value, therefore, in discussing the concept of accountability at this point, but a brief review of the role of the pupil personnel staff in providing a career education program may be justified.

Career education as a term has enjoyed the privilege of finding definition and conceptual design as the broad ideas have been incorporated into the educational programs of the nation. In the early days of the usage of the term, it was generally accepted as a way of expanding vocational education to all levels of education. Subsequent analysis, however, revealed that supporters of the idea viewed the concept as something far broader than a simple new change of title for an old area of education. It soon became apparent that the suggestions made by proponents included a significant shift in the direction of curriculum content toward a career orientation for all students. The justification for the concept appeared to depend on a way to achieve the educational objectives which had been stated and restated for well over half a century. Objectives that emphasized economic efficiency were pointed out as areas of failure in the educational program, since so few graduates were capable of entering a post school life in an efficient manner. It was observed that a vast majority of graduates of the high school lacked skills to enter upon a gainful occupation and, even more importantly, they seemed to lack the knowledge to make a choice, nor did they receive direction from the school in the selection process. Such a condemnation of the educational process posed a threat to the entire structure and proved especially painful to the members of the pupil personnel staff, since they had attempted to institute services to prevent the occurrence of the very things for which the schools were being criticized.

Early expressions of interest in the career education concept came from many sources, but it was not until the U.S. Office of Education became a very active proponent in 1969 that educators really realized that the idea had more than the potential of being just another educational fad. Congress appropriated significant sums of money for the support of exemplary programs, and the departments of education in the various states became partners in support of the career emphasis. The endorsement of these professional agencies, plus the support of the lay public, legislatures, and concerned agencies in society, led to a major movement to institute a career-oriented curriculum. An example of the results of such support was reviewed in Chapter 7.

Scope of the Term

Many attempts have been made to define *career education*. The early proposals approached the problem from a negative view point by stating what the concept was not. The more recent suggestions have reversed this by offering a specific definition. Two of the definitions are to be found in a publication by Hoyt et el.[7] One of the co-authors defines *career education* as "the total effort of the community to develop a personally satisfactory succession of opportunities for service through work, paid or unpaid, extending throughout life." In the same publication Hoyt offers a similar definition but introduces the element of the integration of an individual's value system and the value system of the work-oriented society. This is implied in the first definition, but the added element may serve to answer an important question that many educators have had as to the precise meaning of the proposal.

Another attempt to define the career education proposal has been proposed by Goldhammer and Taylor.[8] These authors recognize the need for more study of the emerging role of the idea before an exact definition is adopted, but one statement in their general definition of the term seems to clarify the meaning of *career education*. "*Career education* is designed to capacitate individuals for their several life roles: economic, community, home, avocational, religious, and aesthetic." Other definitions will probably be forthcoming, but at this

407

point in time it appears that the career education concept is directed at curriculum revision that includes greater orientation to careers at all grade levels.

The definition of a career is also undergoing some change as it is used increasingly to cover the totality of experiences of an individual, which typically include some combination of vocational and avocational involvement. It may be defined further by stating that the rewards of such activity may be in the activity itself or the final product. Within this frame of reference, the present author suggests the following definition for the new idea.

Career education is a philosophical concept for the reorganization of life-long education. The concept focuses on careers as a primary thrust of the school experiences from kindergarten through the adult years. A program of this kind, for the traditional twelve years of school, encompasses all or part of the scope of activities identified as career planning. In addition, it provides for curricular reorganization, and includes training and experience-centered activities leading to a development of skills in all students for direct entry into employment or for additional training.

Career Education or Vocational Guidance

The student of the guidance movement history is well aware that the first guidance courses, the first professional guidance organization, and much of the early counseling carried the prefacing title of *vocational*. The early exponents in the professional field were dedicated to helping an individual find an appropriate occupational outlet following an exposure to the world of work and some analysis of himself in relationship to the opportunities. Gradually, the field expanded into various other facets of the services to help others with problems not necessarily oriented to an occupation, and the prominence of vocational guidance in the total spectrum of pupil personnel work was diminished. In spite of this, however, there has remained a sizable group of professional people with a strong desire to serve in this role, and many of them wonder what is new about career education since this is what they have been trying to accomplish for the past three quarters of a century.

It may be an oversimplification of the relationship of the new term to vocational guidance to say that the goals are the same but the approach is different. It would be more accurate perhaps to say that the newer title for career activity builds on the principles set forth by proponents of vocational guidance and projects these into a more prominent place in professional education. A precise set of differences are probably not too important since the basic objectives of both are very similar. A few differences seem to be apparent and are noted here.

1. Career education suggests greater curriculum change then that usually proposed in a program of vocational guidance.
2. Career education demands an increase in the participation of the instructional staff that exceeds that suggested in most vocational guidance programs.
3. Career education requires more direct exposure of students to instructional experiences related to the world of work than has been set forth in most vocational guidance plans.
4. Career education exacts more service from the school counselor in areas of consultation and coordination of career programs than has the vocational guidance programs of the past. It does not eliminate the role of the counselor in dealing with the individual student in a counseling relationship, but it does require professional leadership in the other two areas of counselor activity.

Other differences could be noted regarding the two terms, but they would fall into a category of "nit-picking." Academic arguments that develop from efforts to define precise differences and roles are usually counterproductive, since the ultimate goals of the proponents of both concepts are the same. The supporters of the vocational guidance programs might do well to welcome the support of additional staff and resources made possible under the banner of career education and move in consort toward the most effective vocational guidance program in the history of American education. It now appears that this is the direction the two movements are taking.

Coordination and Consultation

The role of the pupil personnel staff in providing for coordination and consultation in career education programs has been noted above. The nature of this role needs more experimentation, but several activities are sufficiently obvious to be enumerated at this point. The suggestions are predicated on the assumption that the pupil personnel worker, primarily the school counselor, should be one of the most sophisticated members of the school staff in certain areas of career education programs. His training should have included: the theory of vocational choice; sources of occupational, educational, and social information; career unit design and other elements not usually found in the training backgrounds of other school staff. Training of this kind makes him a natural leader in the coordination of the career education program and a very valuable asset in consulting with the instructional staff in the development of career education activities.

COORDINATION

The success or failure of the career education programs of the future will undoubtedly rest more on the success the school district has in coordinating all of the possible activities from kindergarten into adult programs than any other factor. The mass of information available, the number of individuals involved, and the transitional character of career opportunities demand aggressive coordination if the program is to succeed. To do less than this is to invite major omissions and unfortunate duplications in a vertical learning program that cannot afford to waste time or resources.

It has been noted that the career education emphasis is one of curricular alteration. An emphasis of this kind would suggest that the coordination of career education is most appropriately done as a function of the instructional component of education. Should this be the case, the role of the pupil personnel staff in assisting with the implementation of the career education could face a serious administrative obstruction, since there would be divided responsibility. Such a condition is not an uncommon occurrence in the administration of various aspects of education, but it does represent an unfortunate situation for which a remedy must be found if the program is to be one of significance.

The preceding chapters contain various administrative models which may have transfer to the coordination of the career education program. The characteristic of flexibility to meet the demands of a local situation is apparent in most of the suggestions. This may prove to be the primary guide to a staff faced with the coordination of a career curriculum. In this case, the staff may be assisted in their decision by asking questions, leading to the obvious answer. The following questions seem the most pertinent:

1. Is a particular staff member responsible for the coordination of the instructional program? If the answer is "yes," the individual assigned to coordinate the career educational program should become a member of his staff.
2. Is there an individual responsible for the coordination of the pupil

personnel program? If the answer is "yes," a plan must be adopted that permits maximum cooperation between these two components in planning, implementing, and evaluating the career education program.

3. Is an individual available who has both administrative and pupil personnel competencies? If the answer is "none in the system," it may be necessary to go outside the district to obtain a qualified person, since nothing would be more detrimental to the success of the program than to have leadership that could best be described as the "blind leading the blind."

4. Is there an individual in each building who has the interest and ability to serve as coordinator of career education in that building? If the answer is "no," a way should be found to obtain such a person, since the demands of an efficient program require constant liaison between all facets of the district. The person selected may perform these duties on a part-time basis, provided adequate time is available for the coordination of responsibilities.

5. Will the school district have a model for career education which designates an emphasis on careers at certain levels of the school program? If the answer is "no," then some model such as "career awareness" for the primary grades, "career exploration" for the middle grades, and "career preparation" for the high school should be adopted. A model usually results in easier definition of responsibility by teachers at the various levels and permits a program to evolve in proper sequence, minimizing omission and duplication.

Answers to the above questions should go a long way in resolving the problem of coordination. In all probability the future experiences of schools with the career concept will point the way to the best administrative arrangement for program coordination. In the meantime, the staff may find the growing amount of professional writing on the subject helpful in the resolution of particular problems of model design and program implementation. One of these is a revision of a well-known book by Norris et el., which provides considerable insight into the ways by which this new idea can be incorporated into the curriculum.[10] Another excellent reference, dealing with program design, has been written by Hansen, which offers guidelines in the determination of a proper model for the career program.[11]

CONSULTATION

The role of the pupil personnel staff in providing consultative services to members of the staff responsible for the initiation of *career education* is much easier to define because the training of a qualified

411

counselor dictates the role he may play while consulting with other members of the school staff. Based upon this premise the following consultative activities seem to be logical topics:

1. Review the model for the career education program to see if it tends to be defensible in terms of accepted theories of vocational choice.
2. Assist in the identification of materials to be used in the presentation and analysis of career information.
3. Aid teachers in the formulation of instructional units and courses.
4. Design plans for the storage and dissimination of career information.
5. Assist in the evaluation of the program.
6. Report on apparent information duplications or omissions as they are revealed in the counseling relationship.

This list is by no means complete, but it does represent a basic number of consultative activities which the school counselor should be expected to perform. Other members of the pupil personnel staff have unique consultative competencies which may be utilized in program improvement. For example, the placement director, the attendance coordinator, and school nurse will have very pertinent information which should be used in the shaping of the career education program. The placement director will have insights into the needs of the local labor market, the attendance coordinator should be able to provide information about student concerns with the limitations of the current educational offering, and the nurse is a valuable resource person in the development of instructional units built around health careers. Other members will have different but significant contributions; however, these members, as well as those mentioned previously, may not offer their assistance unless the services are requested. The alert program coordinator will not permit these rich resources to go untapped.

A Point of View

It is impossible, at this point in time, to predict the future of the career education concept. Currently it enjoys the support of the major administrative units of American education and seems to be gaining acceptance among various instructional groups. The latter, however, have indicated some reservation and caution and have not embraced the idea with the enthusiasm that will be needed if the complete program is implemented. Continued clarification of the meaning of the concept may remove the objections of some groups to the term, and experience with various aspects of the program may insure greater acceptance. In any event, the pupil personnel staff should find the objectives of the career education concept consistent with the objectives of a good personnel program and deserving of a major effort to insure success.

STAFF ROLES AND SPECIAL INTEREST GROUPS

The traditional and accepted role for members of the pupil personnel team has been reviewed in some length in earlier sections of this book. Precise definition has been slow in coming in some cases, but there now seems to be general understanding among many educators as to the role each professional plays in a given setting. Evidence, however, indicates that when an administrator faces a new student-related problem he is prone to draft the counselor or some other member of the pupil personnel staff to help him cope with the new issues. This has created many administrative problems for the pupil personnel staff, since the new dimension of responsibility may not be consistent with role expectation, and it may well be that the counselor lacks the background to meet the issue with confidence. In addition, the pupil personnel worker is frequently judged by his ability to handle any new or strange issue which might represent a major threat to his professional competence.

Some of the most common crisis problems were discussed earlier in this chapter, but another major issue—that of dissent or discontent of minority groups was not included in that review. The limitations of space and the purposes of this book preclude all but a brief notation of this critical issue which faces the pupil personnel administrator. The problems may be identified by sex, race, or ethnic background, and the members of minority groups have become extremely articulate in recent years. Their voices are being heard in all communities; and the schools, as a major social agency, face the task of adjusting programs to meet the challenges of these groups.

The extent and nature of the adjustments to be made in pupil personnel programs in order to meet the unique demands of minority groups remain to be resolved in the years ahead. To some extent, training programs have been adjusted to develop trainees' awareness, for example, of the particular problems of the underprivileged youngster. Professional writing has contributed much in recent years to help the practitioner gain some insight into the needs

413

of special groups. In addition, efforts are being made to make the professional worker more aware of other movements in the social order. The growing role of women in society occupies increased space in the professional literature. For example, an entire issue of *The Personnel and Guidance Journal* was devoted to the role of women.[12] Other writings are also appearing to help the counselor cope with the special needs of certain groups. A new book by Smith should prove especially helpful in understanding how a group with different cultural backgrounds view their educational opportunities.[13] These examples are but a mere beginning of a professional reading program that must be instituted in a staff if the real concerns of the special groups are to be understood. Such a program need not result in major changes in roles, but it should bring about a change in attitude and practice that is more consistent with the rightful expectations of any group of our citizens.

THE INSTRUCTIONAL STAFF AND GUIDANCE SERVICES

The role of the instructional staff in support of the pupil personnel program was outlined in Chapter 6. Instances of teacher roles were either noted or implied in the five school district descriptions (Chapters 7–11). In spite of this recognition, however, there seems to be a tendency to take the teacher's role in a guidance program for granted, thereby failing to recognize an imperative element to the success of the program. This role is so essential it deserves special recognition in this concluding section.

The typical guidance services were enumerated in Chapter 1 and have been alluded to throughout the text. The three which have received the primary attention are the inventory, information, and counseling services of a guidance program. Counseling has probably enjoyed the most prominent place, since it is conducted by a pupil personnel staff member and since it is usually considered the most significant of all the guidance services. It, however, would probably be of limited value unless the contributions of the other two services, provided primarily by the teaching staff, were readily available. The teacher is expected to observe and record pertinent information about each youngster, to provide instructional experiences that include information about careers and human behavior, and to create a classroom atmosphere that complements the objectives of the total pupil personnel program. A role of such magnitude suggests that the basic foundation for a program of guidance services is to be found in the classroom and under the control of the instructional staff.

The Teacher and the Inventory Service

The classroom teacher is both a contributor to and a recipient of the components of the inventory service. As a contributor, the teacher is expected to provide pupil information to the personnel record of each youngster by utilizing such tools and techniques as autobiographies, anecdotal reports, sociometric evaluations, rating scales, standardized test results, and other techniques designed to identify each pupil as a unique individual. As a recipient of the service, the teacher is expected to combine the observations of other teachers with her own observations to bring about a more objective understanding of each pupil and to use the information in combinations for increased understanding of the youngster. For example, she may use the scattergram to combine scholastic aptitude norms with academic achievement to discover the overachiever or underachiever. In all these situations, the instructional staff plays a vital role but may need some assistance from the pupil personnel staff if maximum results are anticipated. The point to be remembered is that the teacher is a significant part of the guidance program and must be included in the implementation of the services and helped to attain the best product possible.

The Teacher and the Information Service

Authorities in the field of guidance for many years have identified a role for the teacher in providing information to students that includes occupational, educational, and personal-social components. This role now has taken on an increased dimension with the advent of the career education concept. The classroom teacher in such a setting becomes the key member of the delivery system for that aspect of information where awareness may be the most significant objective. A teacher is expected to select curriculum materials, to invite resource speakers, to plan trips, and to conduct sociodramas that broaden the pupil's understanding of his current and future environment. Here again, the instructional staff plays an essential role in the program but will need the consultative services of members of the pupil personnel staff. In addition, the instructional staff will need direction and coordination of the information service if it is to be free of unnecessary duplication and major omissions.

415

The Teacher and the Counseling Service

In the early days of the guidance movement, it was fairly common to overhear a heated debate among educational staff members relative to the role of a teacher as a counselor. There is still some evidence to indicate that some educators are willing to call the teacher a counselor. In the more sophisticated professional circles, however, this type of academic discussion has disappeared. It is agreed, generally, that counseling is performed by an individual with special training for the task, and this person is the counselor. It also is agreed that the teacher plays a vital role in assisting the counseling process but does this from her role as an instructional staff member. In such a framework, the counselor is the primary catalyst to the counseling process, while the teacher controls the pupil's environment that can make that process more effective. Both the catalytic element and the environmental element are important in a counseling program, but the significant differences in the roles of the counselor and the teacher seem to dispel the semantic confusion that tends to persist relative to the teacher's role in counseling.

The instructional staff has a role in two very common educational activities that are frequently identified as personnel activities. They are also closely related to the work of the school counselor. These two activities are known as parent-teacher conferences and case studies. The former has become a practice in most school systems and grew out of a desire to provide a better reporting system to parents and a wish to involve parents more in the education of their child. The case study, on the other hand, has been utilized by pupil personnel workers for many years as a way of resolving difficult adjustment problems and at the same time serve as an in-service program for the instructional staff. In both of these cases, the goals of the counseling service may be attained in a more rapid and effective manner if teachers are helped by counselors to conduct better conferences with parents and if they are allowed to participate in the sequence of a total case study. The pupil personnel administrator should find these two activities especially beneficial to the furtherance of a solid program of guidance services.

IN SUMMARY

This brief review of the role of the instructional staff, plus that noted in Chapter 6, is but a minute picture of the potential of such a staff in providing a good program of guidance services. Complete

416

books have been written on the subject and professional periodicals continue to devote extensive coverage to various contributions of the classroom teacher to such a program. Yet, it is not uncommon to find pupil personnel programs which seem to minimize the role of the instructional staff and appear to lose this important base from which a good program can be developed. It is to be hoped that all programs of the future will encompass this important segment of the educational staff.

Adaptability an Obvious Slogan

The authors of this book have tried to note and discuss the major issues facing the present-day pupil personnel administrator. The application of the ideal in the current practices of five widely scattered and diverse programs were described, and the issues they face were noted. In other sections of the book, staff roles were defined and desirable practices described. In most of these, the reader was made aware of the inherent value in remaining adaptable to the demands of the situation since a vital program must be one that can adjust to the challenge of a new problem or issue. The authors have made an effort to identify practices which the reader should find helpful in any situation; but in so doing, they hope that the administrator who follows their suggestions will leave room for adaptability in his particular program. Progress will not be achieved in any other atmosphere.

1. Henry E. Butler, Jr., K. D. Moran, and Floyd A. Vanderpool, Jr., *Legal Aspects of Student Records* (Topeka, Kan.: National Organization on Legal Problems of Education, 1972), 62 pp.
2. August Gribbin, "No-Help Helpers," *The National Observer* (Jan. 20, 1973), 12(3):1.
3. "Counseling and the Social Revolution," *The Personnel and Guidance Journal* (May 1971), 49(9), 96 pp.
4. C. Gilbert Wrenn, *The World of the Contemporary Counselor* (Boston: Houghton Mifflin Company, 1973), 293 pp.
5. Jerome Kagan and Robert Coles, eds., *12 to 16 Early Adolescence* (New York: W. W. Norton and Co., 1972), pp. 197–257.
6. Merville C. Shaw, *School Guidance Systems* (Boston: Houghton Mifflin Company, 1973), pp. 5–86.
7. Kenneth B. Hoyt, Rupert N. Evans, Edward F. Mackin, and Garth Mangum, *Career Education: What It Is and How To Do It* (Salt Lake City, Utah: Olympus Publishing Co., 1972), p. 1.
8. Keith Goldhammer and Robert E. Taylor, *Career Education: Perspective and Promise* (Columbus, Ohio: Charles E. Merrill Publishing Co., 1972), p. 6.
9. Siegfried C. Dietz, "Counselor Role, Function, and Job Satisfaction," *Counselor Education and Supervision* (Dec. 1972), 12(2):150–55.
10. Willa Norris, F. R. Zeran, R. N. Hatch, and J. R. Engelkes, *The Information Service in Guidance: For Career Development and Planning*, 3rd ed. (Chicago: Rand McNally & Co., 1972) pp. 417–59.
11. L. Sunny Hansen, "A Model for Career Development Through Curriculum," *The Personnel and Guidance Journal* (Dec. 1972), 51(4):243–50.
12. "Women and Counselors," *The Personnel and Guidance Journal* (Oct. 1972), 51(2):84–160.
13. Elsie J. Smith, *Counseling the Culturally Different Black Youth* (Charles E. Merrill Publishing Co., 1973), 145 pp.

Appendix A-1
COUNSELOR JOB DESCRIPTION
SANTANA HIGH SCHOOL

The primary function of the counselor is to assist each student to actively participate in his own development and become the person whom he desires to be, assuming the responsibility for the consequences of his own decisions and having full respect for the worth and dignity of self and others.

I. Services to Students
  A. *The counselor assists students to develop self-understanding, a sense of identity, healthy interpersonal relationships, and a system of personal values.*
    1. Provides ongoing personal and supportive relationship with students throughout high school program.
    2. Counsels individually with students regarding personal problems.
    3. Counsels with students regarding academic performance.
    4. Acts as facilitator for teachers and students regarding in-class problems.
    5. Assists students in identifying and implementing positive behaviors which will help achieve individual goals.
    6. Makes home visits.
    7. Acts as student's advocate when needed.
  B. *The counselor assists students in developing, implementing, and achieving educational and vocational plans and goals.*
    1. Administers and interprets tests, such as: State mandated, OVIS, Kuder, SVIB, PSAT, NMSQT.
    2. Assists student in planning his total high school program in order that he qualifies for graduation, and employment, training, or post high school education.
    3. Provides vocational information to students, including specific information on work experience, career entry, apprenticeship programs, on-the-job training, and specific district vocational programs.
    4. Disseminates information regarding military service, registration, the draft and other alternatives, ROTC, and the service academies.
    5. Disseminates information regarding college entrance requirements, program offerings, scholarships, and financial aids.
    6. Prepares and disseminates senior bulletin.
    7. Maintains Career Center.
    8. Maintains liaison with colleges and universities, business schools, private trade schools, and similar institutions.
    9. Arranges for appropriate educational and vocational visitations.
    10. Facilitates plans for early or late graduation.
    11. Supervises the maintainance of cumulative folders.
    12. Provides information to colleges, armed services, probation department, community agencies, and vocational agencies.

419

C. *The counselor assists students to participate meaningfully in the curricular and co-curricular opportunities of the school.*
   1. Places students in proper classes as related to: grade and ability level; interests; college, vocational, and graduation requirements.
   2. Conducts orientation and registration of new students.
   3. Conducts exit interviews and processes necessary paperwork for student check-out.
   4. Conducts programming of students.
   5. Issues special permits.
   6. Initiates homework requests for temporarily incapacitated students.
   7. Adjusts student's programs for special activities, programs, and needs.
   8. Maintains accumulative record cards.
D. *The counselor assists students to be aided by special programs, services and agencies, such as those listed after item number three below.*
   1. Determines eligibility and makes referrals.
   2. Participates in diagnostic staffing conferences.
   3. Provides liaison between school, home, agency, program and/or service.
   Examples of Special Programs:
   High School College Credit Program, Regional Occupation Program, Vocational programs, Continuation School, EMR, EH, Adaptive P.E., Work Experience, special studies on campus, special studies off campus, ESEA—Title I, and gifted.
   Examples of Special Services:
   Home Study, Speech Therapy, Visually Handicapped, Free Lunch, Psychological Services, Social Work(er), Nursing and Health Services, and Child Welfare and Attendance.
   Examples of Special Agencies:
   Neighborhood Youth Corp, Youth Employment Service, Probation Department, Welfare Department, Community Mental Health, Drug Education For Youth, Crisis House, and the Bridge.

II. Services to Teachers and Other Certificated Staff Members
   A. *The counselor assists in developing the optimum learning environment necessary to meet the specific needs of the student.*
      1. Assists teachers in the development of instructional approaches for particular learning disabilities.
      2. Acts as representative to departmental meetings.
      3. Consults with teachers regarding special needs of students, including health, learning, home problems, and personal problems if they affect the student's classroom performance.
      4. Serves as liaison between teachers and district level personnel regarding special programs and classes, in-service functions, etc.
      5. Serves as consultant to teachers regarding personal and/or student problems.
      6. Assists teachers to work effectively with students.
      7. Arranges for and participates in parent/teacher/student conferences at school and in the home.
      8. Initiates referrals of students to district social worker, speech therapist, or school nurse.
      9. Cooperates with school psychologist regarding interpretation of test results and implementation of recommendations with teaching staff and parents.

420

10. Works with the social worker regarding student home problems, drugs, etc.

III. Services to the Administrative Staff:
  A. *The counselor assists the administration in providing the optimum learning environment, educational opportunity, and effective communications as they pertain to students, parents, and staff.*
    1. Cooperates with the administrative staff in resolving student-centered problems.
    2. Participates in staffing meetings for Adaptive P.E. and E.H. Placement.
    3. Works to bring about modifications of existing educational practices, curriculum offerings, and basic policies and procedures.
    4. Works with elementary school personnel in articulation of elementary and high school programs.
    5. Participates in planning and implementing the registration of all students.
    6. Assists in the development of the master schedule.
    7. Implements master schedule adjustments.
    8. Conducts follow-up studies and surveys.
    9. Participates in the local school Assessment and Referral Committee.
    10. Co-ordinates the Driver Training Program.
    11. Refers staff personnel problems to the appropriate administrator.
    12. Certifies eligibility for student government candidates.

IV. Services to the Parents and the Community
  A. *The counselor assists parents and the community by facilitating cooperative inter-relationships between the school and the community, providing information and services, and encouraging open communication and involvement.*
    1. Initiates and participates in conferences regarding interpretation of individual test results and recommendations for special programs.
    2. Arranges for and participates in parent conferences regarding student progress and/or problems, necessary home re-enforcement of positive behaviors, realistic student goals, etc.
    3. Contacts the home regarding lengthy student absences, outstanding achievements, failures, interim progress reports, etc.
    4. Participates in parent orientation programs.
    5. Disseminates information to parents and community.
    6. Participates at area-wide meetings initiated by the school or community.
    7. Fosters positive relationships with public agencies, groups, clubs, colleges, trade schools, armed services, etc.
    8. Participates actively within the community to communicate local school and district policies, procedures, goals, and objectives.

V. Services to Self and Department
  A. *The counselor seeks personal and professional growth in order to maximize his effectiveness within the guidance profession.*
    1. The counselor attempts to perform this function in the following ways:
       a. Develops skills in counseling techniques and interpretation of student records, test data, etc.
       b. Promotes a continuing development of professional proficiencies.
       c. Arranges and/or attends conferences which include students, parents, teachers, administrators, and/or special service personnel.

Appendix A-2
SAN DIEGO CITY SCHOOLS
PERSONNEL DIVISION

PSYCHOLOGIST

Brief Description of Position:
Provides psychologiscal services to schools including testing, counseling, and consulting to assist them in meeting the educational needs of pupils.

Major Duties and Responsibilities:
1. Administers to pupils (on an individual basis) intelligence tests (Binet, WISC, WAIS, Leiter), achievement tests, personality tests, and tests to measure perceptual and motor development.
2. Evaluates and interprets all testing and makes recommendations for school and class placements for the following programs: educable mentally retarded, trainable mentally retarded, educationally handicapped, neurologically handicapped, severe learning problems, state and local gifted, and physically handicapped.
3. Interprets test findings to parents as requested; counsels with parents regarding pupil's potential, achievement level, and personality adjustment; recommends to parents ways of helping pupil or recommends sources from which they may seek further counseling.
4. Confers with teachers, administrators, and other professional staff on findings of individual tests and helps them in their efforts to better understand and place each pupil.
5. Consults with other agencies, both public and private, regarding individual cases.
6. Consults with other psychologists, psychiatrists, and physicians for the purpose: of correlating all available information regarding individual cases.
7. Makes recommendations in cases of exemption, nonpromotion, acceleration and other cases upon request.
8. Counsels individual pupils regarding tests findings, academic problems, social or emotional problems, and general vocational goals upon request of the school administration.
9. Performs other duties as assigned.

Other Duties and Responsibilities:
1. Writes complete report on each pupil tested and files with test record; keeps required monthly records and files in Guidance Services Office; and makes appropriate entries on cumulative record for each pupil tested.
2. Participates in faculty meetings, PTA meetings, and other community groups as a representative of the Guidance Services Department upon request.

Supervision Exercised or Received:
Under the general direction of the Supervising School Psychologist. Under the immediate direction of the site administrator while performing services on the

school site. May be called upon to consult with and provide professional-technical advice to one or more psychometrists.

POSITION QUALIFICATIONS

Minimum Qualifications:
1. *Credential:* General Pupil Personnel Services with the authorization to serve as a Psychologist; or Standard Designated Services in Pupil Personnel with the Psychologist authorization.
2. *Education:* Bachelor's degree, including all courses needed to meet credential requirements.
3. *Experience:* Successful classroom teaching and counseling experience is desirable. Advanced work in clinical psychology beyond level of work required for credential is desirable.
4. *Personal Qualities:* Appearance, grooming and personality which establish a desirable example for pupils. Ability to meet district standards for physical and mental health. Better than average recommendations from student supervisors or other professionals who have observed the personal characteristics, scholastic attainment, and performance of the teacher. Must possess mature judgment and ability to exercise individual initiative. Must be able to develop empathy with parents and pupils.

Appendix B-1

OSSEO JUNIOR HIGH SCHOOL COUNSELING ACTIVITIES,
AUGUST 1971 THROUGH JANUARY 1972

I. *Classroom Work.* Counselors have been involved in five major classroom projects. These include: (a) a three-week unit to help seventh grade students adjust to junior high and to facilitate communication among students and teachers; (b) a three-week unit to establish rapport among students and between class and teacher through the media of group activities and introduction of communication skills; (c) consulting and helping plan and coordinate activities for a block program involving three seventh grade teachers (math, science, and social) and ninety seventh grade students; (d) a two-day seventh grade classroom presentation centered around "How you became you"; and (e) a two-day seventh grade classroom presentation about group and individual testing.

II. *Group Work.* Counselors have been using group procedures with students, teachers and parents in the following instances: (a) they are conducting counseling sessions with one group from each grade level one day per week for an hour each; (b) they met with a group of interested teachers after school for seven weeks to conduct sessions dealing with a study of principles of behavior development, to help them share practical classroom management experiences that worked, to generate solutions for crisis situations, and to help them set individual goals; (c) they met with a group of students interested in helping other students —a "Big Sister-Big Brother" approach to life at school; and (d) a counselor and a school psychologist teamed to conduct four biweekly sessions with a group of four couples to study and practice communication skills and other approaches to ease home pressures.

III. *Committee Work.* (a) At least one counselor is a member of the Parent Teacher Conference Committee and of the 1972–73 School Day Schedule Committee; (b) counselors work with a committee designed to centralize teacher concerns about students with academic and/or behavior problems and to coordinate efforts to help such students. The counselor's roles involve: chairing the meeting, planning the agenda, and providing necessary background information about students on the agenda; and (c) counselors have organized and acted as chairman for student case conferences; have attended all building staff meetings; and attended all counselor meetings (Pyramid, district, and building).

IV. *Miscellaneous.* Other activities to which counselors have devoted time are: (a) seeing recommended and self-referred students in individual counseling sessions; (b) administering and interpreting the Lorge-Thorndike group test to seventh and ninth grade students, individual intelligence tests to some individuals, and an interest inventory to a selected group of ninth grade students; (c) supervising the maintenance of student cummulative record files; (d) initiating, planning, and implementing activities for a guidance resource center devoted to the exploration of career development; (e) working on establishing department goals and objectives; (f) registering new students and developing a new schedule change procedure; (g) providing crisis intervention services to students and teachers; (h) helping plan and implement preschool teachers' workshops; and (i) making home visitations.

424

Appendix B-2
EXCERPTS OF TARGET PUBLICS AND PROPOSED PROJECTS
for 1972–73 SCHOOL YEAR
BROOKLYN JUNIOR HIGH SCHOOL

I.   Target Public: *Parents*
     Projects to increase cooperation between parents and school and assist parents
     in working more effectively with their children include:
     A.   Developing a parent guidance advisory committee.
     B.   Developing and offering class for parents in child-rearing attitudes and
          practices.
     C.   Providing walk-in group or individual counseling services one evening each
          week to parents of the East Pyramid.
II. Target Public: *Teachers*
     Projects to assist teachers in working more effectively with students include:
     A.   Holding Open House for the purpose of discussing school issues and receiv-
          ing feedback from teachers.
     B.   Creating a guidance committee to get teacher input on projects proposed
          by the guidance department.
     C.   Conducting a Classroom Communication and Guidance course for teachers.
     D.   Setting up a career resource room with an employed aid to serve teachers
          and students.
III. Target Public: *Students*
     Projects to assist a student in self-development and personal effectiveness in-
     cludes:
     A.   Cooperating with the English/Social block department in conducting
          groups in self-development.
     B.   Developing and/or teaching a unit in How-to-Study skills.
     C.   Preparing and developing career units with the classroom teacher.
IV. Target Public: *Administrators*
     Projects to assist the principals of the buildings include:
     A.   Process observing staff and faculty meetings.
     B.   Working with principals on special surveys and projects.
V.   Target Public: *Community*
     Projects to assist community resource personnel include:
     A.   Implementing a "big brother" type plan for fatherless boys with cooperation
          from a district committee.

425

Index

in, 218–19; vs. vocational guidance, 408–9

"Career Education Program," 194

Career Exploration System, 139

Career guidance: in Central Bucks County, 382; in Denver, 263–64; in Osseo, Minn., 313–14; in San Diego County, 233, 241–43

Career Information Center, 241

CBRU, 246

Center for Vocational and Technical Education, 121

Central Bucks County: budget of, school, 386–89; community needs of, 363–64; community setting of, 349–60; costs of pupil personnel services in, 388; facilities for pupil personnel in, 367, 368–69; population of, 359–60; pupil personnel services of, 367–86; school enrollment of, 366, 367; school issues and alternatives of, 392–94; schools of, 364–67; special education in, 362, 363, 383–86; unique characteristics of personnel services in, 389–92

Civil rights, pupils', 102–4, 105

Classrooms, today's, 202–4

Codes of ethics: of APGA, 83; of ASCA, 76, 84–85; and group activities, 111; implementation of, 82–91; and pupil personnel staff, 86–93; for school social workers, 28–29; statement of, 80–82; suggestions for activating, 93–95. See also Ethical standards.

Colleague relationship, 194–95

College and scholarship counselors, 264–65

Comprehensive Vocational Guidance System, 139

Computer-Assisted Exploration System (CACEO), 139

Computer-Based Automated Counseling Simulation Situation for Vocational Decisions (ISVD), 138

Computer-Based Resource Units, 246

Computerized Vocational Information System (CVIS), 138, 148–49

Computer-managed instruction (CMI), 138

Computers, 132–49: administration use of, 137; applicability of, 150; communication with, 149–50; costs of, 151; educational use of, 136, 137; functioning of, 133–36; historical development of,

132–33; instructional use of, 137; pupil personnel guidance use, 138–39, 149–51, 152–53; reliability of, 150; research use, 137; vocational counseling use, 139–49

Confidentiality, 76, 77: and APGA, 97–98; and counselors, 76, 88–89; and court cases, 101–2; and ethical standards, 106–7; meaning of, 105; and pupil personnel facilities, 80–81; and pupil personnel staff, 80–81, 97, 105–6; and rights of minors, 102–4; and student records, 77, 96–97

Continuing education of personnel staff, 62

Corrective vs. preventive action, 38

Costs, pupil personnel services: in Bronx District 7, 345–46; in Central Bucks County, 388; in Denver, 258–59, 266–67; in Osseo, Minn., 297, 298, 299; in San Diego County, 239–40

Counseling, 187: ethics in, 75; general system for, 123; and group approaches, 111, 353; individual and group, 36; mobile program for, in San Diego County, 241–42. See also Counselors, school; Guidance.

Counseling Information System (CIV), 139

Counselor aides and assistants: duties of, 180–81; ethical standards for, 89–90

Counselors, school, 32–34, 175–76, 189–90; as advocates, 90; in Bronx District 7, 334, 341–43; California requirements for, 230; in Central Bucks County, 371, 372; changing role of, 320, 402–5; and computer-based vocational guidance, 139–43; and confidentiality, 76, 88–89, 106–7; as consultants, 34; as coordinator and participant, 34; and court cases, 102; criticism of, 33, 404–5; in Denver, 262–64, 266; duties of, 34, 175–76; education of, 95; and ethical standards, 82, 84–85, 87–89, 90–91, 93; and knowledge of legal problems, 96; and malpractice suits, 110; minority representation among, 275, 392; policies to recognize role of, 196–98; in Osseo, Minn., 294–95, 306–7, 308, 309, 315, 320; and parents, 311–12; and privileged communication, 78, 98; responsibilities of, 175–76; roles of, 32–34, 90, 189–90; in San Diego

County, 230–33; and student records, 96–97, 102; and supportive legislation, 112; and teachers, 88–89, 210–12

Court cases: on access to pupil records, 108; and provision of information, 101–2

Criterion-referenced measurements (CRM), 65, 68–71

Cumulative records, and use of information, 98–102

Curriculum: resource units, 246; and teacher's role in building, 219–20; types of, 205–6

Data collection, 136

Delegation of authority, 16

Denver, Colorado: community setting of, 251–53; major community problems of, 252; population of, 251

Denver public schools, 253–56: attendance office in, 273; budget allocations for, 256, 258–59, 266–67; career counselor in, 263–64; college counselor in, 264–65; costs of pupil personnel services in, 258–59; drug education in, 272; elementary schools of, 254; enrollment in, 254; facilities for pupil personnel in, 267–70; general counselor in, 262–63; guidance services of, 272; health services of, 254; high schools in, 254–55; issues and alternatives in, 274–78; junior high schools in, 254; organizational structure of, 253–54; psychologist in, 261–62, 272–73; pupil personnel budget of, 266–67; pupil personnel services of, 257–74; pupil personnel staff of, 255–56; social worker in, 259–61, 273; special education in, 273–74; unique characteristics of pupil personnel in, 270–74

Developmental programs, 37–38

Dial-A-Career Program, 243

Differential staffing, 275, 392

Division of labor, 16–17

Drug programs: in Bronx District 7, 327, 337, 345; in Denver schools, 272

Educable retarded programs: in Central Bucks County, 384–87; in Osseo, Minn., 295, 316–17

Educational objectives, 5–6

Educational organization, components of, 7–9

Educationally handicapped, 237, 246

Education of pupil personnel, 94–95

Elementary counseling and guidance: in Bronx District 7, 341–42; in Central Bucks County, 371; in Denver, 266, 277–28; in Osseo, Minn., 321; in San Diego County, 233–35

Elementary schools: in Bronx District 7, 329–30, 331–32; in Central Bucks County, 366; in Denver, 254; in Osseo, Minn., 292; in San Diego County, 227

Ethical and legal aspects, 37, 74–117

Ethical standards: and APA, 75–76, 81, 83–84; and APGA, 76, 81, 85, 89, 109; and ASCA, 81, 84, 91; codes of, 75–76; and confidentiality, 106–7; and counselors, 82, 84–85, 87–89, 90–91, 93; factors impeding, 86–91; and legal guidelines, 104–5; and paraprofessionals, 89–90, 111–12; and psychologists, 75–76, 83–84, 109; and research with human subjects, 109–10; revision of, 94; and student records, 89, 108–9; statement of, 80–82; suggestions for activating, 93; and training of pupil personnel staff, 89. *See also* Codes of ethics.

Evaluation: Criterion-referenced, 65, 68–71; defined, 65; formative, 63; normative, 67; norm-referenced, 65, 68–71; of pupil personnel services, 62, 64–70, 277–78, 354–56; summative, 67–68

Facilities, pupil personnel, 62–63; in Bronx District 7, 347–48, 355; in Central Bucks County, 367, 368–69; in Denver, 267–70; and ethical standards, 90–91; in Osseo, Minn., 301–6; in San Diego County, 224–25, 231

Family assistant, 336–37, 345

Filmstrips and slides, in guidance, 132

Formative evaluation, 67

Fullerton, Calif., Union High School district goals, 47–48

Gardner, John W., 46–47

Gifted programs, 238

Goals: of education, 44–47; of pupil personnel services, 43–44, 47–51

Group activities, and codes of ethics, 111

Guidance programs: and career planning, 36; in Bronx District 7, 341–43, 349; computer-assisted, 143–48; computer-based vocational, 139–43; and computer reports, 138; in Denver, 272; general system for, 123, 124; and media applications, 129–31; major elements of, 35–36; and media research,

127–29; in Osseo, Minn., 321; and placement and follow-up, 36; policies to recognize roles of, 196–98; role of principal in, 178–79; role of teacher in, 178, 217–20, 230; in San Diego County, 233–35; and student appraisal, 35; and supervisory staff, 179; systems approach to, 124, 125; and systems technology, 119–26; and use of media, 126–33; use of paraprofessionals in, 89–90, 180–81; and use of microfilm, 30. *See also* Counseling.

Health services, 29–30: in Bronx District 7, 335–36; in Central Bucks County, 377–79; in Denver public schools, 254. *See also* Nurse, school.

Helping services. *See* Pupil personnel services.

High school counselors, 177–78; in Bronx District 7, 341, 342–43; in Central Bucks County, 372, 381–82; in Denver, 262–65; in Osseo, Minn., 294–95; in San Diego, 231

High schools: in Bronx District 7, 330; 333; in Central Bucks County, 366–67; in Denver, 354–55; in Osseo, Minn., 290–91; in San Diego County, 227

House high school, 203–4

Human research subjects. *See* Research with human subjects.

Individual differences, 9

Individual rights, vs. research on human subjects, 109–10

Information System for Vocational Decisions (ISVD), 143–48

In-service training, 220

Instructional staff, 7, 8, 137, 202–22

Intermediate schools, in Bronx District 7, 332. *See also* Junior high schools.

Interprofessional Research Commission on Pupil Personnel Services, 10

Invasion of privacy, 96, 398. *See also* Right of privacy.

IRCOPPS, 10, 11

Junior high schools: in Bronx District, 7, 330, 332, 342; in Central Bucks County, 366, 380; counselors in, 177; in Denver, 254–55; in Osseo, Minn., 287, 291; in San Diego County, 233

Laws: governing pupil personnel workers, 95; related to students' rights, 96; and student records, 98–102

Legal guidelines and limitations, 398–99:

and ethical standards, 104–5; for pupil personnel workers, 74–75, 76–80; on research with human subjects, 109

Legislation, and pupil personnel workers, 112

Libel and slander, 78–79, 96, 99, 108–9

Line-and-staff organization: in large school systems, 171; in modal school systems, 167–68

Malpractice: cases of, 96, 110–11; explained, 110; vs. professional behavior, 110–11

Media: applications in guidance, 129–31; audio recordings, 131; classification of, 127; filmstrips and slides, 132; in guidance, 126–33, microfilm, 130–31; multimedia approach, 132–33, in research, 127–29; television and films, 132; video tape recordings, 132

Mental health trainees, 344

Mentally retarded, education of: in Central Bucks County, 283–86; in Denver, 273–74; in Osseo, Minn., 300, 301; in San Diego County, 236–37

Microfilm use for guidance, 130–31

Minority representation in staffing, 275, 392

Minors, rights of, 102–4

Multimedia approach in guidance, 132

Norm-referenced measurements (NRM), 65, 68–71

National Association of Pupil Personnel Administration, 12, 48–49

National Association of Social Workers, 28

National Education Association, 75

National Vocational Guidance Association (NVGA), 75–76, 88

Nurse, school, 29–31, 173–75: as first auxiliary service, 165–66; in Bronx District 7, 344; in Central Bucks County, 372, 377–79; as consultant, 31; as coordinator and participant, 31; in Denver, 286; duties of, 31, 174–75; in Omaha, 30–31; in Osseo, Minn., 295–96; responsibility of, 174–75; role of, 30–31, 173–75; in San Diego County, 238; and teacher, 215–17. *See also* Health services.

Objectives: defined, 51; of pupil personnel services, 51–58; 397–98

Omaha Public Schools nurse, 30–31

Open-space school, 203

Organizational framework of schools, 14–

15; of Bronx District 7, 328–29; of Central Bucks County, 364–66; of Denver, 253, 254, 255; of Osseo, Minn., 286–87, 290–92; of San Diego County, 227–29

Osseo, Minnesota, 280–323: community setting of, 280; costs of pupil personnel services in, 297, 298, 299; cultural and educational facilities of, 284; ethnic factors of, 281; facilities for pupil personnel staff in, 301–6; major community needs of, 284–85; population of, 280–81; organizational structure of schools in, 286–87, 290–92; pupil personnel services of, 292–301; school enrollment of, 280, 283; schools of, 286–92; socioeconomic factors in, 281; special education in, 316–19; special guidance program of, 303–6; unique characteristics of pupil personnel services in, 306–15

Overlapping responsibilities, 9

Paraprofessionals: in Bronx District 7, 339, 344, 345, 350; in Central Bucks County, 392; and ethical standards, 89–90, 111–12; in San Diego County, 233; use of, in guidance, 180–81

Parents: and counselors, 102–3, 311–12; and teacher conferences, 219

Personal notes and confidentiality, 100–1, 108

Physically handicapped: in Central Bucks County, 383; in Osseo, Minn., 300, 301; in San Diego County, 236–37

Placement activities, 36

Privacy, right of. *See* Right of privacy.

Privileged communication, 97–98, 397; and counselors, 78, 98; defined, 97, 105; and personal notes, 80; and psychologists, 78, 98; and pupil personnel staff, 78; and social workers, 78; and state laws, 77–78

Problem-solving model, 52, 53

Professionalism, 59–60, 110–11

Project VIEW, 131, 241

Project VOGUE, 131

Psychiatrist, in Bronx District 7, 344

Psychological testing, and right of privacy, 104

Psychologist, 26–27, 181–83; in Bronx District 7, 343–44; California requirements for, 235; in Central Bucks County, 371, 374–75; as a consultant, 27; as a coordinator and participant,

27–28; definition of, 26; in Denver, 261–62, 272–73; ethical standards of, 75–76, 83–84, 109; in Osseo, Minn., 295, 305; and privileged communication, 78, 98; responsibilities of, 26–27, 182–83; roles of, 26–28, 181–83; in San Diego County, 235–36; and teacher, 212–14

Psycho-social skills, 208–10

Pupil personnel administrator, 21–25; in Bronx District 7, 334, 337–38; in Central Bucks County, 373; characteristics of, 24; in Osseo, Minn., 287; program objectives and assessment by, 41–73; and role of, 21–25; in San Diego County, 238–39; title of, 22, 23

Pupil personnel services, 9–14, 59–64; and accountability, 36–37, 198, 406; adjustments and changes in, 413–14; in Bronx District 7, 333–56; in Central Bucks County, 367–86; concept of, 3–4; defined, 10–11; in Denver, 257–74; and developmental programs, 37–38; emerging trends and issues in, 36–38; and ethical and legal constraints, 37; facilities for, 90; goals of, 43–44, 47–51; issues in, 186–87; objectives of, 51–58, 397–98; and organizational plans, 17–19; in Osseo, Minn., 293–322; programs of, 58–64; renewing vitality of, 188–99; role of individual services in, 25–26; in San Diego County, 229–48; special education and, 13–14; and team approach, 38; and technology, 37; typical services of, 11–12. *See also* Costs, pupil personnel services.

Pupil personnel staff, 8–9, 59–62; accountability of, 198, 248, 275, 278, 318, 319–20, 406; codes of ethics for, 86–93; and confidentiality, 80–81, 97, 105–6; and continuing education, 62; duties and responsibilities of, 184–85; effecting changes in relationships of, 194–98; and ethical standards, 63–64, 75–76, 80–82, 89; evaluation of, 62; expanding sphere of influence of, 247–48; facilities for, 62–63; financial constraints on, 63; functions of, 164; and legal constraints, 75–76, 95–104; in large schools, 171–73; and malpractice, 110–11; in modal school systems, 167–71; organization of, 164; and privileged information, 78; and professionalism, 59–60; question-

431

able practices of, 92; and rights of minors, 102–4; role perceptions of, 20–35; selection of, 61–62; in small school systems, 164–67; and teachers, 207–8; training of, 61, 89, 94, 95; updating roles and functions of, 93–94

Purposes of education, 5–6

Qualified privilege, 77, 78–79, 99

Questionable practices, 92

Public records, 98–99

Rafferty, Max, 46

Remedial worker, 34–35

Research: and computer use, 137; and media use, 127–28; with human subjects, 109–10

Right of privacy, 98: and collection of student information, 107–8; and 4th amendment, 108; and modern technological systems, 107–8; and student records, 399–400; and testing, 104; and use of student information, 107–8

San Diego County, 223–50; budget of, educational, 239–40; budget of, pupil personnel services, 239–40; community setting of, 223–26; counselors in, school, 230–33; Curricular Services Division of, 229; facilities for pupil personnel services, 224–25; gifted programs in, 238; guidance services in, 230–33; nurse in, school, 238; population of, 251; and Project VIEW, 131, 241; psychologists in, school, 235–36; pupil personnel services of, 223–50; school enrollment of, 233; school issues and alternatives, 247–48; social workers in, school, 239; schools of, 226–39; special education services in, 236–37, 245–46; unique characteristics of pupil personnel services of, 240–47

San Diego Personnel and Guidance Association, 92–93

School consolidation programs, 6

School nurse. See Nurse, school.

School psychologist. See Psychologist, school.

School systems: administrative component of, 7–8; of Bronx District 7, 328–33; of Central Bucks County, 364–67; of Denver, 253–56; improvement programs and practices of, 247; instructional component of, 7; organizational framework of, 14–15; organizational plans of, 17–19; of Osseo, Minn., 286–

92; pupil personnel component of, 8–9; of San Diego County, 226–39

Scope of Pupil Personnel Services, 11

SEARCH, 246

Secondary School Counselors, 95

Selection of personnel staff, 61–62

Slander. *See* Libel and slander.

Social worker, school, 28–29: in Bronx District 7, 343; in Central Bucks County, 371, 375–77; code of ethics for, 28–29; as a consultant, 29; as a coordinator and participant, 29; in Denver, 259–61, 273; duties of, 29, 185, 214; and privileged communication, 78; role definition of, 28–29; in San Diego County, 238; and teacher, 214–15

Special education 13–14; in Bronx District 7, 331, 333, 354; in Central Bucks County, 362, 367, 372–73; 383–86, 393; in Denver, 273–74; in Osseo, Minn., 293, 294, 300–1, 316–19; in San Diego County, 236–37, 245–46; staff, 34–35

SPOP format, 54–58

Student appraisal, 35

Student records: confidentiality of, 77, 96–97; and court cases, 101–2; and defamation suits, 108–9; and ethical standards, 89; and legal guidelines for use of, 98–102; and parents, 103; and privileged communication, 78, 98; and right of privacy, 107–8, 399–400; and school policy, 101; and technological systems, 107–8; and use of microfilm, 130–31

Students' rights, 96

Summative evaluation, 67–68

System Development Corporation, 138, 139

Systems approach and concepts: advantages of, 120; application of, in guidance, 121–23; characteristics of, 121; defined, 120; and objectives, 120; and guidance, 124, 125; and research projects, 124

Tape recorders, 131–32

Task schedules, 124, 125

Teacher: accountability of, 198, 218; and counselor, 88–89, 210–12; and guidance role, 178, 204–8, 217–20; new strategies for, 206–7; and nurse, school, 215–17; and parent conferences, 219; and psychologist, school, 212–14; and pupil personnel services, 350; and so-

432